Independent Component Analysis:
Principles and Practice

Independent Component Analysis: Principles and Practice

Edited by
Stephen Roberts
Richard Everson

CAMBRIDGE UNIVERSITY PRESS
Cambridge, New York, Melbourne, Madrid, Cape Town, Singapore,
São Paulo, Delhi, Dubai, Tokyo, Mexico City

Cambridge University Press
The Edinburgh Building, Cambridge CB2 8RU, UK

Published in the United States of America by Cambridge University Press, New York

www.cambridge.org
Information on this title: www.cambridge.org/9780521792981

First published 2001

A catalogue record for this publication is available from the British Library

ISBN 978-0-521-79298-1 Hardback

Contents

Preface

In recent years there has been an explosion of interest in the application and theory of independent component analysis (ICA). This book is aimed to provide a self-contained introduction to the subject as well as offering a set of invited contributions which we see as lying at the cutting edge of ICA research.

ICA is intimately linked with the problem of blind source separation—attempting to recover a set of underlying *sources* when only a noisy mapping from these sources, the *observations*, is given—and we regard this as the canonical form of ICA. Until recently this mapping was taken to be linear (but see Chapter 4) and "traditionally" (if tradition is allowed in a field of such recent developments) noiseless with the number of observations being equal to the number of hypothesised sources. It is surprising that even the simplest of ICA models can be invaluable and offer new insights into data analysis and interpretation. This, at first sight unreasonable, claim may be supported by noting that many observations of physical systems *are* produced by a linear combination of underlying sources. Furthermore, in many applications, it is an end in itself to produce a set of "sources" which are statistically *independent* rather than just decorrelated (see Chapter 1) and for this ICA would appear an ideal tool.

This book was born from discussions with researchers in the ICA community and aims to provide a snapshot of some current trends in ICA research. Wherever possible, the contributors use a common nomenclature and symbol set, especially for the most frequently used terms. The book has a single *global* set of references and index items which may be found at the end of the book.

A web site dedicated to the book and containing links to author web pages and other useful sites along with code and data related to ICA may be found at http://www.dcs.ex.ac.uk/ica

Structure of the book

Chapter 1 offers an introduction to independent component analysis. This chapter aims to give the reader an accessible way into the techniques, issues and jargon of ICA. The field is an extensive one and we have attempted to keep to ideas which we regard as instructive in the key issues of ICA, rather than give a complete description of every sub-method and algorithm modification.

Chapter 2 details one of the most popular approaches to ICA based on polynomial approximations to the mutual information, that of *Fast ICA*. Hyvärinen details in this chapter the theoretical development of the approximations, their justification and the rapid fixed-point algorithm by which the sources are recovered. Background material on the relationship between learning algorithms is also presented along with results on a number of datasets.

Chapter 3 pitches ICA into the important context of graphical models, whereby the relationships between model parameters are represented by a directed acyclic graph. Attias, in this chapter, considers flexible ICA methods (sometimes known as Independent Factor Analysis, IFA) in which the source densities are modelled by mixtures of Gaussians and an explicit additive (sensor) noise term exists. Inference is performed using a *variational learning* approach (see also Chapter 8).

Chapter 4 extends ICA from a general *linear* model of source mixing to the nonlinear case. Karhunen explores in detail the issues involved with forming learning paradigms for such nonlinear ICA and develops promising algorithms to deal with nonlinear mixing. The chapter is illustrated with comparative examples.

Chapter 5 extends ICA to consider the issue of source non-stationarity. Parra and Spence show how the higher order statistics used to locate independent components arise naturally in non-stationary signals. They examine whether linear mixing is a good model for acoustic signals and natural images. Exploiting the property of non-stationarity they show how good blind separation may be achieved using multiple linear decorrelation.

Chapter 6 offers a different perspective on the separation of non-stationary sources. Cardoso and Pham derive an elegant methodology in which non-stationarity may be handled and indeed utilised to aid in the unmixing process.

Chapter 7 considers source separation in the case when the sources are represented by a *sparse* mixture from a signal dictionary (such as wavelet packets). Under these circumstances ICA naturally seeks sources which are as sparse in their representation as possible. This extra information enables Zibulevsky, Pearlmutter, Bofill and Kisilev to obtain impressive results in situations when there are *more* sources than observations.

Chapter 8 pitches ICA as a graphical model with densities over variables being inferred using a variational learning framework. As both *parameters* and *hyper-parameters* of the model are inferred as part of a single learning strategy, this approach is referred to as *ensemble* learning. Miskin and MacKay consider mixture of Gaussian source models and show results from model-selection on real-world problems. They also show that a positivity constraint on the hypothesised mixing process gives rise to ICA solutions which are more local in their support.

Chapter 9 applies ICA to the domain of image decomposition and processing. By assuming that natural images are generated by a linear combination of independent sources (textures and edges for example) ICA may be used to estimate, given an image, a basis for decomposition. Lee and Lewicki show that this basis has an intuitively appealing form (typically that of local filters) and show how ICA may thence be utilised to perform image denoising.

Chapter 10 regards ICA as a general linear transform of the same form as the linear discriminant of pattern classification. Using a nested hierarchy of ICA decompositions of real data, Girolami shows that excellent results may be obtained in difficult unsupervised classification problems. He then proceeds to consider the process of visualisation of high-dimensional data (mapping to a two-dimensional space, for example) as an ICA-like procedure for which learning rules may be obtained.

Chapter 11 allows a model in which the mixing matrix of a linear ICA model is considered to be *non-stationary*. This matrix may thence be tracked using a particle filter. The approach is shown to be very effective when tracking non-stationary mixing of temporally uncorrelated sources. Some solutions to the more difficult problem of tracking mixtures of temporally correlated sources are presented.

Chapter 12 extends the standard ICA model by allowing the source density models to be *dynamic* rather than static. This is achieved by the use of linear dynamic models within the ICA framework. The authors also consider the important issue of model order selection to determine the most probable number of underlying sources. Results are presented for a variety of datasets.

Acknowledgements

There are many people we would like to thank for their contributions to this book. In particular we thank Iead Rezek, Dirk Husmeier, Peter Sykacek, Will Penny and Riz Choudrey for interesting and enlightening conversations. We are especially grateful to Will Penny for a careful reading of the entire book as it neared completion. We would also like to thank David Tranah, our editor at CUP, for his unfailing support for the project, even as the deadline approached and went.

The editors would like to express thanks to the other contributors for their hard work and their patience and help during the editing process.

SR would like to say a big thanks, with much love, to Anna, Rebecca and Elise.

RE thanks Frances, Gwyneth and Juliet for their love and endurance.

Stephen Roberts
Richard Everson

Contributors

Hagai Attias
hagaia@microsoft.com
Microsoft Research 113/3359,
One Microsoft Way,
Redmond, WA 98052-6399,
USA.

Pau Bofill
pau@ac.upc.es
Departament d'Arquitectura de
Computadors,
Universitat Politècnica de Catalunya,
Campus Nord,
Sergi Girona s/n,
08071 Barcelona,
Spain.

Jean-Francois Cardoso
cardoso@tsi.enst.fr
CNRS and ENST,
ENST, Dept TSI,
46, rue Barrault,
75634 Paris CEDEX 13,
France.

Richard Everson
reverson@exeter.ac.uk
Department of Computer Science,
University of Exeter,
Exeter EX4 4PT,
UK.

Mark Girolami
mark.girolami@paisley.ac.uk
Department of Computing and
Information Systems,
University of Paisley,
High Street,
Paisley, PA1 2BE,
Scotland, UK.

Aapo Hyvärinen
Aapo.Hyvarinen@hut.fi
Neural Networks Research Centre,
P.O. Box 5400,
Helsinki University of Technology,
FIN-02015 TKK,
Finland.

Juha Karhunen
Juha.Karhunen@hut.fi
Helsinki University of Technology,
Laboratory of Computer and
Information Science,
P.O. Box 5400,
FIN-02015 HUT,
Finland.

Pavel Kisilev
paulk@tx.technion.ac.il
Electrical Engineering Department,
Technion Israel Institute of
Technology,
Haifa 32000, Israel.

Te-Won Lee
tewon@salk.edu
INC, UC San Diego,
L a Jolla,
CA 9093-0523,
USA.

Michael S. Lewicki
lewicki@cnbc.cmu.edu
CMU/CNBC,
Mellon Inst. 115,
4400 Fifth Avenue,
Pittsburgh, PA 15213,
USA.

David MacKay
mackay@mrao.cam.ac.uk
Cavendish Laboratory,
Madingley Road,
Cambridge, CB3 0HE,
UK.

James Miskin
jwm1003@mrao.cam.ac.uk
Cavendish Laboratory,
Madingley Road,
Cambridge, CB3 0HE,
UK.

Lucas Parra
lparra@sarnoff.com
Sarnoff Corporation, CN5300,
Princeton, NJ, 08543-5300,
USA.

Barak Pearlmutter
bap@cs.unm.edu
Computer Science Department,
FEC 313,
University of New Mexico,
Albuquerque, NM 87131,
USA.

William Penny
wpenny@robots.ox.ac.uk
Robotics Research Group,
Department of Engineering Science,
University of Oxford,
Oxford OX1 3PJ,
UK.

Dinh-Tuan Pham
Dinh-Tuan.Pham@imag.fr
CNRS IMAG-LMC,
51 rue des Mathématiques,
B. P. 53,
38041 Grenoble Cedex 9,
France.

Stephen Roberts
sjrob@robots.ox.ac.uk
Robotics Research Group,
Department of Engineering Science,
University of Oxford,
Oxford OX1 3PJ,
UK.

Clay Spence
cspence@sarnoff.com
Sarnoff Corporation, CN5300,
Princeton, NJ, 08543-5300,
USA.

Michael Zibulevsky
michael@cs.unm.edu
Electrical Engineering Department,
Technion Israel Institute of
Technology,
Haifa 32000,
Israel.

1

Introduction

S.J. Roberts

R.M. Everson

1.1 Introduction

Independent Component Analysis (ICA) has recently become an important tool for modelling and understanding empirical datasets as it offers an elegant and practical methodology for *blind* source separation and deconvolution. It is seldom possible to observe a pure unadulterated signal. Instead most observations consist of a mixture of signals usually corrupted by noise, and frequently filtered. The signal processing community has devoted much attention to the problem of recovering the constituent sources from the convolutive mixture; ICA may be applied to this Blind Source Separation (BSS) problem to recover the sources. As the appellation *independent* suggests, recovery relies on the assumption that the constituent sources are mutually independent.

Finding a natural coordinate system is an essential first step in the analysis of empirical data. Principal component analysis (PCA) has, for many years, been used to find a set of basis vectors which are determined by the dataset itself. The principal components are orthogonal and projections of the data onto them are linearly decorrelated, properties which can be ensured by considering only the second order statistical characteristics of the data. ICA aims at a loftier goal: it seeks a transformation to coordinates in which the data are maximally statistically independent, not merely decorrelated.

Perhaps the most famous illustration of ICA is the 'cocktail party problem', in which a listener is faced with the problem of separating the independent voices chattering at a cocktail party. Humans employ many different strategies, often concentrating on just one voice, more or less successfully [Bregman, 1990]. The computational problem of separating

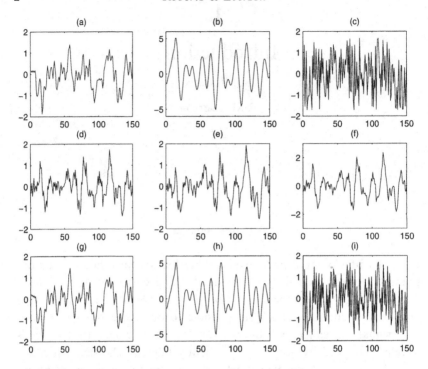

Figure 1.1. *Mixing and separation of music and noise.* Top row: 150 samples of the original sources, $s_m(t)$ ($f_{samp} = 11.3\,kHz$). Middle row: mixtures of the sources, $\mathbf{x}(t)$. Bottom row: the estimated sources, $a_m(t)$. To facilitate comparison both the sources and the recovered sources have been normalised to unit variance.

the speakers from audio mixtures recorded by microphones is challenging, especially when echoes and time delays are taken into account.

To make the ideas and notation concrete we consider a simple example with three sources. The sources were two fragments of music (a Beethoven string quartet and an old recording of a Bessie Smith blues ballad) and uniform noise. Writing the source signals at the instant t in vector form, $\mathbf{s}(t) = [s_1(t), s_2(t), s_3(t)]^\mathsf{T}$, observations $\mathbf{x}(t) \in \mathbb{R}^3$ were generated by mixing the sources by a *mixing matrix*, A, whose elements were chosen at random:†

$$\mathbf{x}(t) = A\mathbf{s}(t). \tag{1.1}$$

The top and middle rows of figure 1.1 show 150 samples from original sources, $\mathbf{s}(t)$, and the mixture $\mathbf{x}(t)$. The aim of BSS is to recover the

† $A = \begin{bmatrix} 0.2519 & 0.0513 & 0.0771 \\ 0.5174 & 0.6309 & 0.4572 \\ 0.1225 & 0.6074 & 0.4971 \end{bmatrix}$

original sources from the observations alone, without any additional knowledge of the sources or their characteristics. Independent component analysis accomplishes the separation relying on the assumption that the sources are independent. It seeks a *separating matrix* (or *filter matrix*) W which, when applied to the observations, recovers estimated sources, $\mathbf{a}(t)$; thus

$$\mathbf{a}(t) = W\mathbf{x}(t).$$

Optimising W to maximise the statistical independence between the components of $\mathbf{a}(t)$ finds estimated sources which are shown in the bottom row of figure 1.1. It is clear that the algorithm has done a good job in separating the sources: the noisy blues recording is estimated together with its noise (plots (a) and (g)), while the string quartet is uncontaminated (plots (b) and (h)). To the ear the recovered sources are indistinguishable from the originals, and in particular there is no trace of music in the unmixed noise.†

Blind source separation has been a practical possibility since the early work of Herault & Jutten [1986] which was analysed from a statistical point of view in [Comon *et al.*, 1991] and further developed by Jutten & Herault [1991], where the phrase 'independent component analysis' first appeared. In a seminal paper Comon [1994] proposed the use of mutual information to measure independence and advanced separation algorithms based on approximations to mutual information.

Work by Linsker [1989, 1992] and Nadal & Parga [1994] on mappings which maximise transmitted information showed that the optimal mappings are those which lead to factorised source probability density functions (p.d.f.s). Bell & Sejnowski [1995] and Roth & Barum [1996] each derived stochastic gradient algorithms to find the optimal mapping, and a similar algorithm was suggested by Cardoso & Laheld [1996].

Generative models and maximum likelihood approaches to ICA were proposed and developed by Gaeta & Lacoume [1990] and Pham *et al.* [1992]. However, MacKay [1996], Pearlmutter & Parra [1996] and Cardoso [1997] established that the infomax objective function of Bell & Sejnowski was indeed a likelihood (in the zero noise limit).

Since the mid-nineties there has been an explosion of work on ICA and BSS. Maximum likelihood methods have been extended to incorporate observational noise [Attias, 1999a] and schemes have been developed

---

† Files with the sources, mixtures and estimated sources may be retrieved from http: //www.dcs.ex.ac.uk/ica

to permit the separation of sub-Gaussian as well as super-Gaussian†
sources (see, for example, [Pham, 1996, Lee *et al.*, 1999b, Everson &
Roberts, 1999a]). Pearlmutter & Parra [1996] exploited the temporal
structure of sources to improve the separation of timeseries data; extensions of this work appear in Chapter 12 of the present book. Girolami
& Fyfe [1997a, 1997b] elucidated the connection between projection pursuit and non-Gaussian sources, and have applied ICA to data mining
problems; in Chapter 10 of the present book Girolami gives details
of recent work on data classification and visualisation. ICA for nonlinear mappings was considered along with early work on linear ICA
[Karhunen & Joutsensalo, 1994]. Karhunen describes recent advances in
nonlinear ICA in Chapter 4. The generative model formulation of ICA
permits Bayesian methods for incorporating prior knowledge, assessing
the number of sources and evaluating errors. Early work was done on
Bayesian approaches by Roberts [1998] and Knuth [1998a] and more
recently by Mohammad-Djafari [1999]. The application of ensemble
learning (or variational) methods has greatly simplified the computation
required for Bayesian estimates; see Chapter 8 of the present book and
[Lappalainen, 1999]. Recent theoretical work (dealt with in the present
book) has also examined non-stationary sources (Chapters 5 and 6) and
non-stationary mixing (Chapter 11).

Chapter overview This book concentrates mainly on the generative model
formulation of ICA as it permits principled extensions. In this introduc-
tory chapter we examine ICA from a number of perspectives. Starting
from a fairly general point of view, noisy and noiseless models for mixing
and the hierarchy of ICA models are discussed first. In subsection 1.2.2
we discuss mutual information as a measure of independence, after which
the more general framework of 'contrast functions' is introduced. The
introduction of generative models permits maximum likelihood separating matrices to be found; the advantages of a Bayesian approach to ICA
are discussed in subsection 1.2.5. ICA has strong links with principal
component analysis. PCA and related methodologies are obtained if the
sources are Gaussian distributed, as is discussed in section 1.3.

Abandoning Gaussian source distributions permits richer notions of
independence to be employed, but also complicates learning the separat-

---

† A random variable is called sub-Gaussian if its kurtosis is negative and super-Gaussian
if its kurtosis is positive. Loosely, the tails of a super-Gaussian p.d.f. decay more slowly
than a Gaussian density, while the tails of a sub-Gaussian density decay more rapidly
than a Gaussian. See pages 27 and 76.

ing matrix, which can no longer be achieved purely by linear algebra. We attempt to distinguish between the ICA objective or contrast function which is to be extremised and the precise optimisation algorithm. This and the relations between various approaches to noiseless ICA are the subjects of sections 1.4 and 1.6.

Extensions to the basic ICA model are introduced in section 1.8, and finally we briefly describe some applications of ICA.

1.2 Linear mixing

We begin by considering a general model of mixing, which will subsequently be simplified and approximated to permit tractable calculations to be made. The basic model is a discrete time model in which M sources $s_m(t)$ are instantaneously mixed and the resulting mixture, possibly corrupted by noise, is observed. Writing the source signals at the instant t† in vector form, $\mathbf{s}(t) = [s_1(t), s_2(t), \ldots, s_M(t)]^\mathsf{T}$, the N-dimensional observations, $\mathbf{x}(t) = [x_1(t), x_2(t), \ldots, x_N(t)]^\mathsf{T}$, are generated by a, possibly nonlinear, mixture corrupted by additive observational or sensor noise $\mathbf{n}(t)$ as follows:

$$\mathbf{x}(t) = \mathbf{f}(\mathbf{s}(t)) + \mathbf{n}(t), \tag{1.2}$$

where $\mathbf{f} : \mathbb{R}^M \rightarrow \mathbb{R}^N$ is an unknown function.

The goal of blind source separation is to invert the mixing function $\mathbf{f}$ and recover the sources. The qualifier *blind* signifies that little is known about the quantities on the right hand side of equation (1.2); the mixing function and the noise and, of course, the sources themselves are unknown and must be estimated. Even with infinite data the unmixing problem is very ill-posed without some additional *a priori* knowledge or assumptions about the sources $\mathbf{s}$, the nature of the mixing $\mathbf{f}$ and the observational noise $\mathbf{n}$. In Chapter 4 Karhunen examines recent approaches to blind source separation with nonlinear mixing. Traditional treatments of ICA, however, make the assumption that the sources are *linearly* mixed by a *mixing matrix* $A \in \mathbb{R}^{N \times M}$. Thus observations are assumed to be generated by

$$\mathbf{x}(t) = A\mathbf{s}(t) + \mathbf{n}(t). \tag{1.3}$$

---

† Although we call t 'time', for most ICA models t is really an index. Most models do not assume any causal dependence of $s_m(t_2)$ on $s_m(t_1)$ when $t_2 > t_1$. See section 1.5 and Chapters 12 and 11.

For simplicity it is usually assumed that **s** and **n** have mean zero, and consequently **x** has zero mean.

Although the nonlinear mixing function has been replaced with an (unknown) matrix the problem of identifying **s** is still under-determined, because there are $N + M$ unknown signals (the noises and the sources) and N known signals (the observations). Progress is only possible with additional assumptions about the nature of the sources and noise.

The principal assumption which permits progress is that the sources are *independent*, which incorporates the idea that each source signal is generated by a process unrelated to the other sources. For example, the voices at a cocktail party might be regarded as independent. Independent Component Analysis is therefore a method for blind source separation, and if independent components can be found they are identified with the (hidden) sources.

1.2.1 *Hierarchy of ICA models*

Although all ICA models assume the sources to be independent, assumptions about the characteristics of the noise and the source densities lead to a range of ICA models, whose relationships are summarised in figure 1.2.

An important class of models is obtained by assuming that both the sources and noise are Gaussian distributed. Factor Analysis describes the linear model with Gaussian sources and a diagonal noise covariance matrix; restricting the covariance matrix to be isotropic yields Probabilistic Principal Component Analysis (PPCA), and Principal Component Analysis emerges in the absence of noise. These models are described in section 1.3.

Gaussian source models, although historically important and computationally attractive, are, however, seriously limited in their ability to separate sources and recent work on source separation depends crucially on the assumption that the sources are non-Gaussian.

Attias [1999a] has developed an ICA model with linear mixing and observational noise; see Chapter 3 of the present book. The majority of classical ICA models, however, are noiseless so that observations are generated according to

$$\mathbf{x} = A\mathbf{s}. \tag{1.4}$$

Variations of these models depend upon the probabilistic model used for the sources: flexible source models, which depend continuously upon

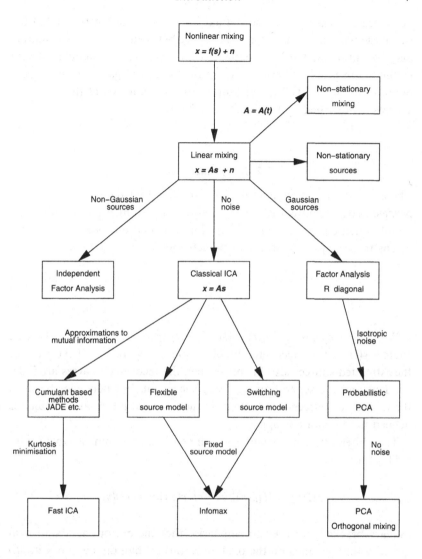

Figure 1.2. *Hierarchy of ICA Models*

their parameters, and schemes which switch between two source models dependent upon the moments of the recovered sources are discussed in section 1.4. If the source model is fixed to be a single function with no explicit parameters, the Bell & Sejnowski Infomax algorithm [Bell & Sejnowski, 1995] is recovered (subsection 1.5). These models all recover sources which are maximally independent. The degree of independence is measured by the mutual information (subsection 1.2.2) between the recovered sources. Independence between the recovered sources may be approximated by cumulant based expansions. Cumulant based methods are briefly described in section 1.4. An elegant and fast fixed-point technique, FastICA, which maximises the kurtosis of the recovered sources is described by Hyvärinen in Chapter 2.

1.2.2 Independent sources

The assumption underlying all ICA models is that the sources are *independent*. The M sources together generate an M-dimensional probability density function (p.d.f.) $p(\mathbf{s})$. Statistical independence between the sources means that the joint source density factorises as

$$p(\mathbf{s}) = \prod_{m=1}^{M} p(s_m(t)). \tag{1.5}$$

We denote by $\mathbf{a}(t) = [a_1(t), a_2(t), \dots, a_M(t)]^{\mathsf{T}}$ the estimates of the true sources $\mathbf{s}(t)$ that are recovered by blind source separation. If the p.d.f. of the estimated sources also factorises then the recovered sources are independent and the separation has been successful. Independence between the recovered sources is measured by their mutual information, which is defined in terms of entropies.

The (differential) entropy of an M-dimensional random variable $\mathbf{x}$ with p.d.f. $p(\mathbf{x})$ is

$$H[\mathbf{x}] = H[p(\mathbf{x})] \stackrel{\text{def}}{=} - \int p(\mathbf{x}) \log p(\mathbf{x}) \, d\mathbf{x}. \tag{1.6}$$

(Square brackets are used to emphasise that the entropy is a statistical quantity that depends on the p.d.f. of $\mathbf{x}$, rather than directly on $\mathbf{x}$ itself.) The entropy measures the average amount of information that $\mathbf{x}$ encodes, or, alternatively, the average amount of information that observation of $\mathbf{x}$ yields [Cover & Thomas, 1991]. If base 2 logarithms are used the entropy is measured in bits.

The joint entropy $H[\mathbf{x}, \mathbf{y}]$ of two random variables $\mathbf{x}$ and $\mathbf{y}$ is defined as

$$H[\mathbf{x}, \mathbf{y}] = - \int p(\mathbf{x}, \mathbf{y}) \log p(\mathbf{x}, \mathbf{y}) \, d\mathbf{x} \, d\mathbf{y}. \tag{1.7}$$

The conditional entropy of $\mathbf{x}$ given $\mathbf{y}$ is

$$H[\mathbf{x}|\mathbf{y}] = -\int p(\mathbf{x},\mathbf{y}) \log p(\mathbf{x}|\mathbf{y}) \, d\mathbf{x} \, d\mathbf{y}. \tag{1.8}$$

from which it follows that

$$H[\mathbf{x},\mathbf{y}] = H[\mathbf{x}] + H[\mathbf{y}|\mathbf{x}] \tag{1.9}$$
$$= H[\mathbf{y}] + H[\mathbf{x}|\mathbf{y}]. \tag{1.10}$$

Equation (1.9) may be interpreted to mean that the (average) information that $\mathbf{x}$ and $\mathbf{y}$ jointly encode is the sum of the information encoded by $\mathbf{x}$ alone and the information encoded by $\mathbf{y}$ given a knowledge of $\mathbf{x}$.

The mutual information between two random variates $\mathbf{x}$ and $\mathbf{y}$ is defined in terms of their entropies.

$$I[\mathbf{x};\mathbf{y}] \stackrel{\text{def}}{=} H[\mathbf{x}] + H[\mathbf{y}] - H[\mathbf{x},\mathbf{y}] \tag{1.11}$$
$$= H[\mathbf{x}] - H[\mathbf{x}|\mathbf{y}] \tag{1.12}$$
$$= H[\mathbf{y}] - H[\mathbf{y}|\mathbf{x}]. \tag{1.13}$$

The mutual information is thus the difference in the information that is obtained by observing $\mathbf{x}$ and $\mathbf{y}$ separately or jointly. Alternatively, as (1.13) shows, the information $H[\mathbf{x}]$ encoded by $\mathbf{x}$ that cannot be obtained by observing $\mathbf{y}$ is $I[\mathbf{x};\mathbf{y}]$. The mutual information is zero if and only if $\mathbf{x}$ and $\mathbf{y}$ are independent (i.e., $p(\mathbf{x},\mathbf{y}) = p(\mathbf{x})p(\mathbf{y})$). The mutual information is non-negative [Cover & Thomas, 1991] which follows from the fact that more information may be obtained by observing $\mathbf{x}$ and $\mathbf{y}$ separately than jointly.

With a slight abuse of notation, the mutual information between the *components* of $\mathbf{a}$ (sometimes called the *redundancy* of $\mathbf{a}$) is written as

$$I[\mathbf{a}] \stackrel{\text{def}}{=} I[\mathbf{a};\{a_m\}] \tag{1.14}$$

$$= \sum_{m=1}^{M} H[a_m] - H[\mathbf{a}] \tag{1.15}$$

$$= \int p(\mathbf{a}) \log \frac{p(\mathbf{a})}{\prod_{m=1}^{M} p_m(a_m)} \, d\mathbf{a}. \tag{1.16}$$

The first term of (1.15) is the sum of the information carried by the recovered sources individually, and $H[\mathbf{a}]$ is the information carried jointly. $I[\mathbf{a}]$ is therefore the information common to the variables and thus measures their independence. It is again non-negative and equal to zero if and only if the components of $\mathbf{a}$ are mutually independent, so that there is no common information and the joint density factorises: $p(\mathbf{a}) =$

$\prod_{m=1}^{M} p(a_m)$. If the estimated sources carry no common information then nothing can be inferred about a recovered source from a knowledge of the others and the recovered sources are independent, $I[\mathbf{a}] = 0$. In this case the blind source separation has been successful.

The Kullback-Leibler (KL) divergence between two p.d.f.s $p(\mathbf{x})$ and $q(\mathbf{x})$ is defined as

$$\mathrm{KL}[p \parallel q] \stackrel{\text{def}}{=} \int_{\mathbf{x}} p(\mathbf{x}) \log \frac{p(\mathbf{x})}{q(\mathbf{x})} \, d\mathbf{x}. \tag{1.17}$$

Note that $\mathrm{KL}[p \parallel q] \neq \mathrm{KL}[q \parallel p]$. Comparison of equations (1.16) and (1.17) shows that the mutual information between the recovered sources is identical to the Kullback-Leibler divergence between the joint density $p(\mathbf{a})$ and the factorised density $\prod_{m=1}^{M} p(a_m)$. Independent component analysis attempts therefore to find a separating transform (a matrix when the mixing is linear) that minimises this KL divergence.

Scaling and permutation ambiguities The linear generative model (1.3) introduces a fundamental ambiguity in the scale of the recovered sources. The ambiguity arises because scaling a source by a factor λ ($s_m(t) \mapsto \lambda s_m(t)$) is exactly compensated by dividing the corresponding column of the mixing matrix by λ. In terms of the mutual information, we see that mutual information is independent of the scale of the recovered sources: the degree of independence between variables does not depend upon the units in which they are measured.† Therefore $I[\mathbf{a}] = I[D\mathbf{a}]$ for any diagonal matrix D ($D_{ii} \neq 0$). Furthermore, the order in which the components of $\mathbf{a}$ are listed is immaterial to their independence, so $I[\mathbf{a}] = I[P\mathbf{a}]$ for any permutation matrix P. Putting these together, $I[\mathbf{a}] = I[PD\mathbf{a}]$ which shows that the sources can only be recovered up to an arbitrary permutation and scaling.

In the zero noise limit a separating matrix W, which inverts the mixing, is sought so that $\mathbf{a} = W\mathbf{x}$. In this case, rather than $WA = I$, the best that may be achieved is

$$WA = PD, \tag{1.18}$$

because $I[\mathbf{s}] = I[W\mathbf{s}] = I[PDW\mathbf{s}]$. In the presence of isotropic observational noise the scaling and permutation ambiguities remain. Anisotropic noise destroys the permutation ambiguity, though the scaling ambiguity remains.

---

† More generally, mutual information is invariant under component-wise invertible transformations [Cover & Thomas, 1991].

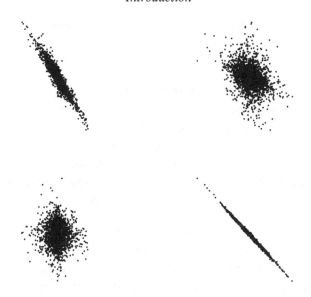

Figure 1.3. *Source separation by direct minimisation of mutual information.* Scatterplots of recovered sources versus true sources after direct minimisation of the mutual information between the recovered sources.

Direct minimisation of mutual information Measuring the mutual information between the components of **a** involves estimating the joint density $p(\mathbf{a})$. Accurate and reliable estimates are difficult to obtain with (usually) small amounts of data (see Fraser & Swinney [1986], Everson & Roberts [2000c]). Nonetheless, rudimentary blind source separation may be carried out by optimising the elements W_{ij} of the separating matrix so that the mutual information $I[W\mathbf{x}]$ is minimised.

As an example a logistic source and a Laplacian source were mixed by $A = \left[\begin{smallmatrix} 2 & 1 \\ 3 & 1 \end{smallmatrix}\right]$ to form 2000 two-dimensional observations. The measured mutual information between the components of $\mathbf{x}(t)$ was 1.73. A quasi-Newton (BFGS) algorithm [Press *et al.*, 1992] was used to find the W that minimised $I[W\mathbf{x}]$. Figure 1.3 shows that fairly good separation of the sources can be achieved, although there clearly exists some residual correlation between them. The measured mutual information between the recovered sources is 0.097, although the mutual information between the original sources is indistinguishable from zero. Straightforward ICA algorithms do much better, for example the algorithm presented on page 47 recovers sources with $I[\mathbf{a}]$ also indistinguishable from zero. Learning rules for ICA when A is square and there is no observational noise may be regarded as minimising the mutual information; see section 1.4.

1.2.3 Contrast functions

We have seen how the mutual information between the recovered sources can be used as an objective or *contrast function* which can be extremised. An ICA method consists of two distinct components. Firstly the formulation of a valid contrast function and secondly the use of an algorithm for extremising the contrast function, thereby estimating the free parameters of the system (A, $\mathbf{a}$ and perhaps some parameters in a source density model).

The so-called contrast function (or simply 'contrast') is the objective function of blind source separation methods, and the nomenclature has come into the language of ICA. For our purposes we define a contrast function, $\psi : \mathbb{R}^n \to \mathbb{R}$, as operating on a *probability density* and adopt the nomenclature of Cardoso [1998a] such that

$$\psi[\mathbf{a}] \stackrel{\text{def}}{=} \psi(p(\mathbf{a})). \qquad (1.19)$$

The contrast function has monotonicity such that

$$\psi[\mathbf{a}] \geqslant \psi[\mathbf{s}] \qquad (1.20)$$

with equality *iff* $\mathbf{a}$ is statistically equivalent† to $\mathbf{s}$.

As Cardoso [1998a] discusses, the *canonical* form of the ICA contrast function may be regarded as being that derived from the mutual information of the source estimates,

$$\psi_{\text{MI}} = I[\mathbf{a}] \qquad (1.21)$$

as it expresses purely the key property of ICA, namely the *independence* of the sources. As we saw in the last section, the difficulty in its direct use lies in the fact that it is extremely difficult, if not impossible, to make good estimates of the densities involved.

A good many alternative contrast functions have been proposed. However, the majority are applicable only to noiseless mixing. Noiseless mixing is, nonetheless, an important aspect of ICA research and the relations between different contrast functions are discussed in section 1.4. Much recent research into ICA has concentrated on modelling the process by which the sources and noise are combined to form the observations. The

---

† The indeterminacy in the ICA problem, $\psi[PD\mathbf{s}] \equiv \psi[\mathbf{s}]$, where P, D are permutation and scaling matrices (cf. page 10), means that we may not, in general, recover $\mathbf{a} \equiv \mathbf{s}$.

prime advantage of the 'generative model approach' is that a noise model is included in the formulation, permitting blind source separation in the presence of noise. It also permits modelling in the case where the number of sources is different from the number of observations and, ultimately, allows inference of the appropriate number of sources (see section 1.7 and Chapters 8 and 12).

1.2.4 Generative models and likelihood

Equations (1.2) and (1.3) explicitly model the process by which the observations are generated and may therefore be termed *generative models* [Everitt, 1984]. The linear generative model of equation (1.3), described in terms of the hidden (or *latent*) variables, $\mathbf{a}(t)$, is parameterised by three sets of numbers: first, the elements A_{nm} of the mixing matrix; second, parameters describing the source densities, which, for now, we summarise as a vector, $\boldsymbol{\theta}$;† and last, parameters describing the statistics of the observational noise. To be specific we assume that the observational noise is Gaussian distributed with mean zero and covariance $R_{\mathbf{n}}$; thus $\mathbf{n}(t) \sim \mathcal{N}(0, R_{\mathbf{n}})$.

The probability or *likelihood* of the observation given the model may therefore be found as follows. The likelihood is the probability that the recovered sources, $\mathbf{a}$, actually generated the datum, $\mathbf{x}$.‡ Hence

$$\ell(\mathbf{x}) \stackrel{\text{def}}{=} p(\mathbf{x} \,|\, A, \boldsymbol{\theta}, R_{\mathbf{n}}) = \int p(\mathbf{x} \,|\, A, \mathbf{a}, R_{\mathbf{n}}) p(\mathbf{a} \,|\, \boldsymbol{\theta}) \, d\mathbf{a}. \tag{1.22}$$

Using the fact that $\mathbf{x} - A\mathbf{a}$ is Gaussian distributed together with the independence of the sources, the likelihood is seen to be the convolution:

$$\ell(\mathbf{x}) = \int \mathcal{G}(\mathbf{x} - A\mathbf{a}, R_{\mathbf{n}}) \prod_{m=1}^{M} p_m(a_m \,|\, \theta_m) \, d\mathbf{a}. \tag{1.23}$$

Here $\mathcal{G}(\mathbf{y}, R_{\mathbf{n}})$ denotes the Gaussian function with mean zero and covariance $R_{\mathbf{n}}$:

$$\mathcal{G}(\mathbf{y}, R_{\mathbf{n}}) \stackrel{\text{def}}{=} \frac{1}{\sqrt{\det 2\pi R_{\mathbf{n}}}} \exp\left\{-\mathbf{y}^{\mathsf{T}} R_{\mathbf{n}}^{-1} \mathbf{y}/2\right\}. \tag{1.24}$$

Assuming that observations are independent, the likelihood for a batch

---

† Strictly the parameters $\boldsymbol{\theta}$ should include the unknown *number* of sources, M; methods for estimating M are examined in section 1.7.

‡ For now we omit the explicit dependence of $\mathbf{x}, \mathbf{s}, \mathbf{a}$ on t.

of observations $X \stackrel{\text{def}}{=} \{\mathbf{x}(t)\}_{t=1}^{T}$ is

$$p(X|A,\boldsymbol{\theta},R_{\mathbf{n}}) = \prod_{t=1}^{T} p(\mathbf{x}(t)|A,\boldsymbol{\theta},R_{\mathbf{n}}). \qquad (1.25)$$

It is often more convenient to consider the (normalised) log likelihood:

$$\mathcal{L}(X|A,\boldsymbol{\theta},R_{\mathbf{n}}) = \frac{1}{T} \sum_{t=1}^{T} \log p(\mathbf{x}(t)|A,\boldsymbol{\theta},R_{\mathbf{n}}). \qquad (1.26)$$

Given an expression for the likelihood, the mixing matrix A, the source parameters $\boldsymbol{\theta}$ and the noise covariance $R_{\mathbf{n}}$ may be estimated by adjusting them until the likelihood (or equivalently, the log likelihood) is maximised. An appropriate contrast function is therefore†

$$\psi_{\text{gen}} \stackrel{\text{def}}{=} -\mathcal{L}. \qquad (1.27)$$

We remark that the scaling and permutation ambiguities in source recovery persist here. The likelihood is invariant if any source is multiplied by a factor λ and the corresponding column of A is divided by λ. Likewise, the likelihood is invariant under permutations of the sources if the observational noise is isotropic.

Note that the form of the source model has not yet been specified; we have only formally written that the model depends on parameters $\boldsymbol{\theta}$. Choice of a particular source model gives rise to a number of well known ICA algorithms, several of which are discussed in section 1.4 and section 1.8. The numerical method used to optimise the likelihood is properly distinct from the choice of source model and a number of common methods are discussed in section 1.6.

Classical ICA models (e.g., Bell & Sejnowski [1995], Cardoso & Laheld [1996], Hyvärinen [1999a]) frequently omit the observational noise term and perform, for example, gradient ascent to a maximum likelihood solution. Noiseless mixing models of this kind are examined in section 1.4. Even if observational noise is included in the generative model the covariance matrix $R_{\mathbf{n}}$ is often assumed to be known (or is estimated separately from A and $\boldsymbol{\theta}$) and optimisation of $\mathcal{L}$ is carried out over A and $\boldsymbol{\theta}$.

Likelihood landscape It is possible to visualise the likelihood landscape for two-dimensional mixing. Since the likelihood is invariant under rescaling of the columns of A, we may write A in column-normalised form,

---

† This contrast may be regarded as $\psi_{\text{gen}}[\mathbf{x}]$ as it is a measure based on the observation density given the model.

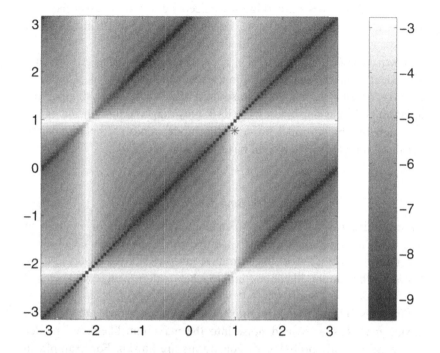

Figure 1.4. **Likelihood landscape.** *Likelihood for a mixture of a Laplacian and a Gaussian source. The log likelihood $\mathcal{L}$ is plotted as a function of angles θ_1 and θ_2 parameterising each column of A. Dark grey indicates low likelihood matrices and white indicates high likelihood matrices. A maximum likelihood matrix is indicated by the *.*

i.e., so that $\sum_i A_{ij}^2 = 1$, $\forall j$. Each two-dimensional column is therefore parameterised by a single angle, thus

$$A = \begin{bmatrix} \cos\theta_1 & \cos\theta_2 \\ \sin\theta_1 & \sin\theta_2 \end{bmatrix}. \tag{1.28}$$

Figure 1.4 shows the log likelihood for a mixture of a Gaussian and a Laplacian source ($p(s) \propto e^{-|s|}$) in the zero noise limit.

The striking symmetry of the figure is conferred by the invariance of the likelihood under permutation of the sources, $\mathcal{L}(X|A,\theta,R_n) = \mathcal{L}(X|PA,\theta,R_n)$ for any permutation matrix P. Also the likelihood is unchanged if the sources are multiplied by -1, corresponding to a translation by π in the figure. The maximum likelihood is therefore achieved for several (θ_1,θ_2) corresponding to different matrices related by symmetry. One instance is marked with a star in the figure. The maximum likelihood matrix lies on a ridge with steep sides and a nearly flat top; in subsection 1.6.4 we show how the ridge lies close to the manifold of matrices which recover *linearly* decorrelated sources.

When $\theta_2 = \theta_1 + n\pi$ $(n = \pm 1, \pm 2, \ldots)$ the columns of A are linearly dependent, and the generative model predicts that $x_2(t)$ is a multiple of $x_1(t)$ for all t. In the zero noise limit the likelihood is singular (cf. equation (1.53)) as depicted by the dark grey diagonal lines in the figure. Inclusion of observational noise in the model removes the singularity, but these singular mixtures still have very low likelihood.

1.2.5 Bayesian ICA

By maximising $\mathcal{L}(X \mid A, \theta, R_n)$, the maximum likelihood formulation of ICA finds a single mixing matrix, source model parameters and noise covariance which are most likely to have given rise to the observed data. However, maximum likelihood approaches suffer from two principal difficulties.

First, it is difficult to incorporate additional prior knowledge about the mixing matrix, sources and noise into the maximum likelihood model, particularly if only probabilistic constraints are known. For example, in some image processing applications it is not straightforward to enforce the known constraint that the mixing is positive, $A_{nm} \geqslant 0$. This problem is treated by Miskin and MacKay in Chapter 8. Secondly, the likelihood alone does not limit the complexity (the number of parameters) in a model. In fact, even if a model exactly describes the method by which the observations were generated, a maximum likelihood model will always choose a more complex model because the extra degrees of freedom may be used to model the noise. The tendency of maximum likelihood models to over-fit the data has led to several schemes, such as the Akaike Information Criterion (AIC, [Akaike, 1973]), Minimum Description Length (MDL, [Rissanen, 1978]) and Minimum Message Length (MML, [Wallace & Boulton, 1968]), to limit the fitted model complexity by penalising over-complex models.

Adoption of a Bayesian methodology [Roberts, 1998, Knuth, 1999, Mohammad-Djafari, 1999] can overcome both of these difficulties in a natural way.† Although a Bayesian formulation applies equally to the nonlinear case, we restrict the discussion to linear ICA, in which we are interested in learning about the sources, the mixing and the noise

† A good introduction to Bayesian data analysis is given by Sivia [1996].

covariance having observed data $X = \{\mathbf{x}(t)\}_{t=1}^{T}$. We denote the particular model by $\mathcal{H}$. Bayes' theorem can be used to write

$$p(A, \theta, R_n | X, \mathcal{H}) = \frac{p(X | A, \theta, R_n, \mathcal{H}) p(A, \theta, R_n | \mathcal{H})}{p(X | \mathcal{H})}. \tag{1.29}$$

The first factor in the numerator is recognised as the data likelihood given a particular model (1.25). The second factor, $p(A, \theta, R_n | \mathcal{H})$, expresses prior information (before the data have been observed) about the model. The normalising factor in the denominator is constant for any particular model. It is known as the *Bayesian evidence* and may be used in model order selection in a manner that naturally penalises complex models (see section 1.7). The left hand side is known as the *posterior* density as it describes the knowledge about the model after the data have been observed.

The mixing matrix, model parameters and noise covariance which maximise the posterior density are known as the *maximum a posteriori* (MAP) estimates. In addition the p.d.f. of solutions allows sensible error bars to be attached to the single most probable estimate. A final valuable property of the Bayesian formulation is that the posterior density may be used as a prior density if more observations become available (see Chapter 11).

Since the mixing matrix, which describes the mixing of the sources, is independent of the sources themselves, and the sensor noise is independent of the details of the mixing and sources, the prior probability may be factorised to give

$$p(A, \theta, R_n | X, \mathcal{H}) \propto p(X | A, \theta, R_n, \mathcal{H}) p(A | \mathcal{H}) p(\theta | \mathcal{H}) p(R_n | \mathcal{H}). \tag{1.30}$$

The noise covariance, for example, may thence be treated as a nuisance parameter and marginalised by integrating over all possible values:

$$p(A, \theta | X, \mathcal{H}) \propto \left\{ \int p(X | A, \theta, R_n, \mathcal{H}) p(R_n | \mathcal{H}) \, dR_n \right\} p(A | \mathcal{H}) p(\theta | \mathcal{H}). \tag{1.31}$$

Of course a natural choice for a prior density over the sources is just a factorised density (1.5); however, the Bayesian formulation shows how to relax the assumption of independence and how additional constraints on the sources may be incorporated into $p(\theta | \mathcal{H})$. Likewise, prior information about the elements of the mixing matrix may be incorporated into $p(A | \mathcal{H})$.

Roberts [1998] shows how the integrals occurring in the likelihood (1.31) may be approximated to provide a practical scheme for finding

MAP estimates. More recently ensemble learning methods have been used with success; see Chapter 8 and [Lappalainen, 1999]. Knuth [1998a] exploits the Bayesian approach in a model for electroencephalography (EEG) in which the mixing matrix elements are dependent upon source location. Parra *et al.* [2000] incorporate prior information about both sources and mixing into a model for hyperspectral imagery. Model order estimation is treated from a Bayesian point of view in section 1.7, and in Chapters 8 and 12.

1.3 Gaussian sources

The ubiquity of the Gaussian distribution in nature and the analytic tractability that it lends to many problems give it a central role in many probabilistic methods. Here we consider the special cases that arise when the sources in the ICA generative model are Gaussian, namely Principal Component Analysis (PCA), Factor Analysis (FA), and a recent generalisation of PCA which sets it on a firm probabilistic footing, known as Sensible PCA (SPCA, [Roweis, 1997]) or Probabilistic PCA (PPCA [Tipping & Bishop, 1997]).

Gaussian densities are completely described by second-order statistics, namely the mean and covariance. In fact, for Gaussians the notion of independence is equivalent to decorrelation, so that if a joint Gaussian density has a diagonal covariance matrix the marginal densities are independent because

$$\mathcal{G}(\mathbf{s}, \text{diag}(\sigma_1^2, \sigma_2^2, \dots, \sigma_M^2)) = \prod_{m=1}^{M} \mathcal{G}(s_m, \sigma_m^2). \qquad (1.32)$$

In addition, if the sources and observational noise are each Gaussian, with covariances R_s and R_n respectively, then so are the observations:

$$p(\mathbf{x}) = \mathcal{G}(\mathbf{x}, AR_sA^\mathsf{T} + R_n). \qquad (1.33)$$

Principal Component Analysis   Principal Component Analysis (PCA, [Jolliffe, 1986]), which dates back to Pearson [1901] describes the situation in which the sources are Gaussian and there is no observational noise:

$$\mathbf{x}(t) = A\mathbf{s}(t) \qquad (1.34)$$

The fundamental ambiguity alluded to on page 10 between the scale of the sources and the magnitude of A persists when the sources are Gaussian. In the PCA formulation the ambiguity is resolved by choosing the sources to have unit variance: $\mathbf{s} \sim \mathcal{N}(0, I)$. A general mixing matrix may be written in terms of its singular value decomposition (SVD; see, for example, [Horn & Johnson, 1985]), thus

$$A = U\Sigma V^\mathsf{T} \tag{1.35}$$

where $U \in \mathbb{R}^{N \times M}$ and $V \in \mathbb{R}^{M \times M}$ are matrices with orthonormal columns and Σ is diagonal. However, since V is orthogonal, $|\det V| = 1$ and straightforward transformation of probabilities [Papoulis, 1991] shows that $V^\mathsf{T}\mathbf{s}$ is itself Gaussian with covariance I. Hence A can, without loss of generality, be written in the form

$$A = U\Sigma. \tag{1.36}$$

Thus in the Gaussian case a further ambiguity, in addition to the scaling and permutation ambiguities, is present; namely, A can only be determined up to a rotation.

The predicted covariance of the data is therefore (see equation (1.33)):

$$R_\mathbf{x} = AR_s A^\mathsf{T} = U\Sigma^2 U^\mathsf{T}. \tag{1.37}$$

The orthonormal matrix U and the scaling factors Σ may now be identified by equating the sample covariance of the dataset $\hat{R}_\mathbf{x}$ and the predicted covariance (see equation (1.37)):

$$\hat{R}_\mathbf{x} = \frac{1}{T} \sum_{t=1}^{T} \mathbf{x}(t)\mathbf{x}(t)^\mathsf{T} = U\Sigma^2 U^\mathsf{T} = R_\mathbf{x}. \tag{1.38}$$

Rearranging obtains an eigenvalue equation,

$$\hat{R}_\mathbf{x} U = U\Sigma^2. \tag{1.39}$$

The eigenvectors, which form the columns of U, are known as the *principal components* of the data, and the eigenvalues σ_m^2 measure the variance (or power) of the M sources. The eigenvalues (which are non-negative because $R_\mathbf{x}$ is Hermitian) are usually arranged in decreasing order, $\sigma_1 \geqslant \sigma_2 \geqslant \cdots \geqslant \sigma_M \geqslant 0$.

The goal of ICA, to find a separating matrix W so that the recovered sources $\mathbf{a}(t) = W\mathbf{x}(t)$ are decorrelated and therefore independent, is achieved with $W = \Sigma^{-1}U^\mathsf{T}$. Here U^T projects the data into the M-dimensional source space and Σ^{-1} scales the projections to have unit variance. Of course, $\hat{W} = QA = Q\Sigma^{-1}U^\mathsf{T}$, where Q is any orthogonal matrix, also recovers decorrelated Gaussian sources, which may equally well be interpreted as the original sources. However, PCA chooses $Q = I$, which means that $\mathbf{u}_1$ is the direction in which the data have greatest variance, and $\mathbf{u}_2$ is the direction orthogonal to $\mathbf{u}_1$ with greatest variance, etc. This characterisation of the principal components may also be used as a starting point from which to derive (1.39).

PCA is often approached from the point of view of finding a new (low-dimensional) orthogonal basis for the data with the property that the least mean squared error is made when approximating the data using this basis. The motivation is that the low-dimensional basis will capture the important features of the data while discarding the unimportant directions (which are probably dominated by noise, although there is no proper noise model). Let the columns of $U \in \mathbb{R}^{N \times M}$ be some orthonormal basis. Then a datum $\mathbf{x} \in \mathbb{R}^N$ is represented by the M-dimensional vector $U^T\mathbf{x}$.

In the original space the approximation to $\mathbf{x}$ (or the reconstruction of $\mathbf{x}$) is the projection

$$\hat{\mathbf{x}} = UU^T\mathbf{x}. \tag{1.40}$$

The approximation error is

$$\epsilon^2 = \| \mathbf{x} - \hat{\mathbf{x}} \|^2 \tag{1.41}$$

$$= \| \mathbf{x} - UU^T\mathbf{x} \|^2 \tag{1.42}$$

$$= \mathbf{x}^T\mathbf{x} - \mathbf{x}^T UU^T\mathbf{x}. \tag{1.43}$$

The mean squared error over all the data is therefore

$$E = \frac{1}{T} \sum_{t=1}^{T} \epsilon^2 = \frac{1}{T}[\mathrm{Tr}(R_\mathbf{x}) - \mathrm{Tr}(UR_\mathbf{x}U^T)]. \tag{1.44}$$

Maximising $\mathrm{Tr}(UR_\mathbf{x}U^T)$ subject to the constraint that the columns of U be orthonormal leads again to the eigenvalue equation (1.39) (Bishop [1995] provides a clear derivation.). This shows that on average the PCA basis commits the smallest reconstruction error among all linear bases.

Figure 1.5 shows the two principal components for a two-dimensional mixture of two Gaussian sources. The first principal component lies in the direction of maximum variance, while $\mathbf{u}_2$ is orthogonal to $\mathbf{u}_1$ and lies in the direction of the remaining variance. Note that even though the sources are Gaussian (and thus are well described by the PCA model), projection onto either principal component fails to recover a source. This is because rotation of the recovered sources by any orthogonal matrix, Q, accounts for the data equally well: PCA makes the arbitrary choice that $\mathbf{u}_1$ lies in the direction of maximum variance. For the same reason ICA is unable to separate the sources.

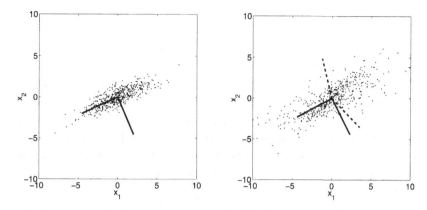

Figure 1.5. **PCA and ICA.** *Left: principal components of a mixture of two Gaussian distributed sources. Each point is an observation* **x**(t) *and the lines show the direction of the principal components. Right: Principal components (solid) and independent component basis vectors (dashed) of a mixture of a Laplacian and a Gaussian source.*

Figure 1.5 also shows the principal components for a mixture of a Gaussian source and a Laplacian source ($p(s) \propto e^{-|s|}$), for which the Gaussian source model is clearly incorrect. The first principal component lies in the direction of maximum variance, but, again both principal components fail to capture either source. Also shown are the directions of the rows $\mathbf{w}_1$ and $\mathbf{w}_2$ of the separating matrix found by ICA using a generalised exponential source model (section 1.5). The rows of the separating matrix are *independent component basis vectors*. The ICA model, which gives up the requirement of finding an orthogonal basis in return for a more flexible source model, is able to correctly locate the constituent sources and projections onto $\mathbf{w}_1$ and $\mathbf{w}_2$ correctly separate the sources.

If the data are arranged as the columns of a matrix $X \in \mathbb{R}^{N \times T}$ PCA is equivalent to a singular value decomposition [Horn & Johnson, 1985] of X:

$$X = U \Sigma V^\mathsf{T} \tag{1.45}$$

where $U \in \mathbb{R}^{N \times N}$ and $V \in \mathbb{R}^{N \times T}$ are matrices with orthonormal columns and $\Sigma \in \mathbb{R}^{N \times N}$ is a matrix with non-negative entries on the diagonal and zeros elsewhere. The equivalence to PCA can be seen by forming the sample covariance matrix:

$$\hat{R}_x = \frac{1}{T}XX^\mathsf{T} = \frac{1}{T}U\Sigma^2 U^\mathsf{T}. \tag{1.46}$$

Thus the columns of U are the eigenvectors of $\hat{R}_x$, namely the principal components.

When $N < T$ it is efficient to calculate the principal components by solving the eigenvalue equation (1.39), which takes $O(N^3)$ operations.† When $T < N$ (for example, when the observations are images) a more efficient procedure is to form the $T \times T$ matrix

$$K = \frac{1}{T}X^\mathsf{T}X = \frac{1}{T}V\Lambda^2 V^\mathsf{T}. \tag{1.47}$$

As equation (1.47) shows, K has the same eigenvalues, σ_i^2, $i = 1, \ldots, T$, as $\hat{R}_x$, but can be diagonalised in $O(T^3)$ operations to find V^T, after which the principal components may be found from $U = XV\Sigma^{-1}$. These observations form the basis of the *snapshot* method [Sirovich, 1987, Sirovich & Everson, 1992]. Note, however, that Roweis [1997] describes a method to find the first k principal components in $O(kNT)$ operations.

PCA with noise PCA, although widely used, does not strictly embody a proper generative model, because the noise term is absent. Consequently only observations which lie in the range of A can be sensibly assigned a likelihood. There are, however, a number of linear generative models with Gaussian sources and observational noise. In both Factor Analysis [Everitt, 1984] and Probabilistic PCA [Tipping & Bishop, 1997, Tipping & Bishop, 1999]‡ observations are modelled as being generated by a mixture of a (small number of) Gaussian distributed latent variables or sources:

$$\mathbf{x}(t) = A\mathbf{s}(t) + \mathbf{n}(t), \qquad \mathbf{n}(t) \sim \mathcal{N}(0, R_n). \tag{1.48}$$

In FA the sources are known as *factors*. The difference between the models lies in the modelling of the noise covariance. In both cases the covariance matrix is assumed to be diagonal, which makes the observations conditionally independent given the sources. PPCA makes the

---

† In contrast to solving an eigenvalue equation, most ICA methods must, more or less slowly, iteratively ascend a likelihood gradient.

‡ Roweis [1997] uses the same generative model as PPCA, but calls it Sensible PCA; we refer to both methods as PPCA.

further restriction that the noise variance at each sensor is identical so that $R_n = r^2 I$.

No closed form solution for the FA model is available, so A and R_n must be estimated iteratively. On the other hand, Tipping & Bishop were able to show that the first M columns of the maximum likelihood A span the same subspace as the first M principal components, and may be computed from them via eigendecomposition of the sample covariance matrix. The fact that they span the same subspace also implies that the mean squared reconstruction error for PPCA is identical to that for PCA, and is therefore minimum among all linear bases.

If the sources are permitted to be non-Gaussian we recover ICA models. With simple observational noise models we obtain Independent Factor Analysis (IFA [Attias, 1999a], see Chapter 3 of the present book) or Probabilistic ICA (PICA, see Chapter 12). When the observational noise is zero and the mixing matrix is square, but the source priors are non-Gaussian, classical ICA models are obtained; these are discussed in the following section. It is interesting to note that Roweis & Ghahramani [1999] provide an interpretation of ICA in which the sources are Gaussian, but the mixing is nonlinear.

1.4 Noiseless (square mixing) ICA

Bell & Sejnowski's [1995] seminal paper, which has inspired much recent work, treated ICA without observational noise and with a square mixing matrix, $N = M$. We now examine noiseless mixing with a square mixing matrix, from a number of different aspects. In this section some general facts about the noiseless, square mixing case are established and the relationships between different information theoretic characterisations of ICA are examined (see [Lee *et al.*, 2000b] for an extensive review). In the following section we examine the effect of particular choices of source models, which give rise to several well known algorithms. Throughout these two sections we concentrate on the objective function, or *contrast* function, which is to be maximised, and defer discussion of specific optimisation methods and related ICA algorithms to section 1.6.

Likelihood The likelihood in the noiseless case can be found by allowing the Gaussian in equation (1.23) to become infinitely sharp. Replacing the Gaussian by a Dirac delta function and carrying out the integration gives an expression for the likelihood of a single observation $\mathbf{x}(t)$ in the noiseless case:

$$p(\mathbf{x}|A,\mathbf{s}) = \frac{1}{|\det A|} \prod_{m=1}^{M} p(s_m). \tag{1.49}$$

This expression is also simply obtained by noting that

$$p(\mathbf{x}) = \frac{p(\mathbf{s})}{|\det J|}, \tag{1.50}$$

where $J_{ij} = \partial x_i / \partial s_j = A_{ij}$ is the Jacobian of the transformation from $\mathbf{s}$ to $\mathbf{x}$ [Papoulis, 1991].

Note that, like PCA, since there is no noise term the ICA model $\mathbf{x} = A\mathbf{s}$ cannot be considered to be a true generative model, and no likelihood can properly be assigned to an observation that is not in the range of A. Nonetheless, we shall refer to this pseudo-likelihood as the plain likelihood.

Since there is no noise, ICA amounts to seeking a separating matrix $W = A^{-1}$, which, when applied to the observations, recovers the latent sources $\mathbf{a} = W\mathbf{x}$. It is often useful to write the likelihood in terms of the separating matrix W and the recovered sources. Thus the log likelihood for a single observation is [MacKay, 1996]

$$\log \ell(\mathbf{x}) = \log p(\mathbf{x}|W,\mathbf{a}) = \log|\det W| + \sum_{m=1}^{M} \log p(\mathbf{a}_m). \tag{1.51}$$

For a batch of T observations the log likelihood is

$$\mathcal{L} = \log|\det W| + \frac{1}{T} \sum_{t=1}^{T} \sum_{m=1}^{M} \log p(\mathbf{a}_m(t)) \tag{1.52}$$

$$= \log|\det W| + \frac{1}{T} \sum_{t=1}^{T} \sum_{m=1}^{M} \log p\left(\sum_{j} W_{mj}\mathbf{x}_j(t)\right) \tag{1.53}$$

$$= \log|\det W| - \sum_{m=1}^{M} H_m[a_m], \tag{1.54}$$

where

$$H_m[a_m] = -\frac{1}{T} \sum_{t=1}^{T} \log p(a_m(t)) \tag{1.55}$$

$$\approx -\int p(a_m) \log p(a_m) \, da_m \tag{1.56}$$

is an estimate of the entropy of the mth recovered source. Equation (1.53) forms the basis of many source separation algorithms. For a particular choice of source model (that is, $p(\mathbf{a}_m)$), differentiation of $\mathcal{L}$ with respect to the elements of W gives the gradient of the log likelihood which can be ascended to find the maximum likelihood separating matrix. Particular source models are discussed in section 1.5.

Mutual information The maximum likelihood separating matrix is equivalent to the separating matrix which gives the most independent recovered sources. The equivalence was first demonstrated by MacKay [1996] and Cardoso [1997], and can be seen in the following way. The mutual information between the recovered sources (or equivalently the KL divergence between the joint source density and the product of the individual marginal densities) is given by

$$I[\mathbf{a}] = \mathrm{KL}[\mathbf{a} \parallel \{a_m\}] \tag{1.57}$$

$$= \int p(\mathbf{a}) \log \frac{p(\mathbf{a})}{\prod_{m=1}^{M} p(a_m)} \, d\mathbf{a} \tag{1.58}$$

$$= \int p(\mathbf{a}) \log p(\mathbf{a}) \, d\mathbf{a} + \sum_{m=1}^{M} H_m[a_m] \tag{1.59}$$

$$= -\log |\det W| + H[\mathbf{x}] + \sum_{m=1}^{M} H_m[a_m], \tag{1.60}$$

where $H[\mathbf{x}] = \int p(\mathbf{x}) \log p(\mathbf{x}) \, d\mathbf{x}$ is the entropy of the observations. Comparison of equations (1.54) and (1.60) shows that

$$I[\mathbf{a}] = H[\mathbf{x}] - \mathcal{L}. \tag{1.61}$$

Since $H[\mathbf{x}]$ is constant, maximisation of the likelihood is seen to be equivalent to minimising the mutual information between the recovered sources.

As we noted previously and Cardoso [1998a] discusses, the *canonical* form of the ICA contrast function may be regarded as being that derived from the mutual information of the source estimates, $\psi_{\mathrm{MI}} = I[\mathbf{a}]$, as it expresses purely the key property of ICA, namely the *independence* of the sources. As the above discussion shows, if a model (note that this model can be approximate only) for the source densities is used, then $\psi_{\mathrm{ML}} = \mathcal{L} - H[\mathbf{x}]$ may be a natural choice of contrast as it is neatly interpretable as the deviation between the data and the generative model.

Information maximisation Barlow [1961b, 1989] suggested that efficient biological networks should combine their inputs so that each output neuron encodes a feature that is maximally statistically independent of other output neurons in the network; that is the network should minimise the mutual information between its outputs. On the other hand, Linsker [1989, 1992] proposed that the design principle for biological networks should be the maximisation of transmitted information, and Atick & Redlich [1990] have modelled the early visual system using this principle. See Hinton & Sejnowski [1998] for recent ideas in this field. While blind source separation by minimisation of the mutual information between the outputs of a linear network (i.e., between the estimated sources) is clearly analogous to Barlow's suggestion, Bell & Sejnowski [1995] and Roth & Baram [1996] each formulated blind source separation algorithms in terms of information maximisation.

Consider the information transmitted by the mapping $\mathbf{f} : \mathbf{x} \mapsto \mathbf{y}$. Bell & Sejnowski [1995] consider the two-stage mapping, which might be implemented by a single layer feed-forward neural network, as follows:

$$\mathbf{a} = W\mathbf{x}, \tag{1.62}$$

$$\mathbf{y} = \mathbf{g}(\mathbf{a}), \qquad y_m = g_m(a_m), \tag{1.63}$$

where W is a linear transformation and $\mathbf{g}$ is a bounded nonlinearity applied to each individual output, a_m.

The information transmitted by the mapping is the mutual information between the input and the output:

$$I[\mathbf{x}; \mathbf{y}] = H[\mathbf{x}] + H[\mathbf{y}] - H[\mathbf{x}, \mathbf{y}] \tag{1.64}$$

$$= H[\mathbf{y}] - H[\mathbf{y}|\mathbf{x}]. \tag{1.65}$$

The joint entropy of the outputs $H[\mathbf{y}]$ may be written in terms of the mutual information *between* the individual outputs, $I[\mathbf{y}]$, to obtain

$$I[\mathbf{x}; \mathbf{y}] = \sum_{m=1}^{M} H[y_m] - I[\mathbf{y}] - H[\mathbf{y}|\mathbf{x}]. \tag{1.66}$$

If the mapping is deterministic there is no uncertainty in the $\mathbf{y}$ given $\mathbf{x}$. Bell & Sejnowski therefore argue that in the low noise limit the term $H[\mathbf{y}|\mathbf{x}]$ which measures the uncertainty in $\mathbf{y}$ given $\mathbf{x}$ may be ignored. Consequently, the transmitted information is maximised if the individual output entropies are maximised and the mutual information between them simultaneously minimised. Now, if every output of the transformation is bounded the maximum $H[y_m]$ is achieved when y_m is uniformly distributed [Cover & Thomas, 1991] and the minimum $I[\mathbf{y}]$ is achieved when $\mathbf{y}$ factorises. Bell & Sejnowski then make the crucial observation that, since the mutual information is invariant under component-wise monotone transformations, if the y_m are independent then so are the components a_m of $\mathbf{a}$. Blind source separation of $\mathbf{x}$ can therefore be accomplished by optimising $\mathbf{g}$ and A so as to maximise the information transmission by $\mathbf{f}$. Algorithms derived from this perspective are therefore dubbed 'infomax' algorithms.

Nadal & Parga [1994] make this argument more precise by showing that if the observations result from the linear mixing of independent sources, s_m, and if $\mathbf{g}$ is chosen so that $p(s_m) = \partial g_m(s_m)/\partial s_m$ then the transmitted information $I[\mathbf{x};\mathbf{y}]$ is maximised when

$$W = PDA^{-1}, \tag{1.67}$$

for arbitrary diagonal matrix D and permutation matrix P.

Bell & Sejnowski [1995] found that the choice of $g(\cdot)$ is not too crucial. In fact, if $g(\cdot)$ is chosen to be a sigmoidal function[†] then a wide range of platykurtic (heavy tailed) sources can be separated by a learning rule that minimises the mutual information between the output variables. We examine the reason for this spectacular ability in section 1.5.

Cumulant based methods and higher order statistics In the previous section we have seen that many of the commonest approaches to ICA give rise to the same maximum likelihood or *infomax* objective. In this section we consider how approaches based on the statistical *moments* on the estimated sources also give valid contrast functions. These methods are often considerably faster than infomax approaches and, despite their approximative nature, may give excellent results. We note, furthermore, that moment based methods have historical precedence in the signal processing literature (see Comon [1994] for a review).

We first introduce the definition of higher order statistical measures known as *cumulants*, of which the most relevant for ICA are those of second and fourth order, defined respectively as

$$C_{ij}[\mathbf{a}] \stackrel{\text{def}}{=} \mathcal{E}\{a_i a_j\} \tag{1.68}$$

(in which $\mathcal{E}\{.\}$ is the expectation operator) and

$$
\begin{aligned}
C_{ijkl}[\mathbf{a}] \stackrel{\text{def}}{=}\ &\mathcal{E}\{a_i a_j a_k a_l\} - \mathcal{E}\{a_i a_j\}\mathcal{E}\{a_k a_l\} \\
&- \mathcal{E}\{a_i a_k\}\mathcal{E}\{a_j a_l\} - \mathcal{E}\{a_i a_l\}\mathcal{E}\{a_j a_k\}.
\end{aligned}
\tag{1.69}
$$

[†] For example, the standard neural network nonlinearity, $g(a) = 1/(1 + e^{-a})$.

Independence of a_j and a_k means that

$$\mathcal{E}\{g_1(a_j)g_2(a_k)\} = 0 \quad \text{for all} \quad j \neq k \tag{1.70}$$

for arbitrary (up to certain technical conditions) functions g_1 and g_2. When we consider the cumulants of the hypothesised sources, under the assumption of independence, we see therefore that all cross entries are zero and

$$C_{ii}[\mathbf{s}] = \mathcal{E}\{s_i^2\} \stackrel{\text{def}}{=} \sigma_i^2 \tag{1.71}$$

where σ_i^2 is the variance of the ith source. Similarly

$$C_{iiii}[\mathbf{s}] = \mathcal{E}\{s_i^4\} - 3\sigma_i^4 \stackrel{\text{def}}{=} \kappa_i \tag{1.72}$$

where κ_i is the *kurtosis* of the ith source. Signals with positive kurtosis (loosely the tails of their densities decay more slowly than the Gaussian density and so they are sharply peaked around their mean) are known variously as platykurtic, sparse or super-Gaussian, whereas signals with negative kurtosis (rapidly decaying tails) are called leptokurtic or sub-Gaussian.

The paper which introduced the use of mutual information in ICA, Comon [1994] (see also [Hyvärinen, 1999d]), used Edgeworth expansions (see, for example, [Kendal & Stuart, 1969]) to derive an approximation to the mutual information $I[\mathbf{a}] = \text{KL}[\mathbf{a} \parallel \mathbf{s}]$, when the a_m are uncorrelated,[+] as follows:

$$I[\mathbf{a}] \approx c + \frac{1}{48} \sum_{m=1}^{M} \left\{ 4C_{ii}^2(a_m) + C_{iiii}^2(a_m)7C_{iiii}^4(a_m) - 6C_{ii}^2(a_m)C_{iiii}(a_m) \right\}$$

$$\tag{1.73}$$

where c is a constant. Comon proposes an ICA algorithm based on this approximation, and other ingenious algebraic methods based on joint diagonalisation of cross cumulants are given by Cardoso & Comon [1996]. Particularly effective and popular among these is the JADE algorithm [Cardoso & Souloumiac, 1993, Cardoso, 1999b]. This approximation, in a slightly altered guise, forms the basis of ICA methods such as Fast-ICA [Hyvärinen, 1999a], more detail on which is available in subsection 1.6.4 and Chapter 2. We note also that Amari *et al.* [1996] have developed ICA algorithms based on Gram-Charlier expansions instead of Edgeworth expansions.

+ Easily achieved by sphering the observations via PCA, for example.

Simpler measures than (1.73) may, however, be defined using the Euclidean distance between cumulants, namely

$$\psi_2[\mathbf{a}] \stackrel{\text{def}}{=} \sum_{ij} (C_{ij}[\mathbf{a}] - C_{ij}[\mathbf{s}])^2 = \sum_{ij} (C_{ij}[\mathbf{a}] - \sigma_i^2 \delta_{ij})^2$$

and

$$\psi_4[\mathbf{a}] \stackrel{\text{def}}{=} \sum_{ijkl} (C_{ijkl}[\mathbf{a}] - C_{ijkl}[\mathbf{s}])^2 = \sum_{ijkl} (C_{ijkl}[\mathbf{a}] - \kappa_i \delta_{ijkl})^2.$$

As Cardoso [1998a] points out, the first of these measures is not a true contrast in the ICA sense, as it reaches zero when $\mathbf{a}$ is merely *linearly* decorrelated, rather than independent. The use of fourth order information alone, i.e., $\psi_4[\mathbf{a}]$, leads to a valid ICA formalism however.

If the kurtosis $\kappa_m[a_m]$ of all the sources is of the same sign (i.e., they are all sub-Gaussian or, more commonly, all super-Gaussian) Moreau & Macchi [1993] showed that optimising a particularly simple contrast function, namely the sum of the fourth moments

$$\psi[\mathbf{a}] = \sum_{m=1}^{M} \mathcal{E}\{a_m^4\} \tag{1.74}$$

will achieve blind source separation. In Chapter 5 of the present book Parra and Spence give an illuminating discussion of how a common class of non-stationary, short-time Gaussian signals have positive kurtosis.

These cumulant methods are, however, prone to the difficulties inherent in estimating the higher moments from a limited amount of data. More fundamentally the approximations to the mutual information, which are derived via Edgeworth expansions, rely on the recovered sources being not too far from Gaussian.

Negentropy In fact, source separation may be achieved by maximising the non-Gaussianity of the recovered sources. The deviation from Gaussianity of a random variate may be quantified in terms of the *negentropy*:

$$J[\mathbf{a}] \stackrel{\text{def}}{=} H[\boldsymbol{\alpha}] - H[\mathbf{a}], \tag{1.75}$$

where $\boldsymbol{\alpha}$ is a random variate with the same covariance as $\mathbf{a}$. Like mutual information, the negentropy is non-negative and it is zero if and only if $\mathbf{a}$ is Gaussian [Comon, 1994]. Negentropy is related to the mutual information by the relation

$$I[\mathbf{a}] = J[\mathbf{a}] - \sum_{m=1}^{M} J[a_m] + \frac{1}{2} \log \frac{\det \text{diag}(R)}{\det R}, \tag{1.76}$$

where R is the covariance matrix of **a**. When the recovered sources are decorrelated, so that R is diagonal, the last term is zero, giving

$$I[\mathbf{a}] = J[\mathbf{a}] - \sum_{m=1}^{M} J[a_m]. \qquad (1.77)$$

The negentropy is invariant under invertible transforms [Comon, 1994], so maximising the sum of the recovered source negentropies is equivalent to minimising the mutual information. Thus finding directions which maximise the deviation from Gaussian of the recovered sources will achieve separation. Hyvärinen makes simple polynomial approximations to $J[a_m]$ to develop the highly effective FastICA algorithm; Hyvärinen describes this approach in detail in Chapter 2 of the present book.

Note the connection with projection pursuit methods, which also seek directions in data which are 'interesting' in the sense that projections of the data onto them have maximally non-Gaussian densities [Friedman, 1987]. Girolami & Fyfe [1997b, 1997a] used the negentropy as a projection pursuit index to derive a learning rule that is able to separate both sub- and super-Gaussian sources.

1.5 Source models

Linear generative models for ICA (equations (1.3) and (1.4)) must make an *a priori* assumption about the probability density functions of the sources. In this section we examine a number of alternative source models. Although we examine them in the context of noiseless, square mixing, they can also be used in the general noisy case.

Fixed source models The most basic choice for the source probability density is to choose some function with no adjustable parameters. A particularly nice example from an analytic point of view is the reciprocal cosh density,

$$p(s) = \frac{1}{\pi \cosh(s)}, \qquad (1.78)$$

which was one of the functional forms proposed by Bell & Sejnowski [1995]. Once a particular source model has been selected the gradient of the log likelihood may be found and used to find the maximum likelihood unmixing matrix. With a fixed source model the gradient of the log likelihood is found by differentiating equation (1.53):

$$\frac{\partial \log \ell(\mathbf{x})}{\partial W_{ij}} = W_{ij}^{-\mathsf{T}} + \frac{\partial \log p_i(a_i)}{\partial a_i} x_j. \tag{1.79}$$

In fact the source model is frequently defined implicitly by the choice of a nonlinear 'squashing' or 'score' function

$$\phi_m(a_m) \stackrel{\text{def}}{=} -\frac{\partial \log p(a_m)}{\partial a_m} = -\frac{1}{p(a_m)} \frac{\partial p(a_m)}{\partial a_m}, \tag{1.80}$$

which appears in a learning rule based on (1.79). More on particular learning rules appears in section 1.6. In terms of the cumulative source density,

$$P(a) = \int_{-\infty}^{a} p(x)\, dx, \tag{1.81}$$

the function ϕ_m is seen to be

$$\phi_m(a_i) = -\frac{P'(a_i)}{P''(a_i)}. \tag{1.82}$$

Equation (1.80) shows that if $p(a_m)$ is platykurtic, so that its tails decay more slowly than Gaussian (e.g., $p(a_m) \propto \exp\{-|a_m|^r\}$, $r > 2$), $\phi(a)$ has a sigmoidal shape similar to neural network transfer functions. Indeed Bell & Sejnowski used the form

$$\phi_m(a) = \frac{1}{1 + e^{-a}} \tag{1.83}$$

in their neuro-mimetic algorithm. Bell & Sejnowski also interpret the shape of ϕ as the shape that maximises information transfer through a nonlinear network (cf. section 1.4 above). Note that the density corresponding to (1.83) is implicitly defined via (1.80), but does not have an analytic form, although the reciprocal cosh density (1.78) leads to

$$\phi_m(a_i) = \tanh(a_i), \tag{1.84}$$

see figure 1.6. Surprisingly, models with a fixed sigmoidal source density are able to separate a wide range of heavy tailed sources. They are, however, unable to separate leptokurtic sources (i.e., sources with negative kurtosis, for example sources with a uniform density).

This ability turns out to be due to the freedom to adjust the scaling of the rows of the separating matrix without affecting the independence between the recovered sources. As noted on page 10, the mutual information between the recovered sources (or, equivalently, the likelihood)

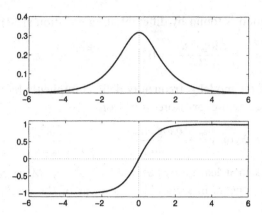

Figure 1.6. ***Reciprocal cosh density and squashing function.*** *[Top] The density* $1/(\pi\cosh(a))$, *and [Bottom] the nonlinear squashing function* $\phi(a) = \tanh(a)$ *which appears in the gradient of the log likelihood.*

is unaffected by multiplying the separating matrix W by a diagonal matrix D. This is only true, however, if the source model corresponds to the true sources; if the assumed source model is different from the true source density the elements of D may be used as additional parameters to tune the model, thereby increasing the likelihood.

Any separating matrix W may be written as $W = D\hat{W}$, where $\hat{W}$ is a *row-normalised* matrix, $\sum_i \hat{W}_{ij}^2 = 1$. The importance of scaling the rows of the separating matrix is illustrated in Figure 1.7, which shows the likelihood of two-dimensional *row-normalised* separating matrices plotted as a function of the angles θ_1, θ_2 parameterising $\hat{W}$:

$$\hat{W} = \begin{bmatrix} \cos\theta_1 & \sin\theta_1 \\ \sin\theta_2 & \cos\theta_2 \end{bmatrix}. \tag{1.85}$$

The left hand plot shows the true likelihood (calculated with a flexible source model), while the right hand plot shows the likelihood calculated with a fixed source model, $p(a) = 1/(\pi\cosh(a))$. Although the likelihood landscapes are broadly similar, with a fixed source model the ridges are not so sharp and the maximum log likelihood is only -3.99, which is to be compared with the true maximum log likelihood of -3.1178. Multiplying the row-normalised mixing matrix by a diagonal matrix, D, opens up the possibility of better fitting the recovered source densities to $1/(\pi\cosh(a))$. Denoting the row-normalised A^{-1} by W^*, figure 1.8 shows the log likelihood of DW^* as a function of D. It is apparent that each row of the maximum likelihood separating matrix is scaled differently.

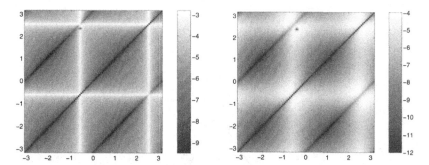

Figure 1.7. **Likelihood with flexible and fixed source models.** *Normalised log likelihood for a mixture of a Laplacian and a Gaussian source plotted in the space of two-dimensional, row-normalised separating matrices, $\hat{W}$, parameterised by angles (θ_1, θ_2). A^{-1} is marked with a star. [Left]: The likelihood is calculated using a flexible source model. [Right]: The likelihood calculated assuming $p(a) = 1/(\pi \cosh(a))$.*

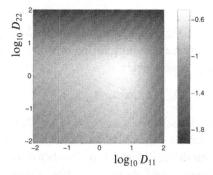

Figure 1.8. **Likelihood of scaled separating matrices with a fixed source model.** *Likelihood of separating matrices DW^* as a function of the elements D_{11} and D_{22} of a diagonal matrix multiplying the true row-normalised separating matrix, W^*. Since the log likelihood becomes very large and negative for large D_{mm}, the grey scale is $-\log_{10}(|\log \mathcal{L}|)$.*

The maximum likelihood with the scaled, fixed source model is -3.1881, much closer to the true likelihood.

The scaling factors D_{mm} may be thought of as adjustable parameters of the source model. To be explicit we write $W = D\hat{W}$, where D is diagonal and $\hat{W}$ is row-normalised, and let $\mathbf{a} = D\hat{\mathbf{a}} = D\hat{W}\mathbf{x}$, so that $\hat{\mathbf{a}}$ are the sources recovered by the row-normalised separating matrix. The nonlinearity occurring in the likelihood gradient (1.79) can therefore be written as

$$\phi_m(a_m) = \phi_m(D_{mm}\hat{a}_m) \stackrel{\text{def}}{=} \hat{\phi}_m(\hat{a}_m). \qquad (1.86)$$

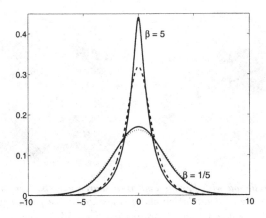

Figure 1.9. **Source models with scaling.** *The function* $[\cosh(\beta a)]^{-1/\beta}$ *plotted for* $\beta = 1$ *(dashed),* $\beta = 5$ *and* $\beta = 1/5$. *A Gaussian with the same variance as the function with* $\beta = 1/5$ *is shown dotted.*

If $\phi_m(a_m) = -\tanh(a_m)$, then $\hat{\phi}_m(\hat{a}_m) = -\tanh(D_{mm}\hat{a}_m)$. The source density modelled by $\hat{\phi}_m$ (for the row-normalised mixing matrix) is discovered by solving (1.80) for p, which yields

$$p(\hat{a}_m | D_{mm}) \propto [\cosh(D_{mm}\hat{a}_m)]^{-1/D_{mm}}. \qquad (1.87)$$

Figure 1.9 shows $p(\hat{a}_m | D_{mm})$ for $D_{mm} = 5, 1, 1/5$. When D_{mm} is large the source model approximates a Laplacian density, while as $D_{mm} \to 0$ a Gaussian density is modelled. Thus a range of heavy tailed densities can be modelled by scaling a 'fixed' density. We note that rescaling the rows of W so that it is row-normalised during learning results in much poorer separation.

Note that no amount of scaling can approximate a density with tails lighter than Gaussian, which explains why learning rules with sigmoidal nonlinearities ϕ are unable to separate mixtures which include light tailed sources (such as a uniform density) or sources with densities which are multi-modal. Two common approaches exist to combat this problem: switching source models and more flexible source models.

Generalised exponentials An alternative to relying on the scaling of the separating matrix and switching source models is to adopt a more flexible density model in the form of a 'generalised exponential', such that

$$p(a_m) = \frac{r_m}{2\sigma_m \Gamma(1/r_m)} \exp\left(-\left|\frac{a_m - \mu_m}{\sigma_m}\right|^{r_m}\right). \qquad (1.88)$$

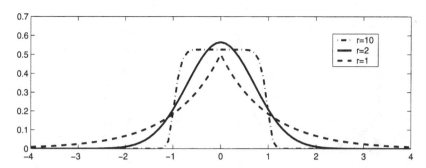

Figure 1.10. *Generalised exponential source models:* Probability densities for $r = 1, 2, 10$, $\mu = 0$ and $\sigma = 1$ from the generalised exponential distribution as defined in equation (1.88).

The parameters μ_m, σ_m, r_m alter the position, width and shape, respectively, of the resultant density function (see [Everson & Roberts, 1999a, Penny et al., 2000, Everson & Roberts, 1999b] for details of this model applied to ICA). Figure 1.10 shows the density of a generalised exponential for $r = 1$ (Laplacian or bi-exponential), $r = 2$ (Gaussian) and $r = 10$ (as $r \to \infty$ so the density approaches that of a uniform distribution) with $\mu = 0$ and $\sigma = 1$.

Maximum likelihood estimates of the parameters r_m, μ_m and σ_m may be found from the estimated sources [Everson & Roberts, 1999a]. Alternatively, they may be estimated from the second and fourth moments of the estimated sources [Choi et al., 1998]. Generalised exponential source models were used to separate the mixture of music sources (super-Gaussian) and uniformly distributed noise (sub-Gaussian) presented in section 1.1.

Mixtures of Gaussians The issue of the source density being skewed or multi-modal is not, however, addressed using the generalised exponential model. One approach which offers a wide degree of flexibility is to model each source density as a mixture of Gaussians (MOG). MOG density models have the desirable property that, with sufficiently many component Gaussians, they are able to approximate a wide class of densities to arbitrary precision. This approach has been taken by several authors [Attias, 1999a, Pham, 1996, Moulines et al., 1997, Choudrey et al., 2001] and is discussed in Chapters 8 and 9 in particular. Figure 1.11 shows the (far from symmetric or unimodal) density of a real (scaled) image along with the maximum likelihood densities from a generalised

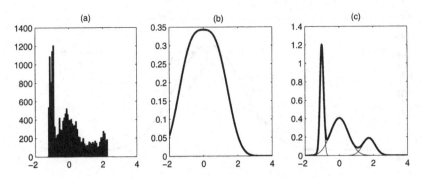

Figure 1.11. **Source models:** *Plot (a) shows the histogram from a (scaled) real image. Note that the density is far from simple. Plots (b) and (c) respectively show the maximum likelihood fits to a generalised exponential model and a three component Gaussian mixture. Note that the latter offers a considerably better source density model.*

exponential model and a three component MOG. We note that the latter offers a very good source density model. The flexibility of the MOG is offset somewhat, however, by the larger number of parameters required to model each source density (three parameters, the mean, variance and a weight, are associated with each Gaussian in the mixture). A variational learning approach offers many advantages in this case [Attias, 1999a]. Empirically it is observed that a mixture of a small number of Gaussians only is required to obtain good results on many real-world problems.

Girolami [1997, 1998] has also used a simplified MOG source model to model sub-Gaussian sources. The symmetric Pearson mixture model [Pearson, 1894] is a mixture of two Gaussians with identical variance, σ^2, placed a distance μ on either side of the origin:

$$p(a) = \frac{1}{2}(\mathcal{G}(a + \mu, \sigma^2) + \mathcal{G}(a - \mu, \sigma^2)). \qquad (1.89)$$

The kurtosis of the mixture (which is bimodal for $\mu > 1$) can be shown [Girolami, 1997] to be

$$\kappa = \frac{-2\mu^4}{(\mu^2 + \sigma^2)^2}. \qquad (1.90)$$

Rather than explicitly learning the parameters μ and σ, however, the Pearson mixture model is principally used as a sub-Gaussian model with the parameters fixed at $\mu = \sigma = 1$, so that $\kappa = -1$. Scaling implicit in the separating matrix is then able to tune the density to a range of sub-Gaussian sources (cf. page 31).

Switching source models Girolami [1998] observed that the nonlinearity ϕ_m corresponding to the Pearson mixture model with $\mu = \sigma = 1$ is $\phi_m(a_m) = a_m - \tanh(a_m)$. Additionally, the nonlinearity $\phi_m(a_m) = a_m + \tanh(a_m)$ corresponds to the super-Gaussian density

$$p(a_m) \propto \mathcal{G}(a_m, 1) \operatorname{sech}^2(a_m). \tag{1.91}$$

He therefore proposed the following simple ϕ_m, which switches between nonlinearities depending upon the kurtosis of the estimated sources:

$$\phi_m(a_m) = \begin{cases} a_m + \tanh(a_m), & \text{super-Gaussian, kurtosis} > 0, \\ a_m - \tanh(a_m), & \text{sub-Gaussian, kurtosis} < 0. \end{cases} \tag{1.92}$$

Scaling, as outlined above, permits adaption to a range of sub- and super-Gaussian densities. Following the analysis by Cardoso [1998b, 2000] (see also page 41) of the stability of learning rules based on the gradient of the likelihood, an alternative algorithm which switches based on these stability criteria has been developed [Lee *et al.*, 1999b]; see Chapter 9 of the present book. Lee *et al.* demonstrate that this algorithm, which is known as the 'extended infomax algorithm' is effective at separating mixtures with both sub- and super-Gaussian sources.

Temporally structured sources The independence assumption of ICA refers to independence *between* the sources. No assumptions are made about the dependence or otherwise of the sample $s_m(t)$ on $s_m(t-1)$ and previous samples. Most ICA models assume that samples from each source are identically and independently distributed, so that temporal shuffling of a batch of observations makes no difference to the independent components which are recovered.

Many sources, such as speech and music, however, are temporally structured, and the temporal dependence *within* sources may be exploited to learn more about each source and thus achieve better separation. Pearlmutter & Parra [1996] commented on and exploited the temporal correlation in what they call 'contextual ICA'; they also note that other non-temporal contextual information (such as lip positions if mixtures of voices are being separated) can be incorporated into the source models. Briefly, the likelihood of the data is now written as the product of conditional densities:

$$\mathcal{L} = p(\mathbf{x}(t), \mathbf{x}(t-1), \dots) \tag{1.93}$$

$$= p(\mathbf{x}(t)|\mathbf{x}(t-1), \mathbf{x}(t-2), \dots)p(\mathbf{x}(t-1)|\mathbf{x}(t-2), \mathbf{x}(t-3), \dots)\dots$$

$$= \prod_{\tau=0}^{\infty} p(\mathbf{x}(t-\tau)|\mathbf{x}(t-\tau-1), \mathbf{x}(t-\tau-2), \dots). \tag{1.94}$$

Using the independence between sources and the transformation of probabilities by the separating matrix W, the probabilities may be expressed in terms of the latent source conditional densities:

$$\mathcal{L} = \prod_{\tau=0}^{\infty} |\det W| \prod_{m=1}^{M} p(a_m(t-\tau)|a_m(t-\tau-1), a_m(t-\tau-2), \dots). \tag{1.95}$$

Pearlmutter & Parra used a linear auto-regressive (AR) model for each source. The AR model makes a linear prediction $\hat{a}_m(t)$ of $a_m(t)$ based on the last p samples of a_m:

$$\hat{a}_m(t) = \sum_{\tau=1}^{p} c_m(\tau)a_m(t-\tau), \tag{1.96}$$

where the $c_m(\tau)$ are the AR coefficients (or linear prediction coefficients) for the mth source. Writing the prediction error as $e_m(t) = \hat{a}_m(t) - a_m(t)$, the probability of $a_m(t)$ conditioned on the previous p samples is simply

$$p(a_m(t)|a_m(t-1), a_m(t-2), \dots, a_m(t-p)) = p(e(t)). \tag{1.97}$$

Pearlmutter & Parra [1996] originally used mixtures of logistic density functions to model the sources, although mixtures of Gaussians have been used subsequently [Parra, 1998a]. With a specific source model the likelihood may be maximised as usual, using one of the methods in the following section. Pearlmutter & Parra [1996] demonstrate that the additional temporal information permits the separation of Gaussian sources with temporal structure; ICA without temporal information is ineffective here, because the likelihood for Gaussian sources is invariant under rotations of the separating matrix (section 1.3). Pearlmutter & Parra are also able to separate audio signals using very simple model source densities (such as a single Gaussian). In Chapter 12 an AR model incorporating generalised exponential source densities is used, and it is shown how the model order p may be estimated.

We also note that mixtures of sources with temporal structure can be separated by insisting that the estimated sources are (linearly) decorrelated for all time shifts; see Chapter 5 and [Molgedey & Schuster, 1994, Koehler & Orglmeister, 1999] for more details.

1.6 Optimisation and algorithms

In this section we consider methods for estimating solutions to the unknowns in the ICA problem. We start with the simplest case, that of *noiseless* ICA with $N = M$, as considered in section 1.4. The unknowns in

$$\mathbf{x} = A\mathbf{s} \tag{1.98}$$

are the elements of the (non-singular) mixing matrix, A, and the sources **s** which we consider as being estimated by a recovered source set **a**.

1.6.1 Gradient information

In the previous section we have seen that many different ICA contrasts may be derived so as to give extremal measures when the source estimates in **a** are independent. An ICA method consists of two distinct components: firstly the formulation of a valid contrast function and secondly the use of an algorithm for estimating the free parameters of the system (W and perhaps some parameters in a source density model). In this section we consider some algorithmic approaches to the issue of parameter estimation.

We firstly consider approaches which rely on the gradient of the contrast to ascend or descend to an extremal contrast measure. It is computationally attractive to have access, therefore, to the analytic form for the gradient of the contrast function with respect to the free parameters. We will consider, as an example, the basis of the contrast function to be that of a generative model approach, such as that defined in equation (1.49). We will work with the log likelihood measure for datum **x**, $q(\mathbf{x}) \stackrel{\text{def}}{=} \log \ell(\mathbf{x})$, noting that *ascending* this likelihood to a maximum is identical to *descending* the contrast function to a minimum.

Consider the derivative of $q(\mathbf{x})$ with respect to element W_{ij} of the separation matrix,

$$\frac{\partial q(\mathbf{x})}{\partial W_{ij}} = W_{ij}^{-\mathsf{T}} + \frac{\partial \ln p_i(a_i)}{\partial a_i} x_j. \tag{1.99}$$

Define the vector $\mathbf{z} \in \mathbb{R}^M$ to have elements

$$z_i \overset{\text{def}}{\equiv} \frac{\partial \ln p_i(a_i)}{\partial a_i}, \tag{1.100}$$

so that $z_i \equiv \phi_i(a_i)$, where ϕ_i is the nonlinear 'squashing function' defined in equation (1.80). Therefore, we may write equation (1.99) as

$$\frac{\partial q}{\partial W} = W^{-\mathsf{T}} + \mathbf{z}\mathbf{x}^{\mathsf{T}}. \tag{1.101}$$

Gradient-ascent, or steepest-gradient, methods require only this first order information and update W in the direction of the gradient. The update rule for W in discrete time $t \leftarrow t + 1$ is hence

$$W(t + 1) = W(t) + \eta(W^{-\mathsf{T}}(t) + \mathbf{z}\mathbf{x}^{\mathsf{T}}). \tag{1.102}$$

where $0 \leqslant \eta \leqslant 1$ is the adaptation parameter.† Note that this learning rule describes an online learning procedure because data are processed sequentially as they are received. Gradient ascent to the likelihood for a batch of T observations is performed with the modified rule

$$W(t + 1) = W(t) + \eta \left\{ W^{-\mathsf{T}}(t) + \frac{1}{T} \sum_{t=1}^{T} \mathbf{z}(t)\mathbf{x}^{\mathsf{T}}(t) \right\}. \tag{1.103}$$

Since the learning rule (1.102) is obtained from (1.103) by dropping the averaging operation it is sometimes called *stochastic gradient ascent*.

The use of *steepest-gradient* techniques to ascend the likelihood to near its (local) supremum was formulated by Bell & Sejnowski [1995] (they took, however, a slightly different approach to the derivation of the above gradient). One of the key problems, however, with steepest-gradient methods is their poor convergence in regions of shallow gradient and in regions where the likelihood landscape is far from isotropic (e.g., long thin ridges). To overcome some of these issues, Bell & Sejnowski utilised *batching*, whereby the mean gradient (1.103) over a set of consecutive samples is utilised rather than the sample-by-sample estimate of equation (1.102), and *sphering*‡ in which a linear decorrelation of $\{\mathbf{x}\}$ was performed prior to analysis. This has the double effect of making the likelihood landscape more isotropic and also removing from the ICA algorithm the burden of removing second order information. The downside, however, is that for large datasets (especially with high dimensionality)

---

† If η is fixed this procedure corresponds to maximum likelihood re-estimation with an exponential weighting over successive samples. In practice η is hence often adapted as $\eta(t) \propto t^{-1}$.

‡ In effect *Principal Component Analysis*, see page 18.

these benefits may be outweighed by the computational overhead of the sphering process.

As is discussed on page 30, the source model determines the form of $z_i = \phi_i(a_i)$. Bell & Sejnowski suggested a number of source models including

$$p_i(a_i) = \frac{1}{\pi \cosh a_i} \tag{1.104}$$

so that the components of $\mathbf{z}$ in equation (1.100) become

$$z_i = -\tanh(a_i). \tag{1.105}$$

They point out that this form of mapping function is commonly used in *neural network* methods and hence they relate the issue of finding W to finding the synaptic weights in a neural network.

1.6.2 Convergence and stability

Amari *et al.* [1997] and Cardoso [1998b, 2000] examined the stability of learning rules based on gradient information, such as (1.102) and (1.103). In particular Cardoso considers general learning rules cast in the form

$$\mathbf{a}(t) = W(t)\mathbf{x}(t), \tag{1.106}$$

$$W(t+1) = \{I - \eta(t)G(\mathbf{a}(t)\} W(t), \tag{1.107}$$

where G is a nonlinearity and $\{\eta(t)\}$ is a sequence of positive learning steps; often $\eta(t)$ is constant for all t. Comparison with equation (1.102) shows that the nonlinearity for standard gradient ascent is

$$G_r(\mathbf{a}) \overset{\text{def}}{=} \phi(\mathbf{a})\mathbf{a}^{\mathsf{T}} - I \tag{1.108}$$

where ϕ is the component-wise nonlinearity with components $\phi(a_i) = -z_i$. Cardoso also considers nonlinearities which force the separating matrix onto the manifold of decorrelating separating matrices (see also subsection 1.6.4).

Gradient-ascent algorithms, of course, suffer from the problem that they may become stuck at a local maximum. If, however, the global maximum likelihood solution is located, then Cardoso shows that its stability depends on the scale of the recovered sources and on $M(M-1)/2$ conditions dependent on the characteristics of each pair of recovered sources.

The scale stability condition is written

$$1 + \mathcal{E}\phi_i'(a_i)a_i^2 > 0, \qquad i = 1, \ldots, M. \tag{1.109}$$

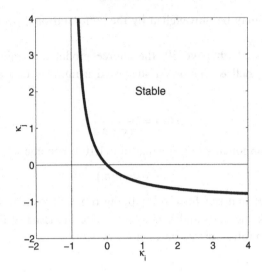

Figure 1.12. **Stability boundaries in the** κ_i, κ_j **plane.** *Learning rules operating to the right of the thick line are stable at the maximum likelihood point. (After Cardoso [1998b].)*

If the nonlinear functions ϕ_i are non-decreasing, these conditions are readily met. The pairwise stability conditions are expressed in terms of the following moments:

$$\kappa_i \overset{\text{def}}{=} \mathcal{E}\phi_i'(a_i)\mathcal{E}a_i^2 - \mathcal{E}\phi_i(a_i)a_i. \tag{1.110}$$

If the maximum likelihood mixing matrix is located at $a_i = \lambda_i s_i$ for some scale λ_i and the expectations in (1.110) are taken over the scaled variables a_i. The stability conditions, which are illustrated in figure 1.12, are then simply expressed as

$$(1 + \kappa_i)(1 + \kappa_j) > 1, \qquad 1 \leqslant i < j \leqslant M, \tag{1.111}$$

$$(1 + \kappa_i) > 1, \qquad 1 \leqslant i \leqslant M. \tag{1.112}$$

Cardoso notes that the conditions are all satisfied if the nonlinearities are chosen so that $\kappa_i > 0$ for all the sources. A Gaussian source has $\kappa_i = 0$, so the stability conditions can never be met if there is more than one Gaussian source. On the other hand, separation of a source with $\kappa_i < 0$ may be achieved if all the other sources have sufficiently large κ_j. Furthermore if ϕ is chosen to match the source density (i.e., in accordance with equation (1.80)) then stability is guaranteed. Cardoso [1998a] gives useful interpretations of the stability conditions in terms of the angle between the recovered source and the source modelled by ϕ. Lee *et al.* [1999b] use the pairwise conditions as the criteria to switch between source models; see section 1.5 above and Chapter 9 of the present book.

1.6.3 Second order optimisation

As mentioned in the previous subsection, steepest gradient methods are poor if the likelihood landscape has, for example, long thin ridges rather than isotropic peaks. Second order methods overcome this by applying a scaling and rotation matrix to the gradient such that the resultant is directed to the likelihood supremum. It is straightforward to show that one possible matrix which will perform this task is the inverse *Hessian* matrix of second derivatives of the likelihood with respect to the parameters. The constant re-estimation of the Hessian and its inversion is computationally infeasible for all but the smallest problems. One may make approximations, however, and still enjoy the benefits of the method. We briefly review here approaches to making these approximations.

Quasi-Newton approaches Consider the gradient of some contrast function $g(W) = \nabla\psi$ as being estimated via a Taylor series about the point of contrast minimum, which occurs at $W = W^*$:

$$g(W) \approx g(W^*) + \frac{d\mathbf{g}}{dW}\bigg|_{W^*} (W - W^*)$$
$$= H(W - W^*) \tag{1.113}$$

where H is the Hessian matrix and the $g(W^*) = 0$. Re-arranging this equation leads to

$$W^* = W \underbrace{-H^{-1}\mathbf{g}}_{\text{Newton step}} \tag{1.114}$$

which can be compared to the standard gradient update of

$$W(t + 1) = W(t) - \eta\mathbf{g} \tag{1.115}$$

to see that the inverse Hessian acts as a rotation and scaling matrix. An exact Newton step will find the minimum of any locally quadratic function *in a single step*. Note that the Newton step vector always points from W to the minimum, not just down the line of steepest gradient. We could use this, but if we are in an area of the error surface which is not locally quadratic then the step we make will not get to a minimum (but would get us closer), and we would have to re-estimate the Hessian and invert it at every step of the optimisation procedure.

We may, however, utilise re-estimation approaches to the inverse Hessian which do not require a full re-calculation. The most widely used method which performs this re-estimation of the inverse Hessian is the *Broyden–Fletcher–Goldfarb–Shanno* (BFGS) method. The derivation of this is out of place here, but can be found in standard texts on optimisation [Gill *et al.*, 1995]. To implement the quasi-Newton approach we need to use the following update equation:

$$W(t+1) = W(t) - \eta(t)\hat{H}^{-1}(t)\mathbf{g}(t) \qquad (1.116)$$

in which $\eta(t)$ is an adaption or step-size parameter, and $\hat{H}^{-1}$ is an approximation to H^{-1} which is constructed iteratively. The step size is typically automatically determined from a *line-search* approach. The interested reader is again referred to texts on optimisation for more details. Several publications have successfully used quasi-Newton methods to estimate ICA parameters (see [Roberts, 1998, Everson & Roberts, 1999a], for example). The clear advantage of such approaches is that there are no 'user-set' variables required.

Natural gradient methods The *natural gradient* approach was pioneered by Amari [1985] and applied to the ICA problem in [Amari *et al.*, 1996]. Amari's key insight lies in the fact that the scaling and rotation matrix is the local Riemannian curvature matrix. Amari considers the Lie group invariance properties of the parameter space of W and considers Euclidean (isotropic) metrics in the space. Consider a Euclidean metric to exist at the identity I of some mapped space, such that dW at W maps to some dX at I in which the space is Euclidean local to I with respect to changes in X. As the X-space is locally Euclidean, a simple gradient update is directed towards the contrast extremum, that is, we may utilise

$$\frac{dX}{dt} = \eta \frac{\partial q}{\partial X} \qquad (1.117)$$

in the update equations. The mapping $dW|_W \mapsto dX|_I$ may be achieved by

$$dX = dW W^{-1} \qquad (1.118)$$

hence

$$\frac{dW}{dt} = \eta \frac{\partial q}{\partial X} W$$
$$= \eta \frac{\partial q}{\partial W} W^{\mathsf{T}} W. \tag{1.119}$$

Thus simple post-multiplication of the standard gradient update equation by $W^{\mathsf{T}}W$ results in an algorithm with considerably improved properties (such as faster convergence). Combining equations (1.119) and (1.102) leads to the natural gradient update rule in discrete time,

$$W(t+1) = W(t) + \eta(W^{-\mathsf{T}}(t) + \mathbf{z}\mathbf{x}^{\mathsf{T}})W^{\mathsf{T}}W$$
$$= W(t) + \eta(W(t) + \mathbf{z}\mathbf{y}^{\mathsf{T}}), \tag{1.120}$$

where we define the vector $\mathbf{y} \stackrel{\text{def}}{=} W^{\mathsf{T}}\mathbf{a}$ and $\mathbf{z}$ is as defined in equation (1.100). MacKay [1996] notes that in this form 'global' information is not required as W is not inverted and hence this approach is more 'biologically plausible' and computationally more efficient, especially for large W. Figure 1.13 shows the convergence of the elements of $W \in \mathbb{R}^{2 \times 2}$ for a simple mixture of music sources (as in section 1.1).

Cardoso & Laheld [1996] (see also page 162) consider a different approach to the problem of ill-posed gradient optimisation for cases when W is square. Cardoso & Laheld define a small transform of $\mathbf{a}$, such that $\mathbf{a} \rightarrow \mathbf{a} + \epsilon\mathbf{a}$, where ϵ is a small perturbation matrix. If we assume that the contrast function ψ is smooth then

$$\psi[\mathbf{a} + \epsilon\mathbf{a}] \approx \psi[\mathbf{a}] + \sum_{ij} \left.\frac{\partial(\mathbf{a} + \epsilon\mathbf{a})}{\partial \epsilon_{ij}}\right|_{\epsilon=0} \epsilon_{ij}. \tag{1.121}$$

The partial derivative components form a square matrix which is referred to as the *relative gradient* [Cardoso & Laheld, 1996]. In particular, if $\mathbf{a} = W\mathbf{x}$ then the relative gradient is given as

$$\nabla\psi[W\mathbf{x}] = W^{\mathsf{T}} \frac{\partial \psi[W\mathbf{x}]}{\partial W}. \tag{1.122}$$

Consequently an update equation, similar to that of natural gradient (equation (1.119)) may be formulated,

$$\frac{dW}{dt} = -\eta W^{\mathsf{T}} \frac{\partial \psi[W\mathbf{x}]}{\partial W}. \tag{1.123}$$

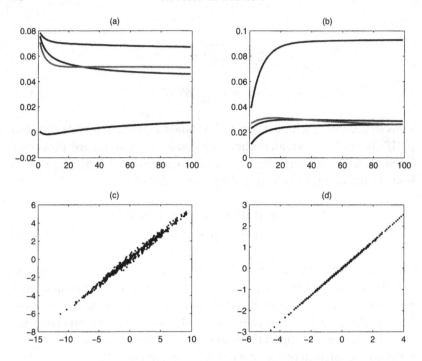

Figure 1.13. **Gradient based optimisation:** *Time course of the elements of W for (a) gradient ascent, (b) natural gradient approaches. Scatterplot of first recovered source against original for (c) gradient ascent and (d) natural gradient approaches. For the standard gradient ascent method the data were 'sphered' first. Both methods utilised a reciprocal cosh source model. The natural gradient method offers a faster convergence rate and slightly improved results in this example. There was no 'batching' of the data and the adaptation rate was fixed at $\eta = 0.1$ in both cases.*

1.6.4 Constrained optimisation

Fixed point methods This approach is due to Hyvärinen [1999a] and makes the common assumption of a noiseless linear mixing. Fixed point algorithms are based on the convergence of iterative function maps of the form $W \leftarrow f(W)$ which has a fixed point at $W_{fp} = f(W_{fp})$. The FastICA approach relies upon the fact that minimisation of differential negentropy in a set of sources (thus making them maximally independent—this is approximately equivalent to the *minimisation* of the mutual information between them). As Hyvärinen describes in Chapter 2 below, minimisation of the negentropy may be approximated by maximisation of a measure of the non-Gaussianity of the recovered sources. The non-Gaussianity of the sources may be maximised by a fixed point algorithm; crucially, maximisation may be performed for each source in turn leading to a fast *deflationary* procedure. Full details are given by Hyvärinen in Chapter 2.

Decorrelating manifold and flexible nonlinearity (DMFN-ICA) approach
Several authors have noted that if the components of a are to be independent, they must be linearly decorrelated. Therefore it is expedient to formulate algorithms which operate on, or close to, the manifold of decorrelating separation matrices [Everson & Roberts, 1999a, Cardoso & Laheld, 1996]. Let us now consider what properties a matrix has if it is to be decorrelating. Linear decorrelation means that the expectation of the product between any pair of different variables is zero, that is

$$\mathcal{E}\{a_j a_k\} = \delta_{j,k} d_j^2 \qquad (1.124)$$

in which a_j is the jth source estimate and d_j is a scale factor corresponding to the power of this jth component. Arrange the observations in a matrix $X \in \mathbb{R}^{N \times T}$ so that the tth row column of X is $\mathbf{x}(t)$. Then the matrix $B = WX$ contains $a_m(t)$ as its mth row. The criterion for linear decorrelation can then be expressed as:

$$BB^\mathsf{T} = WXX^\mathsf{T}W^\mathsf{T} = D^2, \qquad (1.125)$$

where D is a *diagonal* matrix of scaling factors. It is simple to show (see [Everson & Roberts, 1999a]) that if W is to be a decorrelating matrix then it must be of the form

$$W = DQ\Sigma^{-1}U^\mathsf{T} \qquad (1.126)$$

where the columns of U are the first M principal (eigen) components of X, Σ is the (diagonal) matrix of singular values of X, D is some diagonal scaling matrix and $Q \in \mathbb{R}^{M \times M}$ is a real orthogonal matrix. As is shown in by Everson & Roberts [1999a] optimisation of the ICA unmixing matrix, W, may then proceed in the $M(M + 1)/2$ dimensional space of decorrelating matrices rather than in the full NM dimensional space. Furthermore, the resultant matrix is guaranteed to be decorrelating. Optimisation may then proceed using a variety of approaches, such as the BFGS quasi-Newton method [Everson & Roberts, 1999a].

The invariance of ICA to scaling may again be utilised to visualise the manifold of decorrelating matrices. For $W \in \mathbb{R}^{2 \times 2}$ we may parameterise

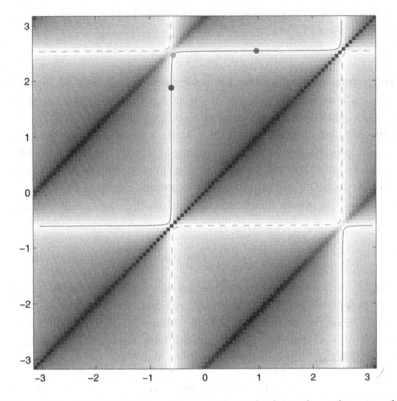

Figure 1.14. **Manifold of decorrelating matrices:** *The figure shows the space of all 2 × 2 matrices (parameterised by two angles, $-\pi \leqslant \theta_1, \theta_2 \leqslant \pi$). The grey scale depicts the likelihood landscape of $q(\mathbf{x})$ and the lines the manifold of decorrelating matrices. Note that the latter reside very close to the ridges of high likelihood. The points indicated represent, from left to right along the manifold, the ICA, ZCA and PCA solutions for W.*

the sum-of-squares row-normalised matrix using just two angles, such that we may view the contrast measure over a two-dimensional plane, i.e., we may write

$$W = \begin{bmatrix} \cos \theta_1 & \sin \theta_1 \\ \cos \theta_2 & \sin \theta_2 \end{bmatrix}.$$

Figure 1.14 depicts the likelihood landscape for a simple mixture of sources drawn from Gaussian and bi-exponential (Laplacian) densities and then mixed. The grey scale depicts the likelihood and the lines show the manifold of decorrelating matrices. Note that the latter reside very close to the ridges of high likelihood. The points indicated represent (from left to right along the manifold) the ICA, ZCA,† and PCA solutions for W. We may achieve an efficient algorithm which operates on the decorrelating manifold by initialising at the PCA solution.

Keeping on the decorrelating manifold may be achieved explicitly, by re-defining the co-ordinates which parameterise W to lie on the decorrelating manifold [Everson & Roberts, 1999a] or by writing the contrast function in a way such that a term penalising off-diagonal elements of $\mathcal{E}\{\mathbf{aa}^\mathsf{T}\}$ exists. Some contrast functions are naturally amenable to this approach [Cardoso & Laheld, 1996].

Comparative example Figure 1.15 shows a comparison of some of the ICA methods discussed in this chapter. We note that FastICA was more rapid in reaching convergence than all the other methods though the decorrelating manifold approach, on this data, was also very rapid (taking 1.5 seconds of CPU time on a SUN ULTRA-10 machine compared to 0.68 seconds for FastICA). FastICA gave unusually poor source estimates, however, on this dataset. It is interesting to note that the steepest gradient approach, which took the longest to converge (some 4.5 seconds) gives very good results. We note that sphering was performed prior to this analysis, however.

1.6.5 Expectation Maximisation

The Expectation Maximisation algorithm [Dempster *et al.*, 1976] is a powerful methodology for parameter estimation in systems of *coupled* nonlinear equations, such as those found in the ICA problem. We give here a brief overview only of the principle behind the method. The interested reader is referred to Attias' [1999a] paper on Independent Factor Analysis which utilised the EM framework and to Chapter 3. Neal & Hinton [1993] give an illuminating discussion and interpretation of the EM algorithm and its variants.

We consider a general system, parameterised by some *visible* variables w. The key to the EM formalism lies in the introduction of a set of *hidden* variables, h say. The simplest example lies in the use of EM in mixture models in which the updating, given some datum X, of parameters within each mixture component is dependent upon the unknown set of mixture

---

† Zero-phase component analysis, as discussed in [Bell & Sejnowski, 1995, Everson & Roberts, 1999a].

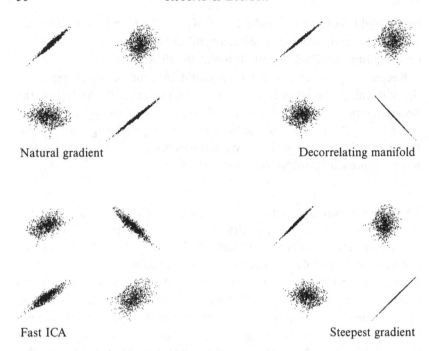

Natural gradient   Decorrelating manifold

Fast ICA   Steepest gradient

Figure 1.15. **Comparative example:** *Scatterplots of true versus estimated sources for various ICA methods. All approaches used the same data: 1000 samples of two music sources linearly mixed with a square mixing matrix. Relative timing shows that FastICA is over twice as fast as the fastest of the other methods (the decorrelating manifold method). FastICA performs unusually poorly, however, on this dataset. The natural gradient and steepest gradient methods used a source model in which $p_i(a_i) \propto 1/\cosh(a_i)$.*

posteriors given the datum, $p(h|X)$, although for brevity we write this as $p(h)$. In this case w corresponds to the model parameters and h to the component posteriors.

We consider a set of data, $X \overset{\text{def}}{=} \{x_t\}_{t=1}^T$, and let the log likelihood of the dataset be $\mathcal{L}(X) = \sum_t \ln p(x_t|w)$. Now suppose that the parameters are re-estimated to some new values. We denote the old and new states with subscripts o and n respectively. The difference in likelihood between old and new system states is

$$\mathcal{L}_n - \mathcal{L}_o = \sum_t \ln \left\{ \frac{p_n(x_t|w)}{p_o(x_t|w)} \right\}. \tag{1.127}$$

We may write the above in terms of the hidden variable set by noting that $p(x|w) = \sum_h p(x|w,h)p(h)$, i.e.,

$$\mathcal{L}_n - \mathcal{L}_o = \sum_t \ln \left\{ \frac{\sum_h p_n(x_t|w,h)p_n(h)}{p_o(x_t|w)} \right\} \tag{1.128}$$

$$= \sum_t \ln \left\{ \frac{\sum_h p_n(x_t|w,h)p_n(h)p_o(h|x_t,w)/p_o(h|x_t,w)}{p_o(x_t|w)} \right\}$$

$$= \sum_t \ln \left\{ \sum_h \left[p_n(x_t|w,h)p_n(h) \right] p_o(h|x_t,w) \right\} + C.$$

where we have collected all terms dependent only on the old system state into the constant C. Jensen's inequality may be utilised to convert the logarithm of the expectation (of the term in square brackets) into the expectation of the logarithm such that

$$\mathcal{L}_n - \mathcal{L}_o \geqslant \sum_t \sum_h p_o(h|x_t,w) \ln \left[p_n(x_t|w,h)p_n(h) \right] + C$$

$$= Q(h,w) + C. \tag{1.129}$$

The EM algorithm thence proceeds in two steps:

E-step in which the set of distributions over h (for each datum) is estimated using the *old* parameters, i.e., $p_o(h|x_t,w)$.

M-step in which the *new* parameter values are estimated so as to maximise $Q(h,w)$.

The advantage of the EM approach is that, as formula (1.129) shows, the likelihood is guaranteed never to decrease from one iteration to the next. The major disadvantage of the approach is that it is inherently a maximum likelihood technique and hence is prone to overfitting. Incorporation of priors over parameters is possible though cumbersome and normally other methods (such as variational approaches; see subsection 1.7.5) are utilised if a Bayesian approach is advocated.

EM finds its main application to ICA when mixture models are used for each source (see section 1.5). In this case we consider the parameters w of the above formalism to be, for example, the elements of the (un)mixing matrix along with any parameters in each source model. The hidden parameters, h, thence are indicator variables specifying which of the component Gaussians was 'responsible' for generating a particular source realisation at each t. The parameters are thence updated in the M-step in the light of this interpretation.

1.7 Model order estimation

Typical ICA methods assume that the number of observations (N) and the hypothesised number of sources (M) are equal. If $N = M$ then the matrices A and W are square and (up to a scaling and permutation) form an inverse pair, so the arguments of the previous sections are applicable. In many applications, however, the number of sources is itself unknown. We restrict our discussion here to the case in which there are more observations than sources, i.e., $N > M$. We note that there is no general solution as yet to the true 'cocktail party problem' in which $M > N$, but see Chapter 7 for recent advances in this direction.

This general problem of finding not only a parameter set but also the intrinsic dimensionality of the system is a well-known and difficult issue, normally referred to as the problem of *model order estimation*. Several approaches have been put forward, some heuristic, others based on more principled approaches. In recent years, however, it has become clear that techniques of the latter category are superior and, at best, heuristic methods may be seen as approximations to some more detailed underlying principle.

1.7.1 The noiseless case

If we have a noiseless ICA model of the form

$$\mathbf{x} = A\mathbf{s}$$

in which A is non-square then the resultant singular value decomposition of $X = \{\mathbf{x}(t)\}_{t=1}^{T}$ will have a rank deficiency of $N - M$ (assuming that the sources are non-zero and not dependent). This deficiency may be estimated by finding singular values close to machine precision, for example, or by visual inspection of the singular spectrum. In this case one may reduce X by retaining only those components associated with non-zero singular values. As described earlier, this is equivalent to projecting X onto the first M principal components (equation (1.40)). As the number of 'observations' in this reduced set is now equal to the number of hypothesised sources, standard, square mixing, approaches may be employed. Figure 1.16 shows the singular values from two sources mixed

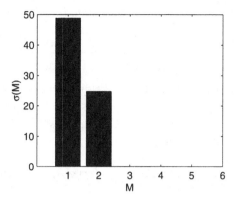

Figure 1.16. *Noiseless non-square mixing: Singular values from six observations mixed from two sources without noise. Note that the last four values are zero and by projecting onto the first two principal components we obtain a square mixing problem.*

to six observation sequences without noise. Note that all singular values save for the first two are zero.

1.7.2 The noisy case

If there is additive noise, $\mathbf{n}$, in the system, such that the ICA model is

$$\mathbf{x} = A\mathbf{s} + \mathbf{n}, \qquad (1.130)$$

then the former approach may not, in general, be taken.† Attias [1999a] refers to the model of equation (1.130) as Independent Factor Analysis (IFA) and this may be seen as a generalisation of ICA which is arguably more suited to 'real-world' application.

Consider an ICA system in which the unknown variables are A, the number of sources M, and the covariance $R_{\mathbf{n}}$ of the noise process (which is normally taken to have a zero-mean Gaussian density). We wish initially to infer a joint density over these quantities, i.e., $p(A, M, R_{\mathbf{n}} | \mathbf{x}, \mathbf{a})$, where $\mathbf{x}$ is an element of the observation dataset and $\mathbf{a}$ is the associated source

---

† It is noted, however, that one may tackle the problem by applying, for example, Bayesian PCA methods to infer the most probable number of components in the noisy case, and indeed an estimate of the noise (co)variance [Rajan & Rayner, 1997, Everson & Roberts, 2000b]. See also Chapter 12 for a comparison of these with other methods.

estimate. Using Bayes' theorem we may write this density as

$$p(A, M, R_n | \mathbf{x}, \mathbf{a}) \propto \underbrace{p(\mathbf{x} | A, M, R_n, \mathbf{a})}_{\text{likelihood}} \underbrace{p(A | M, R_n) p(M) p(R_n)}_{\text{priors}}. \qquad (1.131)$$

This has the form of the product of a likelihood measure and prior terms which act, in an elegant manner, to penalise over-complex solutions. By integrating over the 'latent' variable, $\mathbf{a}$, the posterior density over the unknown parameters is obtained as:

$$p(A, M, R_n | \mathbf{x}) \propto p(A | M, R_n) p(M) p(R_n) \int p(\mathbf{x} | A, M, R_n, \mathbf{a}) p(\mathbf{a}) d\mathbf{a}. \quad (1.132)$$

This equation will not, in general, be analytically tractable and we briefly comment on approaches to its evaluation based on analytic approximations and a sample based method. Considerably more detail is offered in Chapter 8 and in [Knuth, 1999].

1.7.3 Laplace approximation approach

Roberts [1998] considered a set of Laplace approximations to the marginal integral of formula (1.132). The ICA model was that of *non-square* mixing such that $N > M$ and assumed $A = W^+$ and $W = A^+$, in which the Moore-Penrose pseudo-inverse is used, defined as $A^+ \stackrel{\text{def}}{=} (A^T A)^{-1} A^T$.

Let $X = \{\mathbf{x}(t)\}_{t=1}^T$ represent the dataset. The likelihood function of X conditioned on the mixing matrix A is

$$p(X | A, M, R_n) = \prod_t p(\mathbf{x}(t) | A, M, R_n). \qquad (1.133)$$

By marginalising over the latent variable space the likelihood of datum $\mathbf{x}$ is

$$p(\mathbf{x} | A, M, R_n) = \int p(\mathbf{x} | A, M, R_n, \mathbf{a}) p(\mathbf{a}) d\mathbf{a}, \qquad (1.134)$$

where $p(\mathbf{a})$ is, as previously defined, the assumed form of the marginal distribution of the latent variables. Making the assumption (as also made in [MacKay, 1996]) that the density over each noise component is Gaussian with a common variance, given by $1/\beta$, i.e., $R_n \stackrel{\text{def}}{=} \beta^{-1} I$, we may write

$$p(\mathbf{x} | A, M, \mathbf{a}, \beta) = \frac{1}{Z} \exp\left\{ -\frac{\beta}{2} (\mathbf{x} - A\mathbf{a})^2 \right\}, \qquad (1.135)$$

where $1/Z = (\beta/2\pi)^{N/2}$. Making the assumption that the integral is dominated by a sharp peak† at $\mathbf{a} = \hat{\mathbf{a}}$ enables a Laplace approximation of the marginal integral to be made (see [O'Ruanaidth & Fitzgerald, 1996] for example). Defining $h(\mathbf{a}) = (\mathbf{x} - A\mathbf{a})^2$ then

$$\frac{1}{Z} \int \exp\left\{-\frac{\beta}{2}h(\mathbf{a})\right\} p(\mathbf{a})da \approx \frac{1}{Z}p(\hat{\mathbf{a}}) \left(\frac{4\pi}{\beta}\right)^{M/2} \sigma \exp\left\{-\frac{\beta}{2}h(\hat{\mathbf{a}})\right\}$$

(1.136)

where $\sigma = \left|\frac{\partial^2 h(\mathbf{a})}{\partial \mathbf{a}^2}\right|^{-1/2}$ Combining equations (1.134)-(1.136) gives an estimate of the log likelihood (evidence):

$$\ln p(\mathbf{x}|A, M, \beta) = \ln p(\hat{\mathbf{a}}) + \frac{1}{2}(N - M)\ln\left(\frac{\beta}{2\pi}\right)$$
$$- \frac{1}{2}\ln|A^\mathsf{T}A| - \frac{\beta}{2}(\mathbf{x} - A\hat{\mathbf{a}})^2$$

(1.137)

where $\hat{\mathbf{a}} = A^+\mathbf{x}$. Note that if $N = M$ then the above equation reduces to the ICA contrast function ψ_{ML} as the second and final terms vanish and $-\frac{1}{2}\ln|A^\mathsf{T}A| = \ln|W|$ for $A = W^{-1}$.

In order to look at inferring the model order we may integrate out the parameters using another marginal integral, i.e.,

$$p(M|\mathbf{x}, \beta) \propto p(\mathbf{x}|M, \beta) = \int p(\mathbf{x}|A, M, \beta)p(A)dA,$$

(1.138)

and re-estimate the noise variance parameter β using (for example) its maximum likelihood value, $\hat{\beta}$, rather than using a full Bayesian framework (see [Roberts, 1998] for full details). Several assumptions regarding the prior may be made. Two possible choices are: that the elements of A are independent and drawn from a normal distribution; and that the mixing is strictly positive (see page 63) and hence the appropriate prior may be of gamma form. Figure 1.17 shows the model order results obtained from using flat (improper) priors for the elements of A applied to 500 samples of two music sources mixed into a six dimensional observation set with 10% additive noise. Note that the model order was correctly determined and the resultant source estimates are surprisingly good.

We note that, in this case, similar results are obtained from a 'traditional' model order selection based on an asymptotic *minimum description length* (MDL, [Rissanen, 1978]) penalty to the data likelihood measure. The MDL penalised likelihood measure is given as:

$$\text{Penalised Likelihood} = \text{Likelihood } (X) - N_p \ln T$$

(1.139)

† This is, for ICA, a rather strong assumption, it must be noted.

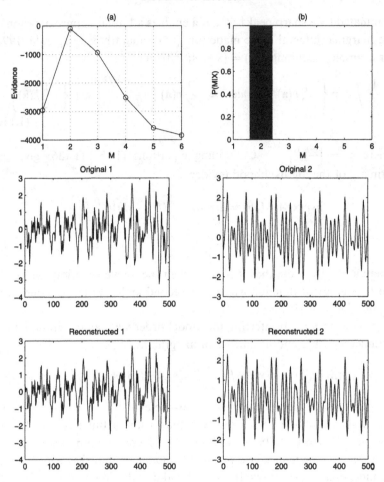

Figure 1.17. *Music data – approximate Bayesian approach:* Top row: Model assessment measures – log model evidence (a) and resultant model posteriors (b). Middle row: Original sources. Bottom row: Estimated sources from $M = 2$ hypothesis.

where the model has N_p free parameters and the dataset consists of T observation vectors.

1.7.4 Sample based approach

We briefly give the example of a sample based approach, in which the joint density over A, M, R_n is inferred using a *reversible-jump* Markov chain Monte Carlo (RJ-MCMC) approach, popularised by Richardson

& Green [1997] in their work on mixture models. The underlying idea is to construct a Markov chain which (when at statistical equilibrium) generates samples from $p(A, M, R_n)$. MacKay [1999] gives a nice introduction to Monte Carlo methods.

A Metropolis-Hastings Markov chain is set up in which moves from A, M, R_n to A', M', R'_n are accepted with probability

$$p_{accept} = \min \left(1, \frac{p(A', M', R'_n | X)}{p(A, M, R_n | X)} \frac{q(A, M, R_n | X)}{q(A', M', R'_n | X)} \; J \right). \qquad (1.140)$$

Here $p(A, M, R_n | X)$ is the (unknown) posterior of interest, q is a *proposal* density and J is the ratio of Jacobians for the proposal moves between the primed and non-primed spaces (Richardson & Green [1997] provide considerably more detail). An appropriate proposal for A is to draw each element from a normal distribution with zero mean and to draw the noise covariance from a *Wishart* distribution. In the following example a simple isotropic noise covariance was assumed, i.e., $R_n \stackrel{\text{def}}{=} \beta^{-1}I$ and the precision parameter β was drawn from a gamma distribution. The same example as in the previous subsection was used, that of two music sources mixed to six observations with 10% additive Gaussian noise. Figure 1.18 shows the results obtained. The top graph depicts the evolution of the model order with the Markov chain and the lower subplots give the resultant recovered sources.

1.7.5 Variational learning

In many situations we wish to infer posterior distributions over the parameters of interest. Such distributions may be given as marginal integrals. Unfortunately, such integrals are often non-analytic and in the previous subsections we have briefly discussed two approaches to this problem. Recently such Bayesian inference problems have been tackled using a particularly powerful approximative approach known as *variational learning*. This has been successfully applied to the ICA problem [Attias, 1999b] and to the related issue of probabilistic PCA [Bishop, 1999]. Chapters 3 and 8 of the present book and Choudrey *et al.* [2001] deal in considerably more detail with the application of variational learning to ICA and a brief introduction only is presented here.

Variables in the problem are divided into two classes: the visible or observed variables v (the data, for example); and the hidden variables, h, whose distribution we wish to infer. In ICA problems the hidden variables

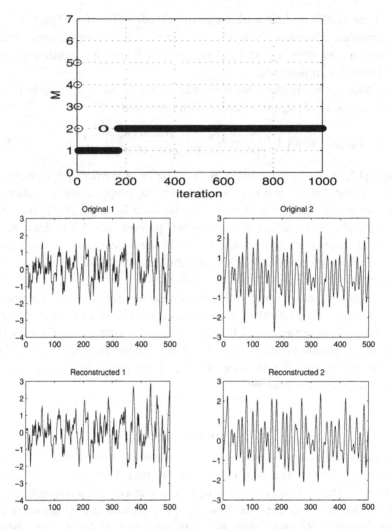

Figure 1.18. *Music data – RJ-MCMC approach:* Top row: Evolution of model order during the chain. The first 500 samples constitute a 'burn-in' period. Middle row: Original sources. Bottom row: estimated sources. Note that these source estimates are very close to those obtained by the approximative Bayesian method (*Figure 1.17*).

may be the parameters of A, the noise covariance matrix, any parameters in the source density models and all associated *hyperparameters* including the model order.

Given the *visible* variables, v, we wish to evaluate the conditional probability $p(h|v)$. Since Bayes' theorem allows the posterior distribution of the hidden variables to be written as

$$p(h|v) = \frac{p(v|h)p(h)}{p(v)}, \qquad (1.141)$$

it is of interest to evaluate the *evidence* of the generative model, namely

$$p(v) = \int p(v|h)p(h)dh = \int p(h,v)dh.$$

A strict lower bound for this marginalised evidence may be given as

$$\ln p(v) \geqslant \int q(h) \ln \frac{p(h,v)}{q(h)} dh, \qquad (1.142)$$

where $q(h)$ is the *variational approximation* to $p(h|v)$. This may be rewritten as

$$\ln p(v) \geqslant F \stackrel{\text{def}}{=} \int q(h) \ln p(h,v) \, dh + H[q(h)], \qquad (1.143)$$

in which F, by analogy with statistical mechanics, is the negative of the *variational free energy*. It is straightforward to show that the difference between this variational bound and the true marginalised likelihood is the KL divergence between $q(h)$ and $p(h|v)$. Simply performing an *unconstrained* minimisation of the KL divergence leads to the same problems of intractability as in a direct approach. Variational learning avoids this by using a form for $q(h)$ which results in a tight bound in formula (1.142) yet is simple in the sense that it makes the computations tractable. One very popular form for $q(h)$ takes the approximating density over the hidden variables to be factorised in such a way that the computation of F becomes tractable [MacKay, 1995, Attias, 1999b, Attias, 1999a]. We note that as the hidden variables consist of an *ensemble* of all free parameters the approach is often (and more accurately) referred to as *ensemble learning*.

There are two promising approaches to source-number determination using variational learning approaches. Firstly, as Attias [1999b] observes, as the negative variational free energy, F, forms a close bound to the true evidence, it may be used directly in a model selection process. One may choose, for example, the model for which F is maximal.† Secondly, the scheme of *Automatic Relevance Determination* (ARD, see [Bishop, 1995]) may be applied, which acts to suppress sources which are unsupported by the data. One method of applying ARD in the ICA case is to take a

---

† This presumes a flat prior over models.

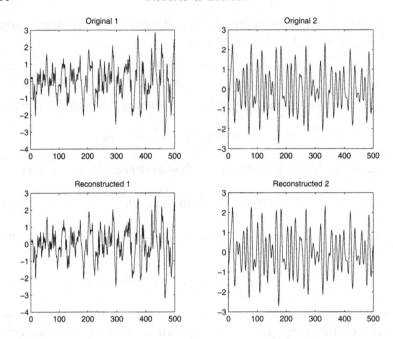

Figure 1.19. **Music data – variational approach:** *[top] Original sources and [bottom] estimated sources. The other four sources (not shown) were suppressed by the ARD scheme.*

Gaussian prior over the elements of W with separate variances for each row (corresponding to each hypothesised source). The variance hyperparameters of those sources which do not contribute to modelling the observations (i.e., through duplication) tend to very small values. The resultant source estimates are therefore very small and the source models do not move significantly from their priors. More details of this scheme may be found in Chapter 8 of the present book and in [Choudrey *et al.*, 2001].

Figure 1.19 shows the recovered sources using the same music data as in the previous examples. Four other sources (there being six observations) were suppressed by the ARD priors by two orders of magnitude and are not shown here. The sources are well recovered and the approach was considerably faster than either approximate Bayesian or sample based methods.

1.8 Extended ICA models

1.8.1 Dynamic ICA models

The standard ICA model consists of observations which are generated via a linear mixing of a set of *stationary* sources in which the mixing

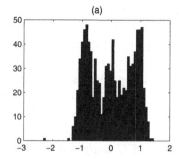
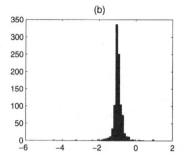

Figure 1.20. *Simple noisy sine wave source: plot (a) shows the p.d.f. of a sinusoid with 10% additive Gaussian noise. Note that the p.d.f. ideally requires a multi-modal source density (e.g., a MOG). If, however, an autoregressive model acts as the source process in the ICA model the resultant 'source' has a p.d.f. which is amenable to simple ICA source models (e.g., a reciprocal cosh distribution).*

is assumed static, i.e., A is not time-varying. Recently attempts have been made to overcome some of the problems associated with these assumptions. In [Penny *et al.*, 2000] the fact that sources (in this case biomedical signals) were likely to have multi-modal densities and be non-stationary was tackled by allowing the source model for the ICA process to be that of a generalised autoregressive (GAR) model which acts to transform the domain in which ICA operates from the raw signals to that of the parameters of the GAR model. A similar methodology was taken previous to this work by Pearlmutter & Parra [1996]. This approach does not alleviate the problems of source non-stationarity but allows a less complex source model to be used in the ICA algorithm. To see why this might be the case we refer to Figure 1.20(a) in which the density of a noisy sinusoidal source is shown. We note that the density is clearly multi-modal. Plot (b) shows the coefficient obtained from a first order autoregressive model of this source. The resultant 'source' has a unimodal p.d.f. which is well-suited to simple source models, such as the 'traditional' reciprocal-cosh approach. Penny *et al.* showed that when the noise is small (so the 'true' source p.d.f.s of a linear mix of near sinusoidal signals are very multi-modal) the autoregressive observation model gives considerably improved results over standard ICA.

The issue of allowing the mixing matrix itself, A, to have time varia-tion has been tackled recently in different ways. A piece-wise stationary approach may be taken by incorporating ICA into a switching state (hidden Markov) model, in which different, but static, mixing regimes are modelled [Penny *et al.*, 2000]. The model of Penny *et al.* allows switching between different mixing matrices whilst the sources remain the same (in the analogy of speakers in a room, changing from one set of microphones to another whilst the speakers continue talking). It also permits the converse problem, of a fixed A but switching sources, to be solved (i.e., the microphones remain fixed, but the speakers are changed). Thus the switching between different stationary source models and/or mixing matrices allows non-stationary sources to be modelled. Chapter 12 covers some of these issues in more detail and Chapter 6 discusses the issue of non-stationarity of the sources from a more fundamental perspective in which non-stationarity in the sources is used to aid the ICA algorithm.

Whilst this switching-state approach was well suited to the application (biomedical signal processing) it is not a generic solution in cases where the mixing may be constantly changing. One may, however, allow A to be a continuously time-varying parameter which evolves according to a parameterised dynamic model. Recent work shows that, with some caveats, this is possible [Everson & Roberts, 1999b]. Chapter 11 in the present book gives more details on this approach.

1.8.2 Different prior models

In previous sections we have seen that the ICA problem may be cast in a principled way as a probabilistic inference problem. Such an approach naturally codes prior information regarding the model. We briefly comment here on these priors and discuss the opportunities for alternatives.

Conditionally dependent sources Hyvärinen *et al.* [2000] considers the assumptions of *complete* independence between sources to be unrealistic in many situations. In particular, correlation of source energies is considered. This means that

$$\text{cov}(s_i^2, s_j^2) = \mathcal{E}\{s_i^2 s_j^2\} - \mathcal{E}\{s_i^2\}\mathcal{E}\{s_j^2\} \neq 0. \qquad (1.144)$$

Of particular interest is the case in which these correlations between the sources are *topographic* in nature. Hyvärinen *et al.* consider the case in which, given the variances, the sources are independent. A simple example is that of two independent components z_i and z_j and a common modulation σ which give rise to a hypothesised set of sources via multiplication, i.e., $s_i = z_i\sigma$ and $s_j = z_j\sigma$. These sources are *uncorrelated* but their energies are not.

The topographic aspect of this approach lies in the generative model for the set of σ_i. Sources which are 'closer' in a pre-defined sense are modelled as having stronger correlation (coupling) between their modulation parameters, σ_i. Hyvärinen *et al.* show that this approach gives rise to ICA decompositions in which the basis vectors (the rows of W) are naturally ordered topographically.

Priors on the mixing process The standard formulation of ICA makes strong assumptions regarding the independence of the sources, although these assumptions may be relaxed as discussed in the previous subsection. The mixing process itself is typically left vague in the sense that an *explicit* prior over A is not made.† Knuth [1999] considers the role of priors over A and details how a variety of more efficient algorithms are obtained, for particular analysis problems, by the incorporation of prior information. In particular, for fixed source dimensionality (i.e., M is assumed known *a priori*), the prior over A appears in the ICA equations as

$$p(A \mid \mathbf{x}) \propto p(A) \int p(\mathbf{x} \mid A, \mathbf{a}) p(\mathbf{a}) d\mathbf{a}. \qquad (1.145)$$

Knuth considers the case of separation of *a priori* decorrelated signals and imposes a prior on A which ensures the orthogonality of estimates for A. He also considers the case of 'inverse square' mixing in which sources that are believed to lie further from a sensor (which generates an observation sequence) have less mixing in accordance with an inverse square law. This model may be well suited to the problems of locating electrical sources of, e.g., brain activity from a set of electrodes located at different spatial positions on the head. Further details of these approaches may be found in [Knuth, 1999].

As an example of imposing different priors over A we apply a *non-negative* mixing matrix to the two music sources used throughout this chapter. Two priors were used for the elements of A, firstly a broad Gaussian prior and secondly a broad gamma prior.‡ Both priors being broad means that they did not significantly influence the evolution of A save for, in the gamma case, negative elements for A are not obtained. Figure 1.21

---

† The absence of any such explicit prior is equivalent to using an implicit improper flat prior, which plays no part in the ICA process.

‡ The gamma prior on A is taken as $p(A) = \prod_{ij} \frac{A_{ij}^{c-1}}{\Gamma(c)b^c} \exp\left(-\frac{A_{ij}}{b}\right)$. The mean of a gamma distribution with hyperparameters b, c is bc and the variance is $b^2 c$.

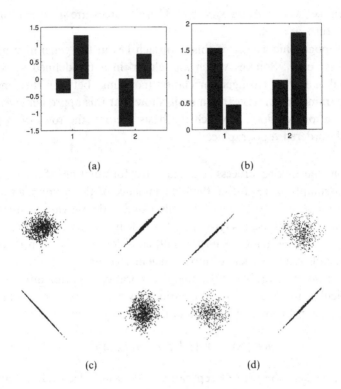

(a)   (b)

(c)   (d)

Figure 1.21. **Non-negativity prior on** A: *Estimates of A obtained using (a) Gaussian prior and (b) gamma prior. The resultant source scatterplots (true against estimated) are shown in (c) (Gaussian) and (d) (gamma).*

shows the resultant estimated unmixing matrices for (a) Gaussian and (b) Gamma priors together with scatterplots of the recovered sources against the true sources. The source estimates in the Gaussian case are very good because although the correct mixing matrix $\left[\begin{smallmatrix} 3 & 1 \\ 1 & 2 \end{smallmatrix} \right]$ has not been located, a mixing matrix which is related by symmetry of the likelihood has been found (cf. page 15) This would imply that as, in most cases, the performance of ICA is assessed by the independence of the sources (or their closeness to the true sources), the estimated mixing and unmixing matrices may not be meaningful in the sense that they may not be close to the true matrices. This is of particular importance in applications of ICA to image analysis in which the ICA basis vectors (rows or columns of the (un)mixing matrix) are imbued with significance.

1.9 Applications

In this section we review some of the applications of independent component analysis. It is impossible to thoroughly survey such a rapidly developing field and we merely give brief descriptions and pointers to some of the relevant literature.

1.9.1 Signals

Convolutive mixtures Ever since Jutten & Herault's pioneering work [1991] ICA has been widely used for the blind separation of a variety of signals, in both toy problems and real-world applications. However, the assumption of instantaneous linear mixing is seldom a very good one, because signals from the sources travel different distances to the microphones and are often reflected from surfaces on the way. Signals may therefore arrive at the sensors with multiple time delays. A more accurate model for the multi-path environment is a finite impulse response (FIR) convolutive filter:

$$\mathbf{x}(t) = \sum_{\tau=0}^{P} A(\tau)\mathbf{s}(t - \tau) + \mathbf{n}(t). \qquad (1.146)$$

Inferring the PNM filter coefficients and estimating the sources is clearly a more difficult problem than inverting instantaneous mixing.

A direct link with the instantaneous mixing case can be made if observations, $x(t)$, are made of the convolution of a filter, h, and a *single* source, $s(t)$, so that

$$x(t) = \sum_{\tau=0}^{P} h(\tau)s(t - \tau). \qquad (1.147)$$

Under the (usually not very good) assumption that the realisations of the source at different time points are independent, we can form an observation vector $\mathbf{x}(t) = [x(t), x(t-1), \dots, x(t-P)]^\mathsf{T}$, and a similar time-delayed vector for the source: $\mathbf{s}(t) = [s(t), s(t-1), \dots, s(t-P)]^\mathsf{T}$. Equation (1.147) can then be written as $\mathbf{x}(t) = A\mathbf{s}(t)$, where the mixing matrix is approximately

$$A = \begin{bmatrix} h(P) & h(P-1) & \dots & h(0) \\ h(P-1) & h(P-2) & \dots & 0 \\ h(P-2) & h(P-3) & \dots & 0 \\ \vdots & & & \vdots \end{bmatrix}. \qquad (1.148)$$

With these approximations the instantaneous ICA methodologies may be applied directly. Work on blind deconvolution has a long history (see, for example, [Haykin, 1994]). Other methods based on contrast functions which maximise the kurtosis of the recovered signal have been developed [Shalvi & Weinstein, 1994]. See also work by Attias & Schreiner [1998] on 'dynamic component analysis'.

However, mixtures of several sources and with time delays are much harder to treat. The inverse of the convolution (1.146) is, in general, an Infinite Impulse Response (IIR) filter which can be implemented by a neural network with a feedback architecture; this approach was adopted by Torkkola [1996a, 1996c] in schemes which maximise an information theoretic contrast. See also [Amari *et al.*, 1998] for a scheme which approximates the IIR filter with an FIR filter. A good introduction to kurtosis based methods for multiple independent sources is given by Douglas & Kung [2000].

Blind deconvolution of temporally correlated and non-stationary signals can be achieved using second order statistics only [Weinstein *et al.*, 1993]. Parra & Spence develop effective algorithms using this approach; they give details of this method and its application to separation of speech in reverberant environments in [Parra & Spence, 2000a] and Chapter 5.

Audio Speech separation is an important and appealing application domain for blind source separation, with applications ranging from voice control of computers to forensic surveillance. In real environments multiple paths are the norm and blind deconvolution is usually necessary. Torkkola [Torkkola, 1999] gives an extensive survey, with many references, of blind separation of audio signals.

Biomedical Ever since the recent upsurge in interest in ICA it has been applied to biomedical data, and in particular human electroencephalograms (EEGs) [Makeig *et al.*, 1996]. The propagation through the head of the electric field resulting from neuronal assemblies is approximately linear, and sufficiently rapid that time-delay effects are insignificant. Consequently a linear model, i.e., a superposition, is not inappropriate for EEG signals. Applications of ICA to EEG have concentrated on source localisation and on artifact removal. The element W_{jk} gives the relative contribution of the signal recorded at the kth sensor to the jth recovered source. A knowledge of the sensor (i.e., recording electrode) locations, therefore, permits the spatial distribution of each recovered source to be mapped back over the head. For work on source localisation in EEG and magnetoencephalography (MEG) the reader is referred to, for example, [Huang *et al.*, 1998, Aine *et al.*, 1998, Vigário *et al.*, 2000].

Eye movement, muscle movement, cardiac signals and extraneous electrical signals all contaminate EEG recordings and ICA has been proposed as a method for cleaning up the signal, by removing the artifactual components [Makeig *et al.*, 1996, Vigário, 1997, Jung *et al.*, 1998, Jung *et al.*, 2000, Jung *et al.*, 2000]. See Ziehe *et al.* [2000] for work on artifact removal in MEG. ICA is not, however, a panacea for artifact removal. In certain cases the linear model may fail [Knuth, 1998b, Everson & Roberts, 2000a] and physiological and experimental conditions (e.g., drying out of electrodes) may lead to non-stationarities in the data which prevent clean separation. Non-stationary mixing models (Chapter 11) and hidden Markov models [Penny *et al.*, 2000] may help to alleviate the problems due to non-stationarity, while nonlinear ICA (Chapter 4) and ICA mixture models (Chapter 9) may help with nonlinear mixing.

We note that ICA is also useful in the analysis and treatment of Event Related Potential (ERP) signals [Makeig *et al.*, 1997a, Jung *et al.*, 1999a, Jung *et al.*, 1999b, Makeig *et al.*, 1999, Vigário *et al.*, 1999], and finds application in other biomedical domains, for example, [Vetter *et al.*, 1999, Barros & Ohnishi, 1999]

Finance The analysis and forecasting of economic timeseries is an attractive goal, and ICA has been applied to the analysis of portfolio returns [Back & Weigend, 1998, Chin *et al.*, 1999]; see also work by Kiviluoto & Oja [1998]. Although the financial timeseries considered can be faithfully reconstructed using a smaller number of independent components than principal components, it is unclear what meaning can be attributed to the small number of sources recovered by a noiseless ICA model applied to financial timeseries which are influenced by a great many factors.

1.9.2 Images

Work to date using ICA on images ignores the two-dimensional nature of images and concatenates rows (or columns) of the image to form a one-dimensional signal.

Biomedical Brain imaging datasets have been the focus of considerable attention in recent years. In both functional magnetic resonance (fMRI) imaging and optical imaging† the goal is to extract independent components that correspond to the neural activity in the brain, while discarding components that describe unrelated physiological activity. See [Makeig et al., 1997b, McKeown et al., 1998a, McKeown et al., 1998b] for work on fMRI. Ensuring that the basis images are linearly decorrelated for all shifts with respect to each other is used for blind source separation in optical imaging [Schießl et al., 1999, Schießl et al., 2000, Schöner et al., 2000].

Hansen [2000] has developed a version of ICA using a Boltzmann learning rule, which he uses to extract independent components from short fMRI sequences.

The majority of optical imaging and fMRI experimental protocols are comprised of an unstimulated (or baseline) period followed by a period during which a stimulus is applied. Porrill et al. [2000] derive a 'weak causal' model which weakly incorporates this prior knowledge, and apply it to optical imaging data. The same group have also developed 'spatio-temporal ICA' which attempts to minimise a linear combination of the mutual independence between the time courses *and* the mutual independence of the basis images; this methodology is applied to fMRI data [Stone et al., 1999].

Faces The hypothesis that human faces are composed from an admixture of a small number of canonical or basis faces was first examined by Sirovich [1987] and Kirby and Sirovich [1990]. It has inspired much research in the pattern recognition [Atick et al., 1995] and psychological [O'Toole et al., 1991a, O'Toole et al., 1991b] communities. Much of this work has focused on *eigenfaces*, which are the principal components of an ensemble of faces and are therefore mutually orthogonal. Recently ICA has been applied to this problem [Bartlett et al., 1998, Everson & Roberts, 1999a]; the basis faces (the rows of the separating matrix) located by ICA are spatially more localised, and their densities are sparser, than the PCA basis faces. Recognition rates using the ICA basis are (slightly) higher than achieved with PCA [Bartlett et al., 1998]. Bartlett et al. [1997] also report that the recognition using independent components is more robust to changes of viewpoint. We note that the effective dimension of 'face space' remains an open question.

---

† A method dependent on the changes in the reflectance of the cortical surface in dance with the underlying neural activity [T'so et al., 1990].

Natural scenes There is a good deal of interest in the statistical properties of natural scenes (see Ruderman [1998] and Wainwright & Simoncelli [2000]) because the early stages of the visual system are likely to be adapted to them. Bell & Sejnowski [1997] discovered that the ICA basis functions (the rows of the separating matrix) are similar to spatial edge filters.

Olshausen & Field [1996] (see also [Olshausen & Field, 1997] and work by Lewicki & Olshausen [1999]) found filters similar to the localised and oriented receptive fields, suggesting that the primary visual cortex is coding visual scenes so that the mutual information between its output is minimum as suggested by Barlow [1961b, 1989]. However, van Hateren & van der Schaaf [1998] found no correspondence between the spatial frequency tuning of the ICA filters and simple cells in the visual cortex. Extension of their work to image sequences gives better correspondence between calculation and experiment [van Hateren & Ruderman, 1998]. See also the discussions by Parra & Spence (page 146) and by Lee & Lewicki (page 239).

Manduchi & Portilla [1999] perform ICA on the result of bandpass filtering textured images at several scales. The marginal p.d.f.s of the latent sources are then used for classification of the texture, and Manduchi & Portilla report more accurate classification with ICA than PCA. In Chapter 9 Lee & Lewicki use mixtures of independent component analysers for classification and segmentation based on texture.

1.9.3 Miscellaneous

Text Isbell & Viola [1999] and Kolenda *et al.* [2000] apply ICA to text corpuses in order to identify groups of documents with independent themes. In Chapter 10 Girolami extends the standard ICA model for use in the unsupervised classification and visualisation of high-dimensional datasets, particularly text.

Mechanics Ypma and Pajunen [1999] analyse the vibration of mechanical systems by simultaneously removing temporal correlations at all lags.

Telecommunications ICA has recently been proposed as a method to remove interfering transmissions in wireless telecommunications systems [Ristaniemi & Joutsensalo, 1999, Chevalier *et al.*, 1999, Deville *et al.*, 1999].

Remote sensing Each pixel of a hyperspectral satellite image provides the ground reflectance at a few hundred wavelengths. Usually each pixel contains a mixture of reflectances from a number of materials on the ground. Parra *et al.* [2000] apply a Bayesian ICA method to find the ratios of the constituent materials.

2

Fast ICA by a fixed-point algorithm that maximizes non-Gaussianity

Aapo Hyvärinen

Non-Gaussianity is of paramount importance in ICA estimation. Without non-Gaussianity the estimation is not possible at all (unless the independent components have time-dependences). Therefore, it is not surprising that non-Gaussianity could be used as a leading principle in ICA estimation.

In this chapter, we derive a simple principle of ICA estimation: the independent components can be found as the projections that maximize non-Gaussianity. In addition to its intuitive appeal, this approach allows us to derive a highly efficient ICA algorithm, FastICA. This is a fixed-point algorithm that can be used for estimating the independent components one by one. At the end of the chapter, it will be seen that it is closely connected to maximum likelihood or infomax estimation as well.

2.1 Whitening

First, let us consider preprocessing techniques that are essential if we want to develop fast ICA methods.

The rather trivial preprocessing that is used in many cases is to centre $\mathbf{x}$, i.e. subtract its mean vector $\mathbf{m} = \mathcal{E}\{\mathbf{x}\}$ so as to make $\mathbf{x}$ a zero-mean variable. This implies that $\mathbf{s}$ is zero-mean as well. This preprocessing is made solely to simplify the ICA algorithms: it does not mean that the mean could not be estimated. After estimating the mixing matrix A with centred data, we can complete the estimation by adding the mean vector of $\mathbf{s}$ back to the centred estimates of $\mathbf{s}$. The mean vector of $\mathbf{s}$ is given by $A^{-1}\mathbf{m}$, where $\mathbf{m}$ is the mean that was subtracted in the preprocessing.

The more sophisticated preprocessing that we want to use here is called whitening, or sphering. This means that before the application of the ICA algorithm (and after centring), we transform the observed vector $\mathbf{x}$ *linearly* so that we obtain a new vector $\tilde{\mathbf{x}}$ which is white, i.e., its components are uncorrelated and their variances equal unity. In other words, the covariance matrix of $\tilde{\mathbf{x}}$ equals the identity matrix:

$$\mathcal{E}\{\tilde{\mathbf{x}}\tilde{\mathbf{x}}^\mathsf{T}\} = I. \tag{2.1}$$

The whitening transformation is always possible. One popular method for whitening is to use the eigenvalue decomposition (EVD) of the covariance matrix $\mathcal{E}\{\mathbf{x}\mathbf{x}^\mathsf{T}\} = EDE^\mathsf{T}$, where E is the orthogonal matrix of eigenvectors of $\mathcal{E}\{\mathbf{x}\mathbf{x}^\mathsf{T}\}$ and D is the diagonal matrix of its eigenvalues, $D = \mathrm{diag}(d_1, ..., d_n)$. Note that $\mathcal{E}\{\mathbf{x}\mathbf{x}^\mathsf{T}\}$ can be estimated in a standard way from the available sample $\mathbf{x}(1), ..., \mathbf{x}(T)$. Whitening can now be done by

$$\tilde{\mathbf{x}} = ED^{-1/2}E^\mathsf{T}\mathbf{x} \tag{2.2}$$

where the matrix $D^{-1/2}$ is computed by a simple component-wise operation as $D^{-1/2} = \mathrm{diag}(d_1^{-1/2}, ..., d_n^{-1/2})$. It is easy to check that now $\mathcal{E}\{\tilde{\mathbf{x}}\tilde{\mathbf{x}}^\mathsf{T}\} = I$.

Whitening transforms the mixing matrix into a new one, $\tilde{A}$. We have from (2.1) and (2.2):

$$\tilde{\mathbf{x}} = ED^{-1/2}E^\mathsf{T}A\mathbf{s} = \tilde{A}\mathbf{s}. \tag{2.3}$$

The utility of whitening resides in the fact that the new mixing matrix $\tilde{A}$ is orthogonal. This can be seen from

$$\mathcal{E}\{\tilde{\mathbf{x}}\tilde{\mathbf{x}}^\mathsf{T}\} = \tilde{A}\mathcal{E}\{\mathbf{s}\mathbf{s}^\mathsf{T}\}\tilde{A}^\mathsf{T} = \tilde{A}\tilde{A}^\mathsf{T} = I. \tag{2.4}$$

Here we see that whitening reduces the number of parameters to be estimated. Instead of having to estimate the n^2 parameters that are the elements of the original matrix A, we only need to estimate the new, orthogonal mixing matrix $\tilde{A}$. An orthogonal matrix contains $n(n-1)/2$ degrees of freedom. For example, in two dimensions, an orthogonal transformation is determined by a single angle parameter. In larger dimensions, an orthogonal matrix contains only about half of the number of parameters of an arbitrary matrix. Thus one can say that whitening solves half of the problem of ICA. Because whitening is a very simple and standard procedure, much simpler than any ICA algorithms, it is a good idea to reduce the complexity of the problem this way.

It may also be quite useful to reduce the dimension of the data at the same time as we do the whitening. Then we look at the eigenvalues d_j of $\mathcal{E}\{\mathbf{x}\mathbf{x}^\mathsf{T}\}$ and discard those that are too small, as is often done in the

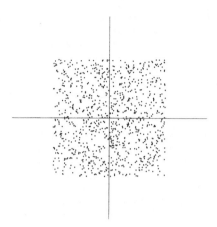

Figure 2.1. *The joint distribution of two independent components with uniform densities.*

statistical technique of principal component analysis. This often has the effect of reducing noise, and may prevent over-learning.

As an illustration, consider two independent components which have uniform densities, i.e. their densities are given by

$$p(s) = \begin{cases} \frac{1}{2\sqrt{3}} & \text{if } |s| \leq \sqrt{3}, \\ 0 & \text{otherwise.} \end{cases} \quad (2.5)$$

Their joint distribution is illustrated in Figure 2.1. These independent components are linearly mixed to obtain the data in Figure 2.2. The effect of whitening can be seen in Figure 2.3, in which the whitened mixtures are shown. The square defining the distribution is now clearly a rotated version of the original square in Figure 2.1. All that is left is the estimation of a single angle that gives the rotation.

In the rest of this chapter, we assume that the data has been preprocessed by centring and whitening. For simplicity of notation, we denote the preprocessed data just by x, and the transformed mixing matrix by A, omitting the tildes.

2.2 'Non-Gaussian is independent'

Now we are ready to discuss the significance of non-Gaussianity in ICA. The Central Limit Theorem, a classical result in probability theory, tells us that the distribution of a sum of independent random variables

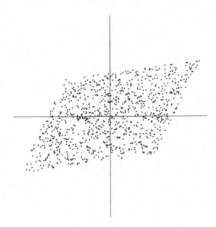

Figure 2.2. *The distribution of the mixtures of two independent components.*

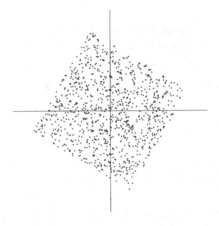

Figure 2.3. *The joint distribution of whitened mixtures of two independent components.*

tends toward a Gaussian distribution, under certain conditions. Loosely speaking, a sum of two independent random variables usually has a distribution that is closer to Gaussian than any of the two original random variables.

Let us thus assume that the whitened data vector **x** is distributed according to the ICA data model:

$$\mathbf{x} = A\mathbf{s}. \tag{2.6}$$

For simplicity, we assume in this section that all the independent components have identical distributions. Estimating the independent components can be accomplished by finding the right linear combinations of the mixture variables, since we can invert the mixing as

$$\mathbf{s} = A^{-1}\mathbf{x}. \qquad (2.7)$$

Thus, to estimate one of the independent components, we can consider a linear combination of the x_i. Let us denote this by $a = \mathbf{w}^\mathsf{T}\mathbf{x} = \sum_i w_i x_i$, where $\mathbf{w}$ is a vector to be determined. If $\mathbf{w}$ were one of the rows of the inverse of A, this linear combination would actually equal one of the independent components.

The question is now: How could we use the Central Limit Theorem to determine $\mathbf{w}$ so that it would equal one of the rows of the inverse of A? In practice, we cannot determine such a $\mathbf{w}$ exactly, because we have no knowledge of matrix A, but we can find an estimator that gives a good approximation.

To see how this leads to the principle of non-Gaussianity, let us make a change of variables, defining $\mathbf{q} = A^\mathsf{T}\mathbf{w}$. Then we have $a = \mathbf{w}^\mathsf{T}\mathbf{x} = \mathbf{w}^\mathsf{T}A\mathbf{s} = \mathbf{q}^\mathsf{T}\mathbf{s}$. Thus a is a linear combination of s_i with weights given by q_i. Since a sum of even two independent random variables is more Gaussian than the original variables, $\mathbf{q}^\mathsf{T}\mathbf{s}$ is more Gaussian than any of the s_i and becomes least Gaussian when it in fact equals one of the s_i. (Note that this is strictly true only if the s_i have identical distributions, as we assumed here.) In this case, obviously only one of the elements q_i of $\mathbf{q}$ is nonzero.

Therefore, we could take as $\mathbf{w}$ a vector that *maximizes the non-Gaussianity* of $\mathbf{w}^\mathsf{T}\mathbf{x}$. Such a vector would necessarily correspond (in the transformed coordinate system) to a $\mathbf{q}$ which has only one nonzero component. This means that $\mathbf{w}^\mathsf{T}\mathbf{x} = \mathbf{q}^\mathsf{T}\mathbf{s}$ equals one of the independent components! Maximizing the non-Gaussianity of $\mathbf{w}^\mathsf{T}\mathbf{x}$ thus gives us one of the independent components. In fact, the optimization landscape for non-Gaussianity in the M-dimensional space of vectors $\mathbf{w}$ has $2n$ local maxima, two for each independent component, corresponding to s_i and $-s_i$ (recall that the independent components can be estimated only up to a multiplicative sign).

We can illustrate the principle of maximizing non-Gaussianity by simple examples. Let us consider two independent components that have uniform densities. Their joint distribution is illustrated in Figure 2.1, in which a sample of the independent components is plotted on the two-dimensional plane. Figure 2.4 also shows, on the left, a histogram

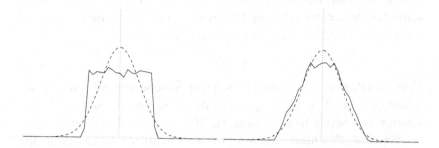

Figure 2.4. *Densities of mixtures: Left: The estimated density of one uniform independent component, with the Gaussian density (dashed curve) given for comparison. Right: The marginal density of a whitened mixture. It is closer to the Gaussian density (given by the dashed curve) than the densities of the independent components.*

estimate of the uniform densities. These variables are then linearly mixed, and the mixtures are whitened as a preprocessing step. The joint density of the whitened mixtures is given in Figure 2.3. It is a rotation of the original joint density.

Now, let us look at the densities of the whitened mixtures. One of these is estimated in Figure 2.4, on the right. One can clearly see that the densities of the mixtures are closer to a Gaussian density than the densities of the independent components in Figure 2.4 on the left.

To recapitulate, we have formulated ICA estimation as the search for directions that are maximally non-Gaussian: each local maximum gives one independent component. Our approach here is somewhat heuristic, but it will be seen in the next section that it has a perfectly rigorous justification.

From a practical point of view, we now have to answer the following questions: How can non-Gaussianity of $w^T x$ be measured? And how can we compute the values of w that maximize (locally) such a measure of non-Gaussianity? The rest of this chapter is devoted to answering these questions.

2.3 Measuring non-Gaussianity by kurtosis

2.3.1 Extrema of kurtosis give independent components

To use non-Gaussianity in ICA estimation, we must have a quantitative measure of non-Gaussianity of a random variable, say x. In this section, we show how to use kurtosis, a classic measure of non-Gaussianity, for ICA estimation.

Kurtosis is the name given to the fourth-order cumulant of a random variable. For simplicity, let us assume that x has zero mean. Then the kurtosis of x, denoted by kurt(x), is defined by

$$\text{kurt}(x) = \mathcal{E}\{x^4\} - 3(\mathcal{E}\{x^2\})^2. \tag{2.8}$$

To further simplify things, we can assume that x has variance equal to one: $\mathcal{E}\{x^2\} = 1$. Then the right-hand side simplifies to $\mathcal{E}\{x^4\} - 3$. This shows that kurtosis is simply a normalized version of the fourth moment $\mathcal{E}\{x^4\}$. For a Gaussian x, the fourth moment equals $3(\mathcal{E}\{x^2\})^2$. Thus, kurtosis is zero for a Gaussian random variable. For most (but not quite all) non-Gaussian random variables, kurtosis is nonzero.

Kurtosis can be either positive or negative. Random variables that have a negative kurtosis are called sub-Gaussian, and those with positive kurtosis are called super-Gaussian. In statistical literature, the corresponding expressions platykurtic and leptokurtic are also used. *Super-Gaussian* random variables have typically a 'spiky' pdf with heavy tails, i.e., the pdf is relatively large at zero and at large values of the variable, while being small for intermediate values. A typical example is the Laplace distribution, whose pdf (normalized to unit variance) is given by

$$p(x) = \frac{1}{\sqrt{2}} \exp(\sqrt{2}|x|). \tag{2.9}$$

This pdf is illustrated in Figure 2.5, on the left. *Sub-Gaussian* random variables, on the other hand, have typically a 'flat' pdf, which is rather constant near zero, and very small for larger values of the variable. A typical example is the uniform distibution, which was used in the examples above. Its density is given in (2.5), and illustrated in Figure 2.5, on the right.

Typically non-Gaussianity is measured by the absolute value of the kurtosis. The square of the kurtosis can also be used. These measures are zero for a Gaussian variable, and greater than zero for most non-Gaussian random variables. There are non-Gaussian random variables that have zero kurtosis, but they can be considered as very rare.

Kurtosis, or rather its absolute value, has been widely used as a measure of non-Gaussianity in ICA and related fields. The main reason is its simplicity, both computational and theoretical. Computationally, kurtosis can be estimated simply by using the fourth moment of the sample data (if the variance is kept constant). Theoretical analysis is

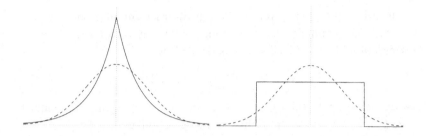

Figure 2.5. *Laplacian and uniform densities: Left: the density function of the Laplace distribution, which is a typical super-Gaussian distribution. For comparison, the Gaussian density is given by a dashed line. Both densities are normalized to unit variance. Right: the density function of the uniform distribution, which is a typical sub-Gaussian distribution.*

simplified because of the following linearity property: if x_1 and x_2 are two independent random variables, it holds that

$$\text{kurt}(x_1 + x_2) = \text{kurt}(x_1) + \text{kurt}(x_2) \tag{2.10}$$

and

$$\text{kurt}(\alpha x_1) = \alpha^4 \text{kurt}(x_1) \tag{2.11}$$

where α is a constant. These properties can be easily proven using the definition.

To illustrate in a simple example what the optimization landscape for kurtosis looks like, and how independent components could be found by kurtosis minimization or maximization, let us look at a two-dimensional model $\mathbf{x} = A\mathbf{s}$. Assume that the independent components s_1, s_2 have kurtosis values $\text{kurt}(s_1), \text{kurt}(s_2)$, respectively, both different from zero. Recall that they have unit variances by definition. We seek for one of the independent components as $a = \mathbf{w}^\mathsf{T}\mathbf{x}$.

Let us again make the transformation $\mathbf{q} = A^\mathsf{T}\mathbf{w}$. Then we have $a = \mathbf{w}^\mathsf{T}\mathbf{x} = \mathbf{w}^\mathsf{T}A\mathbf{s} = \mathbf{q}^\mathsf{T}\mathbf{s} = q_1 s_1 + q_2 s_2$. Now, based on the additive property of kurtosis, we have $\text{kurt}(a) = \text{kurt}(q_1 s_1) + \text{kurt}(q_2 s_2) = q_1^4 \text{kurt}(s_1) + q_2^4 \text{kurt}(s_2)$. On the other hand, we made the constraint that the variance of a is equal to 1, based on the same assumption concerning s_1, s_2. This implies a constraint on $\mathbf{q}$: $\mathcal{E}\{y^2\} = q_1^2 + q_2^2 = 1$. Geometrically, this means that the vector $\mathbf{q}$ is constrained to the unit circle on the two-dimensional plane.

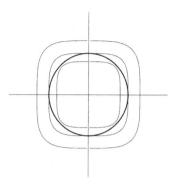

Figure 2.6. *The optimization landscape of kurtosis: The thick curve is the unit circle, and the thin curves are the contours where F in (2.12) is constant.*

The optimization problem is now: What are the maxima of the function $|\text{kurt}(a)| = |q_1^4 \text{kurt}(s_1) + q_2^4 \text{kurt}(s_2)|$ on the unit circle? For simplicity, we may assume that the kurtoses are of the same sign, in which case the absolute value operators can be omitted. Thus we may consider simply the function

$$F(\mathbf{q}) = q_1^4 + q_2^4. \tag{2.12}$$

Some contours of this function, i.e. curves in which this function is constant, are shown in Figure 2.6. The unit circle, i.e. the set where $q_1^2 + q_2^2 = 1$, is shown as well. This gives the 'optimization landscape' for the problem.

It is not hard to see that the maxima are at those points where exactly one of the elements of vector $\mathbf{q}$ is zero and the other nonzero; because of the unit circle constraint, the nonzero element must be equal to 1 or -1. But these points are exactly the ones when a equals one of the independent components $\pm s_i$, and the problem has been solved.

Now we see the utility of preprocessing by whitening. For whitened data $\mathbf{x}$, we seek for a linear combination $\mathbf{w}^\mathsf{T}\mathbf{x}$ that maximizes non-Gaussianity. This simplifies the situation here since we have due to the orthogonality of A

$$\|\mathbf{q}\|^2 = (\mathbf{w}^\mathsf{T} A)(A^\mathsf{T} \mathbf{w}) = \mathbf{w}^\mathsf{T}(AA^\mathsf{T})\mathbf{w} = \|\mathbf{w}\|^2. \tag{2.13}$$

This means that constraining $\mathbf{q}$ to lie on the unit sphere is equivalent to constraining $\mathbf{w}$ to be on the unit sphere. Thus we maximize the absolute value of the kurtosis of $\mathbf{w}^\mathsf{T}\mathbf{x}$ under the constraint that $\|\mathbf{w}\| = 1$.

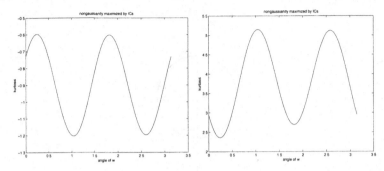

Figure 2.7. **Kurtosis of projections:** *The values of kurtosis for projections as a function of the angle. Vertical axis: kurtosis. Horizontal axis: angle. Left: sub-Gaussian ICs. Kurtosis is minimized, and its absolute value maximized, in the directions of the independent components. Right: super-Gaussian ICs. Here, kurtosis is maximized, as well as its absolute value, in the directions of the independent components.*

As an example, let us consider the whitened mixtures of uniformly distributed independent components in Figure 2.3. We search for a vector $\mathbf{w}$ such that the projection in that direction has maximum non-Gaussianity. We can plot the kurtosis of $\mathbf{w}^T\mathbf{x}$ as a function of the angle in which $\mathbf{w}$ points, as given in Figure 2.7, on the left. The plot shows the kurtosis is always negative, and is minimized in the directions of the independent components. These correspond to the direction in which the absolute value of the kurtosis is maximized.

In the second example, we see the same phenomenon for whitened mixtures of super-Gaussian independent components. Again, we search for a vector $\mathbf{w}$ such that the projection in that direction has maximum non-Gaussianity. We can plot the kurtosis of $\mathbf{w}^T\mathbf{x}$ as a function of the angle in which $\mathbf{w}$ points, as given in Figure 2.7, on the right. The plot shows the kurtosis is always positive, and is maximized in the directions of the independent components. These correspond to the direction in which the absolute value of kurtosis is maximized, as before.

2.4 Measuring non-Gaussianity by negentropy

2.4.1 Critique of kurtosis

Above, we showed how to measure non-Gaussianity by kurtosis, thus obtaining a simple ICA estimation method. However, kurtosis also has some drawbacks in practice, when its value has to be estimated from a measured sample. The main problem is that kurtosis can be very sensitive to outliers. Assume, for example, that a sample of 1000 values of a random variable (with zero mean and unit variance, say) contains one value equal to 10. Then the kurtosis equals at least $10^4/1000 - 3 = 7$, which means that the single value makes the kurtosis large. Thus we see that the value of the kurtosis may depend on only a few observations in the tails of the distribution, which may be erroneous or irrelevant observations. In other words, kurtosis is not a robust measure of non-Gaussianity.

Thus, other measures of non-Gaussianity might be better than kurtosis in some situations. In this section, we shall consider negentropy, which is the second important measure of non-Gaussianity. Its properties are in many ways opposite to those of kurtosis: it is robust but computationally complicated. We also introduce computationally simple approximations of negentropy that more or less combine the good properties of both measures.

2.4.2 *Negentropy as information-theoretic non-Gaussianity measure*

Negentropy is based on the information-theoretic quantity of entropy. Entropy is the basic concept of information theory. The entropy of a random variable can be interpreted as the degree of information that the observation of the variable gives. The more 'random', i.e. unpredictable and unstructured, the variable is, the larger its entropy.

Entropy H is defined for a discrete random variable X as

$$H(X) = -\sum_i P(X = \xi_i) \log P(X = \xi_i) \qquad (2.14)$$

where the ξ_i are the possible values of X. This very well-known definition can be generalized for continuous-valued random variables and vectors. The generalization is often called differential entropy, but for simplicity, we call it just entropy. The (differential) entropy H of a random vector $\mathbf{x}$ with density $p(\mathbf{x})$ is defined as

$$H(\mathbf{x}) = -\int p(\mathbf{x}) \log p(\mathbf{x}) d\mathbf{x}. \qquad (2.15)$$

A fundamental result of information theory is that *a Gaussian variable has the largest entropy* among all random variables of equal variance. This means that entropy could be used as a measure of non-Gaussianity. In fact, this shows that the Gaussian distribution is the 'most random' or the least structured of all distributions. Entropy is small for distributions that are clearly concentrated on certain values, i.e., when the variable is clearly clustered, or has a pdf that is very 'spiky'.

To obtain a measure of non-Gaussianity that is zero for a Gaussian variable and always non-negative, one often uses a normalized version of differential entropy, called negentropy. Negentropy J is defined as follows:

$$J(\mathbf{x}) = H(\mathbf{x}_{gauss}) - H(\mathbf{x}), \tag{2.16}$$

where $\mathbf{x}_{gauss}$ is a Gaussian random variable of the same covariance matrix as $\mathbf{x}$. Due to the above-mentioned properties, negentropy is always non-negative, and it is zero if and only if $\mathbf{x}$ has a Gaussian distribution. Negentropy has the additional interesting property that it is invariant for invertible linear transformations.

The advantage of using negentropy, or, equivalently, differential entropy, as a measure of non-Gaussianity is that it is well justified by statistical theory. In fact, negentropy is in some sense the optimal estimator of non-Gaussianity, as far as statistical properties are concerned. The problem in using negentropy is, however, that it is computationally very difficult. Estimating negentropy using the definition would require an estimate (possibly nonparametric) of the pdf. Therefore, simpler approximations of negentropy are very useful, as will be discussed next.

2.4.3 Approximating negentropy

The estimation of negentropy is difficult, as mentioned above, and therefore this contrast function remains mainly a theoretical one. In practice, some approximations have to be used. Here we introduce approximations that have very promising properties, and which will be used in the following to derive an efficient method for ICA.

The classical method of approximating negentropy is using higher-order cumulants. These approximations typically have a form similar to

$$J(x) \approx \frac{1}{12}\mathcal{E}\{x^3\}^2 + \frac{1}{48}\mathrm{kurt}(x)^2. \tag{2.17}$$

The random variable x is assumed to be of zero mean and unit variance. Actually, this approximation leads to the use of the kurtosis as in the preceding section. This is because the first term on the right-hand side of (2.17) is zero in the usual case of random variables with symmetric distributions. Therefore, the approximation is equivalent to the square of the kurtosis. Maximization of the square of the kurtosis is of course equivalent to maximization of its absolute value. Thus this approximation leads essentially to the method in Section 2.3. In particular, this approximation suffers from the non-robustness encountered with kurtosis. Therefore, we develop here more sophisticated approximations of negentropy.

One useful approach is to generalize the higher-order cumulant approximation so that it uses expectations of general nonquadratic functions, or 'nonpolynomial moments'. We shall not go into details of such an approximation here, the interested reader is referred to [Hyvärinen, 1998a]. In general we can replace the polynomial functions x^3 and x^4 by any other functions G^i (possibly more than two). Thus we obtain a simple way of approximating the negentropy based on the expectations $\mathcal{E}\{G^i(x)\}$. As a simple special case, we can take any two nonquadratic functions G^1 and G^2 such that G^1 is odd and G^2 is even, and we obtain the following approximation:

$$J(x) \approx k_1(\mathcal{E}\{G^1(x)\})^2 + k_2(\mathcal{E}\{G^2(x)\} - \mathcal{E}\{G^2(v)\})^2 \qquad (2.18)$$

where k_1 and k_2 are positive constants, and v is a Gaussian variable of zero mean and unit variance (i.e., standardized). The variable x is assumed to have zero mean and unit variance. Note that even in cases where this approximation is not very accurate, (2.18) can be used to construct a measure of non-Gaussianity that is consistent in the sense that it is always non-negative, and equal to zero if x has a Gaussian distribution. This is a generalization of the moment-based approximation in (2.17), which is obtained by taking $G^1(x) = x^3$ and $G^2(x) = x^4$.

In the case where we use only one non-quadratic function G, the approximation becomes

$$J(x) \propto [\mathcal{E}\{G(x)\} - \mathcal{E}\{G(v)\}]^2 \qquad (2.19)$$

for practically any non-quadratic function G. This is a generalization of the moment-based approximation in (2.17), if x has a symmetric distribution, in which case the first term in (2.17) vanishes. Indeed, taking $G(x) = x^4$, one then obtains a kurtosis-based approximation.

But the point here is that by choosing G wisely, one obtains approximations of negentropy that are better than the one given by (2.17). In particular, choosing a G that does not grow too fast, one obtains more robust estimators. The following choices of G have proved very useful:

$$G_1(x) = \frac{1}{a_1} \log \cosh a_1 x, \qquad (2.20)$$

$$G_2(x) = -\exp(-x^2/2) \qquad (2.21)$$

where $1 \leqslant a_1 \leqslant 2$ is some suitable constant, often taken equal to one. The functions in (2.20)-(2.21) are illustrated in Figure 2.8.

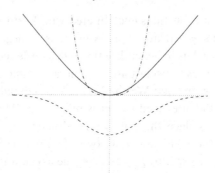

Figure 2.8. **Approximations to negentropy:** *The functions G_1 in Eq. (2.20), G_2 in Eq. (2.21), given by the solid curve and the dashed curve, respectively. The fourth power, as used in kurtosis, is given for comparison by the dash-dotted curve.*

Thus we obtain approximations of negentropy that give a very good compromise between the properties of the two classical non-Gaussianity measures given by kurtosis and negentropy. They are conceptually simple, fast to compute, yet have appealing statistical properties, especially robustness. Therefore, we shall use these contrast functions in our ICA methods. Interestingly, kurtosis can be expressed in this same framework.

2.5 The FastICA algorithm

After we have defined a measure of non-Gaussianity, we have to develop a practical method for maximizing it. The basic method used in this kind of problems is the gradient method. Here we develop, however, a much more powerful algorithm, called FastICA.

FastICA is based on a fixed-point iteration scheme for finding a maximum of the non-Gaussianity of $\mathbf{w}^T\mathbf{x}$, as measured in (2.19). More rigorously, it can be derived as an approximative Newton iteration. The FastICA algorithm using negentropy combines the superior algorithmic properties resulting from the fixed-point iteration with the preferable statistical properties due to negentropy.

2.5.1 Derivation of fixed-point algorithm

In this subsection, we derive the fixed-point algorithm. This subsection can be skipped by the reader not interested in mathematical details.

A trivial method of deriving a fixed-point iteration would be to equate

w to the gradient of the measure of non-Gaussianity. This is because if **w** equals this gradient (multiplied by some constant), then due to normalization to unit norm, this is a fixed point of the gradient method. This immediately suggests the following fixed-point iteration:

$$\mathbf{w} \leftarrow \mathcal{E}\{\mathbf{x}g(\mathbf{w}^\mathsf{T}\mathbf{x})\}, \tag{2.22}$$

which would be followed by normalization of **w**.

The iteration in (2.22) does not, however, have good convergence properties. Therefore, the iteration in (2.22) has to be modified. This is possible because we can add **w**, multiplied by some constant α, on both sides of (2.22) without modifying the fixed points. In fact, we have

$$\mathbf{w} = \mathcal{E}\{\mathbf{x}g(\mathbf{w}^\mathsf{T}\mathbf{x})\} \Leftrightarrow (1+\alpha)\mathbf{w} = \mathcal{E}\{\mathbf{x}g(\mathbf{w}^\mathsf{T}\mathbf{x})\} + \alpha\mathbf{w}, \tag{2.23}$$

and, because of the subsequent normalization of **w** to unit norm, the latter equation (2.23) gives a fixed-point iteration that has the same fixed points. Thus, by choosing α wisely, it may be possible to obtain an algorithm that converges very fast. In fact, such an α *can* be found, as we show here.

The suitable coefficient α, and thus the FastICA algorithm, can be found using an approximative Newton method. The Newton method is a powerful method for solving equations. When it is applied to the gradient, it gives an optimization method that usually converges in a small number of steps. The problem with the Newton method is, however, that it usually requires a matrix inversion at every step. Therefore, the total computational load may not be smaller than with gradient methods. What is quite surprising is that using the special properties of the ICA problem, we can find an approximation of the Newton method that does *not* need a matrix inversion but still converges roughly with the same number of iterations as the real Newton method (at least in theory). This approximative Newton method gives a fixed-point algorithm of the form (2.23).

To derive the approximative Newton method, first note that the maxima of the approximation of the negentropy of $\mathbf{w}^\mathsf{T}\mathbf{x}$ are obtained at certain optima of $\mathcal{E}\{G(\mathbf{w}^\mathsf{T}\mathbf{x})\}$. According to the Kuhn-Tucker conditions, the optima of $\mathcal{E}\{G(\mathbf{w}^\mathsf{T}\mathbf{x})\}$ under the constraint $\mathcal{E}\{(\mathbf{w}^\mathsf{T}\mathbf{x})^2\} = \|\mathbf{w}\|^2 = 1$ are obtained at points where

$$\mathcal{E}\{\mathbf{x}g(\mathbf{w}^\mathsf{T}\mathbf{x})\} + \beta\mathbf{w} = 0 \tag{2.24}$$

where β is some constant. Now let us try to solve this equation by

Newton's method. Denoting the function on the left-hand side of (2.24) by F, we obtain its Jacobian matrix $JF(\mathbf{w})$ as

$$JF(\mathbf{w}) = \mathcal{E}\{\mathbf{x}\mathbf{x}^{\mathsf{T}}g'(\mathbf{w}^{\mathsf{T}}\mathbf{x})\} + \beta I. \qquad (2.25)$$

To simplify the inversion of this matrix, we decide to approximate the first term in (2.25). Since the data is sphered, a reasonable approximation seems to be

$$\mathcal{E}\{\mathbf{x}\mathbf{x}^{\mathsf{T}}g'(\mathbf{w}^{\mathsf{T}}\mathbf{x})\} \approx \mathcal{E}\{\mathbf{x}\mathbf{x}^{\mathsf{T}}\}\mathcal{E}\{g'(\mathbf{w}^{\mathsf{T}}\mathbf{x})\} = \mathcal{E}\{g'(\mathbf{w}^{\mathsf{T}}\mathbf{x})\}I. \qquad (2.26)$$

Thus the Jacobian matrix becomes diagonal, and can easily be inverted. Thus we obtain the following approximative Newton iteration:

$$\mathbf{w} \leftarrow \mathbf{w} - [\mathcal{E}\{\mathbf{x}g(\mathbf{w}^{\mathsf{T}}\mathbf{x})\} + \beta\mathbf{w}]/[\mathcal{E}\{g'(\mathbf{w}^{\mathsf{T}}\mathbf{x})\} + \beta]. \qquad (2.27)$$

This algorithm can be further simplified by multiplying both sides of (2.27) by $\beta + \mathcal{E}\{g'(\mathbf{w}^{\mathsf{T}}\mathbf{x})\}$. This gives, after straightforward algebraic simplification

$$\mathbf{w} \leftarrow \mathcal{E}\{\mathbf{x}g(\mathbf{w}^{\mathsf{T}}\mathbf{x}) - \mathcal{E}\{g'(\mathbf{w}^{\mathsf{T}}\mathbf{x})\}\mathbf{w}\}. \qquad (2.28)$$

This is the basic fixed-point iteration in FastICA.

2.5.2 The algorithm for one independent component

The preceding derivation gives us the FastICA algorithm which can be described as follows.

First, we choose a nonlinearity g, which is the derivative of the non-quadratic function G used in (2.19). For example, we can use the derivatives of the functions in (2.20)-(2.21) which give robust approximations of negentropy. Alternatively, we could use the derivative corresponding to the fourth power as in kurtosis, which leads to the method that was already described in the previous section. Thus we can choose from

$$g_1(u) = \tanh(a_1 u), \qquad (2.29)$$

$$g_2(u) = u\exp(-u^2/2), \qquad (2.30)$$

$$g_3(u) = u^3 \qquad (2.31)$$

where $1 \leqslant a_1 \leqslant 2$ is some suitable constant, often taken as $a_1 = 1$. These functions are illustrated in Figure 2.9.

The basic form of the FastICA algorithm is then as described in Table 2.1.

Note that, as above, convergence means that the old and new values

(i) Whiten the data to give **x**.
(ii) Choose an initial (e.g. random) weight vector **w** of unit norm.
(iii) Let **w** ← $\mathcal{E}\{\mathbf{x}g(\mathbf{w}^T\mathbf{x})\} - \mathcal{E}\{g'(\mathbf{w}^T\mathbf{x})\}\mathbf{w}$, where g is defined e.g. as in (2.29)-(2.31).
(iv) Let **w** ← **w**/‖**w**‖.
(v) If not converged, go back to step (iii).

Table 2.1. *The FastICA algorithm for finding one maximally non-Gaussian direction, i.e. estimating one independent component.*

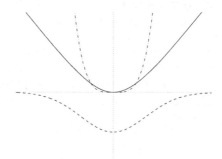

Figure 2.9. **Robust nonlinearities:** *The robust nonlinearities g_1 in Eq. (2.29), g_2 in Eq. (2.30), given by the solid line and the dashed line, respectively. The third power in (2.31), as used in kurtosis-based methods, is given by the dash-dotted line.*

of **w** point in the same direction, i.e. their dot-product is (almost) equal to 1. It is not necessary that the vector converges to a single point, since **w** and −**w** define the same direction.

The FastICA algorithm and the underlying non-Gaussianity measures have a number of desirable properties when compared with other existing methods for ICA.

- The convergence is cubic, or at least quadratic, under the assumption of the ICA data model (for a proof, see [Hyvärinen, 1999a]). This is in contrast to gradient descent methods, where the convergence is only linear. This means a very fast convergence, as has been confirmed by simulations and experiments on real data.
- Unlike with gradient-based algorithms, there are no step size parameters to choose. This means that the algorithm is easy to use.
- The algorithm finds directly independent components of (practically) any non-Gaussian distribution using any nonlinearity g. This is in

contrast to many algorithms, where some estimate of the probability distribution function has to be first available, and the nonlinearity must be chosen accordingly.

- The performance of the method can be optimized by choosing a suitable nonlinearity g. In particular, one can obtain algorithms that are robust and/or of minimum variance, see [Hyvärinen, 1997].
- The independent components can be estimated one by one, which is roughly equivalent to doing projection pursuit (see below).
- FastICA inherits most of the advantages of neural algorithms, from which it was originally derived. It is parallel, distributed, computationally simple, and requires little memory space.

Gradient methods seem to be preferable only if fast adaptivity in a changing environment is required.

The algorithm given above estimates only one independent component. To estimate more independent components, different kinds of decorrelation schemes should be used, as discussed next.

2.5.3 Estimating several independent components

Above, we estimated only one independent component. This is why the algorithms above are called 'one-unit' algorithms. In principle, we could find more independent components by running the algorithm many times and using different initial points. This would not be a reliable method of estimating many independent components, however.

The key to extending the method of maximum non-Gaussianity to estimate more than one independent component is based on the following property: the vectors w_i corresponding to different independent components are orthogonal in the whitened space, as shown in section 2.1. To recapitulate, the independence of the components requires that they are uncorrelated, and in the whitened space we have $\mathcal{E}\{(\mathbf{w}_i^T\mathbf{x})(\mathbf{w}_j^T\mathbf{x})\} = \mathbf{w}_i^T\mathbf{w}_j$, and therefore uncorrelatedness is equivalent to orthogonality.

Thus, to estimate several independent components, we need to run any of the above one-unit algorithms using several units (e.g. neurons) with weight vectors $\mathbf{w}_1, ..., \mathbf{w}_N$, and to prevent different vectors from converging to the same maxima we must *orthogonalize* the vectors after every iteration. We present in the following different methods for achieving decorrelation.

A simple way of orthogonalization is *deflationary orthogonalization* using the Gram-Schmidt method. This means that we estimate the inde-

(i) Whiten the data to give $\mathbf{x}$.

(ii) Choose m, the number of ICs to estimate. Set counter $p \leftarrow 1$.

(iii) Choose an initial value of unit norm for $\mathbf{w}_p$, e.g. randomly.

(iv) Let $\mathbf{w}_p \leftarrow \mathcal{E}\{\mathbf{x}g(\mathbf{w}_p^\mathsf{T}\mathbf{x})\} - \mathcal{E}\{g'(\mathbf{w}_p^\mathsf{T}\mathbf{x})\}\mathbf{w}$, where g is defined e.g. as in (2.29)-(2.31).

(v) Do the following orthogonalization:

$$\mathbf{w}_p \leftarrow \mathbf{w}_p - \sum_{j=1}^{p-1}(\mathbf{w}_p^\mathsf{T}\mathbf{w}_j)\mathbf{w}_j. \tag{2.32}$$

(vi) Let $\mathbf{w}_p \leftarrow \mathbf{w}_p / \|\mathbf{w}_p\|$.

(vii) If $\mathbf{w}_p$ has not converged, go back to step (iv).

(viii) Set $p \leftarrow p + 1$. If $p \leqslant m$, go back to step (iii).

Table 2.2. *The FastICA algorithm with deflationary orthogonalization.*

pendent components one by one. When we have estimated p independent components, or p vectors $\mathbf{w}_1, ..., \mathbf{w}_p$, we run any one-unit algorithm for $\mathbf{w}_{p+1}$, and after every iteration step subtract from $\mathbf{w}_{p+1}$ the 'projections' $(\mathbf{w}_{p+1}^\mathsf{T}\mathbf{w}_j)\mathbf{w}_j, j = 1, ..., p$, of the previously estimated p vectors, and then renormalize $\mathbf{w}_{p+1}$. The resulting FastICA algorithm with deflationary orthogonalization is shown in Table 2.2.

In certain applications, however, it may be desirable to use a symmetric decorrelation, in which no vectors are 'privileged' over others. This means that the vectors $\mathbf{w}_i$ are not estimated one by one; instead, they are estimated in parallel. One motivation for this is that the deflationary method has the drawback that estimation errors in the first vectors are accumulated in the subsequent ones by the orthogonalization. This is done by first doing the iterative step of the one-unit algorithm on every vector $\mathbf{w}_i$, and afterwards orthogonalizing all the $\mathbf{w}_i$ by special symmetric methods.

The *symmetric orthogonalization* of W can be accomplished, e.g., by the classical method involving matrix square roots,

$$W \leftarrow (WW^\mathsf{T})^{-1/2}W. \tag{2.33}$$

The inverse square root $(WW^\mathsf{T})^{-1/2}$ is obtained from the eigenvalue decomposition of $WW^\mathsf{T} = E\,\mathrm{diag}(d_1, ..., d_m)E^\mathsf{T}$ as

$$(WW^\mathsf{T})^{-1/2} = E\,\mathrm{diag}(d_1^{-1/2}, ..., d_m^{-1/2})E^\mathsf{T}. \tag{2.34}$$

A simpler alternative is the following iterative algorithm:

(i) Whiten the data to give **x**.
(ii) Choose m, the number of independent components to estimate.
(iii) Choose initial values for the $\mathbf{w}_i, i = 1,...,m$, each of unit norm.
(iv) For every $i = 1,...,m$, let $\mathbf{w}_i \leftarrow \mathcal{E}\{\mathbf{x}g(\mathbf{w}_i^T\mathbf{x})\} - \mathcal{E}\{g'(\mathbf{w}_i^T\mathbf{x})\}\mathbf{w}$, where g is defined e.g. as in (2.29)-(2.31).
(v) Do a symmetric orthogonalization of the matrix $W = (\mathbf{w}_1,...,\mathbf{w}_m)^T$ by

$$W \leftarrow (WW^T)^{-1/2}W. \tag{2.35}$$

(vi) If not converged, go back to step (iv).

Table 2.3. *FastICA with symmetric orthogonalization.*

(i) Let $W \leftarrow W/\|W\|$.
(ii) Let $W \leftarrow \frac{3}{2}W - \frac{1}{2}WW^TW$.
(iii) If WW^T is not close enough to identity, go back to step (ii).

The norm in step (i) can be almost any ordinary matrix norm, e.g., the 2-norm or the largest absolute row or column sum (but not the Frobenius norm).

Using the former symmetric orthogonalization, we give the corresponding version of the FastICA algorithm in Table 2.3.

2.6 ICA and projection pursuit

It is interesting to note how the approach to ICA described in this Chapter makes explicit the connection between ICA and another technique: projection pursuit.

2.6.1 Searching for interesting directions

Projection pursuit is a technique developed in statistics for finding 'interesting' projections of multidimensional data. Such projections can then be used for optimal visualization of the data, and for such purposes as density estimation and regression.

When projection pursuit is used for exploratory data analysis, we usually compute a couple of the most 'interesting' 1-dimensional projections. (The definition of interestingness will be treated in the next subsection.) Some structure of the data can then be visualised by showing the distribution of the data in the 1-dimensional subspaces, or on 2-dimensional planes spanned by two of the projection pursuit directions. This method

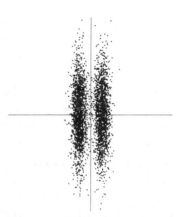

Figure 2.10. **Projection pursuit:** *An illustration of projection pursuit and the 'interesting' directions. The data in this figure is clearly divided into two clusters. The goal in projection pursuit is to find the projection (here, on the horizontal axis) that reveals the clustering or other structure of the data.*

is an extension of the classical method of using PCA for visualization, in which the distribution of the data is shown on the plane spanned by the two first principal components.

An example of the problem can be seen in Figure 2.10. In reality, projection pursuit is of course used in situations where the number of dimensions is very large, but for purposes of illustration, we use here a trivial 2-dimensional example. In the figure, the interesting projection of the data would be on the horizontal axis. This is because that projection shows the clustering structure of the data. In contrast, projections in very different directions (here, projection on the vertical axis) would show only ordinary Gaussian data. It would thus be useful to have a method that automatically finds the horizontal projection in this example.

2.6.2 Non-Gaussian is interesting

The basic question in projection pursuit is thus to define what kind of projections are interesting.

It is usually argued that the Gaussian distribution is the least interesting one, and that the most interesting directions are those that show the least Gaussian distribution. One motivation for this is that distributions that are multimodal, i.e. show some clustering structure, are far from Gaussian. An information-theoretic motivation is that entropy is maximized by the

Gaussian distribution, and entropy can be considered as a measure of the lack of structure.

The usefulness of using the most non-Gaussian projections for visualization can be seen in Figure 2.10. Here the most non-Gaussian projection is on the horizontal axis; this is also the projection that most clearly shows the clustered structure of the data. On the other hand, the projection on the vertical direction, which is also the direction of the first principal component, fails to show this structure. This shows also that PCA does not use the clustering structure. In fact, clustering structure is not visible in the covariance matrix on which PCA is based (cf. section 1.3).

Thus projection pursuit is usually performed by finding the most non-Gaussian projections of the data. This is the same thing as we did in this chapter to estimate the ICA model. This means that all the non-Gaussianity measures and the corresponding ICA algorithms presented in this chapter could also be called projection pursuit 'indices' and algorithms.

It should be noted that in the formulation of projection pursuit, no data model or assumption about independent components is made. If the ICA model holds, optimizing the ICA non-Gaussianity measures produces independent components; if the model does not hold, then what we get are the projection pursuit directions.

2.7 FastICA and maximum likelihood

Finally, we give a version of FastICA that shows explicitly the connection to the well-known infomax or maximum likelihood algorithm. If we express FastICA using the intermediate formula in (2.27), and write it in matrix form, we see that FastICA takes the following form:

$$W \leftarrow W + \text{diag}(\alpha_i)[\text{diag}(-\beta_i) + \mathcal{E}\{g(\mathbf{a})\mathbf{a}^\mathsf{T}\}]W, \qquad (2.36)$$

where $\mathbf{a} = W\mathbf{x}$, $\beta_i = \mathcal{E}\{a_i g(a_i)\}$, and $\alpha_i = 1/(\beta_i - \mathcal{E}\{g'(a_i)\})$. The matrix W needs to be orthogonalized after every step. In this matrix version, it is natural to orthogonalize W symmetrically.

The above version of FastICA could be compared with the stochastic gradient method for maximizing likelihood,

$$W \leftarrow W + \mu[I + \phi(\mathbf{a})\mathbf{a}^\mathsf{T}]W, \qquad (2.37)$$

where μ is the learning rate, not necessarily constant in time. Comparing (2.36) and (2.37), we see that FastICA can be considered as a fixed-point algorithm for maximum likelihood estimation of the ICA data model. In

FastICA, convergence speed is optimized by the choice of the matrices $\text{diag}(\alpha_i)$ and $\text{diag}(-\beta_i)$.

Another advantage of FastICA is that it can estimate both sub- and super-Gaussian independent components, which is in contrast to ordinary ML algorithms, which only work for a given class of distributions. The reason is clear from (2.36): the matrix $\text{diag}(\alpha_i)$ contains estimates on the nature (sub- or super-Gaussian) of the independent components. For the adaptive gradient descent algorithm, the nature of the independent components has to estimated separately.

Note that in FastICA, the outputs a_i are decorrelated and normalized to unit variance after every step. No such operations are needed in the gradient descent rule. The fixed-point algorithm is not stable if these additional operations are omitted. Thus the optimization space is slightly reduced.

2.8 References

This approach of estimating components by non-Gaussianity was first developed in the context of blind deconvolution [Donoho, 1981, Shalvi & Weinstein, 1993]. Blind deconvolution is a linear model not unlike the ICA model, but the mixing is done by convolution of a one-dimensional signal. The principle was probably first used in the context of ICA in [Delfosse & Loubaton, 1995], where the maximality property of kurtosis was proven rigorously, and further developed in [Hyvärinen & Oja, 1997, Hyvärinen & Oja, 1998, Hyvärinen, 1999a]; these papers form the basis for this chapter. From a different starting point, it was also developed in the projection pursuit literature [Huber, 1985, Jones & Sibson, 1987, Friedman, 1987, Cook *et al.*, 1993]. The important connection between kurtosis and negentropy in (2.17) was derived in [Jones & Sibson, 1987]. The ML gradient algorithm can be found in slightly different forms in [Amari *et al.*, 1996, Bell & Sejnowski, 1995, Cardoso & Laheld, 1996, Cichocki & Unbehauen, 1996], and the connection to FastICA was shown in [Hyvärinen, 1999b]. For a discussion of over-learning in ICA, see [Hyvärinen *et al.*, 1999c]. Extensions of FastICA have been developed for noisy data [Hyvärinen, 1999c], complex-valued data [Bingham & Hyvärinen, 2000], and overcomplete bases [Hyvärinen *et al.*, 1999a].

2.9 Conclusion

A fundamental approach to ICA is given by the principle of non-Gaussianity. The independent components can be found by finding directions in which the data is maximally non-Gaussian. Non-Gaussianity can be measured by entropy-based measures or cumulant-based measures like kurtosis. Estimation of the ICA model can then be performed by maximizing such non-Gaussianity measures. This can be done by a fast fixed-point algorithm called FastICA. Several independent components can be found by finding several directions of maximum non-Gaussianity under the constraint of decorrelation. This approach is closely connected to projection pursuit, in which the maximally non-Gaussian directions are considered interesting from the viewpoint of visualization and exploratory data analysis.

3

ICA, graphical models, and variational methods

H. Attias

3.1 Introduction

Early work on ICA [Jutten & Herault, 1991, Comon, 1994, Bell & Sejnowski, 1995] has focused on the case where the number of sources
equals the dimensionality of the data, the mixing is invertible, the data
are noise free, and the source distributions are known in advance. These
assumptions were very restrictive, and several authors have proposed
ways to relax them (e.g., [Lewicki & Sejnowski, 1998, Lee *et al.*, 1998,
Lee *et al.*, 1999b, Attias, 1999a]). This chapter presents one strand of research that aims to deal with the full generality of the blind separation
problem in a principled manner. This is done by casting blind separation as a problem in learning and inference with probabilistic graphical
models.

Graphical models (see [Jordan, 1999] for a review) serve as an increasingly important tool for constructing machine learning algorithms
in many fields, including computer science, signal processing, text modelling, molecular biology, and finance. In the graphical model framework, one starts with a statistical parametric model which describes
how the observed data are generated. This model uses a set of parameters, which in the case of blind separation include, e.g., the mixing
matrix and the variance of the noise. It may contain hidden variables,
e.g., the sources. The machinery of probability theory is then applied
to learn the parameters from the dataset. Simultaneously with learning the parameters, the same machinery also computes the conditional
distributions over the hidden variables given the data. This is done iteratively using the well known Expectation Maximization (EM) algorithm
[Rubin & Thayer, 1982, Neal & Hinton, 1993]. In the case of blind sep-

aration, the hidden variable distributions can be used to reconstruct the sources from data.

This chapter demonstrates, in a tutorial manner, that the framework of graphical models allows, and in fact encourages, systematic and useful extensions of ICA in several directions. In particular, all the restrictions mentioned above can be relaxed. We design an algorithm that learns arbitrary source distributions from data, and extend it to learn temporal properties of the sources as well. We also show how to obtain optimal source reconstructions in the presence of noise with unknown variance. Moreover, the algorithms we develop can handle arbitrary numbers of sources and sensors.

Our discussion starts with the technique of Independent Factor Analysis. IFA, introduced in [Attias, 1999a], provides a tool for modelling N-dimensional data in terms of M unobserved factors. These factors are mutually independent and combine linearly with added noise to produce the observed data. Mathematically, the model is defined by

$$\mathbf{x}_t = A\mathbf{s}_t + \mathbf{n}_t, \tag{3.1}$$

where $\mathbf{s}_t$ is the vector of factor activities at time t, $\mathbf{x}_t$ is the data vector, A is the $N \times M$ mixing matrix, and $\mathbf{n}_t$ is the noise.

The origins of IFA lie in applied statistics on the one hand and in signal processing on the other hand. Its statistics ancestor is ordinary factor analysis (FA), which assumes Gaussian factors. In contrast, IFA allows each factor to have its own arbitrary distribution, modelled semi-parametrically by a 1-dimensional mixture of Gaussians (MOG). The MOG parameters, as well as the mixing matrix and noise covariance matrix, are learned from the observed data by an EM algorithm.

The signal processing ancestor of IFA is the method of ICA for blind source separation [Bell & Sejnowski, 1995, Amari *et al.*, 1996, Pearlmutter & Parra, 1996, Hyvärinen & Oja, 1997, Attias & Schreiner, 1998]. In ICA, the factors are termed *sources*, and the task of blind separation algorithms is to recover them from the observed data with no knowledge of the mixing process. The sources in ICA have non-Gaussian distributions but, unlike in IFA, these distributions are usually fixed by prior knowledge or have quite limited adaptability. IFA allows any M, N (including more sources than sensors, $M > N$), as well as non-zero noise with unknown covariance. In addition, its use of the flexible MOG model often proves crucial for achieving successful separation. IFA therefore generalizes and unifies FA and ICA.

However, IFA and its ancestors suffer from the following shortcoming:

they are oblivious to temporal information since they do not attempt to model the temporal statistics of the data (but for square, noise-free mixing see [Pearlmutter & Parra, 1996]). In other words, the model learned would not be affected by permuting the time indices of $\{\mathbf{x}_t\}$. This is unfortunate since, in general, modelling the data as a time series would facilitate filtering and forecasting, as well as more accurate classification. In particular, for source separation applications, learning temporal statistics would provide additional information on the sources, leading to cleaner source reconstructions.

To see this, one may think of the problem of blind separation of noisy data in terms of two components: source separation and noise reduction. A possible approach might be the following two-stage procedure. First, perform noise reduction using, e.g., Wiener filtering. Second, perform source separation on the cleaned data using, e.g., an ICA algorithm. Notice that this procedure directly exploits temporal (second-order) statistics of the data in the first stage to achieve stronger noise reduction. An alternative approach would be to exploit the temporal structure of the data indirectly, by using a temporal source model. In the resulting single-stage algorithm, the operations of source separation and noise reduction are coupled.

This is the approach taken here. Temporal statistics may be captured by using dynamic probabilistic models for the sources. For this purpose, we will describe each source by a hidden Markov model (HMM). The resulting dynamic model describes a multivariate time series in terms of several independent sources, each having its own temporal characteristics. We will present an EM learning algorithm for the zero-noise case, and an algorithm for the case of isotropic noise. The case of non-isotropic noise turns out to be computationally intractable; we will provide an approximate EM algorithm based on a variational approach.

Whereas the graphical models framework is sufficiently powerful and flexible to facilitate an attack on the problem in its full generality, this comes at a price. The price is that the mathematics involved in doing learning and inference with the models introduced here is somewhat technically involved. We shall start with the simpler case of IFA and work our way toward more complicated models.

Notation The multivariable Gaussian density for a random vector $\mathbf{x}$ with mean μ and covariance matrix Σ is denoted by

$$\mathcal{G}(\mathbf{x} \mid \mu, \Sigma) = \mid 2\pi\Sigma \mid^{-1/2} \exp\left[-(\mathbf{x} - \mu)^{\mathsf{T}}\Sigma^{-1}(\mathbf{x} - \mu)/2\right]. \tag{3.2}$$

We work with T-point time blocks denoted by $\mathbf{x}_{1:T} = \{\mathbf{x}_t\}_{t=1}^T$. The ith coordinate of $\mathbf{x}_t$ is x_t^i. For a function f, $\langle f(\mathbf{x}_{1:T}) \rangle$ denotes averaging over an ensemble of $\mathbf{x}_{1:T}$ blocks.

3.2 IFA with flexible sources: zero noise

The ability to learn source densities $p(s_i)$ from the observed data is crucial. However, existing algorithms usually employ a source model that either is fixed or has only limited flexibility. When the actual source densities in the problem are known in advance, this model can be tailored accordingly; otherwise, an inaccurate model often leads to a bad estimate for A and failed separation. Whereas a flexible parametric form of $p(s_i)$ can in principle be learned by ML, existing algorithms adapt the parameters by gradient ascent, which would result in rather slow learning.

Our solution is based on a source model that (i) is capable of approximating arbitrary densities, and (ii) can be learned efficiently from data by EM. A simple model satisfying both requirements is a mixture of Gaussians. In that case,

$$p(s_i) = \sum_q \pi_q^i \, \mathcal{G}(s_i - \mu_q^i, v_q^i) \tag{3.3}$$

is a weighted sum of n_i Gaussian densities labeled by q, with means μ_q^i, variances v_q^i, and mixing proportions π_q^i. These Gaussians can be viewed as hidden states of the sources. Denoting the state of source i by q_i, its signal s_i is generated by selecting a state q with probability $p(q_i = q)$ independently at each time point t, followed by sampling from the corresponding Gaussian; the data are then generated via $x_i = \sum_j A_{ij} s_j$. This is a probabilistic generative model for the data, defined by

$$p(q_i = q) = \pi_q^i,$$
$$p(s_i \mid q_i = q) = \mathcal{G}(s_i - \mu_q^i, v_q^i),$$
$$p(\mathbf{x}) = |\det W| \prod_{i=1}^M p(s_i), \tag{3.4}$$

where the last equation follows from $\mathbf{s} = W\mathbf{x}$, with $W = A^{-1}$.

The model density $p(\mathbf{x} \mid V)$ defined by (3.4) is parametrized by $V = \{W_{ij}, \mu_q^i, v_q^i, \pi_q^i\}$. An EM algorithm can be derived in the stantard way. Here we provide a derivation based on [Neal & Hinton, 1993], which presents a generalized but non-standard view of the EM algorithm. Whereas this generalization is unnecessary in the current case, it becomes crucial later, so we take the opportunity to become familiar with it in the present, simpler context.

We begin by bounding the log-likelihood $\mathcal{L} = \log p(\mathbf{y})$ from below:

$$\mathcal{L} \geqslant \log | W | + \sum_i E_{p'} \log p(q_i, s_i) - E_{p'} \log p', \qquad (3.5)$$

where $E_{p'}$ denotes averaging over the hidden states $\mathbf{q} = (q_1, ..., q_M)^\mathsf{T}$ using an arbitrary posterior $p' = p'(\mathbf{q} \mid \mathbf{s})$.

E-step In EM, p' is computed at each iteration from (3.4) via Bayes' rule, but using the parameters V obtained in the previous iteration. This can be derived from maximizing the bound above with respect to p'. Notice that this posterior factorizes into a product of $\gamma_q^i = p(q_i = q \mid s_i)$ over i, which depends on the data via $s_i = \sum_j W_{ij} x_j$.

M-step Following the calculation of γ_q^i, the lower bound above is maximized again, this time with respect to the new parameters V. The maximization with respect to W is performed by gradient ascent using

$$\delta W = \epsilon W - \epsilon \phi(\mathbf{s}) \mathbf{s}^\mathsf{T} W, \qquad (3.6)$$

where

$$\phi(s_i) = \sum_q \gamma_q^i \frac{s_i - \mu_q^i}{v_q^i}, \qquad (3.7)$$

and ϵ is a properly chosen learning rate. The relative gradient [Amari et al., 1996, Cardoso & Laheld, 1996] was used to derive (3.6). For the source parameters we obtain the update rules

$$\mu_q^i = \frac{E\gamma_q^i s_i}{E\gamma_q^i}, \quad v_q^i = \frac{E\gamma_q^i s_i^2}{E\gamma_q^i} - \mu_{i,q}^2, \quad \pi_q^i = E\gamma_q^i, \qquad (3.8)$$

where E denotes averaging over the data instances.

Scaling. In the blind separation problem, the sources and mixing matrix can be identified only to within an order permutation and scaling of the sources; in other words, the likelihood is invariant under these transformations. The continuous degrees of freedom added by the scaling invariance may delay convergence and cause numerical problems (e.g., W_{ij} may acquire arbitrarily large values). These effects can be minimized by scaling each source s_j and row j of W at each iteration by a factor σ_j, which is determined by the source variance or by the norm of the corresponding row. It is easy to show that this scaling leaves the likelihood function unchanged.

The algorithm (3.6–3.8) may be used in several possible generalized EM schemes. An efficient one is given by the following two-phase procedure: (i) freeze the source parameters and learn the separating matrix W using (3.6); (ii) freeze W and learn the source parameters using (3.8), then go back to (i) and repeat. Notice from the above definition of ϕ that for our source model (3.4),

$$\phi(s_i) = -\frac{\partial \log p(s_i)}{\partial s_i}. \tag{3.9}$$

Hence, the rule (3.6) formally coincides with the ICA rule of Bell & Sejnowski [1995], which was derived for the special case $p(s_i) \propto 1/\cosh(s_i)$. We also recognize (3.8) as the EM learning rules for a 1-dimensional MOG. Therefore, in phase (i) our algorithm separates the sources using a generalized ICA rule, whereas in phase (ii) it learns a MOG model for each source.

Remark Often one would like to model a given N-variable time series in terms of a smaller number $M \leqslant N$ of factors. In the framework of our noise-free model $\mathbf{x}_t = A\mathbf{s}_t$, this can be achieved by applying the above algorithm to the M largest principal components of the data; notice that if the data were indeed generated by M factors, the remaining $N - M$ principal components would vanish. Equivalently, one may apply the algorithm to the data directly, using a non-square $M \times N$ unmixing matrix W.

3.3 IFA with flexible sources: non-zero noise

We now turn to the general problem, where the number of sources may differ from the number of sensors and noise is present. We model the noise density by a zero-mean Gaussian with covariance matrix Λ. The ML estimation problem is now more difficult, as is evident from examining the likelihood:

$$p(\mathbf{y} \mid V) = \int d\mathbf{s} \, \mathcal{G}(\mathbf{x} - A\mathbf{s}, \Lambda) \prod_i p(s_i). \tag{3.10}$$

For non-Gaussian $p(s_i)$, one might expect that approximations (see [Lewicki & Sejnowski, 1998] for fixed Laplacian densities) or numerical methods must be used to perform the integration over the sources.

3.3.1 Few sources: an exact EM algorithm

However, MOG sources allow performing all the probabilistic calculations, including the above M-dimensional integral, analytically and exactly. An EM algorithm is derived by first noting that in the noisy case, both the source signals s_i and states q_i are hidden variables. This is in contrast to the noise-free case where the s_i are deterministically related to the observed data. We begin, as before, with a lower bound on the log-likelihood:

$$\mathcal{L} \geqslant E_{p'} \log p(\mathbf{x} \mid \mathbf{s}) + \sum_{i=1}^{M} E_{p'} \log p(q_i, s_i) - E_{p'} \log p', \qquad (3.11)$$

where $E_{p'}$ denotes averaging using a posterior density $p' = p'(\mathbf{q}, \mathbf{s} \mid \mathbf{x})$ over the hidden variables. Due to our noise model,

$$p(\mathbf{x} \mid \mathbf{s}) = \mathcal{G}(\mathbf{x} - A\mathbf{s}, \Lambda). \qquad (3.12)$$

The joint source-state density $p(q_i, s_i)$ is defined by (3.4).

E-step Here we calculate the posterior in terms of the previous iteration parameters V'. First, given a state configuration $\mathbf{q} = (q_1, ..., q_M)^{\mathsf{T}}$, the data have a Gaussian density $p(\mathbf{x} \mid \mathbf{q}) = \mathcal{G}(\mathbf{x} - A\boldsymbol{\mu}_\mathbf{q}, A\Gamma_\mathbf{q} A^{\mathsf{T}} + \Lambda)$, where the vector $\boldsymbol{\mu}_\mathbf{q} = (\mu_{1,q_1}, ..., \mu_{M,q_M})^{\mathsf{T}}$ and diagonal matrix $\Gamma_\mathbf{q} = \mathrm{diag}(v_{1,q_1}, ..., v_{M,q_M})$ are determined by the means and variances of the individual sources. The probability density $p(\mathbf{x})$ for generating a data vector is therefore a mixture of $\prod_i n_i$ Gaussians, with mixing proportions $p(\mathbf{q}) = \prod_i \pi_{q_i}^i$. The state posterior $\gamma_\mathbf{q}(\mathbf{x}) = p(\mathbf{q} \mid \mathbf{x})$ is obtained via Bayes' rule.

Next, when both the data vector and state configuration are fixed, it is easily shown that the sources are jointly Gaussian,

$$p(\mathbf{s} \mid \mathbf{q}, \mathbf{x}) = \mathcal{G}(\mathbf{s} - \rho_\mathbf{q}, \Sigma_\mathbf{q}), \qquad (3.13)$$

with covariance

$$\Sigma_\mathbf{q} = (A^{\mathsf{T}} \Lambda^{-1} A^{\mathsf{T}} + \Gamma_\mathbf{q}^{-1})^{-1} \qquad (3.14)$$

and data-dependent mean

$$\rho_\mathbf{q}(\mathbf{x}) = \Sigma_\mathbf{q}(A^{\mathsf{T}} \Lambda^{-1} \mathbf{x} + \Gamma_\mathbf{q}^{-1} \boldsymbol{\mu}_\mathbf{q}). \qquad (3.15)$$

All the quantities required for the M-step below can be expressed in terms of $\gamma_\mathbf{q}$, $\rho_\mathbf{q}$, and $\Sigma_\mathbf{q}$.

M-step Maximization with respect to the model parameters V produces

$$A = Ex\langle s^\mathsf{T} \rangle (E\langle ss^\mathsf{T} \rangle)^{-1},$$
$$\Lambda = Exx^\mathsf{T} - Ex\langle s^\mathsf{T} \rangle A^\mathsf{T},$$
$$\mu_q^i = \frac{E\langle s_i \rangle_q}{E\gamma_q^i}, \qquad\qquad (3.16)$$
$$v_q^i = \frac{E\langle s_i^2 \rangle_q}{E\gamma_q^i} - \mu_{i,q}^2,$$
$$\pi_q^i = E\gamma_q^i,$$

with the conditional source mean

$$\langle s \rangle = \sum_q \gamma_q \rho_q \qquad\qquad (3.17)$$

and covariance

$$\langle ss^\mathsf{T} \rangle = \sum_q \gamma_q (\rho_q \rho_q^\mathsf{T} + \Sigma_q). \qquad\qquad (3.18)$$

The state-conditioned averages are given by

$$\langle s_i \rangle_q = \sum_q {}' \gamma_q (\rho_q)_i,$$
$$\langle s_i^2 \rangle_q = \sum_q {}' \gamma_q (\rho_q \rho_q^\mathsf{T} + \Sigma_q)_{ii}, \qquad\qquad (3.19)$$

where $\sum_q'$ denotes summation over $\{q_{j \neq i}\}$, holding $q_i = q$ fixed. Finally,

$$\gamma_q^i = \sum_q {}' \gamma_q. \qquad\qquad (3.20)$$

We point out that in the limit $\Lambda \to 0$, this algorithm does *not* reduce to the noise-free separation algorithm from the previous section. In fact, the rule for the mixing matrix becomes $A \to R_x A (A^\mathsf{T} R_x A)^{-1} A^\mathsf{T} A$, where $R_x = Exx^\mathsf{T}$ is the data covariance matrix. This rule can be shown to perform principal component analysis: after learning, A will contain the eigenvectors of R_x that correspond to its largest M eigenvalues.

Scaling The discussion in section 3.2 should be repeated, with the jth row of W replaced by the jth column of A.

Source reconstruction There are two special cases where the sources are reconstructed from the data by a linear estimator: the noise-free case discussed above, where $\hat{s} = Wx$, and the noisy case with Gaussian sources where $\hat{s} = (A^T\Lambda^{-1}A + I)^{-1}A^T\Lambda^{-1}x$. In general, a linear estimator is sub-optimal. Here we consider two non-linear source estimators, based on different optimality criteria. The first is the maximum a-posteriori probability (MAP) estimator $\hat{s}^{MAP}$, obtained by maximizing the source posterior $p(s \mid x)$ with respect to s. A gradient-ascent learning rule can be derived and is given by

$$\delta\hat{s} = \epsilon A^T\Lambda^{-1}(x - A\hat{s}) - \epsilon\phi(\hat{s}), \tag{3.21}$$

where ϕ is the negative log-derivative of the source density as before, and ϵ is a properly chosen learning rate.

Alternatively, one may use the least mean square (LMS) estimator, which minimizes the error $E(\hat{s} - s)^2$. The LMS estimator is given by

$$\hat{s}^{LMS} = \langle s \rangle, \tag{3.22}$$

where the conditional mean is expressed above as a sum over state configurations q of the terms ρ_q that are linear in x, weighted by the terms γ_q that are non-linear in x. In computer simulations, we found that whereas $\hat{s}^{LMS}$ indeed minimizes the mean square error, $\hat{s}^{MAP}$ yields a lower cross-talk level.

3.3.2 Many sources: a variational EM algorithm

The exact E-step of the algorithm described above becomes intractable as the number of sources becomes large, since it requires summing over all possible source configurations $(q_1, ..., q_M)$ (see, e.g., the expression for $\langle s \rangle$) whose number $\prod_i n_i$ depends exponentially on M. As long as we focus on separating a small number of sources (treating the rest as noise) and describe each source by a small number n_i of states, the E-step is tractable, but separating, for example, $M = 13$ sources with $n_i = 3$ states each would involve ($3^{13} \approx 1.6 \times 10^6$)-element sums at each iteration. The intractability problem stems from the fact that, while the sources are independent, the sources *conditioned on a data vector* are correlated, resulting in a large number of hidden configurations. Notice that this problem does not arise in the noise-free case, where the posterior over the sources factorizes.

The intractability of exact learning is shared by many probabilistic models. In general, approximations must be made. The approximation developed below is based on the variational framework introduced by [Saul & Jordan, 1996, Saul *et al.*, 1996]. The lower bound (3.11) served as a starting point; note that the inequality holds for an arbitrary p'. In EM, p' is chosen as the true posterior, parametrized by the model parameters V. In the variational approach, we choose p' of a form that differs from the true posterior, but that makes the E-step tractable. It has a separate set of parameters V', which are optimized to tighten the lower bound on $\mathcal{L}$.

E-step We consider the factorized form

$$p'(\mathbf{q}, \mathbf{s} \mid \mathbf{x}, V') = \prod_i p'(q_i, s_i \mid \mathbf{x}), \qquad (3.23)$$

with

$$p'(q_i = q \mid \mathbf{x}) = v_q^i(\mathbf{x}),$$
$$p'(s_i \mid q_i = q, \mathbf{x}) = \mathcal{G}\left[s_i - \psi_q^i(\mathbf{x}), \xi_q^i\right]. \qquad (3.24)$$

The form (3.24) of the posterior is analogous to that of the prior in (3.29) below, with the parameters allowed to depend on the data. Of course, the true posterior does couple the sources given the data. To best approximate it, the variational parameters $V' = \{v_q^i, \psi_q^i, \xi_q^i\}$ are optimized by maximizing the bound on $\mathcal{L}$ with respect to V', or equivalently by minimizing the KL distance between p' and the true posterior. This requirement leads to the fixed-point equations

$$\xi_q^i = \left(\bar{H}_{ii} + \frac{1}{\gamma_q^i}\right)^{-1},$$

$$\sum_{j \neq i} \sum_{q'=1}^{n_j} \bar{H}_{ij} v_{q'}^j \psi_{q'}^j + \frac{1}{\xi_q^i} \psi_q^i = (A^\mathsf{T} \Lambda^{-1} \mathbf{y})_i + \frac{\mu_q^i}{\gamma_q^i}, \qquad (3.25)$$

$$v_q^i = \frac{1}{z_i} \gamma_q^i \exp\left[\frac{1}{2}\left(\log \xi_{i,q}^2 + \frac{\psi_{i,q}^2}{\xi_q^i}\right) - \frac{1}{2}\left(\log v_{i,q}^2 + \frac{\mu_{i,q}^2}{v_q^i}\right)\right],$$

where $\bar{A} = A^\mathsf{T} \Lambda^{-1} A$, and z_i in the last equation are set so that $\sum_q v_q^i = 1$. The variances ξ_q^i are data-independent; the means ψ_q^i and mixing proportions v_q^i are obtained by solving the last two coupled equations in (3.25) iteratively for each data vector $\mathbf{x}$. To do this, we first initialize $v_q^i = \gamma_q^i$, and obtain ψ_q^i using the fact that the second equation is a linear $(\sum_i n_i) \times (\sum_i n_i)$ system and can be solved using standard methods. These ψ_q^i are used to update v_q^i, and the process is repeated until convergence. In practice, we found that an average of 7 to 8 iterations is required.

M-step Maximization of the bound on the log-likelihood with respect to the model parameters V produces the following adaptation rules:

$$A = E\mathbf{x}\langle \mathbf{s}^\mathsf{T}\rangle(E\langle \mathbf{ss}^\mathsf{T}\rangle)^{-1},$$
$$\Lambda = E\mathbf{xx}^\mathsf{T} - E\mathbf{x}\langle \mathbf{s}^\mathsf{T}\rangle A^\mathsf{T},$$
$$\mu_q^i = \frac{Ev_q^i \psi_q^i}{Ev_q^i}, \qquad (3.26)$$
$$v_q^i = \frac{Ev_q^i(\psi_{i,q}^2 + \xi_q^i)}{Ev_q^i} - \mu_{i,q}^2,$$
$$\pi_q^i = Ev_q^i,$$

where the conditional averages are given by

$$\langle s_i\rangle = \sum_q v_q^i \psi_q^i,$$
$$\langle s_i^2\rangle = \sum_q v_q^i(\psi_{i,q}^2 + \xi_q^i), \qquad (3.27)$$
$$\langle s_i s_{j\neq i}\rangle = \sum_{qq'} v_q^i v_{q'}^j \psi_q^i \psi_{q'}^j.$$

These rules have the same form as the EM rules (3.16), but with the conditional means and probabilities given in terms of the variational parameters, and require only n_i-element sums.

Source reconstruction In the previous subsection, the LMS and MAP source estimators were given in terms of V. Notice that, being part of the E-step, computing the LMS estimator exactly quickly becomes intractable as the number of sources increases. In the variational approximation it is replaced by the tractable sum

$$\hat{s}_i = \sum_q v_q^i \psi_q^i. \qquad (3.28)$$

In contrast, the MAP estimator remains unchanged (but the parameters V on which it depends are now learned by variational EM); note that its computational cost is only weakly dependent on M.

3.4 IFA with flexible dynamic sources: zero noise

The MOG source model employed in the previous sections has the advantages that (i) it is capable of approximating arbitrary densities, and (ii) it can be learned efficiently from data by EM. The Gaussians correspond to the hidden states of the sources, labeled by q. Assume that at time t, source i is in state $q_t^i = q$. Its signal s_t^i is then generated by sampling from a Gaussian distribution with mean μ_q^i and variance v_q^i. In this section and the following one, we extend this model to incorporate temporal statistical properties of the sources.

For this purpose, we endow the model sources with temporal structure by introducing a transition matrix $a_{q'q}^i$ between the states. Focusing on a time block $t = 1, ..., T$, the resulting probabilistic model is defined by

$$
\begin{aligned}
p(q_t^i = q \mid q_{t-1}^i = q') &= a_{q'q}^i, \\
p(q_0^i = q) &= \pi_q^i, \\
p(s_t^i \mid q_t^i = q) &= \mathcal{G}(s_t^i - \mu_q^i, v_q^i), \\
p(\mathbf{s}_{1:T}) &= |\det W|^T p(\mathbf{s}_{1:T}),
\end{aligned}
\tag{3.29}
$$

where $p(\mathbf{s}_{1:T})$ is the joint density of all sources $s_t^i, i = 1, ..., M$, at all time points, and the last equation follows from $\mathbf{s}_t = W\mathbf{x}_t$ with $W = A^{-1}$ being the unmixing matrix. As usual in the noise free scenario, we are assuming that the mixing matrix is square and invertible.

The graphical model for the observed density $p(\mathbf{x}_{1:T} \mid V)$ defined by (3.29) is parametrized by $V = \{W_{ij}, \mu_q^i, v_q^i, \pi_q^i, a_{q'q}^i\}$. This model describes each source as a first-order HMM; it reduces to a time-independent model if $a_{q'q}^i = \pi_q^i$. Whereas temporal structure can be described by other means (see, for example, [Pearlmutter & Parra, 1996, Attias & Schreiner, 1998]), the HMM is advantageous since it models high-order temporal statistics and facilitates EM learning.

It is easy to go through the derivation for noise free IFA and extend it to the case of HMM sources. Maximization with respect to W_{ij} results in the incremental update rule

$$
\delta W = \epsilon W - \epsilon \frac{1}{T} \sum_{t=1}^{T} \phi(\mathbf{s}_t)\mathbf{s}_t^\mathsf{T} W,
\tag{3.30}
$$

where $\phi(s_t^i) = \sum_q [\gamma_t^i(q)(s_t^i - \mu_q^i)/v_q^i]$, and ϵ is a suitably chosen learning rate. For the source parameters we obtain the update rules

$$
\begin{aligned}
\mu_q^i &= \frac{\sum_t \gamma_t^i(q) s_t^i}{\sum_t \gamma_t^i(q)}, \\
v_q^i &= \frac{\sum_t \gamma_t^i(q)(s_t^i - \mu_q^i)^2}{\sum_t \gamma_t^i(q)}, \\
a_{q'q}^i &= \frac{\sum_t \xi_t^i(q', q)}{\sum_t \gamma_{t-1}^i(q')},
\end{aligned}
\tag{3.31}
$$

with the initial probabilities updated via $\pi_q^i = \gamma_0^i(q)$. We used the standard HMM notation

$$\gamma_t^i(q) = p(q_t^i = q \mid s_{1:T}^i),$$
$$\xi_t^i(q', q) = p(q_{t-1}^i = q', q_t^i = q \mid s_{1:T}^i). \tag{3.32}$$

These posterior densities are computed in the E-step for each source, which is given in terms of the data via $s_t^i = \sum_j W_{ij} x_t^j$, using the forward-backward procedure [Rabiner & Juang, 1993].

As in noise free IFA, the algorithm (3.30–3.31) may be used in several possible generalized EM schemes. An efficient one is given by the following two-phase procedure: (i) freeze the source parameters and learn the separating matrix W using (3.30); (ii) freeze W and learn the source parameters using (3.31), then go back to (i) and repeat. Notice that the rule (3.30) is similar to a natural gradient version of the ICA rule of Bell & Sejnowski [1995]; in fact, the two coincide for time-independent sources where $\phi(s_i) = -\partial \log p(s_i)/\partial s_i$. We also recognize (3.31) as the Baum-Welch method. Hence, in phase (i) our algorithm separates the sources using a generalized ICA rule, whereas in phase (ii) it learns an HMM for each source.

3.5 IFA with flexible dynamic sources: isotropic noise

We now turn to the case of non-zero noise $\mathbf{n}_t \neq 0$. We assume that the noise is white and has a zero-mean Gaussian distribution with covariance matrix Λ. In general, this case is computationally intractable (see section 3.6). The reason is that the E-step requires computing the posterior distribution $p(\mathbf{q}_{0:T}, \mathbf{s}_{1:T} \mid \mathbf{x}_{1:T})$ not only over the source states (as in the zero-noise case) but also over the source signals, and this posterior has a quite complicated structure. We now show that if we assume isotropic noise, i.e. $\Lambda_{ij} = \lambda \delta_{ij}$, as well as square invertible mixing as above, this posterior simplifies considerably, making learning and inference tractable. This is done by adapting an idea suggested in [Lee *et al.*, 2000a] to our dynamic probabilistic network.

We start by pre-processing the data using a linear transformation that makes their covariance matrix unity, i.e., $\langle \mathbf{x}_t \mathbf{x}_t^\mathsf{T} \rangle = I$ ('sphering'). Here $\langle \cdot \rangle$ denotes averaging over T-point time blocks. From (3.1) it follows that $A \mathbf{s} \mathbf{s}^\mathsf{T} A^\mathsf{T} = \lambda' I$, where $\mathbf{s} = \langle \mathbf{s}_t \mathbf{s}_t^\mathsf{T} \rangle$ is the diagonal covariance matrix of the sources, and $\lambda' = 1 - \lambda$. This, for a square invertible A, implies that $A^\mathsf{T} A$ is diagonal. In fact, since the unobserved sources can be determined only to within a scaling factor, we can set the variance of each source to unity and obtain the *orthogonality property* $A^T A = \lambda' I$. It can be shown that the source posterior now factorizes into a product over the individual sources,

$$p(\mathbf{q}_{0:T}, \mathbf{s}_{1:T} \mid \mathbf{x}_{1:T}) = \prod_i p(q_{0:T}^i, s_{1:T}^i \mid \mathbf{x}_{1:T}), \qquad (3.33)$$

where

$$p(q_{0:T}^i, s_{1:T}^i \mid \mathbf{x}_{1:T}) \propto \left[\prod_{t=1}^{T} \mathcal{G}(s_t^i - \eta_t^i, \sigma_t^i) \cdot v_t^i p(q_t^i \mid q_{t-1}^i) \right] v_0^i p(q_0^i). \quad (3.34)$$

The means and variances at time t in (3.34), as well as the quantities v_t^i, depend on both the data $\mathbf{x}_t$ and the states q_t^i; in particular, $\eta_t^i = (\sum_j A_{ji} x_t^j + \lambda \mu_s^i)/(\lambda' v_s + \lambda)$ and $\sigma_t^i = \lambda v_s^i/(\lambda' v_s + \lambda)$, using $q = q_t^i$. The transition probabilities are the same as in (3.29). Hence, the posterior distribution (3.34) effectively defines a new HMM for each source, with $\mathbf{x}_t$-dependent emission and transition probabilities.

To derive the learning rule for A, we should first compute the conditional mean $\langle \mathbf{s}_t \rangle$ of the source signals at time t given the data. This can be done recursively using (3.34) as in the forward-backward procedure. We then obtain

$$A = \sqrt{\lambda'} C(C^T C)^{-1/2}, \qquad C = \frac{1}{T} \sum_{t=1}^{T} \mathbf{x}_t \bar{\mathbf{s}}_t^T. \qquad (3.35)$$

This fractional form results from imposing the orthogonality constraint $A^T A = \lambda' I$ using Lagrange multipliers and can be computed via a diagonalization procedure. The source parameters are computed using a learning rule (omitted) similar to the noise free rule (3.31). It is easy to derive a learning rule for the noise level λ as well; in fact, the ordinary FA rule would suffice. We point out that, while this algorithm has been derived for the case $M = N$, it is perfectly well defined (though sub-optimal: see below) for $M \leqslant N$.

3.6 IFA with flexible dynamic sources: non-isotropic noise

The general case of non-isotropic noise and non-square mixing is computationally intractable. This is because the exact E-step requires summing over all possible source configurations $(q_{t_1}^1, ..., q_{t_M}^M)$ at all times $t_1, ..., t_M = 1, ..., T$. The intractability problem stems from the fact that, while the sources are independent, the sources *conditioned on a data vector* $\mathbf{x}_{1:T}$ are correlated, resulting in a large number of hidden configurations. This problem does not arise in the noise free case, and can be avoided in the case of isotropic noise and square mixing using the orthogonality property; in both cases, the exact posterior over the sources factorizes.

The EM algorithm derived below is based on a variational approach. As mentioned above, this approach was introduced in the context of sigmoid belief networks (see [Saul *et al.*, 1996]), but constitutes a general framework for ML learning in intractable probabilistic networks. Ghahramani & Jordan [1997] applied variational ideas to a factorial HMM model that bears some similarity to our case. The idea in the variational approach is to use an approximate but tractable posterior to place a lower bound on the likelihood, and optimize the parameters by maximizing this bound.

As before, a starting point for deriving a bound on the likelihood $\mathcal{L}$ is the Neal & Hinton [1993] formulation of the EM algorithm:

$$\mathcal{L} = \log p(\mathbf{y}_{1:T})$$

$$\geqslant \sum_{t=1}^{T} E_{p'} \log p(\mathbf{x}_t \mid \mathbf{s}_t) + \sum_{i=1}^{M} E_{p'} \log p(q_{0:T}^i, s_{1:T}^i) - E_{p'} \log p', \quad (3.36)$$

where $E_{p'}$ denotes averaging with respect to an arbitrary posterior density over the hidden variables given the observed data, $p' = p'(\mathbf{q}_{0:T}, \mathbf{s}_{1:T} \mid \mathbf{x}_{1:T})$. Exact EM, as shown in [Neal & Hinton, 1993], is obtained by maximizing the bound (3.36) with respect to both the posterior p' (corresponding to the E-step) and the model parameters V (M-step). However, the resulting p' is the true but intractable posterior. In contrast, in variational EM we choose a p' that differs from the true posterior, but facilitates a tractable E-step.

E-step We use

$$p'(\mathbf{q}_{0:T}, \mathbf{s}_{1:T} \mid \mathbf{x}_{1:T}) = \prod_i p'(q_{0:T}^i \mid \mathbf{x}_{1:T}) \prod_t p'(\mathbf{s}_t \mid \mathbf{x}_{1:T}), \quad (3.37)$$

parametrized as

$$\begin{aligned} p'(q_t^i = q \mid q_{t-1}^i = q', \mathbf{x}_{1:T}) &\propto \lambda_{q,t}^i a_{q'q}^i, \\ p'(q_0^i = q \mid \mathbf{x}_{1:T}) &\propto \lambda_{q,t}^i \pi_q^i, \\ p'(\mathbf{s}_t \mid \mathbf{x}_{1:T}) &= \mathcal{G}(\mathbf{s}_t - \boldsymbol{\rho}_t, \Sigma_t). \end{aligned} \quad (3.38)$$

Thus, the variational transition probabilities in (3.38) are described by multiplying the original ones $a^i_{q'q}$ by the parameters $\lambda^i_{q,t}$, subject to the normalization constraints. The source signals s_t at time t are jointly Gaussian with mean ρ_t and covariance Σ_t. The means, covariances and transition probabilities are all time- and data-dependent, i.e., $\rho_t = f(x_{1:T}, t)$ etc. This parametrization scheme is motivated by the form of the posterior in (3.34); notice that the quantities $\eta^i_t, \sigma^i_t, v^i_{q,t}$ there become the *variational parameters* $V' = \{\rho^i_t, \Sigma^{ij}_t, \lambda^i_{q,t}\}$ of (3.38). A related scheme was used by Ghahramani & Jordan [1997]. Since these parameters will be adapted independently of the model parameters, the non-isotropic algorithm is expected to give superior results compared to the isotropic one.

Of course, in the *true* posterior the s_t are correlated, both temporally among themselves and with q_t, and the latter do not factorize. To best approximate it, the variational parameters V' are optimized to maximize the bound on $\mathcal{L}$, or equivalently to minimize the KL distance between p' and the true posterior. This requirement leads to the fixed point equations

$$
\rho_t = (A^\mathsf{T}\Lambda^{-1}A + B_t)^{-1}(A^\mathsf{T}\Lambda^{-1}x_t + b_t),
$$
$$
\Sigma_t = (A^\mathsf{T}\Lambda^{-1}A + B_t)^{-1}, \tag{3.39}
$$
$$
\lambda^i_{q,t} = \frac{1}{z^i_t}\exp\left[-\frac{1}{2}\log v^i_q - \frac{(\rho^i_t - \mu^i_q)^2 + \Sigma^{ii}_t}{2v^i_q}\right],
$$

where $B^{ij}_t = \sum_q [\gamma^i_t(q)/v^i_q]\delta_{ij}$, $b^i_t = \sum_q [\gamma^i_t(q)\mu^i_q/v^i_q]$, and the factors z^i_t ensure normalization. The HMM quantities $\gamma^i_t(q)$ are computed by the forward-backward procedure using the *variational* transition probabilities (3.38). The variational parameters are determined by solving eqs. (3.39) iteratively for each block $x_{1:T}$; in practice, we found that less than 20 iterations are usually required for convergence.

M-step The update rules for W are given for the mixing parameters by

$$
A = \left[\sum_t x_t\rho^\mathsf{T}_t\right]\left[\sum_t (\rho_t\rho^\mathsf{T}_t + \Sigma_t)\right]^{-1},
$$
$$
\Lambda = \frac{1}{T}\sum_t (x_t x^\mathsf{T}_t - x_t\rho^\mathsf{T}_t A^\mathsf{T}), \tag{3.40}
$$

and for the source parameters by

$$\mu_q^i = \frac{\sum_t \gamma_t^i(q) \rho_t^i}{\sum_t \gamma_t^i(q)},$$

$$v_q^i = \frac{\sum_t \gamma_t^i(q)((\rho_t^i - \mu_q^i)^2 + \Sigma_t^{ii})}{\sum_t \gamma_t^i(q)}, \tag{3.41}$$

$$a_{q'q}^i = \frac{\sum_t \xi_t^i(q', q)}{\sum_t \gamma_{t-1}^i(q')},$$

$$\pi_q^i = \gamma_0^i(q),$$

where the $\xi_t^i(q', q)$ are computed using the variational transition probabilities (3.38). Notice that the learning rules for the source parameters have the Baum-Welch form, in spite of the correlations between the conditioned sources. In our variational approach, these correlations are hidden in V', as manifested by the fact that the fixed point equations (3.39) couple the parameters V' across time points (since $\gamma_t^i(q)$ depends on $\lambda_{q,t=1:T}^i$) and sources.

Source reconstruction From $p'(\mathbf{s}_t \mid \mathbf{x}_{1:T})$ (see equation (3.38)), we observe that the MAP source estimate is given by

$$\hat{\mathbf{s}}_t = \rho_t(\mathbf{x}_{1:T}), \tag{3.42}$$

and depends on both V and V'. We point out that, as mentioned in the introduction, noise reduction and source separation are performed simultaneously and in an integrated manner, resulting in a Bayes optimal source estimate. This is a consequence of working on the problem in the framework of graphical models.

3.7 Conclusion

An important issue that has not been addressed here is model selection. When applying our algorithms to an arbitrary dataset, the number of factors and of HMM states for each factor should be determined. Whereas this could be done using cross-validation, the required computational effort would be fairly large. Alternatively, the Bayesian framework instructs us to compute the *evidence* (also called marginal likelihood) for different models with different numbers of sources, and choose the one which maximizes the evidence. This works since the evidence includes a built-in penalty for complex models. Until recently, evidence computations were intractable in all but the simplest probabilistic models, and in particular in models with hidden variables. However, Waterhouse *et al.* [1996], Bishop [1999], Attias [2000], and Ghahramani & Beal [2000] have developed a new approach to Bayesian model selection and model averaging, based on vartiational ideas. This framework, termed *Variational Bayes* (VB), produces EM-like algorithms which approximate full posterior distributions over not only hidden variables but also parameters and model structure, in an analytical manner. Consequently, the evidence and various predictive quantities can be obtained analytically. The VB approach is directly applicable to the models presented here, as demonstrated in [Attias, 2000].

Another issue which has not been discussed in this chapter is convolutive mixing. In real acoustic environments, this mixing is not instantaneous. The source signals take a finite time to propagate in a medium on their way to the sensors, and are modified by the impulse response of the environment. The signal may also be reflected from walls and obstacles, resulting in multipath propagation. These effects are termed *reverberations*, and are described mathematically by convolution:

$$x_t^i = \sum_j \sum_\tau A_\tau^{ij} s_{t-\tau}^j + u_t^i, \tag{3.43}$$

where A_τ^{ij} is the impulse response of the filter which convolves the jth source signal on its way to the ith sensor. Hence, the mixing matrix becomes a matrix of filters.

The case of convolutive mixing with zero noise and an equal number of sources and sensors was addressed by Torkkola [1996b] and Lee *et al.* [1997]. Attias [1999a] derived a family of algorithms for this case, based on spatio-temporal graphical models. However, algorithms for convolutive mixing, while often successful on synthetic data, generally perform poorly when applied to real world cases. Moreover, whereas for zero noise the maximum likelihood problem is solvable, the case of non-zero noise is computationally intractable. Hence, blind separation of convolutive mixtures is still an open problem. We believe that the methods presented in this chapter will make important contributions to its solution.

4

Nonlinear Independent Component Analysis

J. Karhunen

This chapter deals with independent component analysis and blind source separation for nonlinear data models. A fundamental difficulty, especially in the nonlinear ICA problem, is that it is highly non-unique without a suitable regularization. After considering this, two methods for solving the nonlinear ICA and BSS problems are presented in more detail. The first one is a maximum likelihood method based on a modified generative topographic mapping. The second approach applies Bayesian ensemble learning to a flexible multi-layer perceptron model for finding the sources and nonlinear mixing mapping that have most probably given rise to the observed mixed data. Finally, other techniques introduced for the nonlinear ICA and BSS problems are briefly reviewed.

4.1 Introduction

Independent Component Analysis [Lee, 1998, Oja *et al.*, 1997, Girolami, 1999b] is a statistical technique which tries to represent the observed data in terms of statistically independent component variables. ICA is closely related to the blind source separation (BSS) problem [Cardoso, 1998a, Amari *et al.*, 1996, Lee, 1998, Oja *et al.*, 1997, Girolami, 1999b], where the general goal is to separate mutually independent but otherwise unknown source signals from their observed mixtures without knowing the mixing process.

The basic linear data model used in ICA and BSS has the following form. Denote by $\mathbf{x}(t) = [x_1(t), \ldots, x_N(t)]^\mathsf{T}$ the N-dimensional tth observation or data vector. The vectors $\mathbf{x}(t)$ have a common unknown zero-mean non-Gaussian statistical distribution. In basic ICA and BSS, one tries to

113

fit to the data $\mathbf{x}(t)$ the linear expansion

$$\mathbf{x}(t) = A\mathbf{s}(t) = \sum_{j=1}^{M} s_j(t)\mathbf{e}_j. \tag{4.1}$$

Here the source vector $\mathbf{s}(t) = [s_1(t), \ldots, s_M(t)]^{\mathsf{T}}$ contains the M source signals or independent components $s_j(t)$ for the data vector $\mathbf{x}(t)$. $A = [\mathbf{e}_1, \ldots, \mathbf{e}_M]$ is a constant full-rank $N \times M$ matrix, called the mixing matrix. The vectors $\mathbf{e}_j$, $j = 1, \ldots, M$, are the basis vectors of ICA; see [Lee, 1998, Oja et al., 1997]. In this section, the number of independent components or sources M is usually assumed to be at most equal to the number of mixtures N, and often $M = N$.

The independent components and source signals $s_j(t)$ are determined by finding an $M \times N$ inverse mapping (separating matrix) W so that the M-vector

$$\mathbf{a}(t) = W\mathbf{x}(t) \tag{4.2}$$

becomes an estimate $\mathbf{a}(t) = \hat{\mathbf{s}}(t)$ of the source vector $\mathbf{s}(t)$. To this end, several efficient algorithms have been proposed; see for example [Lee, 1998, Oja et al., 1997, Girolami, 1999b, Amari et al., 1996] for further information and reviews. The estimate of the mixing matrix A can be computed as the pseudoinverse of W. Because of the blind nature of the linear ICA/BSS problem, the estimated sources or independent components can appear in any order in $\mathbf{a}(t)$, and their scaling and sign can be chosen arbitrarily. Usually the estimated sources are scaled so that their variance equals unity.

The basic linear model (4.1) is often too simple for describing the observed data $\mathbf{x}(t)$ adequately. A natural extension is to consider the respective ICA or BSS problems for nonlinear data models. For instantaneous mixtures, the nonlinear data model has the general form

$$\mathbf{x}(t) = \mathbf{f}(\mathbf{s}(t)) \tag{4.3}$$

where $\mathbf{f}$ is an unknown real-valued N-component vector function. The ICA problem is now to estimate the realizations of the independent components $s_i(t)$ using only observations of the mixtures $x_j(t)$. In its full generality this nonlinear generalization of ICA is intractable, since the indeterminacies in the separating solutions are much more severe than in the linear case. This is discussed in more detail in the next section.

4.2 Nonlinear ICA and BSS

Assume now for simplicity that the number of independent components or source signals M equals the number of mixtures N. The nonlinear ICA problem now consists of finding an inverse mapping $\mathbf{h} : \mathbb{R}^N \to \mathbb{R}^N$ which gives estimates of the independent components as

$$\mathbf{a}(t) = \mathbf{h}(\mathbf{x}(t)) \tag{4.4}$$

This important problem has drawn increasing attention lately, see for example the papers [Hyvärinen & Pajunen, 1999, Parra *et al.*, 1996, Pajunen & Karhunen, 1997, Lin *et al.*, 1997, Yang *et al.* 1998, Taleb & Jutten, 1999, Lee, 1998, Cichocki *et al.*, 1999] and the references therein. However, nonlinear ICA is often difficult to apply for reasons discussed below.

First, solution of the nonlinear ICA problem is usually highly non-unique [Hyvärinen & Pajunen, 1999]. Basically, this results from the fact that if x and y are two independent random variables, any functions $f(x)$ and $g(y)$ are also independent. Thus if some ICA solution is found for the data model (4.3), it may be quite different from the solution of the respective nonlinear BSS problem, where one should find the original sources $\mathbf{s}(t)$.

It is worth emphasizing that while the solutions of ICA and BSS problems coincide for the basic linear model (4.1), they are clearly different for the nonlinear data model (4.3). Finding the true source signals $\mathbf{s}(t)$ that have generated the observed data is usually a clearly more meaningful and also more unique problem than the nonlinear ICA problem. However, solving it is not easy, and generally requires additional prior information or suitable regularizing constraints.

The question of existence and uniqueness of solutions for nonlinear independent component analysis has been addressed by Hyvärinen & Pajunen [1999]. The authors show that there always exists an infinity of solutions if the space of the nonlinear mixing functions $\mathbf{f}$ is not limited. They also present a method for constructing parameterized families of nonlinear ICA solutions. A unique solution (up to a rotation) can be obtained in the two-dimensional special case if the mixing mapping $\mathbf{f}$ is constrained to be a conformal mapping together with some other assumptions; see [Hyvärinen & Pajunen, 1999] for details.

Several authors have recently studied separation of so-called *post-nonlinear* mixtures; see, for example, [Lee, 1998, Yang *et al.*, 1998, Taleb & Jutten, 1999]. They are a special case of the general nonlinear mixing model (4.3) where each mixture has the form

$$x_i(t) = f_i \left(\sum_{j=1}^{N} a_{ij} s_j(t) \right), \qquad i = 1, \dots, N. \qquad (4.5)$$

Here a_{ij} is the element on the ith row and jth column of the mixing matrix A. Thus the sources $s_j(t)$, $j = 1, \dots, N$, are first mixed linearly according to the basic ICA/BSS model (4.1), but after that a nonlinear function f_i is applied to them to get the final observations $x_i(t)$. It can be shown [Taleb & Jutten, 1999] that for the post-nonlinear mixtures, the indeterminacies in the ICA and BSS problems are the same as for the basic linear instantaneous mixing model (4.1). The post-nonlinearity assumption is useful in signal processing because it can be thought of as a model for a nonlinear sensor distortion. In more general situations, it is a restrictive and somewhat arbitrary constraint.

Lin [1999] has recently derived some interesting theoretical results on ICA that are useful in describing the non-uniqueness of the general nonlinear ICA problem, too. Let the matrices H_s and H_x denote the Hessians of the logarithmic probability densities $\log p_s(\mathbf{s})$ and $\log p_x(\mathbf{x})$ of the source vector $\mathbf{s}$ and mixture (data) vector $\mathbf{x}$, respectively. Then for the basic linear ICA model (4.1) it holds that [Lin, 1999]

$$H_s = A^\mathsf{T} H_x A, \qquad (4.6)$$

where A is the mixing matrix. If the components of $\mathbf{s}$ are truly independent, H_s should be a diagonal matrix. Due to the symmetry of the Hessian matrices H_s and H_x, (4.6) imposes $N(N-1)/2$ constraints for the elements of the $N \times N$ matrix A. Thus a constant mixing matrix A can be solved by estimating H_x at two different points, and assuming some values for the diagonal elements of H_s [Lin, 1999].

If the nonlinear mapping (4.3) is twice differentiable, we can approximate it locally at any point by the linear mixing model (4.1). There A is defined by the first order term $\partial \mathbf{f}(\mathbf{s})/\partial \mathbf{s}$ of the Taylor series expansion of $\mathbf{f}(\mathbf{s})$ at the desired point. But now A generally changes from point to point, so that the constraint conditions (4.6) still leave $N(N-1)/2$ degrees of freedom for determining the mixing matrix A (omitting the diagonal elements).

Another difficulty in the general nonlinear BSS (or ICA) methods proposed thus far is that they tend to be computationally rather demanding. Moreover, the computational load usually increases very rapidly with the dimensionality of the problem, preventing in practice the application of nonlinear BSS methods to high-dimensional data sets.

Nonlinear ICA and BSS methods can be broadly divided into generative approaches and signal transformation approaches [Lappalainen *et al.*, 2000a]. In the generative approaches, the goal is to find a specific model which explains how the observations were generated. In our case, this amounts to estimating both the source signals $s(t)$ and the unknown mixing mapping $f(\cdot)$ that have generated the observed data $x(t)$ through the general mapping (4.3). In the signal transformation methods, one tries to estimate the sources directly using the inverse transformation (4.4). In these methods, the number of estimated sources is the same as the number of observed mixtures [Lappalainen *et al.*, 2000a].

In the following, two generative approaches are discussed in more detail. The first one uses a maximum likelihood method assuming an RBF (radial-basis function) type network structure [Haykin, 1998, Bishop, 1995] for the generative mapping. The second approach uses a Bayesian ensemble learning method, modelling the generative mixing mapping by a multi-layer perceptron (MLP) network structure.

4.3 A maximum likelihood approach

4.3.1 Background

One of the earliest ideas [Pajunen *et al.*, 1996] for achieving nonlinear ICA was to use the well-known self-organizing map (SOM) [Kohonen, 1995]. The justification is that an SOM roughly defines a uniform density on a rectangular map with suitable choices of topology and learning mechanism. The marginal densities in the directions of the sides of the rectangle are then statistically independent, and hence provide a nonlinear ICA solution.

However, when this idea is applied to nonlinear blind source separation, the serious indeterminacies in the nonlinear case can cause problems. If the sources are uniformly distributed, then it can be heuristically justified that the regularization of the nonlinear separating mapping provided by the SOM approximately separates the sources. But when the true sources have non-uniform probability distributions, the separating mapping providing uniform densities inevitably causes distortions, which are in general the more serious the farther the true source densities are from the uniform ones.

A few years ago, Bishop, Svensen and Williams introduced the so-called generative topographic mapping (GTM) method as a principled alternative to SOM. Their method is presented in detail in [Bishop, 1998]. In the basic GTM method, mutually similar plain delta functions that are uniformly distributed on a rectangular grid are used to model the discrete uniform density in the space of latent variables [Bishop, 1998], or the joint density of the sources in our case. The mapping from the sources to the observed data, corresponding in our nonlinear BSS problem to the nonlinear mixing mapping (4.3), is then modelled using a mixture-of-Gaussians model. The parameters of the mixture-of-Gaussians model, defining the mixing mapping, are then found using a maximum likelihood method realized by the expectation maximization (EM) algorithm [Bishop, 1995, Haykin, 1998]. It is well-known that any continuous smooth enough mapping can be approximated with arbitrary accuracy using a mixture-of-Gaussians model with sufficiently many Gaussian basis functions [Haykin, 1998, Bishop, 1995]. This provides roughly stated the theoretical basis of the GTM method.

Using the basic GTM method instead of SOM for nonlinear blind source separation does not yet bring out any notable improvement, because the densities of the sources are still assumed to be uniform. However, it is straightforward to generalize the GTM method to *arbitrary known* source densities [Pajunen & Karhunen, 1997]. The advantage of this approach is that we can directly regularize the inverse of the mixing mapping by using the known source densities. The modified GTM method is then used for finding a non-complex mixing mapping. The modified GTM method originally described in [Pajunen & Karhunen, 1997] differs from standard GTM [Bishop, 1998] in that the required joint density of the sources or latent variables is defined as a weighted sum of delta functions. The weighting coefficients are determined by discretizing the known source densities.

4.3.2 Modified GTM algorithm

Only the main points of the GTM algorithm are presented here, with emphasis on the modifications. See [Bishop, 1998] for a complete description. Generally, GTM is inspired by and closely related to the self-organizing map. Its key benefit is a firm theoretical foundation which helps to overcome some of the limitations of SOM. This provides also the basis of generalizing the GTM approach to arbitrary source densities.

The mixture mapping is modelled as a linear combination of basis functions:

$$\mathbf{x} = \mathbf{f}(\mathbf{s}; V) = VF(\mathbf{s}), \quad F = [f_1, f_2, \dots, f_M]^\mathsf{T} \tag{4.7}$$

where the f_j are a suitable fixed basis function (for example Gaussians). In GTM, one tries to maximize the (log) likelihood of the data

$$\mathcal{L}(V, \beta) = \sum_n \log p(\mathbf{x}(n)|V, \beta) = \sum_n \log \int p(\mathbf{x}(n)|\mathbf{s}, V, \beta) p(\mathbf{s}) d\mathbf{s}, \tag{4.8}$$

where β^{-1} is the variance of $\mathbf{x}$ given $\mathbf{s}$ and V. It is assumed that the density of $\mathbf{s}$ is known, and can be approximated by the product of marginal densities $p(\mathbf{s}) = \prod_i p_i(s_i)$, where each marginal density is a discrete density with corresponding sample points to the vectors $\mathbf{s}_{ij}$ below. For easier notation, only two sources are considered here, yielding $p(\mathbf{s}) = \sum_{i,j} \alpha_{ij} \delta(\mathbf{s} - \mathbf{s}_{ij})$. The vectors $\mathbf{s}_{ij}$ are fixed in the source signal space, and the coefficients $\alpha_{ij} = p_1(i) p_2(j)$ where p_1 and p_2 are the discrete approximations of the marginal densities of $\mathbf{s}$. From (4.8), one gets

$$\mathcal{L}(V, \beta) = \sum \log \left(\sum_{i,j} p(\mathbf{x}(n)|\mathbf{s}_{ij}, V, \beta) \right). \tag{4.9}$$

Setting the derivatives of the likelihood to zero yields the equation allowing the update of the weight matrix V:

$$F^\mathsf{T} G F V^\mathsf{T} = F^\mathsf{T} R X, \tag{4.10}$$

where $X = [\mathbf{x}(1), \dots, \mathbf{x}(T)]^\mathsf{T}$, G is a matrix with elements $g_{ij} = \sum_n R_{ijn}(V, \beta)$, and the elements of R are

$$R_{ijn} = \frac{\alpha_{ij} p(\mathbf{x}(n)|\mathbf{s}_{ij}, V, \beta)}{\sum_{k,l} \alpha_{kl} p(\mathbf{x}(n)|\mathbf{s}_{kl}, V, \beta)}. \tag{4.11}$$

Then the parameter β can be updated by

$$\frac{1}{\beta} = \frac{1}{TN} \sum_{i,j} \sum_n R_{ijn} \|\mathbf{f}(\mathbf{s}_{ij}; V) - \mathbf{x}(n)\|^2. \tag{4.12}$$

In GTM, the well-known EM algorithm is used for maximizing the likelihood. Here the E-step (4.11) consists of computing R_{ijn}, and the M-steps (4.10), (4.12) of updating V and β. The above derivation is quite similar to the original GTM method [Bishop, 1998], only the prior density coefficients α_{ij} have been added to the model.

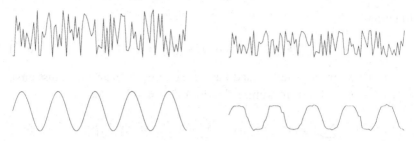

Figure 4.1. *A nonlinear source separation example. Left: The original source signals. Right: Separated signals.*

4.3.3 An experiment

In the following, a simple experiment involving two sources (Figure 4.1) and three noisy nonlinear mixtures is described. Linear mixtures of the sources were transformed using a multi-layer perceptron network with a volume conserving architecture (see [Deco & Brauer, 1995]). Such an architecture was chosen for ensuring that the total mixing mapping is bijective and therefore reversible. Also very complex distortions of the source densities are avoided. This choice also makes the total mixing mapping more complex than the post-nonlinear model used for example in [Taleb & Jutten, 1999] and [Yang *et al.*, 1998]. Finally, additive Gaussian noise was added.

The mixture can be written as

$$\mathbf{x} = A\mathbf{s} + \tanh(UA\mathbf{s}) + \mathbf{n} \qquad (4.13)$$

where U is an upper-diagonal matrix with zero diagonal elements, and $\mathbf{n}$ denotes the noise vector. The nonzero elements of U were drawn from a standard Gaussian distribution. The matrix U ensures volume conservation of the nonlinearity applied to $A\mathbf{s}$. The two-dimensional joint densities of the mixtures are shown in Figure 4.2. They clearly reveal the nonlinearity of the mixing mapping.

The algorithm presented above was used to learn a separating mapping. For reducing scaling effects, the mixtures were first whitened. After whitening, the mixtures are uncorrelated and have a unit variance. Then the modified GTM algorithm was run for eight iterations using a 5×5 map. The separated sources are compared to the original sources in Figure 4.1. The waveforms of the original sources are approximately recovered, even though there is some inevitable distortion due to the noise, discretization, and the difficulty of the problem. Also the joint

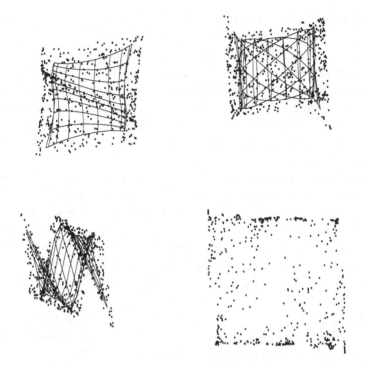

Figure 4.2. *Joint mixture densities with superimposed maps.* Top left: $p(x_1, x_2)$. Top right: $p(x_1, x_3)$. Bottom left: $p(x_2, x_3)$. Bottom right: output signal joint density.

density of the separated sources shown in Figure 4.2 indicates that a factorizable density has been approximately obtained. The superimposed maps were obtained by mapping a 10×10 grid of vectors **s** to the mixture space.

4.4 An ensemble learning approach to nonlinear BSS

4.4.1 Ensemble learning

In this section, we present a promising new generative approach for nonlinear blind source separation or independent component analysis. Here the nonlinear mapping (4.3) from the unknown sources **s**(t) to the known observations **x**(t) is modelled using the familiar multi-layer perceptron (MLP) network structure [Haykin, 1998, Bishop, 1995]. However, the learning procedure is based on unsupervised Bayesian ensemble learning. It is quite different from standard back-propagation learning which minimizes the mean-square representation error in MLP networks in a supervised manner [Haykin, 1998, Bishop, 1995].

A flexible model family, such as MLP networks, provides infinitely many possible explanations of different complexity to the observed data. Choosing too complex a model results in overfitting, where the model tries to make up meaningless explanations for the noise in addition to the true sources or independent components. Choosing too simple a model results in underfitting, leaving hidden some of the true sources that have generated the data.

An appropriate solution to this problem is that no single model should actually be chosen. Instead, all the possible explanations should be taken into account and weighted according to their posterior probabilities. This approach, known as Bayesian learning [Bishop, 1995], optimally solves the tradeoff between under- and overfitting. All the relevant information needed in choosing an appropriate model is contained in the posterior probability density functions (p.d.f.) of different model structures. The posterior p.d.f. of too simple models are low, because they leave a lot of the data unexplained. Also too complex models occupy little probability mass, even though they often show a high but very narrow peak in their posterior p.d.f. corresponding to the overfitted parameters.

In practice, exact treatment of the posterior p.d.f. of the models is impossible. Therefore, some suitable approximation method must be used. Ensemble learning [Barber & Bishop, 1998, Lappalainen & Miskin, 2000], also known as variational learning, is a recently developed method for parametric approximation of posterior p.d.f.s where the search takes into account the probability *mass* of the models. Therefore, it does not suffer from overfitting. The basic idea in ensemble learning is to minimize the misfit between the posterior pdf and its parametric approximation.

Let us denote $X = \{\mathbf{x}(t)|t\}$ and $S = \{\mathbf{s}(t)|t\}$, and let θ denote all the unknown parameters of the model. Furthermore, let $P(\theta|X)$ denote the exact posterior pdf and $Q(\theta)$ its parametric approximation. The misfit is measured with the Kullback-Leibler (KL) divergence C_{KL} between P and Q, defined by the cost function

$$C_{KL} = E_Q\left\{\log\frac{Q}{P}\right\} = \int d\theta\, Q(\theta)\log\frac{Q(\theta)}{P(\theta|X)}. \qquad (4.14)$$

Because the KL divergence involves an expectation over a distribution, it is sensitive to probability mass rather than to probability density.

4.4.2 Model structure

In this approach, MLP networks are used for modelling the nonlinear mixing mapping $\mathbf{f}(\cdot)$. They have the universal approximation property [Haykin, 1998] for smooth continuous mappings, and suit well modelling both strongly and mildly nonlinear mappings.

The data model used in this approach is as follows [Lappalainen & Honkela, 2000, Lappalainen *et al.*, 2000b]. Let $\mathbf{x}(t)$ denote the observed data vector at time t, and $\mathbf{s}(t)$ the vector of source signals (latent variables) at time t. The matrices B and A contain the weights of the output and the hidden layer of the network, respectively, and $\mathbf{b}$ is the bias vector of the hidden layer. The vector of nonlinear activation functions is denoted by $\mathbf{g}(\cdot)$, and $\mathbf{n}(t)$ is a Gaussian noise vector corrupting the observations. It can generally have a nonzero mean vector here. Using these notations, the data model is

$$\mathbf{x}(t) = B\left[\mathbf{g}\left(A\mathbf{s}(t) + \mathbf{b}\right)\right] + \mathbf{n}(t). \tag{4.15}$$

As the activation function, the hyperbolic tangent nonlinearity $g(y) = \tanh(y)$ is used, which is a typical choice in MLP networks. Other continuous activation functions could be used, too. The sources are assumed to be independent, and they are modelled by mixtures of Gaussians. The independence assumption is natural, because the goal of the model is to find the underlying independent components of the observations. By using mixtures of Gaussians, one can model sufficiently well any non-Gaussian distribution of the sources [Bishop, 1995]. This type of representation has earlier been successfully applied to the standard linear ICA model in [Lappalainen, 1999].

The parameters of the network are: (1) the weight matrices A and B and the vector of biases $\mathbf{b}$; (2) the parameters of the distributions of the noise, source signals and column vectors of the weight matrices; (3) the hyperparameters used for defining the distributions of the biases and the parameters in group (2). For a more detailed description, see [Lappalainen & Honkela, 2000, Lappalainen *et al.*, 2000b]. All the parameterised distributions are assumed to be Gaussian except for the sources, which are modelled as mixtures of Gaussians. This does not limit the generality of the approach severely, but makes computational implementation simpler and much more efficient. The hierarchical description of the distributions of the parameters of the model used here is a standard procedure in probabilistic Bayesian modelling. Its strength lies in the fact that knowledge about equivalent status of different parameters can be easily incorporated. For example all the variances of the noise components have a similar status in the model. This is reflected by the fact that their distributions are assumed to be governed by common hyperparameters.

4.4.3 *Learning procedure*

Usually MLP networks learn the nonlinear input-output mapping in a supervised manner using known input-output pairs, for which the mean-square mapping error is minimized using the back-propagation algorithm or some alternative method [Haykin, 1998, Bishop, 1995]. In our case, the inputs are the *unknown* source signals $s(t)$, and only the outputs of the MLP network, namely the observed data vectors $x(t)$, are known. Hence, unsupervised learning must be applied. Due to space limitations, we give an overall description of the proposed unsupervised learning procedure only in this chapter. A more detailed account of the method and discussion of potentially appearing problems can be found in [Lappalainen & Honkela, 2000, Lappalainen *et al.*, 2000b].

The practical learning procedure used in all the experiments was the same. First, linear PCA (principal component analysis) is applied to find sensible initial values for the posterior means of the sources. Even though PCA is a linear method, it yields clearly better initial values than a random choice. The posterior variances of the sources are initialized to small values. Good initial values are important for the method because the network can effectively prune away unused parts. Initially the weights of the network have random values, and the network has quite a bad representation for the data. If the sources were adapted from random values, too, the network would consider many of the sources useless for the representation and prune them away. This would lead to a local minimum from which the network might not recover.

Therefore the sources were fixed at the values given by linear PCA for the first 50 sweeps through the entire data set. This allows the network to find a meaningful mapping from sources to the observations, thereby justifying using the sources for the representation. For the same reason, the parameters controlling the distributions of the sources, weights, noise and the hyperparameters are not adapted during the first 100 sweeps. They are adapted only after the network has found sensible values for the variables whose distributions these parameters control.

Furthermore, we first used a simpler nonlinear model where the sources had Gaussian distributions instead of mixtures of Gaussians. This is called *nonlinear factor analysis* in the following. After this phase, the sources were rotated using an efficient linear ICA algorithm called 'Fast-ICA' (see chapter 2 and [Hyvärinen, 1998b]). The rotation of the sources was compensated by an inverse rotation of the weight matrix A of the hidden layer. The final representation of the data was then found by continuing learning using now the mixture-of-Gaussians model for the sources. In [Lappalainen & Honkela, 2000], this representation is called *nonlinear independent factor analysis*.

4.4.4 Computation of the cost function

In this subsection, the Kullback-Leibler cost function C_{KL} defined earlier in equation (4.14) in considered in more detail. For approximating and then minimizing it, we need two things: the exact formulation of the posterior density $P(\theta|X)$ and its parametric approximation $Q(\theta)$.

According to Bayes' rule, the posterior p.d.f. of the unknown variables S and θ is

$$P(S,\theta|X) = \frac{P(X|S,\theta)P(S|\theta)P(\theta)}{P(X)}. \quad (4.16)$$

The factor $P(X|S,\theta)$ is obtained from equation (4.15). Let us denote the mean vector of $\mathbf{n}(t)$ by μ and the variance vector of the noise term $\mathbf{n}(t)$ by σ^2. The distribution $P(x_i(t)|\mathbf{s}(t),\theta)$ is thus Gaussian with mean $\mathbf{b}_i^T\mathbf{g}(A\mathbf{s}+\mathbf{b}) + \mu_i$ and variance σ_i^2. Here $\mathbf{b}_i^T$ denotes the ith row vector of B. As usual, the noise components $n_i(t)$ are assumed to be independent, and therefore $P(X|S,\theta) = \prod_{t,i} P(x_i(t)|\mathbf{s}(t),\theta)$.

The factors $P(S|\theta)$ and $P(\theta)$ in (4.16) are also products of simple Gaussian distributions, and they are obtained directly from the definition of the model structure [Lappalainen & Honkela, 2000, Lappalainen *et al.*, 2000b]. The term $P(X)$ does not depend on the model parameters and can be neglected.

The approximation $Q(S,\theta)$ must be simple for mathematical tractability and computational efficiency. We assume that it is a Gaussian density with a diagonal covariance matrix. This implies that the approximation is a product of independent distributions: $Q(\theta) = \prod_i Q_i(\theta_i)$. The parameters of each Gaussian component density $Q_i(\theta_i)$ are its mean $\bar{\theta}_i$ and variance $\tilde{\theta}_i$.

Both the posterior density $P(\theta|X)$ and its approximation $Q(\theta)$ are products of simple Gaussian terms, which simplifies the cost function (4.14) considerably: it splits into expectations of many simple terms. The terms of the form $E_Q\{\log Q_i(\theta_i)\}$ are negative entropies of Gaussians, having the exact values $-(1 + \log 2\pi\tilde{\theta}_i)/2$. The most difficult terms are of the form $-E_Q\{\log P(x_i(t)|\mathbf{s}(t), \boldsymbol{\theta})\}$. They are approximated by applying second order Taylor series expansions of the nonlinear activation functions as explained in [Lappalainen & Honkela, 2000, Lappalainen *et al.*, 2000b]. The remaining terms are expectations of simple Gaussian terms which can be computed as in [Lappalainen, 1999].

The cost function C_{KL} is a function of the posterior means $\bar{\theta}_i$ and variances $\tilde{\theta}_i$ of the source signals and the parameters of the network. This is because instead of finding a point estimate, the joint posterior p.d.f. of the sources and parameters is estimated in ensemble learning. The variances give information about the reliability of the estimates.

Let us denote the two parts of the cost function (4.14) by $C_p = -E_Q\{\log P\}$ and $C_q = E_Q\{\log Q\}$. The variances $\tilde{\theta}_i$ are obtained by differentiating (4.14) with respect to $\tilde{\theta}_i$ [Lappalainen & Honkela, 2000, Lappalainen *et al.*, 2000b]:

$$\frac{\partial C}{\partial \tilde{\theta}} = \frac{\partial C_p}{\partial \tilde{\theta}} + \frac{\partial C_q}{\partial \tilde{\theta}} = \frac{\partial C_p}{\partial \tilde{\theta}} - \frac{1}{2\tilde{\theta}}. \tag{4.17}$$

Equating this to zero yields a fixed-point iteration for updating the variances:

$$\tilde{\theta} = \left[2\frac{\partial C_p}{\partial \tilde{\theta}}\right]^{-1}. \tag{4.18}$$

The means $\bar{\theta}_i$ can be estimated from the approximate Newton iteration [Lappalainen & Honkela, 2000, Lappalainen *et al.*, 2000b]:

$$\bar{\theta} \leftarrow \bar{\theta} - \frac{\partial C_p}{\partial \bar{\theta}}\left[\frac{\partial^2 C}{\partial \bar{\theta}^2}\right]^{-1} \approx \bar{\theta} - \frac{\partial C_p}{\partial \bar{\theta}}\tilde{\theta}. \tag{4.19}$$

4.4.5 Experimental results

In all the simulations, the total number of sweeps was 7500, where one sweep means going through all the observations $\mathbf{x}(t)$ once. As explained before, a nonlinear factor analysis (or nonlinear PCA subspace) representation using plain Gaussians as model distributions for the sources was estimated first. In the experiments, 2000 first sweeps were used for finding this intermediate representation. After a linear ICA rotation, the final mixture-of-Gaussians representation of the sources was then estimated during the remaining 5500 sweeps. In the following, experiments with artificially generated nonlinear data are first presented, followed by separation results on real-world process data.

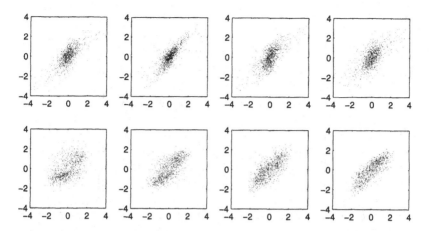

Figure 4.3. *Separation results given by linear ICA.* Original sources are on the x-axis of each scatter plot and the sources estimated by a linear ICA are on the y-axis. Signal-to-noise ratio is 0.7 dB.

In the first experiment, there were eight sources, four sub-Gaussian and four super-Gaussian ones. The data were generated from these sources through a nonlinear mapping, which was obtained by using a randomly initialized MLP network having 30 hidden neurons and 20 output neurons. Gaussian noise having a standard deviation of 0.1 was added to the data. The nonlinearity used in the hidden neurons was chosen to be the inverse hyperbolic sine, $\sinh^{-1}(t)$, which means that the nonlinear source separation algorithm using the MLP network with $\tanh(t)$ nonlinearities cannot use exactly the same weights.

Several different numbers of hidden neurons were tested in order to optimize the structure of the MLP network, but the number of sources was assumed to be known. This assumption is reasonable because it is possible to optimize the number of sources simply by minimizing the cost function as experiments with purely Gaussian sources have shown [Lappalainen & Honkela, 2000, Lappalainen *et al.*, 2000a]. The network which minimized the cost function turned out to have 50 hidden neurons. The number of Gaussians in each of the mixtures modelling the distribution of each source was chosen to be three, and no attempt was made to optimize this number.

The results are depicted in Figures 4.3, 4.4, and 4.5. Each figure shows eight scatter plots, corresponding to each of the eight original sources. The original source which was used for generating the data appears on

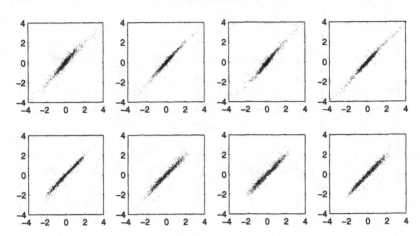

Figure 4.4. **Separation results given by nonlinear factor analysis.** *Scatter plots of the sources after 2000 sweeps of nonlinear factor analysis followed by a rotation with a linear ICA. Signal-to-noise ratio is 13.2 dB.*

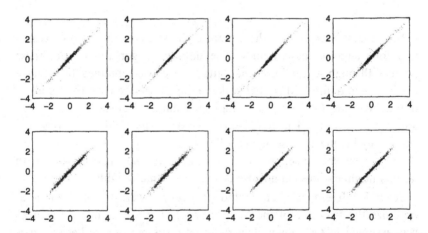

Figure 4.5. **Separation results given by nonlinear ICA.** *The final results after using a mixture-of-Gaussians model for the sources for the last 5500 sweeps. Signal-to-noise ratio is 17.3 dB.*

the x-axis, and the respective estimated source is on the y-axis of each plot. Each point corresponds to one data vector. The upper plots of each figure correspond to the super-Gaussian and the lower plots to the sub-Gaussian sources. Optimal result is a straight line implying that the estimated values of the sources coincide with the true values.

Figure 4.3 shows the result of a linear fixed-point (FastICA) algorithm

[Hyvärinen, 1998b]. The linear ICA is able to retrieve the original sources with only 0.7 dB SNR (signal-to-noise ratio). In practice a linear method could not deduce the number of sources, and the result would be even worse. The poor signal-to-noise ratio shows that the data really lie in a nonlinear subspace. Figure 4.4 depicts the results after 2000 sweeps with Gaussian sources (nonlinear factor analysis) followed by a rotation with linear FastICA. Now the SNR is considerably better, 13.2 dB, and the sources have clearly been retrieved. Figure 4.5 shows the final results after another 5500 sweeps when the mixture-of-Gaussians models have been used for the sources. The SNR has further improved to 17.3 dB.

Another data set consisted of 30 time series of length 2480 measured using different sensors from an industrial pulp process. A human expert preprocessed the measured signals by roughly compensating for the time lags of the process originating from the finite speed of pulp flow through the process.

For studying the intrinsic dimensionality of the data, linear factor analysis was applied to the data. The result is shown in Figure 4.6. The figure also shows the results with nonlinear factor analysis. It is obvious that the data are quite nonlinear, because nonlinear factor analysis is able to explain the data with 10 components equally well as linear factor analysis with 21 components.

Different numbers of hidden neurons and sources were tested with random initializations using Gaussian source models (nonlinear factor analysis). It turned out that the cost function was minimized for a network of 10 sources and 30 hidden neurons. The same network size was chosen for nonlinear blind source separation based on the mixture-of-Gaussians model for the sources. After 2000 sweeps using the nonlinear factor analysis model the sources were rotated with FastICA, and each source was modelled with a mixture of three Gaussian distributions. The resulting sources are shown in Figure 4.7.

Figure 4.8 shows 30 subimages, each corresponding to a specific measurement made from the process. The original measurement appears as the upper time series in each subimage, and the lower time series is the reconstruction of this measurement given by the network. These reconstructions are the posterior means of the outputs of the network when the inputs were the estimated sources shown in Figure 4.7. The original measurements show a great variability, but the reconstructions are strikingly accurate. In some cases it even seems that the reconstruction is less noisy than the original signal.

The experiments suggest that the estimated source signals can have

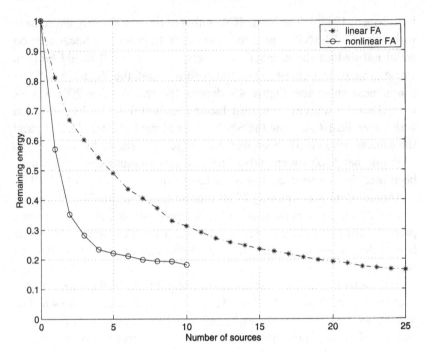

Figure 4.6. *A study of the intrinsic dimensionality of the data.* *The figure shows the remaining energy of the process data as a function of the number of extracted components using linear and nonlinear factor analysis.*

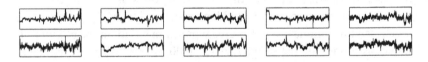

Figure 4.7. *Industrial pulp process: The ten estimated sources. Time increases from left to right.*

meaningful physical interpretations. The results are encouraging, but further studies are needed to verify the interpretations of the signals.

The proposed ensemble learning method for nonlinear blind source separation can be extended in several ways. An obvious extension is inclusion of time delays in the data model, making use of the temporal information often present in the sources. This would probably help in describing the process data even better. Using the Bayesian framework, it is also easy to treat missing observations or only partly known inputs.

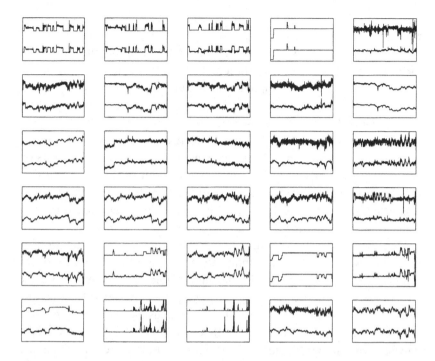

Figure 4.8. **Industrial pulp process:** *The 30 original time series are shown on each plot on top of the reconstruction made from the sources shown in Figure 4.7.*

4.5 Other approaches

Burel [1992] was probably the first to introduce an algorithm for non-linear blind source separation. His method is based on back-propagation type neural learning for parametric nonlinearities, and suffers from computational complexity and problems with local minima. In a series of papers [Deco & Brauer, 1995, Parra *et al.*, 1995, Parra *et al.*, 1996], Deco and Parra with their co-authors developed methods based on volume conserving symplectic transformations for nonlinear independent component analysis. The constraint of volume conservation is, however, somewhat arbitrary, and so these methods are usually not able to recover the original sources. Also their computational load tends to be high.

The idea of using the self-organizing map (SOM) [Kohonen, 1995] for the general nonlinear BSS problem was introduced in [Pajunen *et al.*, 1996]. However, this approach is limited mainly to separation of sources having distributions not too far from the uniform distribution. The nonlinear mixing process is considered to be regular: it is required that the inverse of the mixing mapping should be the least complex mapping which yields independent components [Pajunen *et al.*, 1996]. Also Lin, Grier, and Cowan [Lin *et al.*, 1997] independently proposed using SOM for nonlinear blind source separation in a different manner.

The ensemble learning approach to nonlinear BSS, discussed in more detail earlier in this chapter, is based on using multi-layer perceptron (MLP) networks as a flexible model for the nonlinear mixing mapping (4.3). Several authors have used autoassociative MLP networks for learning similar type mappings. Both the generative model and its inversion are learned simultaneously, but separately without utilizing the fact that the models are connected. Autoassociative MLPs have shown some success in nonlinear data representation [Haykin, 1998], but generally they suffer from slow learning prone to local minima.

Most work on autoassociative MLPs uses point estimates for weights and sources obtained from minimization of the mean-square representation error for the data. It is then impossible to reliably choose the structure of the model, and problems with over- or underfitting can be severe. Hecht-Nielsen [1995, 1996] proposed using so-called replicator networks for universal optimal nonlinear coding of input data. These networks are autoassociate MLP networks, where the data vectors are mapped onto a unit hypercube having a uniform distribution. The coordinates of the data on the axes of the hypercube, called natural coordinates, form then in fact a nonlinear ICA solution, even though this was not noted in the original papers.

Hochreiter & Schmidhuber [1999] have used in context with MLP networks a minimum description length based method which does estimate the distribution of the weights, but has no model for the sources. It is then impossible to measure the description length of the sources. Anyway, their method shows interesting connections with ICA; sometimes it provides a nonlinear ICA solution, sometimes not [Hochreiter & Schmidhuber, 1999]. Another general approach proposed recently for solving the nonlinear BSS or ICA problems is based on state-space modelling [Cichocki *et al.*, 1999].

Various separation methods for the considerably simpler case of the post-nonlinear mixture model (4.5) have been introduced in [Taleb & Jutten, 1999, Lee, 1998, Yang *et al.*, 1998]. In particular, an MLP model is used for separating sources from their post-nonlinear mixtures in [Yang *et al.*, 1998]. This method is an extension of the well-known natural gradient method for linear BSS [Lee, 1998].

In the ensemble learning method discussed before, the necessary regularization for nonlinear ICA is achieved by choosing the model and sources that have most probably generated the observed data. A similar generative model is applied to the linear ICA/BSS problem in [Attias, 1999b] and in chapters 3 and 8. The ensemble learning based method described in this chapter differs from the method introduced in [Attias, 1999a] in that it uses a more general nonlinear data model, and applies a fully Bayesian treatment to the hyperparameters of the network or graphical model, too. Connections of the ensemble learning method with other Bayesian approaches are discussed in more detail in [Lappalainen & Honkela, 2000, Lappalainen *et al.*, 2000a].

Nonlinear blind source separation and independent component analysis are generally difficult problems both computationally and conceptually. Therefore, local linear ICA/BSS methods have received some attention recently as a practical compromise between linear ICA and completely nonlinear ICA or BSS. These methods are more general than standard linear ICA in that several different linear ICA models are used to describe the observed data. The local linear ICA models can be either overlapping as in the mixture-of-ICA methods introduced in [Lee *et al.*, 1999a, Lee *et al.*, 1999c] and chapter 9 or non-overlapping as in the clustering based methods proposed in [Karhunen & Malaroiu, 1999a, Karhunen & Malaroiu, 1999b].

4.6 Conclusions and remarks

In this chapter, generalizations of standard linear ICA and BSS problems to nonlinear data models have been considered. Unlike in the linear case, solutions of the respective ICA and BSS problems usually differ from each other when the data model is nonlinear. In particular the nonlinear ICA problem is ill-posed without some suitable extra constraints or regularization, having in general infinitely many qualitatively different solutions.

Solving the nonlinear ICA or BSS problems appropriately using solely the assumption of independence of the source signals is usually not possible except for simple special cases, for example in the case of post-nonlinear mixtures. Otherwise, suitable additional information on the problem is required. This extra information is often provided in the form of regularizing contraints. Various methods proposed for regularizing the nonlinear ICA or BSS problems have been briefly reviewed in the previous section. Another possibility is to have more information about the sources or mixtures themselves. Examples of this type of approaches are methods developed for separating post-nonlinear mixtures, and the maximum likelihood approach which requires knowledge of the probability distributions of the sources.

A large part of this chapter has been devoted to a recently introduced fully Bayesian approach based on ensemble learning for solving the nonlinear BSS (or ICA) problem. This method applies the well-known MLP network, which is well suited to modelling both mildly and strongly nonlinear mappings. The proposed unsupervised ensemble learning method tries to find the sources and the mapping that have most probably generated the observed data. It is believed that this principle provides an appropriate regularization for the nonlinear source separation problem. The results are encouraging for both artificial and real-world data. The method allows nonlinear source separation for larger scale problems than some previously proposed computationally quite demanding methods, and it can be easily extended in various directions.

A lot of work remains to be done in developing suitable methods for the nonlinear ICA and BSS problems, and understanding better which constraints are most suitable in each situation. A number of different approaches have been proposed, but no comparisons are yet available for assessing their strengths and weaknesses.

Acknowledgments

The author wishes to thank H. Lappalainen, P. Pajunen, A. Hyvärinen, X. Giannakopoulos, and A. Honkela for their co-operation, helpful comments, and useful discussions on the topic of this chapter.

5

Separation of non-stationary natural signals

Lucas C. Parra

Clay D. Spence

Most approaches to the problem of source separation use the assumption of statistical independence. To capture statistical independence higher order statistics are required. In this chapter we will demonstrate how higher order criteria, such as maximum kurtosis, arise naturally from the property of non-stationarity. We will also show that source separation of non-stationary signals can be based entirely on second order statistics of the signals. Natural signals, be they images or time sequences, are for the most part non-stationary. For natural signals therefore we argue that non-stationarity is the fundamental property, from which specific second or higher order separation criteria can be derived. We contrast the linear bases obtained using second order non-stationarity and ICA for the cases of natural images and speech powers. Based on these results we argue that speech powers can in fact be understood as a linear superposition of non-stationary spectro-temporal independent components, while this is not so evident for a spatial basis of images intensities. Finally we demonstrate the practical utility of the second order non-stationarity concept with a separation algorithm for the problem of convolutive source separation. We show its effectiveness on acoustic mixtures in real reverberant environments.

5.1 Second and higher order separation criteria in the context of non-stationary signals

Most approaches to source separation have been based on the condition of statistical independence of the constituent signals. Conventionally, higher order statistics are required to capture statistical independence. In fact if the source signals are identically and independently distributed (i.i.d.) samples of a stationary distribution second order statistics are not sufficient for separation. Fortunately, natural signals are often not stationary, or independently distributed.

Usually natural signals are sampled on a regular lattice, e.g., one-dimensional arrays for time sequences, two-dimensional arrays for images, three-dimensional arrays for image sequences and so on. Neighboring samples on such a lattice are often correlated. Furthermore the statistics of the samples are often not stationary on the lattice, that is, the signals are non-stationary in time or space. This rich spatio-temporal diversity, a result of the spatio-temporal ordering of samples, rather than being a problem, can actually simplify the problem of source separation. In this chapter we try to highlight the statistical properties that arise from non-stationarity that allow us to define useful separation criteria. Other aspects of the non-stationary source separation problem are considered in Chapter 6.

First, we will argue that non-stationarity justifies higher order criteria, in particular maximum kurtosis. The kurtosis of a signal has been used for separation of natural signals, such as speech, or to find independent linear bases for natural images. Therein the assumption is made that the sources of interest have a sparse distribution or high kurtosis. In section 5.2 we show that non-stationarity in fact leads to high kurtosis signals validating the high kurtosis assumption for source separation for natural signals.

It is well known that for temporally correlated sources signal separation can be based entirely on second order statistics [Bradwood, 1978, Bar-Ness *et al.*, 1982, Fety & Van Ulffelen, 1988, Tong & Liu, 1990, Belouchrani *et al.*, 1993, Molgedey & Schuster, 1994]. Less well known is the fact that non-stationary signals can also be separated using decorrelation [Souloumiac, 1995, Matsuoka *et al.*, 1995, Parra & Spence, 2000a]. Almost identical algorithms can be used in both cases, as we will discuss in section 5.3.

Furthermore, for correlated *and* non-stationary signals the more difficult problem of convolutive source separation can be solved using second order statistics as first indicated by [Weinstein *et al.*, 1993] and shown in [Kawamoto *et al.*, 1998, Parra & Spence, 2000a]. We will present a specific algorithm and examples of recovering speech in a reverberant environment in section 5.5.

In section 5.4 we verify our arguments by applying the criterion of non-stationary second order decorrelation to find linear bases for natural images and speech signals. We contrast the results with a standard ICA algorithm. For images, in the past, linear bases for small spatial areas of the visual field have been compared to visual receptive fields [Olshausen & Field, 1996]. Receptive fields in the auditory domain are found to be spectro-temporal patterns [Kowalski *et al.*, 1996, deCharms & Merzenich, 1998, Theunissen & Doupe, 1998]. Different linear bases for small patches of natural images and small spectro-temporal patches of speech powers will be presented in section 5.4. The merits and problems of a linear superposition model of non-stationary independent components will be discussed for both these domains. In essence we argue that acoustic signal powers are well described by such a linear superposition model. We question, however, the concept of linear superposition of image intensities.

5.2 Kurtosis of non-stationary signals

To facilitate the analysis we will first introduce a rather general class of stochastic processes that expresses the main property of non-stationarity we would like to address. Then we will show that this class of non-stationary signals are heavy tailed as measured by their kurtosis.

Assume that at any given instance the signal is specified by a probability density function with zero mean and arbitrary scale or power. Furthermore assume that the signal is non-stationary in the sense that its power varies from one time instance to the next.† A closely related class of signals is the so-called spherical invariant random process (SIRP). If the signals are short time Gaussian and the powers vary slowly the class of signals we have just described are approximately SIRPs. SIRPs have been shown to cover a large range of different stochastic processes with very different higher order properties depending on the distribution of powers. They have been used in a variety of signal processing applications [Goldman, 1976, Rangaswamy *et al.*, 1993, Rupp, 1993]. Band-limited speech in particular has been shown to be well described by SIRPs [Brehm & Stammler, 1987]. Natural images have also been modeled by what in essence is closely related to SIRPs — a finite [Spence & Parra, 2000] or infinite [Wainwright & Simoncelli, 2000] mixture of linear Gaussian features.

Consider a stochastic process with samples $z(t)$ drawn from a zero mean distribution $p_z(z)$. Assume we observe a scaled version of this process, where the magnitude or scale changes over time. If the scale

---

† Throughout this chapter we will refer to signals that are sampled in time. Note that all the arguments apply equally well to a spatial rather than temporal sampling, that is, images rather than time series.

at any instant is given by $s(t) > 0$ sampled from $p_s(s)$ the resulting observable process

$$x(t) = s(t)z(t) \tag{5.1}$$

is distributed according to

$$p_x(x) = \int_0^\infty ds\, p_s(s)\, p_x(x|s) = \int_0^\infty ds\, p_s(s)\, s^{-1}\, p_z\left(\frac{x}{s}\right). \tag{5.2}$$

We refer to $p_x(x)$ as the long term distribution and $p_z(z)$ as the instantaneous distribution. In essence $p_x(x)$ is a mixture distribution with infinitely many kernels $s^{-1}p_z(\frac{x}{s})$. We would like to relate the sparseness of $p_z(z)$, as measured by the kurtosis, to the sparseness of the observable distribution $p_x(x)$. Kurtosis is defined as the ratio between the fourth and second cumulants of a distribution [Kendal & Stuart, 1969]. As such it measures the length of the distribution's tails, or the sharpness of its mode. For a zero mean random variable x this reduces (up to a constant†) to

$$K[x] = \frac{\langle x^4 \rangle_x}{\langle x^2 \rangle_x^2}. \tag{5.3}$$

The expectation over $p_x(x)$ is denoted by $\langle f(x) \rangle_x = \int dx f(x) p_x(x)$.

We will show now that the kurtosis of the long term distribution is always larger than the kurtosis of the instantaneous distribution unless the scale is stationary, i.e., $K[x] \geqslant K[z]$, where the equality holds for $p_s(s) = \delta(s - c)$ for any arbitrary constant c.

Since z and s are independent it is easy to show that

$$\langle x^n \rangle_x = \langle s^n \rangle_s \langle z^n \rangle_z. \tag{5.4}$$

With this we can write the kurtosis $K[x]$ of the long term distribution in terms of the kurtosis $K[z]$ of the instantaneous distribution as

$$K[x] = K[z] \frac{\langle s^4 \rangle_s}{\langle s^2 \rangle_s^2}. \tag{5.5}$$

For any density of a positive random variable, $p_s(s) \geqslant 0$ and $p_s(s) = 0$ for $s < 0$, we know that

$$\int_0^\infty ds\, p_s(s)\, (s^2 - c^2)^2 \geqslant 0 \tag{5.6}$$

---

† The conventional definition is $K[x] = \langle x^4 \rangle_x / \langle x^2 \rangle_x^2 - 3$. We neglect for convenience the constant -3 in our definition.

for arbitrary c. Equality holds only when the integrand vanishes everywhere, i.e., if and only if $p_s(s)$ vanishes except for $s^2 = c^2$. The only distribution that vanishes everywhere except in one point is the Dirac δ-distribution. Therefore equality holds if and only if $p_s(s) = \delta(s - c)$. Rewriting (5.6) we obtain

$$\int ds\, p_s(s)\,(s^4 - 2s^2c^2 + c^4) = \langle s^4 \rangle_s - 2\,\langle s^2 \rangle_s\, c^2 + c^4 \geqslant 0. \quad (5.7)$$

The minimum with respect to c occurs at $\langle s^2 \rangle_s^{1/2}$. Inserting this gives

$$\frac{\langle s^4 \rangle_s}{\langle s^2 \rangle_s^2} \geqslant 1. \quad (5.8)$$

We have therefore

$$K[x] \geqslant K[z]. \quad (5.9)$$

The equality holds if and only if $p_s(s) = \delta(s - c)$. This result was first published by Beale & Mallows [1959] for symmetric $p_z(z)$.

This result means that if the scale $s(t)$ is fixed, i.e., the magnitude of the signal is stationary, the kurtosis will be minimal. Inversely, non-stationary signals, defined as a variable scaling of an otherwise stationary process, will have increased kurtosis.

In the discussion above, the time t did not play a particular role other than to indicate that we sample the random variables over time and that a variable scale translates to scale non-stationarity. We also did not demand that samples be drawn independently. That is, we are implicitly allowing signals that are correlated over time.

In summary we can say that signals with varying power will tend to have high kurtosis.

In our definition a stationary Gaussian signal has kurtosis 3. Non-stationary Gaussian signals will be leptokurtic ($K > 3$). All SIRPs are therefore leptokurtic. The assumption that a distribution is sparse, frequently used in source separation of natural signals, is therefore justified. However, we will not go into the specific approaches of source separation based on higher order statistics as they have been extensively studied and are described elsewhere in this volume. A good overview of higher order contrast functions is given by Cardoso [1999a]. In the following section we will demonstrate how non-stationarity can be used to simplify the problem of source separation by allowing us to use statistics of only second order.

5.3 Separation based on non-stationary second order statistics

In this section we will concentrate on instantaneous mixtures. The more complex case of convolutive mixtures will be presented in the next section. To clarify the notation let us restate the basic problem. Assume M statistically independent sources $s(t) = [s_1(t), ..., s_M(t)]^T$. These sources are mixed in a linear medium leading to N sensor signals $x(t) = [x_1(t), ..., x_N(t)]^T$ that may include additional sensor noise $n(t)$, i.e.,

$$x(t) = As(t) + n(t). \tag{5.10}$$

How can one identify the NM coefficients of the mixture A and how can one find an estimate $\hat{s}(t)$ for the unknown sources?

Early work in the signal processing community proposed that the linearly mixed sources could be recovered by finding the linear transformation W that decorrelates the measured signals, or, more specifically, that diagonalizes the measured auto-correlations at multiple time delays [Bradwood, 1978, Bar-Ness et al., 1982, Fety & Van Ulffelen, 1988, Tong & Liu, 1990]. For an instantaneous mix of non-white signals this is in fact sufficient as discussed in [Molgedey & Schuster, 1994, Van Gerven & Van Compernolle, 1995]. Almost the same approach can be taken if the signals are non-stationary rather than non-white. In this case we can use the covariance estimated during different time intervals instead of the covariance for different delays, as we will now show. This was indicated by Weinstein et al. [1993] and has been explicitly used in [Souloumiac, 1995, Kawamoto et al., 1998].

Note that strictly speaking we are not searching for independent components. We are merely searching for decorrelated model signals that explain a static and instantaneous linear mixture. Certainly statistically independent signals are uncorrelated, but the inverse is not always true.

5.3.1 Forward model estimation

We can formulate the instantaneous covariance $R_x(t)$ of the measured signals at time t with the assumption of independent noise as

$$R_x(t) \equiv \left\langle x(t)x^T(t) \right\rangle = A \left\langle s(t)s^T(t) \right\rangle A^T + \left\langle n(t)n^T(t) \right\rangle$$
$$\equiv A\Lambda_s(t)A^T + \Lambda_n(t). \tag{5.11}$$

Since we assume uncorrelated sources at all times, we postulate diagonal covariance matrices $\Lambda_s(t)$. We also assume uncorrelated noise at each sensor, i.e., diagonal $\Lambda_n(t)$. Any reasonable definition of the average

$\langle f(t) \rangle$ that satisfies these diagonality criteria is applicable, such as the average over an ensemble of independent realizations of the signal $s(t)$ and noise $n(t)$.

Note that any scaling and permutation of the coordinates of $\Lambda_s(t)$ can be absorbed by A. It is well-known that the solution is therefore only specified up to an inherently arbitrary permutation and scaling. Thus we are free to choose the scaling of the coordinates in s. For now we choose $A_{ii} = 1, i = 1, ..., M$, which places M conditions on our solutions.

For non-stationary signals, a set of K equations (5.11) for different times $t_1, ..., t_K$ and the M scaling conditions give a total of $KN(N + 1)/2 + M$ constraints on $MN + MK + NK$ unknown parameters A, $\Lambda_s(t_1), ..., \Lambda_s(t_K)$, $\Lambda_n(t_1), ..., \Lambda_n(t_K)$.† Assuming all conditions are linearly independent‡ we have sufficient conditions if

$$KN(N + 1)/2 + M \geqslant MN + MK + NK. \qquad (5.12)$$

It is interesting to note that in the square case, $M = N$, there are not enough constraints to determine the additional noise parameters unless $N \geqslant 4$, no matter how many more times one considers.§ If we assume zero additive noise, in principle there are sufficient conditions to specify the solution (up to arbitrary permutations) for any $K \geqslant 2$. In that case the problem can be solved as a non-symmetric eigenvalue problem as outlined in [Molgedey & Schuster, 1994]. The covariances at times t_1 and t_2 satisfy

$$R_x(t_1) = A\Lambda_s(t_1)A^{\mathsf{T}}, \qquad (5.13)$$
$$R_x(t_2)^{-1} = A^{-\mathsf{T}}\Lambda_s(t_2)^{-1}A^{-1}, \qquad (5.14)$$

which can be combined to get

$$R_x(t_1)R_x(t_2)^{-1}A = A\Lambda_s(t_1)\Lambda_s(t_2)^{-1}. \qquad (5.15)$$

Equation (5.15) represents a non-symmetric eigenvalue problem. In general its solutions, A, are not orthogonal as expected.

The difficulty with such algebraic solutions, however, is that one does not have perfect estimates of $R_x(t)$. Even if we assume zero noise at best one can assume non-stationary signals and measure the sample estimates

† We will abbreviate the notation in the remainder of the chapter by writing $\Lambda_s(..)$ when we refer to all $\Lambda_s(t_1), ..., \Lambda_s(t_K)$. We use this notation also for $\Lambda_n(t)$.

‡ Conditions on $R_x(t)$ and $\Lambda_s(t)$ for linear independence are outlined in [Molgedey & Schuster, 1994].

§ One can see this by re-writing the inequality as $K(N^2 - 3N) + 2(N - N^2) \geqslant 0$. The second term is never positive, and the first is only positive if $N \geqslant 4$.

$\hat{R}_x(t)$ within some time interval. If we interpret the inaccuracy of that estimation as measurement error

$$E(t) \equiv \hat{R}_x(t) - \Lambda_n(t) - A\Lambda_s(t)A^\mathsf{T}, \qquad (5.16)$$

it is reasonable to estimate the unknown parameters by minimizing the total measurement error for sufficiently large K, i.e.,

$$\hat{A}, \hat{\Lambda}_s(..), \hat{\Lambda}_n(..) = \arg \min_{A,\Lambda_s(..),\Lambda_n(..),A_{ii}=1} \sum_{k=1}^{K} \|E(t_k)\|^2. \qquad (5.17)$$

The matrix norm here is the sum of the absolute squared values of every coefficient. Note that $\|E(k)\|^2 = \mathrm{Tr}[E(k)E^H(k)]$. This is a least squares (LS) estimation problem.

5.3.2 Simultaneous diagonalization with unitary transformations

In the context of source separation it is common to reduce the problem of finding a general linear transformation A to that of finding only a rotation V by first diagonalizing the long term covariance [Cardoso & Souloumiac, 1993, Comon 1994].

This approach is feasible only in the case that the noise is of equal power, σ^2, in all sensors. In addition, for our case this approach requires stationary noise, $\Lambda_n(t) = \sigma^2 I$. Under these constraints the solution to (5.17) can be computed explicitly using an elegant simultaneous diagonalization technique presented in [Cardoso & Souloumiac, 1996].

Consider the long term average $\bar{R}_x = (1/T)\sum_{t=1}^{T} R_x(t)$. To properly account for additive noise, one has to first obtain an estimate of the long term covariance $\bar{R}_y$ of the signal portion in the mixture, $y(t) = As(t)$. Following (5.11) this covariance is given by $\bar{R}_y = \bar{R}_x - \sigma^2 I$. Conventionally for $M < N$ a more stable estimate of $\bar{R}_y$ is obtained using an eigenvalue decomposition of the sample average estimate of $\bar{R}_x$, i.e., $\bar{R}_x = U^\mathsf{T}DU$, where D represents a diagonal matrix with the eigenvalues of $\bar{R}_x$ and U the corresponding matrix of eigenvectors. The eigenvectors with the largest eigenvalues are conventionally referred to as the principal components (page 18). A robust estimate of $\bar{R}_y$ is given by $\bar{R}_y = U^\mathsf{T}\max(D - \sigma^2 I, 0)U$. This is a classic subspace analysis where the N-dimensional data is assumed to originate in an M-dimensional subspace. The average of the $N - M$ smallest eigenvalues provides an estimate for σ^2.†

---

† If, in fact, $\Lambda_n = \sigma^2 I$, in principle the smallest eigenvalues should all have the same mag-

One can show that $\bar{R}_y$ is diagonalized, i.e., $Q\bar{R}_yQ^\mathsf{T} = I$, by a whitening operation $Q = (D - \sigma^2 I)^{-1/2}U$.† Furthermore, for any arbitrary rotation V the matrix

$$A = Q^+ V \bar{\Lambda}_s^{-1/2} \tag{5.18}$$

satisfies $\bar{R}_x = A\bar{\Lambda}_s A^\mathsf{T} - \bar{\Lambda}_n$, which is precisely the diagonalization condition (5.11) for the long term averages. Q^+ represents the pseudo-inverse of Q. Both of these results can only be derived for equal power noise. To find the correct A one has to determine V using additional constraints. It is important to note, however, that the problem of finding a general linear transformation A has been reduced to finding a rotation V.

Consider now the whitened signal portion of the mixture, $\mathbf{z} = Q\mathbf{y}(t)$. Using (5.18) its instantaneous covariance can be written as

$$R_z(t) = QR_y(t)Q^\mathsf{T} = QA\Lambda_s(t)A^\mathsf{T}Q^\mathsf{T} = V\Lambda_s(t)\bar{\Lambda}_s^{-1}V^\mathsf{T}. \tag{5.19}$$

We find therefore that the remaining rotation V has to diagonalize $R_z(t)$ for all times. With the same reasoning applied to the minimal estimation error, therefore, we can rewrite (5.11) as

$$E_z(t) \equiv QE(t)Q^\mathsf{T} = \hat{R}_z(t) - V\Lambda_s(t)\bar{\Lambda}_s^{-1}V^\mathsf{T}, \tag{5.20}$$

$$\hat{V}, \hat{\Lambda}_s(..) = \arg \min_{V=V^\mathsf{T}, \Lambda_s(..)} \sum_{k=1}^{K} \|E_z(t_k)\|^2 . \tag{5.21}$$

This is exactly the problem addressed in the approximate joint eigenspace algorithm described in [Cardoso & Souloumiac, 1996].

Note that $R_y(t)$ can only be properly estimated if $\Lambda_n(t)$ is known. This is why we required stationary noise powers that may be estimated with the subspace analysis outlined above. Additionally we had to demand equal noise powers. There might be cases where these conditions are too restrictive. In addition, as we will discuss in section 5.5, one may wish to place other constraints on A. In such a case direct optimization with respect to A as in (5.17) may be desired.

---

nitude σ^2. However, a sample average is never exact and sampling average instabilities require us to use $\max(D - \sigma^2 I, 0)$.

† In the case that $M < N$ only the M rows of Q corresponding to non-negative values of $D - \sigma^2 I$ have to be considered.

5.3.3 Gradient based diagonalization

To find the extrema of the LS cost $J = \sum_{k=1}^{K} \|E(t_k)\|^2$ in (5.17) let us compute the gradients with respect to its parameters. The result is†

$$\frac{\partial J}{\partial A} = -4 \sum_{k=1}^{K} E(t_k) A \Lambda_s(t_k), \tag{5.22}$$

$$\frac{\partial J}{\partial \Lambda_s(t_k)} = -2 \operatorname{diag} \left(A^{\mathsf{T}} E(t_k) A \right), \tag{5.23}$$

$$\frac{\partial J}{\partial \Lambda_n(t_k)} = -2 \operatorname{diag} \left(E(t_k) \right). \tag{5.24}$$

We can find the minimum with respect to A and $\Lambda_s(t_k)$ with a gradient descent algorithm using the gradients (5.22) and (5.23). The optimal $\Lambda_n(t_k)$ for given A and $\Lambda_s(t_k)$ at every gradient step can be computed explicitly by setting the gradient in (5.24) to zero, which yields $\hat{\Lambda}_n(t_k) = \operatorname{diag} \left(\hat{R}_x(t_k) - A \Lambda_s(t_k) A^{\mathsf{T}} \right)$.

5.3.4 Estimation of source signals

In the case of a square and invertible mixing matrix $\hat{A}$, the signal estimates are trivially computed to be $\hat{\mathbf{s}} = \hat{A}^{-1} \mathbf{x}$. In the non-square case for $M < N$ we can compute the LS estimate

$$\hat{\mathbf{s}}_{\mathrm{LS}}(t) = \arg \min_{\mathbf{s}(t)} \|\mathbf{x}(t) - \hat{A}\mathbf{s}(t)\| = (\hat{A}^{\mathsf{T}} \hat{A})^{-1} \hat{A}^{\mathsf{T}} \mathbf{x}(t). \tag{5.25}$$

If we assume the additive noise to be short term Gaussian, but not necessarily white or stationary, we can compute the maximum likelihood (ML) estimate

$$\hat{\mathbf{s}}_{\mathrm{ML}}(t) = \arg \max_{\mathbf{s}(t)} p\left(\mathbf{x}(t) \mid \mathbf{s}(t); \hat{A}, \hat{\Lambda}_n(t) \right)$$

$$= \left[\hat{A}^{\mathsf{T}} \hat{\Lambda}_n(t)^{-1} \hat{A} \right]^{-1} \hat{A}^{\mathsf{T}} \hat{\Lambda}_n(t)^{-1} \mathbf{x}(t) \tag{5.26}$$

where $p()$ is the Gaussian probability density given by the noise density.

If we further assume the signal to be short term Gaussian, again not necessarily white or stationary, we can compute the maximum a posteriori probability (MAP) estimate. For Gaussian densities the MAP estimate is

---

† The diagonalization operator here zeroes the off-diagonal elements, i.e.,

$$\operatorname{diag}(A)_{ij} = \begin{cases} A_{ij}, & i = j, \\ 0, & i \neq j \end{cases}.$$

equal to the conditional expectation $E[\mathbf{s}(t)|\mathbf{x}(t); \hat{A}, \hat{\Lambda}_n(t), \hat{\Lambda}_s(t)]$.

$$\hat{\mathbf{s}}_{\text{MAP}}(t) = \arg \max_{\mathbf{s}(t)} p(\mathbf{s}(t) \mid \mathbf{x}(t); \hat{A}, \hat{\Lambda}_n(t), \hat{\Lambda}_s(t))$$

$$= E[\mathbf{s}(t)|\mathbf{x}(t); \hat{A}, \hat{\Lambda}_n(t), \hat{\Lambda}_s(t)] \qquad (5.27)$$

$$= \left[\hat{A}^\mathsf{T} \hat{\Lambda}_n(t)^{-1} \hat{A} + \hat{\Lambda}_s(t)^{-1}\right]^{-1} \hat{A}^\mathsf{T} \hat{\Lambda}_n(t)^{-1} \mathbf{x}(t).$$

Note however that the resulting estimates may not be uncorrelated. Assuming that the model is correct and that we found the correct estimate $\hat{A} \approx A$, we get

$$\langle \hat{\mathbf{s}}_{\text{LS}} \hat{\mathbf{s}}_{\text{LS}}^\mathsf{T} \rangle \approx \langle \mathbf{s}\mathbf{s}^\mathsf{T} \rangle + (\hat{A}^\mathsf{T} \hat{A})^{-1} \hat{A}^\mathsf{T} \Lambda_n \hat{A} (\hat{A}^\mathsf{T} \hat{A})^{-1}. \qquad (5.28)$$

Since the second term may not be diagonal, the resulting estimates can be correlated. However, this is not a problem since the correlation is entirely due to correlated noise and the signal portion of the estimates remains uncorrelated.

Instantaneous source separation based on second order statistics has found applications to image processing [Schießl *et al.*, 2000], magneto-encephalography [Wübbeler *et al.*, 2000, Tang *et al.*, 2000] and other bio-magnetic recordings [Ziehe *et al.*, 2000]. The following two sections will demonstrate two applications of source separation. First we will compare the criteria of independence and non-stationary decorrelation in the case of natural images and the time-frequency representation of speech. Then in section 5.5 the strength of the non-stationarity condition is demonstrated on the more complex problem of convolutive source separation in a real acoustic environment.

5.4 Linear basis of images and sounds

In the first two sections we have argued that for non-stationary signals high kurtosis and multiple decorrelation can both be used to find linear combinations of independent sources. If the basic model of linearly mixed sources does not strictly apply, however, it is not evident that the two criteria will lead to the same results. In this section we will use this to verify the modeling assumptions for two different domains, natural images and speech signals.

For images, in the past, linear bases for small spatial areas of the visual field have been compared to visual receptive fields [Olshausen & Field, 1996]. Receptive fields in the auditory domain are found to be spectro-temporal patterns [Kowalski *et al.*, 1996, deCharms & Merzenich, 1998,

Theunissen & Doupe, 1998]. We will therefore analyze spatial segments in images and spectro-temporal segments in speech signals.

In the following we find independent components using the simultaneous approximate joint diagonalization of cumulant matrices algorithm (JADE) [Cardoso & Souloumiac, 1993]. This algorithm assumes that there are non-Gaussian independent sources. On the other hand the multiple decorrelation algorithm described in the previous section assumes that there are non-stationary sources. Both algorithms assume a stationary linear mixture.

5.4.1 Spatial basis of image intensities

ICA has often been used to find a linear basis for images. This may be useful for image coding since independent components are the linear representation with minimal redundancy and maximize therefore coding efficiency [Deco & Obradovic, 1996]. It has also been suggested that when applied to natural images the resulting independent bases resemble receptive fields observed in the visual cortex [Bell & Sejnowski, 1997, van Hateren & Ruderman, 1998]. The high kurtosis distributions and reduced redundancy (sparseness in space and across stimuli) correspond to the sparseness reported for V1 neurons [Olshausen & Field, 1996]. In fact minimum redundancy has been proposed for many years as an organizing principle of visual processing [Barlow, 1961a, Atick & Redlich, 1990].

The question arises, however, if a linear basis also expresses something about the generation process of images. It has been argued that independent sources can be considered as underlying causes and that an image patch represents a linear combination of those independent causes [Bell & Sejnowski, 1997]. Others have argued that occlusion is the predominant characteristic of image generation. Light in any image region stems from a single opaque object in contradiction with the concept of a linear superposition [Ruderman, 1998].

We maintain that an intrinsic property of natural signals is non-stationarity. If that is correct, and image patches are in fact a linear combination of independent sources, ICA and our multiple decorrelation algorithm should give the same results. Otherwise one of the assumptions has to be dismissed, i.e., images are not a linear combination of independent sources, or the sources are stationary.†

---

† We consider the possibility of non-stationary independent components with long term Gaussian distribution to be unlikely.

PCA

MDA

ICA (JADE)

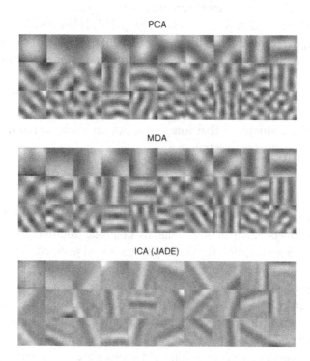

Figure 5.1. *Linear bases of natural images: Linear bases in a 30 dimensional sub-space for* 15×15 *image patches of natural images.*

For a set of natural images we computed the linear basis with ICA and our multiple decorrelation algorithm (MDA) as described in subsection 5.3.2. The results are compared to those of the well-known principal components algorithm.† These components are particularly relevant here since both algorithms (JADE and MDA) use principal component analysis (PCA) to reduce the dimensionality of the problem as a first step of the processing.

Figure 5.1 shows the three basis sets obtained for the natural images used in [Bell & Sejnowski, 1997]. A total of 15842 image patches of 15×15 pixels were used as input. The bases were computed in the subspace of the first 30 principal components. Separate correlations for each image were computed for MDA. We see that components obtained using non-stationarity are not much different from the principal components and differ quite considerably from the independent components.

† In subsection 5.3.2 the vectors in U with the largest eigenvalues.

The independent components reported here vary also from the components obtained in [Bell & Sejnowski, 1997]. This is because in that work specific higher order statistics are used to find the linear components, while JADE makes no particular assumption on the statistics of the components other than non-Gaussianity.

In summary, we conclude that while independent components for images may be useful for coding and for a compact representation of the data, the assumption that image patches are linear combinations of independent causes is questionable.

5.4.2 Spectro-temporal basis of speech powers

The situation is quite different for sounds. It is well known that the signal *powers* of independent acoustic signals combine additively. The linear superposition assumption for signal powers is well justified. The question is whether there are independent components and if these components are non-stationary.

In section 5.5 we will consider the case in which there are multiple sound sources in a reverberant environment and one makes multiple observations of those sources by using multiple microphones. In that case it is reasonable to assume that the sources are independent and the basic physics of acoustics indicates that *amplitudes* combine additively (barring nonlinear phenomena in the microphones and amplifiers). The difficulty there however is that the linear combination is convolutive rather than instantaneous.

In this section we want to analyze the statistical properties of the *powers* of a *single source*, in particular for speech signals. We are interested in the frequency and time properties of signal powers. We will therefore look for a basis that contains spectral as well as temporal information. Guided by what is known of auditory perception we compute the frequency components on a Bark scale for short consecutive time intervals [Pinter, 1996]. For computational reasons we must limit the number of bands and neighboring time slices used. We choose to find a basis for a segment of 21 Bark scale bands and 8 neighboring time slices corresponding to 128 ms of signal between 0 and 4 kHz.† A set of 7808 such spectro-temporal segments were sampled from a 200 s recording of clean speech of a female speaker with signal to noise ratios of at least 30 dB. Figure 5.2 shows the results obtained for a subspace of 15 components.

---

† We used half overlapping windows of 256 samples such that for an 8 kHz signal neighboring time slices are 16 ms apart.

"We had a barbecue over the weekend at my house."

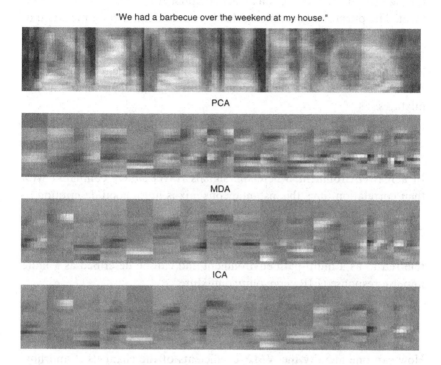

PCA

MDA

ICA

Figure 5.2. *Spectro-temporal linear basis representation of speech:* One pixel in the horizontal direction corresponds to 16 ms. In the vertical direction 21 Bark scale power bands are displayed. The upper diagram shows the log-powers for a 2.5 s segment of the 200 s recording used to compute the different linear bases. The three lower diagrams show three sets of 15 linear basis components for 21 × 8 spectro-temporal segments of the speech powers. The sets correspond to PCA, MDA, and ICA respectively. Note that these are not log-powers, hence the smaller contribution of the high frequencies as compared to the log-power plot on top.

One can see that the components obtained with MDA are quite similar to the result of ICA and differ considerably from the principal components.

From this we conclude that speech powers can, in fact, be thought of as a linear combination of non-stationary independent components. The relevance of this result for auditory receptive fields should not be over-emphasized, however. The linear superposition model applies to speech powers, while it is generally believed that auditory sensitivity scales with the logarithm of power. In that case a linear superposition is no longer correct.

These results were interesting from a theoretical point of view. The following section concentrates on an actual application in a realistic environment. The purpose of presenting this here is to demonstrate the strength of these second order methods in the case that the non-stationarity, independence, and linear superposition assumptions are strictly met. In a real acoustic environment however the mixing problem is more complicated as we have to consider convolutive rather than instantaneous mixtures.

5.5 Convolutive source separation of non-stationary signals

In a real environment, where the signals travel slowly compared with their correlation time, the instantaneous mix is not a good description of the linear superposition. The signals arrive at the different sensors with different time delays. In fact, the signals may be reflected at boundaries and arrive with multiple delays at a particular sensor. This scenario is referred to as a multi-path environment and can be described as a finite impulse response (FIR) convolutive mixture,

$$\mathbf{x}(t) = \sum_{\tau=0}^{P} A(\tau)\mathbf{s}(t - \tau). \qquad (5.29)$$

How can one identify the NMP coefficients of the channels A and how can one find an estimate $\hat{\mathbf{s}}(t)$ for the unknown sources? This situation is considerably more complicated than in the previous sections as one has now a matrix of filters rather than a matrix of scalars. Even once the channel has been identified, inverting it is a more difficult task as in principle the inverse should be a recursive, and therefore potentially an unstable, infinite impulse response (IIR) filter.

Alternatively one may formulate an FIR inverse model W,

$$\hat{\mathbf{s}}(t) = \sum_{\tau=0}^{Q} W(\tau)\mathbf{x}(t - \tau), \qquad (5.30)$$

and try to estimate W such that the model sources $\hat{\mathbf{s}} = [\hat{s}_1(t), ..., \hat{s}_M(t)]^\mathsf{T}$ are statistically independent. Since any convolution of the individual model sources will keep the sources statistically independent this criterion specifies $\hat{\mathbf{s}}$ only up to arbitrary convolutions.

In order to simplify the notation and concentrate the discussion on the difficulties stemming from the convolution we have ignored additive noise in this section. A complete treatment including additive noise can be found in [Parra & Spence, 2000a].

5.5.1 Cross-correlations, circular and linear convolution

First consider the cross-correlations $R_\mathbf{x}(t, t + \tau) = \langle \mathbf{x}(t)\mathbf{x}(t + \tau)^\mathsf{T} \rangle$. For stationary signals the absolute time does not matter and the correlations depend on the relative time, i.e., $R_\mathbf{x}(t, t + \tau) = R_\mathbf{x}(\tau)$. Denote by $R_\mathbf{x}(z)$ the z-transforms of $R_\mathbf{x}(\tau)$. We can then write

$$R_\mathbf{x}(z) = A(z)\Lambda_s(z)A(z)^H, \tag{5.31}$$

where $A(z)$ represents the matrix of z-transforms of the FIR filters $A(\tau)$, and $\Lambda_s(z)$ are the z-transform of the auto-correlation of the sources, which again is diagonal due to the independence assumptions.

For practical purposes we have to restrict ourselves to a limited number of sampling points of z. Naturally we will take T equidistant samples on the unit circle such that we can use the discrete Fourier transform (DFT). For periodic signals the DFT allows us to express circular convolutions as products such as that in (5.31). However, in (5.29) and (5.30) we assumed linear convolutions. A linear convolution can be approximated by a circular convolution if $P \ll T$ and we can write

$$\mathbf{x}(\omega, t) \approx A(\omega)\mathbf{s}(\omega, t), \text{ for } P \ll T, \tag{5.32}$$

where $\mathbf{x}(\omega, t)$ represents the DFT of the frame of size T starting at t, $[\mathbf{x}(t), ..., \mathbf{x}(t + T)]$, and is given by $\mathbf{x}(\omega, t) = \sum_{\tau=0}^{T-1} e^{-i2\pi\omega\tau}\mathbf{x}(t + \tau)$ and corresponding expressions for $\mathbf{s}(\omega, t)$, $A(\omega)$, and $W(\omega)$. In the following the time and frequency domain are identified by their argument τ or ω.

For non-stationary signals the cross-correlation will be time dependent. Estimating the cross-correlation at the desired resolution of $1/T$ is difficult if the stationarity time of the signal is in the order of magnitude of T or smaller. We are content, however, with any cross-correlation estimate which gives a diagonal result for the source signals. One such sample average is

$$\hat{R}_\mathbf{x}(\omega, t) = \frac{1}{L} \sum_{n=0}^{L-1} \mathbf{x}(\omega, t + nT)\mathbf{x}^H(\omega, t + nT). \tag{5.33}$$

We can then write for such averages

$$\hat{R}_\mathbf{x}(\omega, t) \approx A(\omega)\Lambda_s(\omega, t)A^H(\omega). \tag{5.34}$$

If L is sufficiently large we can assume that $\Lambda_s(\omega, t)$ can be modeled as diagonal again due to the independence assumption. For equations (5.34) to be linearly independent for different times t it will be necessary that $\Lambda_s(\omega, t)$ changes over time for a given frequency, i.e., the signals are non-stationary.

5.5.2 Backward model

Given a forward model A it is not guaranteed that we can find a stable inverse. In the two dimensional square case the inverse channel is easily determined from the forward model [Weinstein *et al.*, 1993, Thi & Jutten, 1995]. However it is not apparent how to compute a stable inversion for arbitrary dimensions. Therefore we prefer to directly estimate a stable multi-path backward FIR model such as (5.30).

From the condition for statistical independence of the model sources $\hat{s}$ it follows that their cross-power spectrum is diagonal at all times,

$$\Lambda_s(\omega, t) = W(\omega)\hat{R}_x(\omega, t)W^H(\omega). \tag{5.35}$$

In order to obtain independent conditions for every time t_k we have to choose averaging periods for $\hat{R}_x(\omega, t_k)$ that will lead to sufficiently different second order statistics. If we set $t_k = kTL$, we obtain non-overlapping averaging periods. Overlapping averaging times could have been chosen if the signals had varied sufficiently quickly.

We again compute an LS estimate of a multi-path channel W that satisfies these equations for K times simultaneously.

$$E(\omega, t_k) = W(\omega)\hat{R}_x(\omega, t_k)W^H(\omega) - \Lambda_s(\omega, t_k),$$

$$\hat{W}, \hat{\Lambda}_s(..) = \arg \min_{\substack{W, \Lambda_s(..) \\ W(\tau) = 0, \tau > Q, \\ W_{ii}(\omega) = 1}} \sum_{\omega=1}^{T}\sum_{k=1}^{K} \|E(\omega, t_k)\|^2. \tag{5.36}$$

The convolution ambiguity is resolved here by fixing the diagonal terms to the unit filter. Alternatively one can also place constant time delays in the diagonal filters which is required under some microphone and user configurations [Yen & Zhao, 1999]. Note also the additional time domain constraint on the filter size Q relative to the frame size T. This condition can be satisfied by choosing short filters or alternatively larger frame sizes T. Up to that constraint it would seem the various frequencies $\omega = 1, ..., T$ represent independent problems. However, the solutions $W(\omega)$ are restricted to those filters that have zero time response for $\tau > Q \ll T$. Effectively we are parameterizing TMN filter coefficients in $W(\omega)$ with QMN parameters $W(\tau)$. Due to this constraint we are forced to use a gradient algorithm to find the LS solutions and can no longer use analytic solutions as in the instantaneous mixture case. We will first compute the gradients with respect to the complex valued filter coefficients $W(\omega)$ and discuss their projections onto the subspace of permissible solutions in the following subsection. The gradients† of the LS cost in (5.36) are

$$\frac{\partial J}{\partial W^*(\omega)} = 2 \sum_{k=1}^{K} E(\omega, t_k) W(\omega) \bar{R}_{\mathbf{x}}(\omega, t_k). \tag{5.37}$$

From this we can find the minimum with respect to $W(\omega)$ with a constrained gradient descent algorithm. The optimal $\Lambda_s(\omega, t_k)$ for given $W(\omega)$ at every gradient step can be computed explicitly by setting the gradient with respect to $\Lambda_s^*(\omega, t_k)$ to zero, which yields $\hat{\Lambda}_s(\omega, t_k) = $ diag $\left(W(\omega)\hat{R}_{\mathbf{x}}(\omega, t_k)W^{\mathsf{T}}(\omega) \right)$.

The algorithm described so far uses all of the data to be filtered in order to find the optimal separating filter matrix. Only after that can the data be filtered. In many realistic scenarios an on-line algorithm is required, whereby the filter is immediately applied to the data and relatively little data can be stored. An efficient on-line version of the batch gradient algorithm presented here is given in [Parra & Spence, 2000b]. Though a more rigorous derivation can be given it basically amounts to removing the sum over times t_k. This converts the exact gradient into a stochastic gradient with updates $\Delta_{t_k} W(\omega)$ given by

$$\Delta_{t_k} W(\omega) = 2\mu(\omega, t_k)E(\omega, t_k)W(\omega)\hat{R}_{\mathbf{x}}(\omega, t_k). \tag{5.38}$$

The current cross-power spectrum $\hat{R}_{\mathbf{x}}(\omega, t_k)$ is estimated as a running average. In order to improve the convergence speed of the on-line algorithm we propose in [Parra & Spence, 2000b] a variable learning rate $\mu(\omega, t_k)$, which is motivated by second derivatives of the cost function.

$$\mu(t, \omega)^{-1} = \sum_{i,j} \frac{\partial^2 \|E(t, \omega)\|^2}{\partial W_{ij}^*(\omega)\partial W_{ij}(\omega)} = 2\|W(\omega)\hat{R}_{\mathbf{x}}(t, \omega)\|^2. \tag{5.39}$$

This amounts to an adaptive power normalization in each frequency bin. In our experiments the resulting updates were stable and converged after processing only a few seconds of data.

5.5.3 *Permutations and constraints*

Note that arbitrary permutations of the coordinates for each frequency ω will lead to the same error $E(\omega, t_k)$. Therefore the total cost will not

---

† For any real valued function $f(\mathbf{z})$ of a complex valued variable $\mathbf{z}$ the gradients with respect to the real and imaginary parts are obtained by taking derivatives formally with respect to the conjugate quantities $\mathbf{z}^*$, ignoring the non-conjugate occurrences of $\mathbf{z}$, i.e., $\frac{\partial f(\mathbf{z})}{\partial \Re(\mathbf{z})} + i\frac{\partial f(\mathbf{z})}{\partial \Im(\mathbf{z})} = 2\frac{\partial f(\mathbf{z})}{\partial \mathbf{z}^*}$ [Brandwood, 1983, Jänich, 1977].

change if we choose a different permutation of the solutions for each frequency ω. This seems to be a serious problem since only consistent permutations for all frequencies will correctly reconstruct the sources.

Arbitrary permutations, however, will not satisfy the condition on the length of the filter, $W(\tau) = 0$ for $\tau > Q \ll T$. Effectively, requiring zero coefficients for elements with $\tau > Q$ will restrict the solutions to be continuous or 'smooth' in the frequency domain, e.g., if $T/Q = 8$ the resulting DFT corresponds to a convolved version of the coefficients with a sinc function eight times wider than the sampling rate.

We can enforce the filter size constraint by projecting the unconstrained gradients (5.37) onto the subspace of permissible solutions. The proper projection is implemented by transforming the gradient into the time domain, zeroing all components with $\tau > Q$, and transforming back to the frequency domain. The unit gain constraint on diagonal filters is enforced by holding the filter coefficient constant at $W_{ii}(\omega) = 1$.

The constraint on filter size Q versus frequency resolution $1/T$ links the otherwise independent frequencies, and picks a particular permutation at each frequency. In addition, it is a necessary condition for equations (5.35) to hold to a good approximation. Note also that it does not limit the actual filter size, as in principle one can choose an appropriately large frame size T for any given Q.

As we will see in the next subsection the current continuity condition on the filters gives acceptable performance in a variety of configurations. More recently however we have established that this constraint in fact may not be appropriate for all circumstances (see also work by [Ikram & Morgan, 2000]). In principle, there is no theoretical argument why smooth filters will give the appropriate separation filters. In fact evidence to the contrary may exist [Liavas & Regalia, 1998]. Selecting appropriate permutations remains a subject of current research.

5.5.4 Separation performance in real room environments

We have applied the algorithm of the previous section in a variety of situations. The following performance results are given as the ratio between the power of the signals and the power of the remaining cross-talk, which is commonly referred to as the Signal to Interference Ratio (SIR). The separation performance varies depending on the particular configuration. We obtained an improvement of the SIR of anywhere between 0 and 18 dB. We studied the dependence on the type and number of micro-

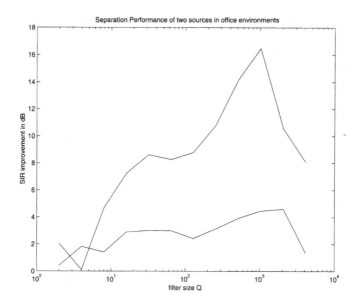

Figure 5.3. **Separation in real room:** *Performance for two speakers recorded with two microphones in two different office environments as a function of separation filter size Q and T/Q = 8. Upper curve: uni-directional microphones in a 3 m × 3.6 m × 2.3 m room, 30 s recordings at 8 KHz, 15 s alternating and 15 s simultaneous speech. Lower curve: 10 s simultaneous speech recorded at 16 KHz in a 4.2 m × 5.5 m × 3.1 m room with omni-directional microphones.*

phones, the number of sources, the user and microphone locations, the size of the room, the size of the filter, and other algorithm parameters.

Results on publicly available signals are shown in Figure 5.3. The graph shows the results for varying filter sizes on the separation of two competing speakers recorded with two microphones. The improvement in SIR can be as high as 16 dB for recordings obtained in an office room using uni-directional (cardioid) microphones (upper curve). Separating two speakers from the recordings in a second room with omni-directional microphones seems more challenging (lower curve).† As expected, the performance initially increases with increasing filter size, since the inverse of the room can be modeled more accurately. However, larger filters may require more training data, and so the performance eventually decreases given the constant amount of data.

We observed in further experiments that separation works better in

† The data for the first example is available from [Parra, 1998b] and that for the second example from [Schoebben, 1998].

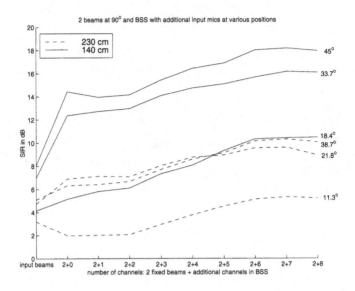

Figure 5.4. *Improvement with increased number of microphones: Performance for the separation of two sources as the number of microphones increases. Broadside and end-fire beams were constructed as two input channels. Besides those a variable number of the microphones were used as additional input channels. The recordings where performed in a moderately reverberant room 422 cm × 372 cm.*

large conference rooms than in small office rooms with stronger reflecting walls, most likely due to the increased reverberation. This was confirmed with simulated environments of varying size [Parra & Spence, 2000a].

The SIRs in Figure 5.3 do not change smoothly, which may be explained by the fact that the algorithm is optimizing multiple decorrelations rather than the SIR. Also, the gradient algorithm may be reaching different local minima of the diagonalization criterion.

Another interesting question is how the performance improves if we use additional microphones, given a constant number of sources. Figure 5.4 shows the performance in separating two simultaneous speakers using a variable number of microphones. In this experiment we used eight cardioid condenser microphones arranged as an equidistant linear array of about 65 cm length. The results are compared to the SIR of broadside and end-fire beams constructed using all eight microphones. While one user is at about 230 cm distance directly at broadside the other user is located at different angles relative to the broadside and at different distances from the array. The data was sampled at 16 kHz with 10 s for training and 10 s for testing and we used $K = 5, Q = 1024, T = 4092$.

Finally we note that a C implementation of this algorithm for two inputs and two sources runs in real time on a 155 MHz Intel Pentium processor at 8 kHz sampling rate and $T = 2048$.

6

Separation of non-stationary sources: algorithms and performance

Jean-François Cardoso

Dinh-Tuan Pham

This chapter shows how to take advantage of the non-stationarity of the source signals to achieve the blind separation of instantaneous mixtures. Off-line and on-line algorithms are developed based on the likelihood principle and the mutual information objective. The analysis of the achievable performance also reveals how non-stationarity and non-Gaussianity both contribute to the separability.

6.1 Introduction

This chapter addresses the problem of separating instantaneous mixtures of non-stationary sources. More to the point, we investigate how to *take advantage* of a possible non-stationarity of the sources in order to achieve separation.

When the source signals are modelled as i.i.d. (independently and identically distributed) sequences, blind separation can be achieved only by exploiting the non-Gaussianity of the sources. In this case, sources *must* be non-Gaussian to be separated; poor results are to be expected when the (marginal) distributions of source signals are too close to a Gaussian distribution. In contrast, the existence of a temporal structure in the source signals makes it possible to separate even Gaussian sources. Two types of temporal structures have been considered in the literature, each corresponding to breaking one 'i' in i.i.d. The first case is that of stationary signals with a temporal dependence, thus having a non-flat spectrum; these are 'non-white' or 'coloured' sequences. Identifiability is granted provided no two sources have proportional spectra (see e.g., [Pham & Garrat, 1993] or [Belouchrani *et al.*, 1997] for more elaborate statements and some algorithms) even when the signals are normally distributed. The second case is that of (possibly white) non-stationary

158

signals. This is the case considered in this chapter: we set out to achieve signal separation by exploiting non-stationarity. Previous contributions to this problem are briefly discussed in section 6.7, and it is addressed from a different perspective in Chapter 5.

The model The exposition is restricted to the simplest possible model able to capture the essence of the problem: instantaneous mixtures and temporally independent sources. Therefore, our working assumptions for deriving separation algorithms are an instantaneous observation model,

$$\mathbf{x}(t) = A\mathbf{s}(t), \tag{6.1}$$

where matrix A is an invertible $M \times M$ matrix, and temporally independent sources, that is, the variable $s_i(t)$, the ith component of $\mathbf{s}(t)$, is zero-mean and independent of $s_j(t')$ for $i \neq j$ or $t \neq t'$.

In most of this chapter, the sources are further modelled as Gaussian variables (only in section 6.6 will we consider a non-stationary and non-Gaussian model). Then the probability of a sequence $\mathbf{x}(1), \ldots, \mathbf{x}(N)$ of N observations is determined by specifying the value of A and the variances $\sigma_i^2(t)$ of $s_i(t)$ for $1 \leqslant i \leqslant M$ and $1 \leqslant t \leqslant N$. The (diagonal) covariance matrix of $\mathbf{s}(t)$ is denoted by

$$\Sigma^2(t) = \mathrm{diag}(\sigma_1^2(t), \ldots, \sigma_M^2(t))$$

where $\mathrm{diag}(\cdot, \ldots, \cdot)$ builds a diagonal matrix from its arguments.

A simple algorithm In order to introduce efficient methods to address the non-stationary problem, we first consider a simple on-line algorithm which, upon reception of a new sample $\mathbf{x}(t)$, updates a separating matrix $W(t)$ according to

$$W(t+1) = W(t) - \lambda G(t)W(t) \tag{6.2}$$

where λ is a small positive constant and $G(t)$ is an $M \times M$ matrix depending on $\mathbf{a}(t) = W\mathbf{x}(t)$. This is a well established technique combining the idea of (stochastic) relative gradient (see [Cardoso & Laheld, 1996] and [Amari, 1997]) and maximum likelihood estimation: in this technique, the entries of matrix $G(t)$ are computed as $G_{ij}(t) = \phi_{it}[a_i(t)]a_j(t) - \delta_{ij}$ where $a_i(t)$ denotes the ith component of $\mathbf{a}(t)$, δ_{ij} is the Kronecker symbol and $\phi_{it}(\cdot)$ is the 'score function' for $s_i(t)$, that is, the negative of the derivative of the hypothesized log probability density of $s_i(t)$. Thus, in the non-Gaussian stationary case, $\phi_{it}(\cdot)$ is a fixed nonlinear function. In contrast, in the non-Gaussian stationary case, the score function is linear but *time dependent*. More specifically, if the distribution of $s_i(t)$ is the Gaussian $\mathcal{N}(0, \sigma_i^2(t))$, then $\phi_{it}[s_i(t)] = s_i(t)/\sigma_i^2(t)$. Therefore, the classic approach (namely: a stochastic relative gradient ascent of the likelihood) leads to $G_{ij}(t) = a_i(t)a_j(t)/\sigma_i^2(t) - \delta_{ij}$ or, equivalently,

$$G(t) = \Sigma^{-2}(t)\mathbf{a}(t)\mathbf{a}(t)^{\mathsf{T}} - I \qquad (6.3)$$

where I denotes the identity matrix.

In the non-Gaussian stationary case, the score functions are time independent and can be replaced by rough estimates (based, for instance, on prior knowledge about the *type* of the source distributions: light-tailed, negative kurtosis, etc.). In the Gaussian non-stationary case, we can also use rough estimates for the score functions (which reduces to estimating the variances $\sigma_i^2(t)$) but it is not realistic to assume that these estimates are available in advance: in most practical situations, one will not know when a source is in a strong or in a weak regime. Therefore, the variance profiles $\sigma_i^2(t)$ must also be estimated from the data themselves. It is clear, however, that these profiles cannot be reliably estimated without some kind of prior assumptions since there are as many values of $\sigma_i^2(t)$ as data points. The most natural approach is to consider the *non-parametric* estimation approach by which $\sigma_i^2(t)$ is simply estimated as a smoothed version of $a_i^2(t)$ for the current value of W. This is equivalent to an implicit assumption of a 'slow' variation of the variance profiles. Typically, the variance profiles could be estimated on-line, for instance as the output of an exponential filter:

$$\hat{\sigma}_k^2(t) = \hat{\sigma}_k^2(t-1) + \rho\,[a_k^2(t) - a_k^2(t-1)] \qquad (6.4)$$

where ρ is a small positive learning step. It would then suffice to replace $\Sigma^2(t)$ in (6.3) with $\hat{\Sigma}^2(t) = \mathrm{diag}(\hat{\sigma}_1^2(t),\dots,\hat{\sigma}_M^2(t))$. Other low-pass filters than (6.4) could be used provided they produce positive output for any positive input. An important point, however, is that λ must be significantly smaller than ρ so that the estimated separating matrix W is nearly constant over a period of time long enough for the source variances and their estimates to vary significantly.

Outline of the chapter We will show how one can significantly improve on the basic algorithm defined by equations (6.2, 6.3, 6.4) by taking into account the specificities of the Gaussian non-stationary model and by considering batch (off-line) algorithms or some mixed approaches. We will also address the issues of achievable performance.

- Section 6.2 examines the Gaussian non-stationary likelihood; a sensible approximation to it yields efficient Newton-like algorithms in section 6.3.

- Section 6.4 considers a piecewise stationary model in which the likelihood objective takes the form of a joint diagonality criterion, yielding a very fast off-line separation algorithm.

- Section 6.5 introduces a Gaussian approximation to mutual information and shows how it relates to maximum likelihood.

- Section 6.6 deals with performance: we exhibit a 'super-efficiency' effect and compute the (asymptotically) achievable performance for non-Gaussian non-stationary sources. As a by-product, we find how non-stationarity and non-Gaussianity jointly govern blind separability.

6.2 Gaussian likelihood

In this section, we study the likelihood function and its derivatives in a Gaussian non-stationary model. The key point is a sensible approximation to the Hessian by which simple Newton-like algorithms can be efficiently implemented.

For a given batch of T data points, we define the *likelihood criterion* C_{ML} as the negative of the normalized log probability of the data set (here 'normalized' refers to the division by the data length):

$$C_{ML} = -\frac{1}{T} \log p[\mathbf{x}(1), \dots, \mathbf{x}(T)].$$

Thus the maximum likelihood estimation is equivalent to the minimization of C_{ML}, which is a function of the $M \times M$ matrix parameter of interest (the 'mixing matrix' A, or its inverse W) and of MT nuisance parameters (the variances of each source at each t).

In the Gaussian model, the log probability density of a source vector $\mathbf{s}(t)$ is $-\frac{1}{2} \sum_{k=1}^{M} \{s_k^2(t)/\sigma_k^2(t) + \log[2\pi\sigma_k^2(t)]\}$ which can also be written as $-\frac{1}{2}(\text{tr}[\Sigma^{-2}(t)\mathbf{s}(t)\mathbf{s}(t)^\mathsf{T}] + \log\det[2\pi\Sigma^2(t)])$ where tr denotes the trace. The probability density $f_{\mathbf{x}(t)}$ of $\mathbf{x}(t) = A\mathbf{s}(t)$ is simply related to the density $f_{\mathbf{s}(t)}$ of $\mathbf{s}(t)$ by $f_{\mathbf{x}(t)}(\mathbf{x}) = |\det A^{-1}| f_{\mathbf{s}(t)}(A^{-1}\mathbf{x}) = |\det W| f_{\mathbf{s}(t)}(W\mathbf{x})$. Therefore, the likelihood criterion C_{ML} is

$$C_{ML} = \frac{1}{T} \sum_{t=1}^{T} \frac{1}{2} \left\{ \text{tr}[\Sigma^{-2}(t)W\mathbf{x}(t)\mathbf{x}(t)^\mathsf{T}W^\mathsf{T}] \right.$$
$$\left. + \log\det[2\pi\Sigma^2(t)] \right\} - \log|\det W|. \qquad (6.5)$$

Derivatives of the likelihood objective The variation of the likelihood criterion with respect to the parameter of interest W is better expressed by considering, as in [Cardoso & Laheld, 1996] for instance, relative variations, that is, the neighbourhood of any given point W is parameterized as $(I + \mathcal{E})W$ and the $M \times M$ matrix $\mathcal{E}$ is the 'relative parameter'. The second order (in $\mathcal{E}$) expansion of the likelihood criterion around a given point W is denoted

$$C_{ML}(W + \mathcal{E}W) = C_{ML}(W) + D_1(\mathcal{E}) + \frac{1}{2}D_2(\mathcal{E}) + o(\|\mathcal{E}\|^2) \qquad (6.6)$$

where $D_1(\mathcal{E})$ is a linear form in $\mathcal{E}$ and $D_2(\mathcal{E})$ is a quadratic form in $\mathcal{E}$. These forms are readily found by reorganizing (6.5) and using $\log\det(I + \mathcal{E}) = \operatorname{tr}\mathcal{E} - \operatorname{tr}\mathcal{E}^2/2 + o(\|\mathcal{E}\|^2)$. The first order term takes the form $D_1(\mathcal{E}) = \operatorname{tr}[G(W)^{\mathsf{T}}\mathcal{E}]$ where the $M \times M$ matrix $G(W)$ is given entry-wise by

$$G_{ij}(W) = \frac{1}{T}\sum_{t=1}^{T}\frac{a_i(t)a_j(t)}{\sigma_i^2(t)} - \delta_{ij}. \qquad (6.7)$$

This matrix is called a *relative gradient* and is nothing but the average of $G(t)$ defined by equation (6.3). The quadratic form is found to be

$$D_2(\mathcal{E}) = \frac{1}{T}\sum_{t=1}^{T}\operatorname{tr}\left[\Sigma^{-2}(t)\mathcal{E}\mathbf{a}(t)\mathbf{a}(t)^{\mathsf{T}}\mathcal{E}^{\mathsf{T}}\right] + \operatorname{tr}\mathcal{E}^2. \qquad (6.8)$$

Note that both the linear and quadratic forms depend on W only via the values of $W\mathbf{x}(t) = \mathbf{a}(t)$. This is a consequence of the equivariant structure of the problem and of considering relative variations.

A block diagonal approximation to the Hessian An interesting approximation to the second order differential D_2 can be obtained as follows. Note that if $\Sigma(t)$ is a slowly varying function of t, the factor $\mathbf{a}(t)\mathbf{a}(t)^{\mathsf{T}}$ in (6.8) can be replaced by its expected value $E[\mathbf{a}(t)\mathbf{a}(t)^{\mathsf{T}}]$. The latter, in turn, can be approximated by $E[\mathbf{s}(t)\mathbf{s}(t)^{\mathsf{T}}] = \Sigma^2(t)$ when the recovered signals $\mathbf{a}(t)$ are close to the true signals $\mathbf{s}(t)$. Thus, we consider approximating D_2 by $\tilde{D}_2$ defined as

$$\tilde{D}_2(\mathcal{E}) = \frac{1}{T}\sum_{t=1}^{T}\operatorname{tr}[\Sigma^{-2}(t)\mathcal{E}\Sigma^2(t)\mathcal{E}^{\mathsf{T}}] + \operatorname{tr}\mathcal{E}^2. \qquad (6.9)$$

The matrix $\Sigma(t)$ being diagonal, we have $\left(\Sigma^{-2}(t)\mathcal{E}\Sigma^2(t)\right)_{ij} = \mathcal{E}_{ij}\sigma_j^2(t)/\sigma_i^2(t)$, so that

$$\tilde{D}_2(\mathcal{E}) = \sum_{1\leqslant i,j\leqslant M} \mathcal{E}_{ij}^2\Omega_{ij} + \mathcal{E}_{ij}\mathcal{E}_{ji} \tag{6.10}$$

where the positive quantities Ω_{ij} are defined by

$$\Omega_{ij} = \frac{1}{T}\sum_{t=1}^T \frac{\sigma_j^2(t)}{\sigma_i^2(t)}. \tag{6.11}$$

This approximation is very valuable because it introduces a *pairwise decoupling* in the second order expansion of the likelihood criterion: combining equations (6.6) and (6.10), the relative variation of $C_{ML}(W)$ around W is approximated by a sum over all the sources and a sum over all the pairs of sources:

$$C_{ML}((I+\mathcal{E})W) \approx C_{ML}(W) + \sum_{1\leqslant i\leqslant M} C_i(\mathcal{E}) + \sum_{1\leqslant i<j\leqslant M} C_{ij}(\mathcal{E}) \tag{6.12}$$

where the linear-quadratic forms $C_i(\mathcal{E})$ and $C_{ij}(\mathcal{E})$ are defined by

$$C_i(\mathcal{E}) = G_{ii}(W)\mathcal{E}_{ii} + \mathcal{E}_{ii}^2,$$

$$C_{ij}(\mathcal{E}) = \begin{bmatrix} G_{ij}(W) \\ G_{ji}(W) \end{bmatrix}^T \begin{bmatrix} \mathcal{E}_{ij} \\ \mathcal{E}_{ji} \end{bmatrix} + \frac{1}{2}\begin{bmatrix} \mathcal{E}_{ij} \\ \mathcal{E}_{ji} \end{bmatrix}^T \begin{bmatrix} \Omega_{ij} & 1 \\ 1 & \Omega_{ji} \end{bmatrix}\begin{bmatrix} \mathcal{E}_{ij} \\ \mathcal{E}_{ji} \end{bmatrix}.$$

The expression for $C_i(\mathcal{E})$ stems from $C_i(\mathcal{E}) = G_{ii}\mathcal{E}_{ii} + \frac{1}{2}(\Omega_{ii} + 1)\mathcal{E}_{ii}^2 = G_{ii}\mathcal{E}_{ii} + \mathcal{E}_{ii}^2$, since $\Omega_{ii} = 1$. Note that the 2×2 matrix in the definition of $C_{ij}(\mathcal{E})$ is positive so long as the sequences $\sigma_j^2(t)$ and $\sigma_i^2(t)$ are not proportional. This is because the Cauchy-Schwarz inequality applied to the sequences $\{T^{-1/2}\sigma_i(t)/\sigma_j(t)\}$ and $\{T^{-1/2}\sigma_j(t)/\sigma_i(t)\}$ yields $\Omega_{ij}\Omega_{ji} > 1$.

6.3 Newton-like separation algorithms

The pairwise decoupling in equation (6.12) means that the relative Hessian of the (approximate) likelihood criterion is a block-diagonal matrix. Thus its inversion reduces to the inversion of 2×2 matrices: the Newton optimization technique can be implemented at low cost.

Off-line algorithm One step of the Newton technique consists in optimizing the second order expansion of the objective function. In our case, it means changing W into $(I+\mathcal{E})W$ with $\mathcal{E}$ minimizing the approximation (6.12). Thus we find that, at step n, the algorithm computes a new separating matrix $W^{(n+1)}$ from the previous $W^{(n)}$ according to

$$W^{(n+1)} = [I - H(W^{(n)})]W^{(n)} \tag{6.13}$$

where $H(W)$ is the matrix with entries $H_{ij}(W)$ given for $i \neq j$ by

$$\begin{bmatrix} H_{ij}(W) \\ H_{ji}(W) \end{bmatrix} = \begin{bmatrix} \Omega_{ij}(W) & 1 \\ 1 & \Omega_{ji}(W) \end{bmatrix}^{-1} \begin{bmatrix} G_{ij}(W) \\ G_{ji}(W) \end{bmatrix} \tag{6.14}$$

and by $H_{ii}(W) = 0$. The values of $G_{ij}(W)$ and $\Omega_{ij}(W)$ appearing in (6.14) are computed using (6.7) and (6.11), with the (unknown) values of $\sigma_i^2(t)$ replaced by estimates $\hat{\sigma}_i^2(t)$ which are obtained by smoothing (low-pass filtering) the sequences $\{a_i^2(t)\}$. It is only required, as in (6.4) for instance, that the low-pass filter guarantees the positiveness of $\hat{\sigma}_i^2(t)$ and has coefficients summing to 1.

Regarding the diagonal terms, since $\Omega_{ii}(W) = 1$, the Newton technique would lead us to choose

$$H_{ii}(W) = \frac{1}{2}G_{ii}(W) = \frac{1}{2T}\sum_t \left(a_i^2(t)/\hat{\sigma}_i^2(t)\right) - 1$$

but this is close to 0 since $\hat{\sigma}_i^2(t)$ is nothing but a smoothed version of $a_i^2(t)$. This is why we set $H_{ii}(W) = 0$ in the above algorithm. This is perfectly consistent with the current approach because the effect of the (i,i)th diagonal term of H is to change the scale of the ith recovered source. It would make sense to change this scale if it were known in advance; it does not make sense to change it when this scale is precisely estimated from the data themselves.

Scale invariance In the source separation model, scales are irrelevant because scale factors can be accounted for by scaling either the estimated source sequence or the corresponding column of A (or row of W). In this respect, it is interesting to investigate to what extent the separation *algorithms* themselves also are scale invariant.

Let us compare the effect of the updating rule (6.13) on $W^{(n)}$ with its effect on a rescaled version of it, that is, on $\tilde{W}^{(n)} = \Lambda W^{(n)}$ where Λ is some invertible diagonal matrix. It is readily checked that the mapping $W \to H(W)$ scales as

$$H(\Lambda W) = \Lambda H(W)\Lambda^{-1} \tag{6.15}$$

for any invertible matrix W and any invertible diagonal matrix Λ. Using this property, one finds that if $W^{(n)}$ is updated by (6.13) to $W^{(n+1)}$, then $\tilde{W}^{(n)} = \Lambda W^{(n)}$ is updated by (6.13) to $\tilde{W}^{(n+1)} = \Lambda W^{(n+1)}$. Therefore, any rescaling of the data is exactly preserved by the rules (6.13-6.14). In this sense, our algorithm is strongly scale invariant. This is not the case for the more straightforward relative gradient algorithm summarized by equations (6.2-6.3) because the relative gradient scales as $G(\Lambda W) = \Lambda^{-1}G(W)\Lambda$, which is to be compared with (6.15) which is of the form granting scale invariance.

The on-line version The batch algorithm (6.13-6.14) admits an on-line version in which the separating matrix is updated upon reception of each sample according to

$$W(t) = W(t-1) - \lambda H(t)W(t-1) \qquad (6.16)$$

where $H(t)$ is the matrix with the diagonal set to zero and off-diagonal elements given by

$$\begin{bmatrix} h_{ij}(t) \\ h_{ji}(t) \end{bmatrix} = \begin{bmatrix} \hat{\omega}_{ij}(t) & 1 \\ 1 & \hat{\omega}_{ji}(t) \end{bmatrix}^{-1} \begin{bmatrix} G_{ij}(t) \\ G_{ji}(t) \end{bmatrix}, \quad G_{ij}(t) = \frac{a_i(t)a_j(t)}{\hat{\sigma}_i^2(t)}. \qquad (6.17)$$

The 2×1 vector on the right hand side of (6.16) is the stochastic (relative) gradient, i.e., the instantaneous value of the summand in (6.7) with the variance profiles estimated on-line by (6.4). The values for the elements of the approximate Hessian are also estimated on-line as

$$\hat{\omega}_{ij}(t) = \hat{\omega}_{ij}(t-1) + \lambda[\hat{\sigma}_j^2(t)/\hat{\sigma}_i^2(t) - \hat{\omega}_{ij}(t-1)]. \qquad (6.18)$$

As already noted, the parameter λ should be much smaller than ρ.

As in the off-line version, we simply set $h_{ii}(t) = 0$ because the effect of the diagonal terms of $H(t)$ is to change the scale of $\hat{s}_i(t)$. By taking $h_{ii}(t) = 0$, we choose not to update W in the directions which change the scales of each output $\hat{s}_i(t)$, hence we choose not to try to control explicitly the scale of the outputs.

The strong scale invariance in the off-line algorithm also holds for the on-line version. However, the lack of explicit control of the scales may become a problem in applications if the system is always in learning mode since then a slow, continuous drift of the scales may accumulate. In such a case, one may wish to control the scales by setting $H_{ii}(t) = \alpha[\hat{s}_i^2(t) - 1]$ with $0 < \alpha \ll 1$ in order to drive gently to 1 the long term average variance of each estimated source signal.

Another remark is that the same learning step λ is used to update W in (6.16) and to update the elements of the Hessian in (6.18). Even though it is possible to choose different steps, using identical steps is suggested by a different derivation of the algorithm described in detail in [Pham & Cardoso, 2000b]. In this derivation of the algorithm, the same learning step does appear in (6.16) and (6.18).

6.4 Piecewise stationarity and joint diagonalization

In this section, we turn to a model of non-stationarity which is 'piecewise stationary' meaning that the variance profiles are modelled as being constant over subintervals. In this model, the likelihood criterion is directly connected to a joint diagonalization criterion for which an efficient optimization exists, as outlined below.

In the piecewise stationary model, the interval $[0, T]$ is divided into L consecutive subintervals $I_1, \ldots, I_L$ such that $\sigma_i^2(t) = \sigma_{i,l}^2$ for $t \in I_l$, for all $i = 1, \ldots, M$. Again, this is a working assumption, intended to capture *some* of the structure of the source sequences: the resulting estimation procedure is applicable to a much larger class of signals than piecewise stationary.

In this model the nuisance parameters are the diagonal matrices $\Sigma_l^2 = \mathrm{diag}(\sigma_{1,l}^2, \ldots, \sigma_{M,l}^2)$ for $1 \leqslant l \leqslant L$ and a sufficient statistic is the set $\hat{R}_1, \ldots, \hat{R}_L$ of sample covariance matrices:

$$\hat{R}_l = \frac{1}{\#I_l} \sum_{t \in I_l} \mathbf{x}(t)\mathbf{x}(t)^\mathsf{T}, \qquad 1 \leqslant l \leqslant L, \tag{6.19}$$

where $\#I_l$ denotes the number of samples in interval I_l. It is a simple matter to re-write the likelihood criterion (6.5) as

$$C_{ML} = \sum_{l=1}^{L} w_l D\{W \hat{R}_l W^\mathsf{T} \mid \Sigma_l^2\} + \text{Constant} \tag{6.20}$$

where $w_l = \#I_l / T$ is the proportion of data points in the lth subinterval and where $D\{R_a \mid R_b\}$ denotes the Kullback-Leibler divergence between two zero-mean M-variate normal densities, with covariance matrices R_a and R_b respectively. This divergence is

$$D\{R_a \mid R_b\} = \frac{1}{2}[\mathrm{tr}(R_b^{-1} R_a) - \log \det(R_b^{-1} R_a) - M]. \tag{6.21}$$

Since $W \hat{R}_l W^\mathsf{T}$ is no other than the sample covariance matrix of the output $\mathbf{a} = W\mathbf{x}$ computed over the lth subinterval, the likelihood criterion takes a simple meaning: it is a weighted measure of mismatch between the covariance matrices of the output and the corresponding covariance matrices of the sources, namely the diagonal matrices $\Sigma_1, \ldots, \Sigma_L$.

As already stressed, the variance of the sources cannot be expected to be known in advance: matrices $\Sigma_1, \ldots, \Sigma_L$ should be estimated from the data. The maximum likelihood estimate of Σ_l for a given value of W is the diagonal matrix which minimizes (6.20), that is, $\Sigma_l^2 = \mathrm{diag}(W \hat{R}_l W^\mathsf{T})$. After this optimization with respect to the nuisance parameters, the C_{ML} criterion depends only on the parameter of interest W and is equal, up to a constant term, to

$$C_{ML}^\star(W) = \sum_{l=1}^{L} w_l \, \mathrm{off}(W \hat{R}_l W^\mathsf{T}) \qquad (6.22)$$

where we define, for a positive matrix R, a measure of deviation from diagonality as

$$\mathrm{off}(R) = D\{R \mid \mathrm{diag} R\} \geqslant 0. \qquad (6.23)$$

The case of equality in (6.23) is when and only when R is diagonal.†

The likelihood in the piecewise stationary model leads to an objective function which is a criterion (6.22) of joint diagonality. This is similar, but not identical, to other joint diagonalization techniques previously reported for non-Gaussian sources in [Cardoso & Souloumiac, 1993] or for coloured processes in [Belouchrani *et al.*, 1997]. In these papers, the measure of diagonality is a quadratic criterion $\mathrm{off}(R) = \sum_{i \neq j} R_{ij}^2$. Such criteria are only approximately related to the likelihood [Cardoso, 1998a] and, in addition, are to be optimized under a decorrelation constraint. As explained in [Cardoso, 1994], this decorrelation constraint bounds the performance and forbids the 'super-efficiency' effect discussed in section 6.6.

Algorithm The minimization of $C_{ML}^\star(W)$ *over all invertible matrices W* can be efficiently implemented thanks to a novel algorithm‡ which is now briefly described (for a full description and a proof of convergence, see the report and a forthcoming paper [Pham, 1999]).

The algorithm uses the classic Jacobi approach of operating by successive transformations, not necessarily orthogonal, on each pair of rows of W. If $W_{i\cdot}$ and $W_{j\cdot}$ denote a pair of rows of W, the algorithm changes

---

† This property can also be derived from the Hadamard inequality which states that $\det R \leqslant \det \mathrm{diag}\, R$ with equality if and only if R is diagonal, see, for example, [Cover & Thomas, 1991].

‡ In a different context, Flury & Gautschi [1986] have considered the problem of minimizing (6.22) but the matrix W is constrained to be orthogonal.

W by changing these rows according to

$$\begin{bmatrix} W_{i\cdot} \\ W_{j\cdot} \end{bmatrix} \leftarrow \begin{bmatrix} W_{i\cdot} \\ W_{j\cdot} \end{bmatrix} - \frac{2}{1 + \sqrt{1 - 4h_{ij}h_{ji}}} \begin{bmatrix} 0 & h_{ij} \\ h_{ji} & 0 \end{bmatrix} \begin{bmatrix} W_{i\cdot} \\ W_{j\cdot} \end{bmatrix}, \qquad (6.24)$$

the other rows being unchanged. The values of h_{ij} are computed as

$$\begin{bmatrix} h_{ij} \\ h_{ji} \end{bmatrix} = \begin{bmatrix} \omega_{ij} & 1 \\ 1 & \omega_{ji} \end{bmatrix}^{-1} \begin{bmatrix} g_{ij} \\ g_{ji} \end{bmatrix} \qquad (6.25)$$

with g_{ij} and ω_{ij} defined as

$$g_{ij} = \sum_{l=1}^{L} w_l \frac{(W \hat{R}_l W^{\mathsf{T}})_{ij}}{(W \hat{R}_l W^{\mathsf{T}})_{ii}}, \qquad \omega_{ij} = \sum_{l=1}^{L} w_l \frac{(W \hat{R}_l W^{\mathsf{T}})_{jj}}{(W \hat{R}_l W^{\mathsf{T}})_{ii}}. \qquad (6.26)$$

These expressions assume that $\sum_{l=1}^{L} w_l = 1$; if this is not the case, the weights must be re-normalized accordingly. The update (6.24) is successively applied to all the pairs of rows. The processing of all the $M(M-1)/2$ pairs is called a *sweep*. The algorithm consists in repeated sweeps until convergence is reached.

It can be shown that (6.24) always decreases the joint diagonality criterion unless $g_{ij} = g_{ji} = 0$. This is very significant since g_{ij} is, for $i \neq j$, nothing but the (i,j)th element of the relative gradient matrix of $C_{ML}^*(W)$. For a proof and a convergence analysis, see [Pham, 1999].

Note that the algorithm does not try to control explicitly the scales of the recovered sources (the criterion $C_{ML}^*(W)$ itself is scale-invariant) but rescaling could be done after convergence if desired. Numerical problems due to large imbalance in scales are not a concern thanks to the very fast convergence (see section 6.6) of the procedure. This algorithm can also be used to minimize the more general mutual information criterion (6.29), described below.

6.5 Likelihood and mutual information

Another approach to the blind source separation problem is as an independent component analysis: finding a transformation matrix W such that the components of $W\mathbf{x}(t)$ are as independent as possible. This section investigates the implementation of this idea in the Gaussian non-stationary case.

Gaussian mutual information In information theory, the mutual information between two random variables is defined as the Kullback-Leibler divergence between their joint distribution and the product of their marginal distributions. This definition extends to any number of random variables and has been proposed by Comon [1994] as an objective function for the separation of non-Gaussian sources. See also page 8. For a zero-mean Gaussian vector $\mathbf{a}$ with covariance matrix R, the mutual information takes a special form: the product of the marginal distributions is again a Gaussian distribution with covariance matrix $\text{diag}(R)$ so that the mutual information (between the elements) of $\mathbf{a}$ is $D\{R \mid \text{diag}(R)\} = \text{off}(R)$ according to definitions (6.21) and (6.23).

We are interested in the mutual information between the reconstructed *sequences* but, under our working assumptions, the observations are temporally independent so that the objective is just the sum over t of the mutual information for $\mathbf{a}(t) = W\mathbf{x}(t)$. Thus the (normalized) mutual information criterion is

$$\frac{1}{T} \sum_{t=1}^{T} \text{off}(W R(t) W^{\mathsf{T}}) \quad \text{where } R(t) = \text{E}[\mathbf{x}(t)\mathbf{x}(t)^{\mathsf{T}}]. \quad (6.27)$$

In practice, the covariance matrix $R(t)$ of $\mathbf{x}(t)$ is unknown and cannot be estimated reliably from the single data point $\mathbf{x}(t)$. An empirical version of (6.27) is obtained by replacing $R(t)$ with some non-parametric kernel estimate $\hat{R}(t)$. We propose to use

$$\hat{R}(t) = \frac{\sum_{\tau=1}^{T} k(\frac{t-\tau}{M})\mathbf{x}(\tau)\mathbf{x}(\tau)^{\mathsf{T}}}{\sum_{\tau=1}^{T} k(\frac{t-\tau}{M})} \quad (6.28)$$

where $k(\cdot)$ is a *positive* kernel function and M is a parameter controlling the window width. The denominator $\sum_{\tau=1}^{T} k(\frac{t-\tau}{M})$ ensures that the right hand side of (6.28) is a weighted average of $\mathbf{x}(\tau)\mathbf{x}(\tau)^{\mathsf{T}}$, but this factor actually has no effect because $\text{off}(\cdot)$ is scale-invariant. The separation procedure then consists of minimizing $\frac{1}{T} \sum_{t=1}^{T} \text{off}[W \hat{R}(t) W^{\mathsf{T}}]$ with respect to W. However, as $\hat{R}(t)$ should vary slowly with t (by the smoothing effect of the kernel), one may approximate this criterion by

$$C_{MI} = \frac{1}{L} \sum_{l=1}^{L} \text{off}[W \hat{R}(lT/L) W^{\mathsf{T}}] \quad (6.29)$$

with L being some integer not exceeding T. In practice L can be chosen much smaller than T, to reduce cost. There is little to gain by choosing a large L, since then the successive matrices $\hat{R}(lT/L)$ would be very similar: if the smoothing kernel has (say) unit width (for any reasonable definition of the width), then $\hat{R}(t)$ varies little over M samples. Thus, it is not computationally efficient to select L such that T/L is much smaller than M: typically, L should be of the same order as T/M.

Connection between likelihood and mutual information The criteria derived from maximum likelihood and minimum mutual information are very similar since both (6.22) and (6.29) measure the joint diagonality of a set of covariance matrices. In fact, the latter covers the former as a special case (at least when the subintervals T_l have the same length) by using a rectangular kernel k.

It is not a coincidence that the two approaches lead to similar criteria. This relationship can be traced back to the general fact that a likelihood criterion (defined, as above, as the negative of the normalized log likelihood) is a sample estimate of the Kullback-Leibler divergence between the distribution of the data and the parameterized distributions of the model. In the stationary non-Gaussian case, it is similarly shown in [Cardoso, 1998a] that – after optimizing with respect to the nuisance parameters describing the distributions of the sources – the large sample limit of the likelihood criterion is the mutual information.

On-line versions of joint diagonalization algorithms We describe an on-line algorithm for the optimization of the mutual information criterion (6.29) which addresses two implementation issues: the storage of many covariance matrices and the cost of computing a joint diagonalization. This efficient on-line implementation can also be used for optimizing (6.22).

We propose to estimate $R(t)$ by a simple low-pass filter

$$\hat{R}(t) = \hat{R}(t-1) + \rho[\mathbf{x}(t)\mathbf{x}(t)^\mathsf{T} - \hat{R}(t-1)] \qquad (6.30)$$

where ρ is a positive number less than 1. It corresponds to using a one-sided exponential kernel function $k(\cdot)$ with a 'window width' $M = 1/\rho$. This estimate guarantees – as required – the non-negativity of matrices $\hat{R}(t)$. Also, it does not require storage of the past values $\mathbf{x}(t')$ for $t' < t$.

In the off-line version (6.29) of the mutual information criterion, the L matrices to be jointly diagonalized are obtained by subsampling the sequence $\hat{R}(t)$ at a rate of one matrix every T/L samples. In the on-line version, we also store L covariance matrices, but they are rather obtained by picking up the value of $\hat{R}(t)$ every m samples. This integer m is a parameter of the on-line algorithm corresponding to the value of T/L in the off-line criterion (6.29). After m new samples have been received, the oldest covariance matrix is discarded and is replaced by the current value of $\hat{R}(t)$. The product mL should be large enough to allow the source variance to significantly vary over mL samples.

Regarding the joint diagonalization, the computational cost for on-line processing can also be reduced because one may perform only a *single* sweep of the joint diagonalization algorithm after a new covariance matrix becomes available (that is once after every m samples). There are at least two reasons for performing only a single sweep once every m samples. Firstly, it should be noted that in the joint approximate diagonalization algorithm, if one starts at the value of the separating matrix obtained at the previous step, then convergence is reached very quickly since the matrices to be diagonalized have not changed much from one time step to the next. Typically, one sweep of the algorithm is expected to be enough. Secondly, it is pointless in the on-line case to compute the absolute best joint diagonalizer with high accuracy since its value will change after the next block is received. In other words, because each sweep is very efficient (with respect to minimizing the criterion), going through more than one single sweep would be wasteful given the (stochastic) variability of the matrices to be diagonalized.

A final remark: after each block of m samples, one sweep is applied to the covariance matrices $\hat{R}(\tau)$ so that the matrices stored in memory are the *transformed* matrices $W\hat{R}(\tau)W^{\mathsf{T}}$ for the current estimate of W, that is, these matrices are estimates for the covariance matrices of the *source* signals. Hence, the following on-line algorithm:

(i) Once every sample:
- An estimate of $\mathbf{s}(t)$ is $\mathbf{a}(t) = W\mathbf{x}(t)$.
- Update $\hat{R}(t)$ according to (6.30).

(ii) Once every m samples:
- Store the current transformed covariance matrix $W\hat{R}(t)W^{\mathsf{T}}$ and discard the oldest one.
- Apply a single sweep of the joint approximate diagonalization algorithm to the L stored covariance matrices.

For the sake of clarity, we note that the single sweep in the last step listed above goes once through all the pairs of sources and amounts to computing an $M \times M$ transform matrix U. In this process, the stored covariance matrices are updated as $\hat{R}(\tau) \leftarrow U\hat{R}(\tau)U^{\mathsf{T}}$ and the transformation matrix is updated as $W \leftarrow UW$.

The piecewise stationary criterion (6.22) can be turned into a 'block on-line' algorithm along the same lines, the only difference being in the way the values of $\mathbf{x}(t)\mathbf{x}(t)^{\mathsf{T}}$ are accumulated into the estimate $\hat{R}(t)$. In this respect, the (implicit) rectangular filtering underlying this criterion offers the same memory-saving implementation as the exponential filtering (6.30): it is only needed to store the current estimates of $\hat{R}(t)$ and of W as well as the matrices to be diagonalized.

6.6 Performance and non-stationarity

Consistency Consistent estimation of all the parameters of the non-stationary model cannot be achieved without strong *a priori* information on the variance profiles $\sigma_i^2(t)$ (such as a *parametric model*) since there are as many data points as values of $\sigma_i^2(t)$ to be estimated. However, the variance profiles are *nuisance* parameters: we are not primarily interested in their estimation. More importantly, variance profiles need not be estimated consistently in order to get a consistent estimate of the parameter of interest (namely, the matrix A) because the stationary points of the estimation algorithm are characterized by the equations

$$\frac{1}{T} \sum_{t=1}^{T} \frac{a_i(t)a_j(t)}{\hat{\sigma}_i^2(t)} = 0 \quad (1 \leqslant i \neq j \leqslant M) \tag{6.31}$$

which express some form of (empirical) decorrelation between the reconstructed sources. Such equations will be satisfied asymptotically by the true sources, whether or not the estimated variance profiles $\hat{\sigma}_i^2(t)$ converge to the true profiles. This does not guarantee that the separating matrix W will converge to A^{-1} (modulo permutation and rescaling) but it is a necessary condition for this to happen and thus points to the possibility of achieving consistency.

Super-efficiency In the noise-free non-stationary setting there is room for 'super-efficiency', that is, for estimating the mixing matrix with an error which decreases faster than $1/\sqrt{T}$ as $T \to \infty$. Assume that the ith source is silent over a given interval $\mathcal{T}$, while the other sources are not always silent over this interval:

$$\forall t \in \mathcal{T} \; s_i(t) = 0 \quad \text{and} \quad \forall j \neq i \; \exists t \in \mathcal{T} \; s_j(t) \neq 0. \tag{6.32}$$

Then there exists a vector $\mathbf{b}_i$ such that $\mathbf{b}_i^{\mathsf{T}}\mathbf{x}(t) = 0$ for all t in this interval. Since this vector must be orthogonal to all the columns of A but the ith column, it is proportional to the ith row of A^{-1}. Thus, in the situation described by (6.32), the ith row of A^{-1} can be estimated *without* error from a finite number of samples.

The possibility of an error-free estimation is preserved when the data in interval $\mathcal{T}$ are summarized by the sample covariance matrix $\hat{R}_{\mathcal{T}} = (\#\mathcal{T})^{-1} \sum_{t \in \mathcal{T}} \mathbf{x}(t)\mathbf{x}(t)^{\mathsf{T}}$. This is because the vector $\mathbf{b}_i$ is also the unique (up to scale) solution of $\mathbf{b}_i^{\mathsf{T}} \hat{R}_{\mathcal{T}} \mathbf{b}_i = 0$. Note that the matrix $\hat{R}_{\mathcal{T}}$, although subject to estimation errors, always has its null space spanned by $\mathbf{b}_i$ and this is all that matters for finding the ith row of A^{-1} without error.

In practice, a situation where (6.32) holds is unlikely to occur (nor can we expect true noise-free instantaneous mixtures). But it is a guarantee of statistical effectiveness of an algorithm that it is capable of super-efficiency when such a possibility exists. In particular, minimizing the criterion $C_{ML}^{\star}$ yields super-efficient estimates (even though not immediately obvious from expression (6.22)) whenever it happens that a given source is silent over one of the subintervals.

Performance bounds for non-Gaussian non-stationary sources Statistical estimates are limited in performance by the Cramér-Rao (CR) bound. Examination of this bound often yields insights on the statistical problem at hand. In the particular case of source separation, we are not directly interested in bounding the variance of an estimate of A but rather in bounding (on the average) the achievable quality of separation. For this reason, rather than considering the deviation of an estimate of A from its ideal value, it is more appropriate to consider the deviation of WA from a non-mixing matrix. Specifically, for a given pair (i, j) of indices, we are more interested in the distribution of $(WA)_{ij}/(WA)_{ii}$ than in the distribution of W_{ij} because the magnitude of the former quantifies (in a scale invariant manner) how well source j is rejected in the estimate of source i.† Another specificity in developing a CR bound to the performance of source separation estimators is that the source model contains an infinite number of nuisance parameters.‡

In spite of these difficulties, the Cramér-Rao bound can still be obtained either as the inverse of a Fisher information matrix (computed as the covariance matrix of the 'relative score') or in a more direct manner. Computations are available in a technical note [Pham & Cardoso, 2000a]. The end result is that under an unbiasedness condition on the separating matrix W, the entries $(WA)_{ij}$ of WA when W is computed from T

---

† It is assumed here that the estimated sources appear in the correct order.
‡ Namely the variances $\sigma_i^2(t)$. The consequence of this is that the bound to be computed is likely to be a strict bound, not even attainable asymptotically by the maximum likelihood method, unless one *knew* the variances profiles.

samples satisfy

$$\mathrm{E}\frac{(WA)_{ij}^2}{(WA)_{ii}^2} \geqslant \frac{1}{N}\frac{\tilde{\omega}_{ji}}{\tilde{\omega}_{ij}\tilde{\omega}_{ji} - 1}\frac{\sum_{t=1}^T \mathrm{E}\,s_i^2(t)}{\sum_{t=1}^T \mathrm{E}\,s_j^2(t)}, \tag{6.33}$$

where, similarly to (6.11) or (6.18), the quantity $\tilde{\omega}_{ij}$ is defined as

$$\tilde{\omega}_{ij} = \frac{1}{N}\sum_{t=1}^T \mathrm{E}\,\phi_{it}^2[s_i(t)]\,\mathrm{E}\,s_j^2(t)\,\frac{\sum_{t=1}^T \mathrm{E}\,s_i^2(t)}{\sum_{t=1}^T \mathrm{E}\,s_j^2(t)} \tag{6.34}$$

with ϕ_{it} denoting, as usual, the score function for the ith source at time t. Our result is obtained *without* assuming Gaussian distributions, so ϕ_{it} is, in general, a nonlinear function. Thanks to this general expression, the CR bound reveals, as seen below, how non-Gaussianity and non-stationarity jointly contribute to separation.

Asymptotic stationarity and extended independence In order to understand the meaning of the CR bound, the meaning of $\tilde{\omega}_{ij}$ could be elucidated in the light of a statistical model for the variations in time of the distributions of the sources. In this chapter, however, we do not assume any specific model but rather impose some broad conditions on sequences of densities $p_{it}(\cdot)$. These conditions are expressed by the convergence of certain 'time averages' as encountered in stationary ergodic processes and are therefore referred to as 'asymptotic stationarity conditions'. For a sequence of random variables $\{X_t\}$ with distribution dependent on t, an operator $\overline{\mathrm{E}}$ is defined as

$$\overline{\mathrm{E}}X = \lim_{T\to\infty}\frac{1}{T}\sum_{t=1}^T \mathrm{E}\,X_t \tag{6.35}$$

if the limit exists. For our purpose, we specifically require that, for all $1 \leqslant i \neq j \leqslant M$, the averages $\overline{\mathrm{E}}\,s_i^2$, $\overline{\mathrm{E}}\,\phi_i^2(s_i)$ and $\overline{\mathrm{E}}[\phi_i^2(s_i)s_j^2]$ exist.

We also need to express not only that the sources are independent, but also that their distributions vary 'independently' in time. Specifically, we have found that simple results emerge if, for any given pair (i, j) of sources, it is further assumed that

$$\overline{\mathrm{E}}[\phi_i^2(s_i)s_j^2] = \overline{\mathrm{E}}[\phi_i^2(s_i)]\,\overline{\mathrm{E}}(s_j^2). \tag{6.36}$$

This condition must be understood as an 'extended independence' condition between the ith and jth sources, since it expresses that the sequence $\{\mathrm{E}\,\phi_i^2[s_i(t)]\}$ is 'uncorrelated' with the sequence $\{\mathrm{E}\,s_j^2(t)\}$ for $i \neq j$. The word 'uncorrelated' is quoted in the previous sentence because these sequences are not random: one should rather talk of a limiting empirical decorrelation between them. This 'empirical decorrelation' condition is expected to hold in many practical situations when the source signals originate from physically independent processes.

Asymptotic results Since we are essentially interested in the ability to separate source signals, the performance of the method should be measured according to this goal. If the source vector is estimated as $W\mathbf{x}$, then the ith source is estimated as $\sum_j (WA)_{ij} s_j$ and thus the average power contributed by the jth source to the estimated ith source is $|(WA)_{ij}|^2 \overline{\mathrm{E}}\, s_j^2$ while the average power contributed by the ith source itself to its estimate is $|(WA)_{ii}|^2 \overline{\mathrm{E}}\, s_i^2$. Hence we use the quantities

$$r_{ij} = T\mathrm{E}\left(\frac{(WA)_{ij}^2}{(WA)_{ii}^2}\right) \cdot \frac{\overline{\mathrm{E}}\, s_j^2}{\overline{\mathrm{E}}\, s_i^2} \tag{6.37}$$

as performance indices. The multiplication by T is introduced to compensate for the effect of sample size, since the variance of a statistical estimator decreases generally as the inverse of the sample size. As we are interested in large sample, we shall consider the limit of this index as $T \to \infty$ (the $\overline{\mathrm{E}}\, s_i^2$ are already defined as limits) and refer to it as the *asymptotic performance index*. The above definition is not only natural, it is also scale-invariant. Using the CR bound (6.33), the asymptotic performance indices are seen to be bounded from below by

$$\rho_{ij} = \frac{\bar{\omega}_{ji}}{\bar{\omega}_{ij}\bar{\omega}_{ji} - 1} \quad \text{where } \bar{\omega}_{ij} = \overline{\mathrm{E}}[\phi_i^2(s_i)s_j^2]\frac{\overline{\mathrm{E}}\, s_i^2}{\overline{\mathrm{E}}\, s_j^2}. \tag{6.38}$$

The asymptotic analysis simplifies greatly under the assumption (6.36) of 'extended independence' since $\bar{\omega}_{ij}$ then reduces to $\overline{\mathrm{E}}[\phi_i^2(s_i)]\overline{\mathrm{E}}\, s_i^2$ which depends only on the distribution of the ith source. Then, the CR bound, as expressed through ρ_{ij} takes the form

$$\rho_{ij} = \frac{R_j + 1}{R_i R_j + R_i + R_j} \tag{6.39}$$

where the nonlinear non-stationary moments R_i are defined as

$$R_i = \overline{\mathrm{E}}\, \phi_i^2(s_i)\overline{\mathrm{E}}\, s_i^2 - 1. \tag{6.40}$$

Thus, the inverse of ρ_{ij} admits a nice decomposition as

$$\rho_{ij}^{-1} = R_i + \frac{R_j}{R_j + 1} \tag{6.41}$$

which shows that good performance depends on having the highest possible values for R_i and R_j. Conversely, performance is at its worst (and blind separation of temporally independent sources becomes impossible) for a given pair (i, j) of sources when $R_i = R_j = 0$. It is thus important to understand the meaning of the R_i moments.

Non-stationarity and non-Gaussianity measures Since our CR bound was obtained for a non-Gaussian non-stationary model, the value of R_i gives a unifying answer to the problem of finding how the non-stationarity *and* the non-Gaussianity of a given source govern the achievable performance of source separation.

By simple algebraic manipulations, each R_i can be re-written as

$$R_i = \alpha_i + \beta_i + \alpha_i \beta_i \tag{6.42}$$

where α_i and β_i are measures of non-Gaussianity and of non-stationarity (respectively) for the ith source defined as follows.

The non-stationarity index β_i is defined as

$$\beta_i = (\overline{E}\,\sigma_i^2)(\overline{E}\,\sigma_i^{-2}) - 1 = \overline{E}\left(\frac{\sigma_i}{(\overline{E}\sigma_i^2)^{1/2}} - \frac{(\overline{E}\sigma_i^2)^{1/2}}{\sigma_i}\right)^2 \tag{6.43}$$

where σ_i should be understood as the sequence $\{\sigma_i(t)\}$ of 'random' variables which are actually deterministic. The last expression shows that $\beta_i > 0$ unless the variance of the ith source does not depend on t, in which case $\beta_i = 0$. Thus β_i actually is a measure of non-stationarity.

The non-Gaussianity index α_i for the ith source is defined as

$$\alpha_i = \frac{\overline{E}(\gamma_i\,\sigma_i^{-2})}{\overline{E}\,\sigma_i^{-2}} \quad \text{where} \quad \gamma_i = \gamma_{it} = E\,\phi_{it}^2[s_i(t)]\,E\,s_i^2(t) - 1. \tag{6.44}$$

This is a weighted average of γ_{it}, weighted by the reciprocal variances. The quantity γ_{it}, on the other hand, is the measure of non-Gaussianity for the density p_{it}, which customarily appears in performance analysis of source separation in the stationary non-Gaussian case (see e.g., [Pham & Garrat, 1997]). It is non-negative and equal to 0 only when p_{it} is a Gaussian distribution.

Therefore, in the case of *stationary non-Gaussian* sources, we have $\beta_i = 0$ and R_i reduces to $R_i = \alpha_i$ while the non-Gaussianity index itself reduces to $\alpha_i = E\,\phi_i^2(s_i)\,E\,s_i^2 - 1$; the results of Pham & Garrat [1997] for the stationary case are recovered with the usual measure of non-Gaussianity.

In the case of *non-stationary Gaussian* sources, the score function is

$\phi_{it}(s_i) = s_i/\sigma_{it}^2$ so that $\gamma_{it} = 0$ and $\alpha_i = 0$. Thus, R_i reduces to $R_i = \beta_i$. It is the particular way in which expression (6.43) measures the deviation of the variance sequence from being constant which quantifies to what extent non-stationarity can be exploited for blind separation.

When the sources are weakly non-Gaussian ($\alpha_i \ll 1$) and weakly non-stationary ($\beta_i \ll 1$), then $R_i \approx \alpha_i + \beta_i$, i.e., the benefits of non-Gaussianity and non-stationarity just *add up*. On the opposite side, for sources which are strongly non-stationary and non-Gaussian, we have $R_i \approx \alpha_i \beta_i$, i.e., the benefits of non-Gaussianity and non-stationarity *multiply* each other to a large value of R_i.

Some experiments We investigate the accuracy of the estimates when the model holds and compare it with our theoretical predictions.

The setting is as follows: $M = 3$ sources are drawn as $s_i(t) = a_i(t)n_i(t)$ where $n_i(t)$ is an i.i.d. Gaussian sequence and the deterministic amplitude is given by $a_i(t) = 1 + \alpha_i \cos(2\pi t/\tau_i + \phi_i)$. The parameter α_i can be varied between 0 (stationary case: $\beta_i = 0$) and 1 (large, potentially infinite, values of β_i). In our experiments, we take $[\alpha_1, \alpha_2, \alpha_3] = [0.4, 0.7, 0.9]$ and $[\tau_1, \tau_2, \tau_3] = [1000, 480, 300]$ for a sample size $T = 4000$. The phases ϕ_i are drawn randomly uniformly on $[0, 2\pi]$.

The rejection rates r_{ij} are evaluated empirically by averaging over $N_e = 1000$ experiments in which the amplitudes $a_i(t)$ are kept fixed and only the sequences $n_i(t)$ are changed for each realization of the source signals. The value of the mixing matrix is irrelevant since we only consider equivariant algorithms.

We report the results of the joint diagonalization algorithm when the block size B is varied. The number L of covariance matrices to be diagonalized is the largest integer smaller than T/B, meaning that an incomplete block (if any) is discarded. We have used block sizes of $B = 10, 20, 40, 80, 160$ samples.

Figure 6.1 is a matrix of $M \times M$ subplots, each subplot showing the variations of some quantities as a function of the block length B. For clarity, the common (logarithmic) scale of the horizontal axis is displayed only on the bottom plots. The off-diagonal (i, j)th subplot shows rejection rates r_{ij} and other quantities related to *pairs* of sources while on-diagonal subplots display quantities related to a single source.

For $i \neq j$, the solid line in the (i, j)th subplot shows the variations of r_{ij} as a function of B, as found in our numerical experiments. In all these plots, it is visible that increasingly large values of B induce too much smoothing and the performance degrades (the rejection rates

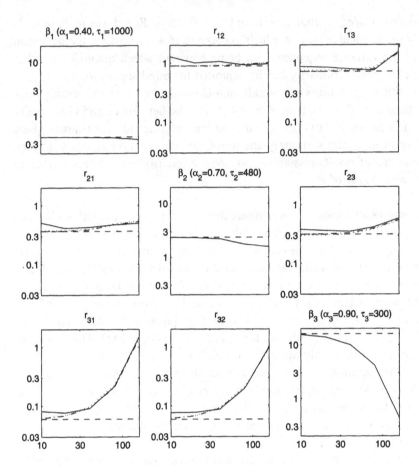

Figure 6.1. **Performance**: *Asymptotic rejection rates achieved by the joint diagonalization algorithm as a function of the block size. Comparison with the Cramér-Rao bound. See text for details.*

r_{ij} increase). However, B cannot be chosen too small either: variances cannot be reliably estimated over a small block, as is also seen on the plots by the increased values of ρ_{ij} for small values of B. However, the loss of accuracy with respect to the optimal block length B appears to be rather small even with blocks as narrow as $B = 10$. Thus, regarding the statistical performance, underestimating the 'optimal' block length seems harmless. There is however a *numerical* price to pay since the number of matrices to be jointly diagonalized is inversely proportional to the block length.

The off-diagonal subplots also show the values predicted by the asymptotic analysis. The dashed horizontal lines show the value of ρ_{ij} deduced from equations (6.33-6.34). This is the theoretical CR bound and does not depend on the block size. The dash-dotted lines show the values of ρ_{ij} computed from (6.38) except that the variance profiles $a_i^2(t)$ are replaced by the smoothed version used in the algorithm, i.e., by their average over a block of size B. Finally, the dotted lines use the same smoothed version of the variance profiles and also the approximation (6.36) or – equivalently – the expression (6.41). There is little difference between the dotted lines and the dash-dotted lines because condition (6.36) is well satisfied in this experiment. More importantly, it shows that the rejection rates are very well predicted by resorting to the asymptotic theory and replacing the various moments by their smoothed versions. This is due to the fact that the algorithm computes the maximum likelihood estimation based on a piecewise stationary model and that maximum likelihood estimation is known to be asymptotically efficient.

The ith on-diagonal subplot displays the non-stationarity index β_i. We show its value computed using the true variance (horizontal dashed line) and the (decreasing) values it takes when computed with the true variance smoothed over blocks of size B. The third source has the highest non-stationarity index and also is the best estimated: see the low values of ρ_{31} and ρ_{32} on the subplots on the same row.

6.7 Conclusions

Related works The algorithms of this chapter extend and improve on previous works. Matsuoka *et al.* [1995], without reference to maximum likelihood or mutual information, consider a criterion which is essentially the Gaussian mutual information. However, it is optimized by a stochastic gradient technique which is bound to be less efficient than the Newton-like technique. Souloumiac [1995] and Tsatsanis & Kweon [1998] consider a simple case of two subintervals of stationarity: then the joint diagonalization of two covariance matrices boils down to solving a generalized eigenvalue problem which can be solved exactly using a standard algorithm. The joint diagonalization algorithm described above can be seen as a generalization of this technique with much more flexibility.

Summary By examining the mutual information and the likelihood criterion in a non-parametric model of Gaussian non-stationarity, several ICA algorithms have been proposed. For block-oriented processing, a new joint diagonalization technique leads to an efficient algorithm (with a 'block on-line' variant) using second order statistics. For on-line ICA, a good approximation of the Hessian of the log-likelihood allows a Newton-like algorithm to be implemented at low cost. The achievable performance using non-stationarity is found via a Cramér-Rao bound which also reveals how non-stationarity and non-Gaussianity contribute to blind separation.

Acknowledgments

The authors would like to thank Prof. Christian Jutten for many stimulating discussions.

7

Blind source separation by sparse decomposition in a signal dictionary

M. Zibulevsky

B.A. Pearlmutter

P. Bofill

P. Kisilev

7.1 Introduction

In blind source separation an N channel sensor signal $\mathbf{x}(t)$ arises from M unknown scalar source signals $s_i(t)$, linearly mixed together by an unknown $N \times M$ matrix A, and possibly corrupted by additive noise $\mathbf{n}(t)$:

$$\mathbf{x}(t) = A\mathbf{s}(t) + \mathbf{n}(t). \tag{7.1}$$

We wish to estimate the mixing matrix A and the M-dimensional source signal $s(t)$. Many natural signals can be sparsely represented in a proper signal dictionary:

$$s_i(t) = \sum_{k=1}^{K} C_{ik}\, \varphi_k(t). \tag{7.2}$$

The scalar functions $\varphi_k(t)$ are called *atoms* or *elements* of the dictionary. These elements do not have to be linearly independent, and instead may form an overcomplete dictionary. Important examples are wavelet-related dictionaries (wavelet packets, stationary wavelets, *etc.*, see for example [Chen *et al.*, 1996, Mallat, 1998] and references therein), or learned dictionaries [Lewicki & Sejnowski, 2000, Lewicki & Olshausen, 1999, Olshausen & Field, 1997, Olshausen & Field, 1996]. Sparsity means that only a small number of the coefficients C_{ik} differ significantly from zero.

We suggest a two stage separation process. First, *a priori* selection of a possibly overcomplete signal dictionary in which the sources are assumed to be sparsely representable. Second, unmixing the sources by exploiting their sparse representability.

In the discrete time case $t = 1, 2, \ldots, T$ we use matrix notation. X is an $N \times T$ matrix, with the i-th component $x_i(t)$ of the sensor signal in row i, S is an $M \times T$ matrix with the signal $s_j(t)$ in row j, and Φ is a

$K \times T$ matrix with basis function $\varphi_k(t)$ in row k. Denoting the matrix of additive noise by $\tilde{N}$, equations (7.1) and (7.2) then take the following simple form:

$$X = AS + \tilde{N}, \qquad (7.3)$$

$$S = C\Phi. \qquad (7.4)$$

Combining them, we get the following when the noise is small:

$$X \approx AC\Phi.$$

Our goal therefore can be formulated as follows:

Given sensor signal matrix X and dictionary Φ, find a mixing matrix A and matrix of coefficients C such that $X \approx AC\Phi$ and C is as sparse as possible.

We should mention other problems of sparse representation studied in the literature. The basic problem is to sparsely represent a scalar signal in a given dictionary (see for example [Chen *et al.*, 1996] and references therein). Another problem is to adapt the dictionary to the given class of signals† [Lewicki & Sejnowski, 2000, Lewicki & Olshausen, 1999, Olshausen & Field, 1997]. This problem is shown to be equivalent to the problem of blind source separation, when the sources are sparse in time [Lee *et al.*, 1998, Lewicki & Sejnowski, 2000]. Our problem is different, but we will use and generalize some techniques presented in these works.

Overview of the chapter

We start the body of this chapter with some motivating examples, which demonstrate how sparsity helps to separate sources (Section 7.2). Then in section 7.3 we present a *clustering* approach, which is one of the most efficient ways to estimate the mixing matrix when the sources are sparse.

Overcomplete dictionary Section 7.4 gives the problem formulation in a probabilistic framework in the most general case of an overcomplete dictionary, when there can be more sources than mixtures, and presents the *maximum a posteriori* approach to its solution.

In section 7.5 we derive another objective function, which provides more robust computations when there are an equal number of sources and mixtures. Section 7.6 presents sequential source extraction using quadratic programming with non-convex quadratic constraints.

† Our dictionary Φ may be obtained in this way.

Non-overcomplete dictionary When the dictionary is non-overcomplete, computationally much faster solutions are possible. In section 7.7 we demonstrate high-quality separation of synthetically mixed musical sounds with a square mixing matrix.

Even when the number of sources is larger than the number of mixtures, we can estimate the mixing matrix beforehand by clustering, and then reconstruct the sources by a *shortest path decomposition*, as shown in section 7.8. Here we present examples of separation of up to six sound sources from two mixtures.

Exploiting multiscale representations In many cases, especially in wavelet-related decompositions, there are distinct groups of coefficients, in which sources have different sparsity properties. Section 7.9 shows how selection of the best groups of coefficients significantly improves the separation quality.

7.2 Separation of sparse signals

In this section we present two examples which demonstrate how sparsity of source signals in the time domain helps to separate them. Many real-world signals have sparse representations in a proper signal dictionary, but not in the time domain. The intuition here carries over to that situation, as shown in subsection 7.4.1.

Example: Two sources and two mixtures Two synthetic sources are shown in figure 7.1a,b. The first source has two non-zero samples, and the second has three. The mixtures, shown in figure 7.1(c,d), are less sparse: they have five non-zero samples each. One can use this observation to recover the sources. For example, we can express one of the sources as

$$\tilde{s}_i(t) = x_1(t) + \mu x_2(t)$$

and choose μ so as to minimize the number of non-zero samples $\|\tilde{s}_i\|_0$, i.e., the l_0 norm of s_i.

This objective function yields perfect separation. As shown in figure 7.2a, when μ is not optimal the second source interferes, and the total number of non-zero samples remains five. Only when the first source is recovered perfectly, as in figure 7.2b, does the number of non-zero samples drop to two, and the objective function achieve its minimum.

Note that the function $\|\tilde{s}_i\|_0$ is discontinuous and may be difficult to optimize. It is also very sensitive to noise: even a tiny bit of noise would

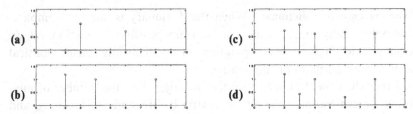

Figure 7.1. **Two sources and two mixtures:** *Sources (a and b) are sparse. Mixtures (c and d) are less sparse.*

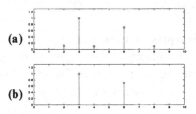

Figure 7.2. **(a) Imperfect separation:** *Since the second source is not completely removed, the total number of non-zero samples remains five.* **(b) Perfect separation:** *When the source is recovered perfectly, the number of non-zero samples drops to two and the objective function achieves its minimum.*

make all the samples non-zero. Fortunately in many cases the l_1 norm $\|\tilde{s}_i\|_1$ is a good substitute for this objective function. In this example, it too yields perfect separation.

Example: Three sources and two mixtures The signals are presented in figure 7.3. These sources have about 10% non-zero samples. The non-zero samples have random positions, and are zero-mean unit-variance Gaussian distributed in amplitude. figure 7.3 shows a scatter plot of the mixtures. The directions of the columns of the mixing matrix are clearly visible. Indeed, if only one source, say $s_1(t)$, were present, the sensor signals would look like

$$
\begin{aligned}
x_1(t) &= A_{11}s_1(t), \\
x_2(t) &= A_{21}s_1(t)
\end{aligned}
$$

and the points at the scatter plot of x_2 versus x_1 would belong to the straight line placed along the vector $[A_{11}, A_{21}]^T$. The same thing happens when all the sources are present but the samples are sparse: at each particular index where a sample of one source is large, there is a high probability that the corresponding samples of other sources are small, and

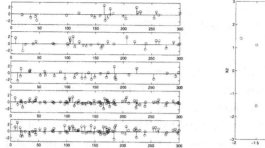 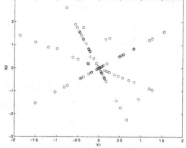

Figure 7.3. *Three sources and two mixtures: Left:* top three panels – sparse sources *(sparsity is 10%); bottom two panels – mixtures. Right: scatter plot of two mixtures x_1 versus x_2. Three distinguished directions, which correspond to the columns of the mixing matrix A, are visible.*

the point in the scatter plot still lies close to the mentioned straight line. This explains the appearance of dominant orientations at the scatter plot.

7.3 Clustering of data concentration directions

The phenomenon of data concentration along the directions of the mixing matrix columns can be used in clustering approaches to source separation [Pajunen *et al.*, 1996, Bofill & Zibulevsky, 2000b]. This works efficiently even if the number of sources is greater than the number of sensors. In order to determine orientations of data concentration, we project the data points onto the surface of a unit sphere† by normalizing corresponding vectors, and then apply a standard clustering algorithm. Our clustering procedure can be summarized as follows:

(i) in order to project data points onto the surface of a unit sphere, normalize the sensor data vectors at every particular time index k: $\mathbf{x}_k = \mathbf{x}_k/\|\mathbf{x}_k\|$. (Before normalization, it is reasonable to remove data points with a very small norm, since these very likely are noisy.);

(ii) move data points to a half-sphere, e.g., by forcing the sign of the first coordinate x_k^1 to be positive: IF $x_k^1 < 0$ THEN $\mathbf{x}_k = -\mathbf{x}_k$; (Without this operation each 'line' of data concentration would yield two clusters on opposite sides of the sphere.);

† One can also use weights, depending on the distance of a data point from the origin, because more distant points are more reliable.

(iii) determine cluster centres using some clustering algorithm; their coordinates will form the columns of the estimated mixing matrix $\tilde{A}$.

In computational examples below in this chapter we use *C-means* clustering [Bezdek, 1981] as implemented in the MATLAB Fuzzy Logic toolbox function FCM. We built also a modification of the C-means algorithm, which allows its input points to be weighted. The optimal choice of the weights, as a function of the distance of a data point from the origin, still requires further investigation. In section 7.8 we use also *potential-function* based clustering [Bofill & Zibulevsky, 2000b].

7.4 Probabilistic framework

In order to derive a maximum *a posteriori* solution, we consider the blind source separation problem in a probabilistic framework [Belouchrani & Cardoso, 1995, Pearlmutter & Parra, 1996]. Suppose that the coefficients C_{ik} in a source decomposition (7.4) are independent random variables with a probability density function (p.d.f.) of an exponential type

$$p_i(C_{ik}) \propto \exp -\beta_i h(C_{ik}). \tag{7.5}$$

This kind of distribution is widely used for modelling sparsity [Lewicki & Sejnowski, 2000, Olshausen & Field, 1997]. A reasonable choice of $h(c)$ may be

$$h(c) = |c|^{1/\gamma}, \qquad \gamma \geqslant 1, \tag{7.6}$$

or a smooth approximation thereof. Here we will use a family of convex smooth approximations to the absolute value,

$$h_1(c) = |c| - \log(1 + |c|), \tag{7.7}$$

$$h_\lambda(c) = \lambda h_1(c/\lambda), \tag{7.8}$$

with λ a proximity parameter: $h_\lambda(c) \to |c|$ as $\lambda \to 0^+$.

We also suppose *a priori* that the mixing matrix A is uniformly distributed over the range of interest, and that the noise $\mathbf{n}(t)$ in (7.3) is a spatially and temporally uncorrelated Gaussian process† with zero mean and variance σ^2.

---

† The assumption that the noise is white is for simplicity of exposition, and can be easily removed.

7.4.1 *Maximum a posteriori approach*

We wish to maximize the posterior probability

$$\max_{A,C} P(A, C|X) \propto \max_{A,C} P(X|A, C) P(A) P(C) \tag{7.9}$$

where $P(X|A, C)$ is the conditional probability of observing X given A and C. Taking into account (7.3), (7.4), and the white Gaussian noise, we have

$$P(X|A, C) \propto \prod_{i,t} \exp -\frac{(X_{it} - (AC\Phi)_{it})^2}{2\sigma^2}. \tag{7.10}$$

By the independence of the coefficients C_{jk} and (7.5), the prior p.d.f. of C is

$$P(C) \propto \prod_{j,k} \exp(-\beta_j h(C_{jk})). \tag{7.11}$$

If the prior p.d.f. $P(A)$ is uniform, it can be dropped† from (7.9). In this way we are left with the problem:

$$\max_{A,C} P(X|A, C) P(C). \tag{7.12}$$

By substituting (7.10) and (7.11) into (7.12), taking the logarithm, and inverting the sign, we obtain the following optimization problem:

$$\min_{A,C} \left\{ \frac{1}{2\sigma^2} \|AC\Phi - X\|_F^2 + \sum_{j,k} \beta_j h(C_{jk}) \right\}, \tag{7.13}$$

where $\|A\|_F = \sqrt{\sum_{i,j} A_{ij}^2}$ is the Frobenius matrix norm.

One can consider this objective as a generalization of [Olshausen & Field, 1997, Olshausen & Field, 1996] by incorporating the matrix Φ, or as a generalization of [Chen et al., 1996] by including the matrix A. One problem with such a formulation is that it can lead to the degenerate solution $C = 0$ and $A = \infty$. We can overcome this difficulty in various ways. The first approach is to force each row A_i of the mixing matrix A to be bounded in norm,

$$\|A_i\| \leqslant 1, \qquad i = 1, \ldots, N. \tag{7.14}$$

The second way is to restrict the norm of the rows C_j from below:

$$\|C_j\| \geqslant 1, \qquad j = 1, \ldots, M. \tag{7.15}$$

† Otherwise, if $P(A)$ is some other known function, we should use (7.9) directly.

A third way is to reestimate the parameters β_j based on the current values of C_j. For example, this can be done using sample variance as follows: for a given function $h(\cdot)$ in the distribution (7.5), express the variance of C_{jk} as a function $f_h(\beta)$. An estimate of β can be obtained by applying the corresponding inverse function to the sample variance,

$$\hat{\beta}_j = f_h^{-1}\left(K^{-1}\sum_k C_{jk}^2\right). \tag{7.16}$$

In particular, when $h(c) = |c|$, $\mathrm{var}(c) = 2\beta^{-2}$ and

$$\hat{\beta}_j = \frac{2}{\sqrt{K^{-1}\sum_k C_{jk}^2}}. \tag{7.17}$$

Substituting $h(\cdot)$ and $\hat{\beta}$ into (7.13), we obtain

$$\min_{A,C}\left\{\frac{1}{2\sigma^2}\|AC\Phi - X\|_F^2 + \sum_j \frac{2\sum_k |C_{jk}|}{\sqrt{K^{-1}\sum_k C_{jk}^2}}\right\}. \tag{7.18}$$

This objective function is invariant to a rescaling of the rows of C combined with a corresponding inverse rescaling of the columns of A.

7.4.2 Experiment: more sources than mixtures

This experiment demonstrates that sources which have very sparse representations can be separated almost perfectly, even when they are correlated and the number of samples is small.

We used the standard wavelet packet dictionary with the basic wavelet *symmlet-8*. When the signal length is 64 samples, this dictionary consists of 448 atoms, i.e., it is overcomplete by a factor of 7. Examples of atoms and their images in the time-frequency phase plane [Coifman & Wickerhauser, 1992, Mallat, 1998] are shown in figure 7.4. We used the ATOMIZER [Chen *et al.*, 1995] and WAVELAB [Buckheit *et al.*, 1995] MATLAB packages for fast multiplication by Φ and Φ^T.

We created three very sparse sources (figure 7.5a), each composed of only two or three atoms. The first two sources have significant cross-correlation, equal to 0.34, which makes separation difficult for conventional methods. Two synthetic sensor signals (figure 7.5b) were obtained as linear mixtures of the sources. In order to measure the accuracy of separation, we normalized the original sources with $\|S_j\|_2 = 1$, and the

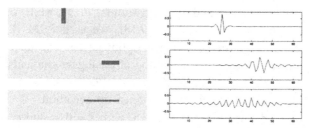

Figure 7.4. **Examples of atoms:** *time-frequency phase plane (left) and time plot (right).*

(a) Sources

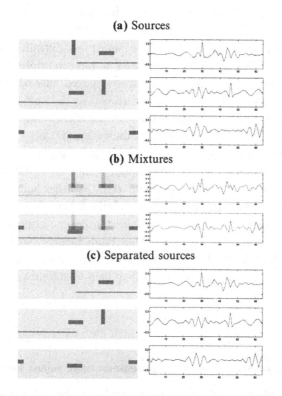

(b) Mixtures

(c) Separated sources

Figure 7.5. **Source separation with wavelets:** *(a) Sources, (b) mixtures, and (c) reconstructed sources, in both time-frequency phase plane (left) and time domain (right).*

estimated sources with $\|\tilde{S}_j\|_2 = 1$. The error was computed as

$$\text{Error} = \frac{\|\tilde{S}_j - S_j\|_2}{\|S_j\|_2} \cdot 100\%. \qquad (7.19)$$

We tested two methods with these data. The first method used the objective function (7.13) and the constraints (7.15), while the second method used the objective function (7.18). We used PBM [Ben-Tal & Zibulevsky, 1997] for the constrained optimization. The unconstrained optimization was done using the method of conjugate gradients, with the TOMLAB package [Holmstrom & Bjorkman, 1999]. The same tool was used by PBM for its internal unconstrained optimization.

We used $h_\lambda(\cdot)$ defined by (7.7) and (7.8) with $\lambda = 0.01$ and $\sigma^2 = 0.0001$ in the objective function. The resulting errors of the recovered sources were 0.09% and 0.02% by the first and the second methods, respectively. The estimated sources are shown in figure 7.5c. They are visually indistinguishable from the original sources in figure 7.5a.

It is important to recognize the computational difficulties of this approach. First, the objective functions seem to have multiple local minima. For this reason, reliable convergence was achieved only when the search started randomly within 10%–20% distance to the actual solution (in order to get such an initial guess one can use a clustering algorithm, as in [Pajunen *et al.*, 1996] or [Bofill & Zibulevsky, 2000b]).

Second, the method of conjugate gradients requires a few thousand iterations to converge, which takes about 5 min on a 300 MHz AMD K6-II even for this very small problem. (On the other hand, preliminary experiments with a truncated Newton method have been encouraging, and we anticipate that this will reduce the computational burden by an order of magnitude or more. Also Paul Tseng's block coordinate descent method (unpublished manuscript) may be appropriate.) Below we present a few other approaches which help to stabilize and accelerate the optimization.

7.5 Equal number of sources and sensors: more robust formulations

The main difficulty in a maximization problem like (7.13) is the bilinear term $AC\Phi$, which destroys the convexity of the objective function and makes convergence unstable when optimization starts far from the solution. In this section we consider more robust formulations for the case when the number of sensors is equal to the number of sources, $N = M$, and the mixing matrix is invertible, $W = A^{-1}$.

When the noise is small and the matrix A is far from singular, WX gives a reasonable estimate of the source signals S. Taking into account (7.4), we obtain a least squares term $\|C\Phi - WX\|_F^2$, so the separation objective may be written

$$\min_{W,C} \left\{ \frac{1}{2} \| C\Phi - WX \|_F^2 + \mu \sum_{j,k} \beta_j h(C_{jk}) \right\}. \tag{7.20}$$

We also need to add a constraint which enforces the non-singularity of W. For example, we can restrict its minimal singular value $r_{min}(W)$ from below,

$$r_{min}(W) \geqslant 1. \tag{7.21}$$

It can be shown that in the noiseless case, $\sigma \approx 0$, the problem (7.20)–(7.21) is equivalent to the maximum *a posteriori* formulation (7.13) with the constraint $\|A\|_2 \leqslant 1$. Another possibility for ensuring the non-singularity of W is to subtract $K \log |\det W|$ from the objective

$$\min_{W,C} \left\{ -K \log |\det W| + \frac{1}{2} \| C\Phi - WX \|_F^2 + \mu \sum_{j,k} \beta_j h(C_{jk}) \right\}, \tag{7.22}$$

which can be seen as a maximum likelihood term [Bell & Sejnowski, 1995, Pearlmutter & Parra, 1996].

When the noise is zero and Φ is the identity matrix, we can substitute $C = WX$ and obtain the BS Infomax objective [Bell & Sejnowski, 1995]

$$\min_W \left\{ -K \log |\det W| + \sum_{j,k} \beta_j h((WX)_{jk}) \right\}. \tag{7.23}$$

Experiment: equal numbers of sources and sensors We created two sparse sources (figure 7.6a) with strong cross-correlation of 0.52. Separation by minimization of the objective function (7.22) gave an error of 0.23%. Robust convergence was achieved when we started from random uniformly distributed points in C and W.

For comparison we tested the JADE [Cardoso, 1999a], FastICA [Hyvä-rinen, 1999a] and BS Infomax [Bell & Sejnowski, 1995, Amari *et al.*, 1996] algorithms on the same signals. All three codes were obtained from public web sites [Cardoso, 1999b, Hyvärinen, 1998b, Makeig, 1999] and were used with default setting of all parameters. The resulting relative errors (figure 7.7) confirm the significant superiority of the sparse decomposition approach.

This still takes a few thousand conjugate gradient steps to converge (about 5 min on a 300 MHz AMD K6-II). For comparison, the tuned

(a) Sources

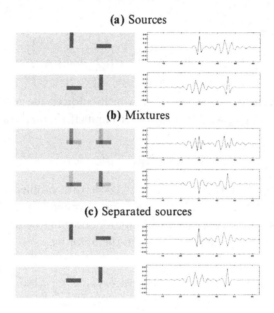

(b) Mixtures

(c) Separated sources

Figure 7.6. ***Equal number of sources & mixtures:*** *(a) Sources, (b) mixtures, and (c) reconstructed sources, in both time-frequency phase plane (left) and time domain (right).*

public implementations of JADE, FastICA and BS Infomax take only a few seconds. Below we consider some options for acceleration.

7.6 Sequential extraction of sources via quadratic programming

Let us consider finding the sparsest signal that can be obtained by a linear combination of the sensor signals $s = w^{\mathsf{T}} X$. By sparsity we mean the ability of the signal to be approximated by a linear combination of a small number of dictionary elements φ_k, as $s \approx c^{\mathsf{T}} \Phi$. This leads to the objective

$$\min_{w,c} \left\{ \frac{1}{2} \| c^{\mathsf{T}} \Phi - w^{\mathsf{T}} X \|_2^2 + \mu \sum_k h(c_k) \right\}, \qquad (7.24)$$

where the term $\sum_k h(c_k)$ may be considered a penalty for non-sparsity. In order to avoid the trivial solution of $w = 0$ and $c = 0$ we need to add a constraint that separates w from zero. It could be, for example,

$$\| w \|_2^2 \geqslant 1. \qquad (7.25)$$

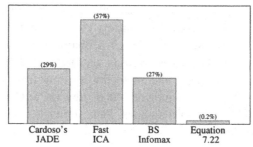

Figure 7.7. **Relative error:** *Percent relative error of separation of the artificial sparse sources recovered by JADE, Fast ICA, Bell-Sejnowski Infomax, and Equation (7.22).*

A similar constraint can be used as a tool to extract all the sources sequentially: the new separation vector w^j should have a component of unit norm in the subspace orthogonal to the previously extracted vectors $w^1, \ldots, w^{j-1}$,

$$\|(I - P^{j-1})w^j\|_2^2 \geqslant 1, \tag{7.26}$$

where P^{j-1} is an orthogonal projector onto Span$\{w^1, \ldots, w^{j-1}\}$.

When $h(c_k) = |c_k|$ we can use the standard substitution

$$c = c^+ - c^-, \quad c^+ \geqslant 0, \quad c^- \geqslant 0,$$

$$\hat{c} = \begin{pmatrix} c^+ \\ c^- \end{pmatrix} \quad \text{and} \quad \hat{\Phi} = \begin{pmatrix} \Phi \\ -\Phi \end{pmatrix}$$

that transforms (7.24) and (7.26) into the quadratic program

$$\min_{w, \hat{c}} \ \frac{1}{2} \|\hat{c}^\mathsf{T} \hat{\Phi} - w^\mathsf{T} X\|_2^2 + \mu e^\mathsf{T} \hat{c}$$

$$\text{subject to } \|w\|_2^2 \geqslant 1, \quad \hat{c} \geqslant 0$$

where e is a vector of ones.

7.7 Fast solution in non-overcomplete dictionaries

In important applications [Tang *et al.*, 1999, Tang *et al.*, 2000], the sensor signals may have hundreds of channels and hundreds of thousands of samples. This may make separation computationally difficult. Here we present an approach which compromises between statistical and computational efficiency. In our experience this approach provides high quality of separation in reasonable time.

Suppose that the dictionary is 'complete,' i.e., it forms a basis in the space of discrete signals. This means that the matrix Φ is square and non-singular. As examples of such a dictionary one can think of the Fourier basis, Gabor basis, various wavelet-related bases, *etc.* We can also obtain an 'optimal' dictionary by learning from a given family of signals [Lewicki & Sejnowski, 2000, Lewicki & Olshausen, 1999, Olshausen & Field, 1997, Olshausen & Field, 1996].

Let us denote the dual basis

$$\Psi = \Phi^{-1} \tag{7.27}$$

and suppose that coefficients of decomposition of the sources

$$C = S\Psi \tag{7.28}$$

are sparse and independent. This assumption is reasonable for properly chosen dictionaries, although of course we would lose the advantages of overcompleteness.

Let Y be the decomposition of the sensor signals

$$Y = X\Psi. \tag{7.29}$$

Multiplying both sides of (7.3) by Ψ from the right and taking into account (7.28) and (7.29), we obtain

$$Y = AC + \zeta, \tag{7.30}$$

where $\zeta = \mathbf{n}\Psi$ is the decomposition of the noise. Here we consider an 'easy' situation, where ζ is white, which assumes that Ψ is orthogonal. We can see that all the objective functions from sections 7.4–7.6 remain valid if we substitute the identity matrix for Φ and replace the sensor signal X by its decomposition Y. For example, the maximum *a posteriori* objectives (7.13) and (7.18) are transformed into

$$\min_{A,C} \left\{ \frac{1}{2\sigma^2} \|AC - Y\|_F^2 + \sum_{j,k} \beta_j h(C_{jk}) \right\} \tag{7.31}$$

and

$$\min_{A,C} \left\{ \frac{1}{2\sigma^2} \|AC - Y\|_F^2 + \sum_j \frac{2\sum_k |C_{jk}|}{\sqrt{K^{-1}\sum_k C_{jk}^2}} \right\}. \tag{7.32}$$

The objective (7.22) becomes

$$\min_{W,C} \left\{ -K \log |\det W| + \frac{1}{2} \| C - WY \|_F^2 + \mu \sum_{j,k} \beta_j h(C_{jk}) \right\}. \quad (7.33)$$

In this case we can further assume that the noise is zero, substitute $C = WY$, and obtain the BS Infomax objective [Bell & Sejnowski, 1995]

$$\min_{W} \left\{ -K \log |\det W| + \sum_{j,k} \beta_j h((WY)_{jk}) \right\}. \quad (7.34)$$

Also other known methods (for example [Lee *et al.*, 1998, Lewicki & Sejnowski, 2000]), which normally assume sparsity of source signals, may be directly applied to the decomposition Y of the sensor signals. This may be more efficient than the traditional approach, and the reason is obvious: typically, a properly chosen decomposition gives significantly higher sparsity for the transformed coefficients than for the raw signals. Furthermore, independence of the coefficients is a more realistic assumption than independence of the raw signal samples.

Experiment: musical sounds   In our experiments we artificially mixed seven five-second fragments of musical sound recordings taken from commercial digital audio CDs. Each of them included 40k samples after down-sampling by a factor of 5 (figure 7.8).

The easiest way to perform sparse decomposition of such sources is to compute a *spectrogram*, the coefficients of a *Short Time Fourier Transform* (STFT).† The sparsity of the spectrogram coefficients (the histogram in figure 7.9, right) is much higher then the sparsity of the original signal (figure 7.9, left)

In this case Y in (7.29) is a real matrix, with separate entries for the real and imaginary components of each spectrogram coefficient of the sensor signals X. We used the objective function in (7.34) with $\beta_j = 1$ and $h_\lambda(\cdot)$ defined by (7.7) and (7.8) with the parameter $\lambda = 10^{-4}$. Unconstrained minimization was performed by a BFGS Quasi-Newton algorithm (MATLAB function FMINU).

This algorithm separated the sources with a relative error of 0.67% for the least well separated source (error computed according to (7.19)). We also applied the BS Infomax algorithm [Bell & Sejnowski, 1995]

---

† We used the function SPECGRAM from the MATLAB signal processing toolbox with a time window of 1024 samples.

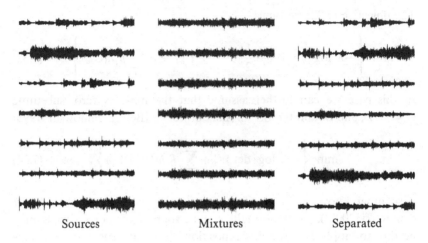

Sources   Mixtures   Separated

Figure 7.8. **Separation of musical recordings:** *Sources were taken from commercial digital audio CDs (five-second fragments).*

implemented in [Makeig, 1999] to the spectrogram coefficients Y of the sensor signals. Separation errors were slightly larger, at 0.9%, but the computing time was improved (from 30 min for BFGS to 5 min for BS Infomax).

For comparison we tested the JADE [Cardoso, 1999a, Cardoso, 1999b], FastICA [Hyvärinen, 1999a, Hyvärinen, 1998b] and BS Infomax algorithms on the raw sensor signals. Resulting relative errors (figure 7.10) confirm the superiority of the sparse decomposition approach.

The method described in this section, which combines a spectrogram transform with the BS Infomax algorithm, is included in the ICA/EEG toolbox [Makeig, 1999].

7.8 Estimating the mixing matrix and the sources separately

As opposed to the case of a square mixing matrix, where finding W amounts to solving the problem $C = WY$, in the case of more sources than mixtures, we are faced with *two* interrelated problems: estimating the mixing matrix A *and* estimating the sources C. Trying to solve both of them at the same time as in equation (7.31) is a difficult multivariate optimization problem.

Another approach consists in estimating the mixing matrix A beforehand. We can do this by clustering (as in section 7.3), using sparsity of sensor coefficients Y. In the experiments of this section we use sparsity of

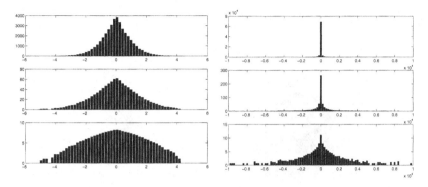

Figure 7.9. **Musical sounds:** *Histogram of sound source values (left) and spectrogram coefficients (right), shown with linear y-scale (top), square root y-scale (centre) and logarithmic y-scale (bottom).*

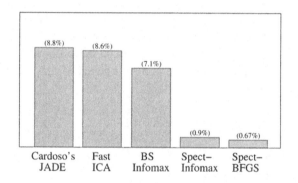

Figure 7.10. **Relative error:** *Percent relative error of separation of seven musical sources recovered by JADE, Fast ICA, Bell-Sejnowski Infomax, Infomax, applied to the spectrogram coefficients, and BFGS minimization of the objective (7.34) with the spectrogram coefficients.*

Short Time Fourier Transform (STFT). The benefits of such an approach are clear in figure 7.11. Six flute signals playing different notes (see the *Six Flutes* example in subsection 7.8.2) were synthetically mixed into two mixtures along equally spaced directions. Figure 7.11a presents a scatter plot of the resulting data ($x_2(t)$ against $x_1(t)$ for every t), showing a single big cloud. As can be seen, the different sources are indistinguishable. Then each mixture was Fast Fourier transformed and the scatter plot of the data in the frequency domain is shown in figure 7.11b (i.e., x_2^ω against x_1^ω for every ω). The difference is extraordinary. Now almost all the data

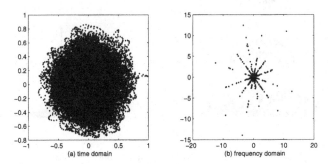

Figure 7.11. **Flute notes:** *Scatter plot X_2 vs X_1 of six flute notes mixed into two mixtures along equally spaced directions in the time (a) and frequency (b) domains.*

points are neatly clustered along the six directions of the columns of the mixing matrix, thus providing very good separability.

If we assume that the matrix A is found, the problem (7.31) can be decomposed into K independent small problems for each data point c^k (here we use $h(\cdot) = |\cdot|$)

$$\min_{\mathbf{c}^k} \left\{ \frac{1}{2\sigma^2} \|A\mathbf{c}^k - \mathbf{y}^k\|^2 + \sum_j |c_j^k| \right\}, \quad \text{for } k = 1, \dots, K. \tag{7.35}$$

Or, in the absence of noise,

$$\min_{\mathbf{c}^k} \left\{ \sum_j |c_j^k| \right\} \quad \text{subject to } A\mathbf{c}^k = \mathbf{y}^k, \quad \text{for } k = 1, \dots, K, \tag{7.36}$$

which can be formulated as a linear programming problem [Chen *et al.*, 1996].

7.8.1 A shortest path decomposition of the sources

We use a simple geometrical approach to the optimization problem (7.36). When the columns of A, $\mathbf{a}^j$, are normalized, the optimal representation of the data point $\mathbf{y}^k = \sum_j \mathbf{a}^j c_j^k$ that minimizes $\sum_j |c_j^k|$ will include at most N of the $\mathbf{a}^j$s, corresponding to the vertices of the *minimal simplex* enclosing the direction of vector $\mathbf{y}^k$ (this leads to the problem of triangulation on the sphere). The non-zero components of the optimal decomposition correspond then to the *shortest path* from the origin to the data point, when only the directions of the mixing matrix may be included in the path.

In particular, for the two sensor case, the shortest path is obtained by choosing the columns $\mathbf{a}^b$ and $\mathbf{a}^a$ whose directions $\tan^{-1}(a_2^b/a_1^b)$ and $\tan^{-1}(a_2^a/a_1^a)$ are the closest from below and from above, respectively, to the direction of the data point $\theta_k = \tan^{-1}(y_2^k/y_1^k)$.

Let $W_r = [\mathbf{a}^b \mathbf{a}^a]^{-1}$ be the *reduced* $N \times N$ inverse matrix, and let $\mathbf{c}_r^k$ be the *reduced* decomposition along directions $\mathbf{a}^b$ and $\mathbf{a}^a$. The components of the sources are then obtained as

$$\mathbf{c}_r^k = W_r \mathbf{y}^k, \tag{7.37}$$

$$c_j^k = 0, \quad \text{for} \quad j \neq b, a. \tag{7.38}$$

In practice, W_r need only be computed once for all data points between any two pairs of mixing directions.

7.8.2 Experiments with estimating the mixing matrix and the sources separately

The approach was first tested using the *Six Flutes* dataset: the sound of a flute playing steady, isolated notes was recorded at high quality in an acoustically isolated booth without reverberation, and sampled at 44.1 kHz with 16 bits resolution. Six 743 ms excerpts (32 768 samples) were selected for the sources, corresponding to the notes a4, d5, f5, g5, c6 and d#6. These six sources were mixed into two mixtures along equally spaced directions. Each of the mixture signals was then processed with a 32 768 sample FFT (i.e., the whole length of the excerpts) and the real and imaginary parts of the positive spectra were used as input to the separation system. We used *potential-function* based clustering [Bofill & Zibulevsky, 2000b]. Results are shown in the first row of Table 7.1.

For the sake of comparison, the next experiment was conducted on the same dataset using the mixtures in the time domain instead of in the frequency domain. The centres of the clusters obtained were no longer in the directions of the mixing matrix, so the resulting estimate was meaningless. The separation was then attempted using the original mixing matrix, but the algorithm totally failed to separate the sources, as shown in Table 7.1, the second row.

Table 7.1. *S/N reconstruction indices (dB) for the different experiments (see text).*

Six flutes (FFT)	50.5	52.5	49.4	43.4	49.1	51.8
Six flutes (time domain)	−1.9	−2.0	−2.2	−2.4	−2.3	−2.4
Four voices (STFT)	21.7	19.4	15.7	16.6		
Five songs (STFT)	15.6	15.5	15.0	15.1	15.2	
Six flute melodies (STFT)	20.4	19.4	14.2	16.1	24.7	29.1

The flute notes in the *Six Flutes* dataset above were very steady, which allowed for a very large FFT window size. The remaining three experiments presented here were performed on much more dynamic signals, and preprocessing was required based on STFT. As before, the sources were first normalized to the same energy level and mixed in the time domain. STFT of the resulting mixtures was produced with a Hanning window of length L, and a 'hop' distance d was used between the starting points of successive frames (yielding an $L - d$ overlap). For each mixture, the input to the separation system was then a single long vector containing the concatenation of the coefficients of real and imaginary parts of the positive spectra among all the frames in that mixture. After the separation the estimated signals were resynthesized by reconstructing the frames, regrouping the real and imaginary parts, taking inverse FFT and inverse windowing. The overlap was removed by keeping only the central part of the frame (thus avoiding the distortion at the edges that often appears after frequency domain manipulation) and the reconstructed signal was obtained by simple concatenation of the resulting pieces.

The experiments were conducted on the following sets of signals: A *Four Voices* dataset with four 2.9 s sentences pronounced by four different people (three females and a male), recorded at 22 050 Hz and 8 bits with a low quality microphone on a home personal computer. The STFT was done with $L = 2048$ and $d = 614$ samples. A *Five Songs* dataset with five 5 s long full-ensemble music pieces (two classical and three pop/folk music) extracted from standard CDs (44 100 Hz/16 bits), down-sampled to 11 025 Hz monophonic and processed with $L = 4096$ and $d = 1228$ samples. Finally, a *Six Flute Melodies* dataset including six 5.7 s long flute melodies (the two voices of a canon, the two voices of a duet and two unrelated melodies) with a high quality registration at 44 100 Hz/16 bits,

(a) Mixtures

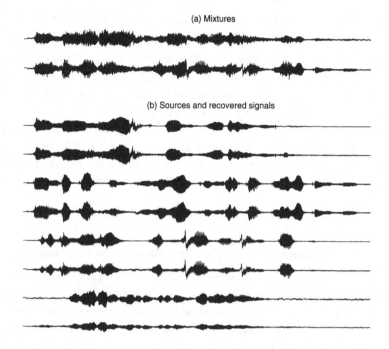

(b) Sources and recovered signals

Figure 7.12. *Four Voices experiment:* (a) Mixtures, (b) sources and recovered signals, pairwise. Taken from [Bofill & Zibulevsky, 2000a].

down-sampled to $22\,050$ Hz and processed with $L = 8192$ and $d = 3276$ samples.

In all three cases the mixing matrix was formed with equally spaced directions. Results of the separation are shown in Table 7.1. Although good enough in themselves, the reconstruction indices of the dynamic signals were significantly poorer than those of the *Six Flutes*, in part due to the intrinsic difficulties of the short term analysis and resynthesis. Reconstruction indices were on the same range for the three examples, regardless of the number of voices, with somehow worse results in the case of the *Five Songs*, probably due to the higher complexity of the sounds. The plot of the recovered signals was in all cases very similar to the plot of the original sources, as illustrated in figure 7.12 for the *Four Voices* case. From a subjective listening point of view, the separation of the *Four Voices* example was remarkable for the high intelligibility of the recovered sentences, in spite of some background noise and cross-talk. Sound examples for the above experiments are available on-line at http://www.ac.upc.es/homes/pau/.

7.9 Source separation using sparsity of multiscale representation

In many cases, especially in wavelet-related decompositions, there are distinct groups of coefficients, in which sources have different sparsity properties. The idea is to select those groups of features (coefficients) which are best suited for separation, with respect to the following criteria: (1) sparsity of coefficients, (2) separability of sources' features. After the best groups are selected, one uses only these in the separation process, which can be accomplished by standard ICA algorithms or by clustering. We present experiments with simulated signals, musical sounds and images which demonstrate the improvement of separation quality.

7.9.1 *Example: sparsity of random blocks in the Haar basis*

Typical block functions are shown in figure 7.13. They are piecewise constant with random amplitude and duration of each constant piece. Let us take a close look at the Haar wavelet coefficients at different resolutions. Wavelet basis functions at the finest resolution are obtained by translation of the Haar mother wavelet:

$$\varphi_j(t) = \begin{cases} -1 & \text{if } t = 0, \\ 1 & \text{if } t = 1, \\ 0 & \text{otherwise.} \end{cases}$$

Taking a scalar product of a function $s(t)$ with the wavelet $\varphi_j(t - \tau)$, we produce a finite differentiation of the function $s(t)$ at the point $t = \tau$. This means that the number of non-zero coefficients at the finest resolution for a block function will correspond roughly to the number of jumps it has. Proceeding to the next, coarser resolution level,

$$\varphi_{j-1}(t) = \begin{cases} -1 & \text{if } t = -1, -2, \\ 1 & \text{if } t = 0, 1, \\ 0 & \text{otherwise,} \end{cases}$$

the number of non-zero coefficients still corresponds to the number of jumps, but the total number of coefficients at this level is halved, and so is the sparsity. If we proceed further in this direction, we will achieve levels of resolution, where the typical width of a wavelet $\varphi_j(t)$ is comparable to the typical distance between jumps in the function $s(t)$. In this case, most of the coefficients are expected to be non-zero, and, therefore, sparsity will fade out.

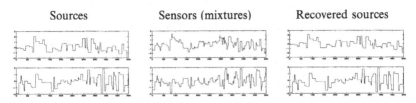

Figure 7.13. *Time plots of block signals.*

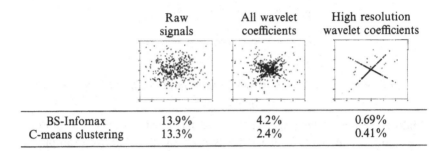

	Raw signals	All wavelet coefficients	High resolution wavelet coefficients
BS-Infomax	13.9%	4.2%	0.69%
C-means clustering	13.3%	2.4%	0.41%

Figure 7.14. *Separation of block signals:* Scatter plots of sensor signals and mean-squared separation errors (%)

To demonstrate how this influences accuracy of a blind source separation, we randomly generated two block-signal sources (figure 7.13, left), and mixed them by the matrix

$$A = \begin{bmatrix} 0.8321 & 0.6247 \\ -0.5547 & 0.7809 \end{bmatrix}.$$

The resulting mixtures, $x_1(t)$ and $x_2(t)$ are shown in figure 7.13, centre. Figure 7.14, first column, shows the scatter plot of $x_1(t)$ versus $x_2(t)$, where there are no visibly distinct features. In contrast, the scatter plot of the wavelet coefficients at the highest resolution (figure 7.14, third column) shows two distinct orientations, which correspond to the columns of the mixing matrix.

Results of separation of the block sources are presented in figure 7.14. The largest error (13-14%) was obtained on the raw data, and the smallest (below 0.7%) on the wavelet coefficients at the highest resolution, which have the best sparsity. Use of all wavelet coefficients leads to intermediate sparsity and performance.

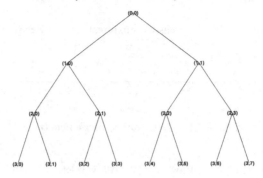

Figure 7.15. **Wavelet packet tree.**

7.9.2 Adaptive selection of sparse subsets of coefficients in wavelet packet tree

Multiresolution analysis Our choice of a particular wavelet basis and of the sparsest subset of coefficients was obvious in the above example: it was based on knowledge of the structure of piecewise constant signals. For sources having oscillatory components (like sounds or images with textures), other systems of basis functions, for example, wavelet packets [Coifman *et al.*, 1992], or multiwavelets [Weitzer *et al.*, 1997], might be more appropriate. The wavelet packet library consists of the triple-indexed family of functions

$$\varphi_{jnk}(t) = 2^{j/2} \varphi_n(2^j t - k), \quad j, k \in \mathbb{Z}, \, n \in \mathbb{N}. \tag{7.39}$$

As in the case of the wavelet transform, j, k are the scale and shift parameters, respectively, and n is the frequency parameter, related to the number of oscillations of a particular generating function $\varphi_n(t)$. The set of functions $\varphi_{jn}(t)$ forms a (j, n) wavelet packet. This set of functions can be split into two parts at a coarser scale: $\varphi_{j-1,2n}(t)$ and $\varphi_{j-1,2n+1}(t)$. It follows that these two form an orthonormal basis of the subspace which spans $\{\varphi_{jn}(t)\}$. Thus, we arrive at a family of wavelet packet functions on a binary tree (figure 7.15). The nodes of this tree are numbered by two indices: the depth of the level $j = 0, 1, .., J$, and the number of nodes $n = 0, 1, 2, 3, ..., 2^j - 1$ at the specified level. Using wavelet packets allows one to analyze given signals not only with a scale-oriented decomposition but also on frequency sub-bands. Naturally, the library contains the wavelet basis.

The decomposition coefficients $c_{jnk} = \langle s, \varphi_{jnk} \rangle$ also split into (j, n) sets corresponding to the nodes of the tree, and there is a fast way to compute them using banks of *conjugate mirror filters*, as is implemented in the fast wavelet transform.

Choice of the best nodes in the tree When signals have a complex nature, it is difficult to decide in advance which nodes contain the sparsest sets of coefficients. That is why we use the following simple adaptive approach.

First, for every node of the tree, we apply a clustering algorithm (see section 7.3), and compute a measure of a cluster's distortion. In our experiments we used a standard *global distortion*: the mean-squared distance of data points to the centres of their own (closest) clusters. (Here again, the weights of the data points can be incorporated.) Second, we choose a few best nodes with the minimal distortion, combine their coefficients into one dataset, and apply a separation algorithm (clustering or Infomax) to these data.

More sophisticated techniques dealing with adaptive choice of best nodes, as well as their number, can be found in [Kisilev *et al.*, 2000].

7.9.3 Experiments with adaptive selection of sparse subsets of coefficients

We evaluated the quality of the proposed wavelet packet based separation method on several types of signals. The first type is the random block signal (see above). The second type of signal is a frequency modulated (FM) sinusoidal signal. In the first case, the carrier is modulated by a sinusoidal function. In the second case, it is modulated by choosing a random frequency and a corresponding random duration; we call this type of signal Block-FM (BFM). The third type of signal is a musical recording of flute sounds. Finally, we apply our algorithm to portrait images.

In order to compare the accuracy of our method with other methods, we form the following features sets: (1) the set of signals, (2) short time Fourier transform (STFT) coefficients, (3) wavelet transform coefficients, and (4) wavelet packet coefficients at the 'best' nodes. In the last case, mixtures of sources were decomposed with the MATLAB wavelet packet toolbox using various families of mother wavelets with different numbers of vanishing moments (smoothness parameter). A typical example of scatter plots of the wavelet packet coefficients at different nodes of the wavelet packet tree is shown in figure 7.16. The upper left scatter plot, labelled 'C', corresponds to the set of coefficients at all nodes. The remainder are the scatter plots of sets of coefficients indexed in a wavelet packet tree above. Generally speaking, the more distinct the directions

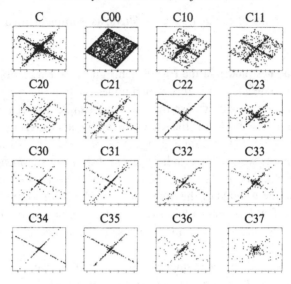

Figure 7.16. *Scatter plots of the wavelet packet coefficients of the FM mixtures.*

appearing on these plots, the more precise the estimation of the mixing matrix, and, therefore, the better the separation.

We applied the fuzzy C-means clustering algorithm with some modifications (see [Kisilev *et al.*, 2000] for details) to each feature set. Table 7.2 summarizes results of our experiments. We compared the quality of separation of random block and BFM signals by performing 100 Monte Carlo simulations and calculating the normalized mean-squared errors (NMSE) for the above feature sets. In the case of deterministic signals, we calculated a normalized squared error (SE). In the case of image separation, we used the two-dimensional Discrete Cosine Transform (DCT) instead of the STFT, and the *Symmlet-8* mother wavelet when using the two-dimensional wavelet transform and wavelet packets.

From Table 7.2 it is clear that the adaptive best nodes method outperforms all other feature sets for each type of signal. Also, as mentioned above, the clustering approach provides a better separation than Infomax. It is clear that using the Haar wavelet function for the wavelet packets representation of the random block signals provides better separation than using some smooth wavelet, e.g., Db8. The reason is that these signals have a sparser representation with the Haar wavelet. In contrast, the flute's signals are better represented with smooth wavelets, and, therefore, these provide best separation. This is another advantage

Table 7.2. **Experimental results:** *normalized mean-squared separation error (%) for signals and images using raw data and decomposition coefficients in different domains. In the case of wavelet packets (WP) we used the best selected nodes.*

Signal	Raw data	STFT	WT, Db8	WT, Haar	WP, Db8	WP, Haar
Blocks	31.89	16.31	4.18	1.94	2.70	**0.43**
BFM sine	49.81	8.17	8.16	15.30	**4.48**	6.65
FM sine	50.57	5.66	10.16	24.71	**4.13**	5.33
Flutes	12.18	5.36	5.96	9.23	**3.93**	8.05
Images	Raw data	DCT	WT, sym8	WT, Haar	WP, sym8	WP, Haar
Portraits	22.11	19.11	10.79	10.57	**6.04**	8.29

of using sets of features at multiple nodes along with various families of 'mother' functions: one can choose best nodes from a number of decomposition trees simultaneously.

More results and comparisons can be found in [Kisilev *et al.*, 2000].

7.10 Conclusions

We showed that the use of sparse decomposition in a proper signal dictionary provides high-quality blind source separation. The maximum *a posteriori* framework gives the most general approach, which includes the situation of an overcomplete dictionary and more sources than sensors. Computationally more robust solutions can be found in the case of an equal number of sources and sensors. We can also extract the sources sequentially using quadratic programming with non-convex quadratic constraints.

Solutions may be obtained much faster by using non-overcomplete dictionaries. Even when the number of sources is larger than the number of mixtures, we can estimate the mixing matrix beforehand by clustering, and then reconstruct the sources by a *shortest path decomposition*.

In many cases, especially in wavelet-related decompositions, selection of a few best groups of coefficients with the highest sparsity brings additional improvement of the separation quality.

Our experiments with artificial signals and digitally mixed musical sounds demonstrate a high quality of source separation, compared to other known techniques.

Acknowledgements

We thank Linda Antas at the University of Washington for the flute performances. This research was partially supported by NSF CAREER award 97-02-311, the National Foundation for Functional Brain Imaging, an equipment grant from Intel Corporation, the Albuquerque High Performance Computing Center, a gift from George Cowan, and a gift from the NEC Research Institute.

8

Ensemble Learning
for blind source separation

J.W. Miskin

D.J.C. MacKay

In this chapter we show how an Ensemble Learning version of Independent Component Analysis (EL–ICA) can be derived by approximating the true posterior distribution over the model parameters by an approximate distribution. We further extend this algorithm to include sources which can only be positive. We show that the blind deconvolution problem is similar to the blind separation problem and derive an algorithm for blind deconvolution.

8.1 Ensemble learning

In many problems we aim to infer a set of model parameters, Θ, from a set of data, D. In the Bayesian framework this can be done by considering the posterior probability of the parameters,

$$P\left(\Theta \,|D, \mathcal{H}\right) = \frac{P\left(D\,|\Theta, \mathcal{H}\right) P\left(\Theta \,|\mathcal{H}\right)}{P\left(D\,|\mathcal{H}\right)}, \tag{8.1}$$

where $\mathcal{H}$ denotes the particular model under consideration.

Commonly the parameters are inferred by maximising the likelihood, $P\left(D\,|\Theta, \mathcal{H}\right)$ (ML methods), or the posterior probability (MAP methods) with respect to the model parameters. These methods can overfit. The model parameters that are obtained can be too specific.

Instead of finding the MAP estimate of the parameters, the correct procedure is to perform inference by averaging over the posterior distribution. This means that instead of being sensitive to regions where the probability density is large, the inferences will be sensitive to regions where the probability mass is large. In many cases it is intractable to perform the averages analytically and so exact inferences must be performed by using Markov chain Monte Carlo (MCMC) sampling. Rather than following a sampling procedure, we could look for a cheaper analytic approximation.

In the Ensemble Learning (EL) approximation [Hinton & van Camp, 1993, MacKay, 1995] we find an approximate posterior distribution, Q, for the model parameters by minimising the Kullback–Leibler divergence between the approximate distribution and the true posterior,

$$D_{KL}\left(Q\,||P\right) = \left\langle \log \frac{Q\left(\Theta\right)}{P\left(\Theta\,|D,\mathcal{H}\right)} \right\rangle_Q \qquad (8.2)$$

where $\langle . \rangle_Q$ denotes the average under the approximate distribution. The divergence is bounded from below by 0, with equality when the approximate distribution is the same as the posterior distribution.

We define a cost function as follows:

$$C_{KL} = D_{KL}\left(Q\,||P\right) - \log P\left(D\,|\mathcal{H}\right),$$
$$= \left\langle \log \left(\frac{Q\left(\Theta\right)}{P\left(D,\Theta\,|\mathcal{H}\right)} \right) \right\rangle_Q,$$
$$\geqslant -\log P\left(D\,|\mathcal{H}\right). \qquad (8.3)$$

Minimising C_{KL} is equivalent to maximising a bound on the evidence, $\log P\left(D\,|\mathcal{H}\right)$, for the model $\mathcal{H}$.

We may wish to compare different models of the observed data and perform model selection. Equation (8.3) shows that by minimising the cost function we obtain a bound on the evidence for the model. We can use Bayes' theorem to obtain the posterior probability of the models,

$$P\left(\mathcal{H}\,|D\right) = \frac{P\left(D\,|\mathcal{H}\right) P\left(\mathcal{H}\right)}{P\left(D\right)}. \qquad (8.4)$$

If we assume a uniform prior over models, constant $P\left(\mathcal{H}\right)$, the model with the highest posterior probability is the model with the highest evidence. Therefore if the bound on the evidence is close to the correct value of the evidence, the model that maximises the posterior probability is the one that minimises C_{KL}.

8.2 Ensemble Learning for ICA

In Independent Component Analysis, the aim is to recover some hidden sources, s_t, from some observed mixtures,

$$\mathbf{x}_t = A\mathbf{s}_t + \mathbf{n}_t \qquad (8.5)$$

where **n** is a noise vector. If the data are noisy, the inverse of the mixing matrix (the separating matrix W) may be ill-defined. Therefore methods that rely on finding the separating matrix could find sub-optimal solutions. We would also like to be able to infer the number of sources in the observations. If MAP or ML methods are used, the number of sources may be overestimated, additional sources may be used to model the noise. Ensemble Learning allows us to handle these problems by providing a method for approximating the posterior distribution over all possible sources and by allowing model selection to select the model with the correct number of sources. Ensemble Learning has been applied to PCA [Bishop, 1999] and to ICA using a fixed form approximation [Lappalainen, 1999]. Here we derive an ICA algorithm using a free form approximation to the true posterior distribution.

As with Independent Factor Analysis [Attias, 1999a] we assign a mixture of L Gaussians prior to the sources and a Gaussian prior to the mixing matrix,

$$P\left(\mathbf{s}_{mt}\,|\mathcal{H}\right) = \sum_{c=1}^{L}\pi_{mc}\mathcal{G}\left(\mathbf{s}_{mt}\,|0,\beta_{mc}\right), \tag{8.6}$$

$$P\left(A_{nm}\,|\mathcal{H}\right) = \mathcal{G}\left(A_{nm}\,|0,\alpha_m\right), \tag{8.7}$$

where

$$P\left(\beta_{mc}\,|\mathcal{H}\right) = \text{Gamma}\left(\beta_{mc}\,|b^{(\beta)},c^{(\beta)}\right), \tag{8.8}$$

$$P\left(\{\pi_{mc}\}_{c=1}^{L}\,|\mathcal{H}\right) = \text{Dirichlet}\left(\{\pi_{mc}\}_{c=1}^{L}\,|c^{(\pi)}\right), \tag{8.9}$$

$$P\left(\alpha_m\,|\mathcal{H}\right) = \text{Gamma}\left(\alpha_m\,|b^{(\alpha)},c^{(\alpha)}\right). \tag{8.10}$$

We choose a Gaussian noise model

$$P\left(\mathbf{x}_t\,|\mu,\Lambda,\mathcal{H}\right) = \mathcal{G}\left(\mathbf{x}_t\,|A\mathbf{s}_t+\mu,\Lambda\right) \tag{8.11}$$

where we have assumed that there is Gaussian noise with mean μ and a diagonal inverse covariance matrix Λ. We use the following hyperpriors:

$$P\left(\mu_n\,|\mathcal{H}\right) = \mathcal{G}\left(\mu_n\,|0,b^{(\mu)}\right), \tag{8.12}$$

$$P\left(\Lambda_{nn}\,|\mathcal{H}\right) = \text{Gamma}\left(\Lambda_{nn}\,|b^{(\Lambda)},c^{(\Lambda)}\right). \tag{8.13}$$

As before, we choose the hyper-parameters to give approximately scale-invariant hyperpriors ($b^{(\alpha)} = c^{(\alpha)} = b^{(\beta)} = c^{(\beta)} = b^{(\mu)} = b^{(\Lambda)} = c^{(\Lambda)} = 10^{-3}$, $c^{(\pi)} = 1$ say).

It is now necessary to assume a separable form for the approximate posterior distribution. One possible form is

$$Q\left(\mathbf{s}, \pi, \beta, A, \alpha, \mu, \Lambda\right) = Q\left(\mathbf{s}\right) Q\left(\pi\right) Q\left(\beta\right)$$
$$\times Q\left(A\right) Q\left(\alpha\right) Q\left(\mu\right) Q\left(\Lambda\right). \tag{8.14}$$

Since the true posterior and the approximate posterior are products of terms, the cost function can be split into a sum of simpler terms:

$$C_{KL} = \left\langle \log\left(\frac{Q\left(\mathbf{s}\right) Q\left(\pi\right) Q\left(\beta\right)}{P\left(\mathbf{s}, \pi, \beta \mid \mathcal{H}\right)}\right)\right\rangle_{Q}$$
$$+ \left\langle \log\left(\frac{Q\left(A\right) Q\left(\alpha\right)}{P\left(A, \alpha \mid \mathcal{H}\right)}\right)\right\rangle_{Q} + \left\langle \log\left(\frac{Q\left(\mu\right) Q\left(\Lambda\right)}{P\left(\mathbf{x}, \mu, \Lambda \mid \mathcal{H}\right)}\right)\right\rangle_{Q}$$
$$= C_{KL}^{(\mathbf{s})} + C_{KL}^{(A)} + C_{KL}^{(\Lambda)}. \tag{8.15}$$

We have to make one final simplification before we can proceed to minimise the cost function. The source prior was a mixture of Gaussians and so we make use of Jensen's inequality to derive

$$-\log P\left(\mathbf{s}_{mt} \mid \mathcal{H}\right) \leqslant \sum_{c=1}^{L} \lambda_{mnc} \log\left(\frac{\pi_{mc}\mathcal{G}\left(\mathbf{s}_{mt} \mid 0, \beta_{mc}\right)}{\lambda_{mnc}}\right), \tag{8.16}$$

where $\{\lambda_{mnc}\}$ are a set of coefficients which obey the constraints

$$\sum_{c=1}^{L} \lambda_{mtc} = 1, \quad \forall m, t. \tag{8.17}$$

This simplified cost function can now be minimised with respect to each of the Q distributions by performing a functional minimisation. Because the priors were chosen to be the set of conjugate priors, the optimal distributions have the same form as the priors and are

$$Q\left(\mathbf{s}_{t}\right) = \mathcal{G}\left(\mathbf{s}_{t} \left| \mathbf{m}_{t}^{(\mathbf{s})}, \Sigma_{t}^{(\mathbf{s})}\right.\right), \tag{8.18}$$

$$Q\left(\{\pi_{mc}\}_{c=1}^{L}\right) = \text{Dirichlet}\left(\{\pi_{mc}\}_{c=1}^{L} \left| \bar{c}_{1}^{(\pi)} \ldots \bar{c}_{L}^{(\pi)}\right.\right), \tag{8.19}$$

$$Q\left(\beta_{mc}\right) = \text{Gamma}\left(\beta_{mc} \left| \bar{b}_{mc}^{(\beta)}, \bar{c}_{mc}^{(\beta)}\right.\right), \tag{8.20}$$

$$Q\left(\mathbf{a}_{n}\right) = \mathcal{G}\left(\mathbf{a}_{n} \left| \mathbf{m}_{n}^{(a)}, \Sigma_{n}^{(a)}\right.\right), \tag{8.21}$$

$$Q\left(\alpha_{mc}\right) = \text{Gamma}\left(\alpha_{mc} \left| \bar{b}_{mc}^{(\alpha)}, \bar{c}_{mc}^{(\alpha)}\right.\right), \tag{8.22}$$

$$Q\left(\mu_{n}\right) = \mathcal{G}\left(\mu_{n} \left| \bar{b}_{n}^{(\mu)}, \bar{c}_{n}^{(\mu)}\right.\right), \tag{8.23}$$

$$Q\left(\Lambda_{nn}\right) = \text{Gamma}\left(\Lambda_{nn} \left| \bar{b}_{n}^{(\Lambda)}, \bar{c}_{n}^{(\Lambda)}\right.\right), \tag{8.24}$$

where $\mathbf{a}_{n}$ is a column vector containing the elements of the nth row of A

and the distribution parameters satisfy

$$\Sigma_t^{(s)} = \text{diag} \left(\sum_{c=1}^{L} \lambda_{mtc} \langle \beta_{mc} \rangle_Q \right) + \langle A^T \Lambda A \rangle_Q, \tag{8.25}$$

$$\mathbf{m}_t^{(s)} = \left(\Sigma_t^{(s)} \right)^{-1} \langle A^T \Lambda (\mathbf{x}_t - \mu) \rangle_Q, \tag{8.26}$$

$$\bar{c}_{mc}^{(\pi)} = c^{(\pi)} + \sum_{t=1}^{T} \lambda_{mtc}, \tag{8.27}$$

$$\bar{b}_{mc}^{(\beta)} = b^{(\beta)} + \frac{1}{2} \sum_{t=1}^{T} \lambda_{mtc} \langle \mathbf{s}_{mt}^2 \rangle_Q, \tag{8.28}$$

$$\bar{c}_{mc}^{(\beta)} = c^{(\beta)} + \frac{1}{2} \sum_{t=1}^{T} \lambda_{mtc}, \tag{8.29}$$

$$\Sigma_n^{(a)} = \text{diag} \left(\langle \alpha \rangle_Q \right) + \langle \Lambda_{nn} \rangle_Q \sum_{t=1}^{T} \langle \mathbf{s}_t \mathbf{s}_t^T \rangle_Q, \tag{8.30}$$

$$\mathbf{m}_n^{(a)} = \langle \Lambda_{nn} \rangle_Q \sum_{t=1}^{T} \langle (\mathbf{x}_{nt} - \mu_n) \mathbf{s}_t^T \rangle_Q \left(\Sigma_n^{(a)} \right)^{-1}, \tag{8.31}$$

$$\bar{b}_{mc}^{(\alpha)} = b^{(\alpha)} + \frac{1}{2} \sum_{n=1}^{N} \langle A_{nm}^2 \rangle_Q, \tag{8.32}$$

$$\bar{c}_{mc}^{(\alpha)} = c^{(\alpha)} + \frac{N}{2}, \tag{8.33}$$

$$\bar{c}_n^{(\mu)} = b^{(\mu)} + T \langle \Lambda_{nn} \rangle_Q, \tag{8.34}$$

$$\bar{b}_n^{(\mu)} = \frac{\langle \Lambda_{nn} \rangle_Q}{\bar{c}_n^{(\mu)}} \sum_{t=1}^{T} \langle (\mathbf{x}_t - A\mathbf{s}_t) \rangle_Q, \tag{8.35}$$

$$\bar{b}_n^{(\Lambda)} = b^{(\Lambda)} + \frac{1}{2} \sum_{t=1}^{T} \langle (\mathbf{x}_t - A\mathbf{s}_t - \mu)^2 \rangle_Q, \tag{8.36}$$

$$\bar{c}_n^{(\Lambda)} = c^{(\Lambda)} + \frac{T}{2}. \tag{8.37}$$

We must also evaluate the set of weights used in approximation (8.16). These weights can be found by minimising C_{KL} subject to the normalisation conditions, (8.17). This results in

$$\log \lambda_{mtc} = \langle \log \left(\pi_{mc} \mathcal{G} \left(\mathbf{s}_{mt} | 0, \beta_{mc} \right) \right) \rangle_Q + \text{constant} \tag{8.38}$$

where the constant is found by satisfying the normalisation conditions.

Although the approximate posterior distribution is assumed to have a separable form, so samples from each distribution are independent, the parameters of the approximate posterior are dependent on the parameters of the other distributions. Therefore the optimal parameters have to be found by repeatedly updating the distributions using equations (8.25-8.37) until C_{KL} converges.

In order to evaluate the evidence bound, we need to be able to evaluate the terms in the split cost function (8.15). If we explicitly find the optimal set of $Q(\alpha)$, using equations (8.25-8.37), prior to evaluating $C_{KL}^{(A)}$, it can be shown that $C_{KL}^{(A)}$ simplifies to

$$
C_{KL}^{(A)} = \sum_{m=1}^{M} \left[\log \frac{\Gamma\left(c^{(\alpha)}\right)}{\Gamma\left(\bar{c}_m^{(\alpha)}\right)} + \bar{c}_m^{(\alpha)} \log \bar{b}_m^{(\alpha)} - c^{(\alpha)} \log b^{(\alpha)} \right]
$$
$$
+ \sum_{n=1}^{N} \left[\frac{1}{2} \log \left|\left| \Sigma_n^{(a)} \right|\right| - \frac{M}{2} \right]. \tag{8.39}
$$

Similarly, if we find the optimal set of $Q(\pi)$, $Q(\beta)$ and $Q(\Lambda)$, we can evaluate the other terms in the cost function:

$$
C_{KL}^{(s)} = \sum_{m=1}^{M} \sum_{c=1}^{L} \left[\log \frac{\Gamma\left(c^{(\beta)}\right)}{\Gamma\left(\bar{c}_{mc}^{(\beta)}\right)} + \bar{c}_{mc}^{(\beta)} \log \bar{b}_{mc}^{(\beta)} - c^{(\beta)} \log b^{(\beta)} \right.
$$
$$
\left. + \log \frac{\Gamma\left(c^{(\pi)}\right)}{\Gamma\left(\bar{c}_{mc}^{(\pi)}\right)} \right] + \sum_{m=1}^{M} \sum_{t=1}^{T} \sum_{c=1}^{L} \lambda_{mtc} \log \lambda_{mtc}
$$
$$
+ \sum_{m=1}^{M} \left[\log \Gamma \left(\sum_{c=1}^{L} \bar{c}_{mc}^{(\pi)} \right) - \log \Gamma \left(\sum_{c=1}^{L} c^{(\pi)} \right) \right]
$$
$$
+ \sum_{t=1}^{T} \left[\frac{1}{2} \log \left|\left| \Sigma_t^{(s)} \right|\right| - \frac{M}{2} \right], \tag{8.40}
$$

$$
C_{KL}^{(\Lambda)} = \sum_{n=1}^{N} \left[\log \frac{\Gamma\left(c^{(\Lambda)}\right)}{\Gamma\left(\bar{c}_n^{(\Lambda)}\right)} + \bar{c}_n^{(\Lambda)} \log \bar{b}_n^{(\Lambda)} - c^{(\Lambda)} \log b^{(\Lambda)} \right]
$$
$$
+ \frac{NT}{2} \log 2\pi. \tag{8.41}
$$

8.2.1 Simpler approximations to the posterior

One possible problem with the algorithm derived above is that there is a poor scaling with M. The approximate distribution for the sources is an M-dimensional Gaussian and so an inverse covariance matrix must be stored for each time step, so the memory requirements scale as $\mathcal{O}\left(M^2\right)$. Additionally the covariance matrix must be evaluated and so the computational time for each iteration scales as $\mathcal{O}\left(M^3\right)$. This means that if there are a large number of sources the algorithm could be prohibitively slow.

We can derive a faster algorithm by making a further assumption about the separability of the approximate posterior distribution. We assume that the distributions are separable into distributions over independent sources:

$$Q\left(\{\mathbf{s}\}_{m=1}^M\right) = \prod_{m=1}^M Q\left(\{\mathbf{s}_m\}_{t=1}^T\right),\tag{8.42}$$

$$Q(A) = \prod_{m=1}^M Q\left(\{A_{nm}\}_{n=1}^N\right),\tag{8.43}$$

We proceed, as before, to minimise C_{KL} with respect to these new approximate distributions. The optimal distributions for $\mathbf{s}$ and A will be

$$Q\left(\mathbf{s}_{mt}\right) = \mathcal{G}\left(\mathbf{s}_{mt}\left|m_{mt}^{(s)}, \Sigma_{mt}^{(s)}\right.\right),\tag{8.44}$$

$$Q\left(A_{nm}\right) = \mathcal{G}\left(A_{nm}\left|m_{nm}^{(A)}, \Sigma_{nm}^{(A)}\right.\right),\tag{8.45}$$

where

$$\Sigma_{mt}^{(s)} = \sum_{c=1}^L \lambda_{mtc}\langle\beta_{mc}\rangle_Q + \sum_{n=1}^N \langle A_{nm}^2\Lambda_{nn}\rangle_Q,\tag{8.46}$$

$$\Sigma_{mt}^{(s)}m_{mt}^{(s)} = \sum_{n=1}^N \left\langle A_{nm}\Lambda_{nn}\left(\mathbf{x}_{nt} - \mu_n - \sum_{m'\neq m}A_{nm'}\mathbf{s}_{m't}\right)\right\rangle_Q,\tag{8.47}$$

$$\Sigma_{nm}^{(A)} = \langle\alpha_m\rangle_Q + \langle\Lambda_{nn}\rangle_Q\sum_{t=1}^T \langle s_{mt}^2\rangle_Q,\tag{8.48}$$

$$\Sigma_{nm}^{(A)}m_{nm}^{(A)} = \langle\Lambda_{nn}\rangle_Q\sum_{t=1}^T \left\langle\left(\mathbf{x}_{nt} - \mu_n - \sum_{m'\neq m}A_{nm'}\mathbf{s}_{m't}\right)\mathbf{s}_{mt}\right\rangle_Q.\tag{8.49}$$

All of the other distributions will remain as before, but the values of the parameters will be different due to the dependence on the expectation of the distributions $Q\left(\mathbf{s}\right)$ and $Q\left(A\right)$. One difference between this version of the EL–ICA algorithm and the previous version that affects optimisation is that one update of the equations (8.46-8.49) will not lead to the optimal distributions for all of the $Q\left(\mathbf{s}\right)$ or all of the $Q\left(\mathbf{A}\right)$. This is because the distributions are coupled and so they must be iteratively optimised. While this means that more iterations may be required, it is not necessarily a handicap because

- each iteration is significantly quicker,
- repeated iterations were already required to reach convergence of the combined distribution $Q(s)Q(A)$.

8.2.2 Toy problem

We test the two algorithms derived above on a set of four sources mixed to obtain ten observed signals. Gaussian noise was added to the mixtures. Figure 8.1 shows how the evidence values for the two algorithms compare. This shows that the simplified approximate posterior results in a marginally worse bound on the evidence, but the difference is insignificant when compared with the variations already present due to varying M.

This suggests one of two possibilities: either the bound on the evidence is very close to the true value of the evidence and there is little that can be done to improve the bound; or correlations between s and A are more important than those between individual elements of s or of A. In either case there is little to be gained by including the covariance terms within the distributions over s or A.

By choosing to ignore the covariance terms in the approximate distributions we are trading off the increase in computational efficiency against an increase in the value of C_{KL}. It should be noted though that this algorithm still has advantages over MAP methods. Firstly, although the covariance between terms is ignored, there is still a distribution over the possible values for the model parameters and so the algorithm will not suffer from overfitting. Secondly, the algorithm gives a bound on the evidence for the model. Therefore it is easy to compare different models. Neglect of the covariance terms means that the bound is not as good as possible, but it is still a rigorous lower bound.

Figure 8.2 shows the correlation between the set of recovered sources and the set of hidden sources using the simplified algorithm. The figure shows that the correct number of sources is identified because four of the recovered sources are correlated with the hidden sources (each column has one straight line, so each hidden source is the same as one of the recovered sources). The remaining recovered sources have zero amplitude since they have been switched off. Since the priors for the model include the idea that independent sources have independent priors, the algorithm

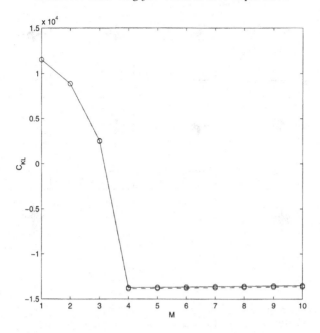

Figure 8.1. **Model selection:** C_{KL} *as a function of the assumed number of sources for a problem consisting of four hidden sources and ten observed noisy mixtures. The dashed line shows the results for the case where the approximate distribution includes correlations within the distributions for $Q(\mathbf{s})$ and $Q(A)$. The solid line shows the results for the case where fully separable distributions are chosen. Choosing the separable distribution results in a worse bound on the evidence, but the difference is insignificant when compared with the variation due to changing M. In each case the correct number of sources is identified.*

can switch off irrelevant sources, in a similar manner to Automatic Relevance Determination [MacKay, 1994].

We can perform model selection to identify the correct number of sources. Figure 8.1 shows how the bound on the evidence varies as a function of the assumed number of hidden sources. This shows a minimum for $M = 4$ and so the correct number of sources is identified.

There are now two possible methods for identifying the number of sources.

- Assume that there are as many sources as observed signals. During optimisation unused sources will be switched off and so the number of sources can be identified.

- Start with one hidden source and optimise the model. Increase the

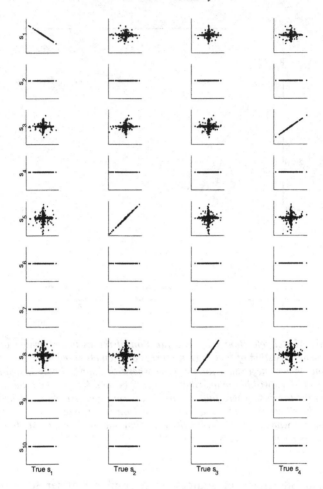

Figure 8.2. *Recovered source correlations: Plots of the correlation between the hidden sources and mean values of the approximate distributions for a problem consisting of four hidden sources and ten observed noisy mixtures. We can see that the correct number of sources (4) has been identified and all remaining reconstructed sources switched off. In addition the recovered sources are equivalent to the hidden sources (to within a rescaling).*

number of sources and optimise the model. Repeat until the evidence no longer increases.

The first method may prove to be too slow if there are a large number of observed sources (if $N \gg M$). The second method may prove to be too slow if there are a large number of hidden sources (if $N \approx M$), in which

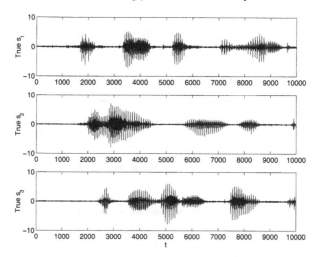

Figure 8.3. *Source samples: The set of source samples used for testing the EL–ICA algorithm. Each sample is speech sampled at 8kHz.*

case the algorithm will have to be run for a large number of models. The method of choice will depend on the specific problem to be tackled.

We test this simpler algorithm on a mixture of 'real world' signals. Figure 8.3 shows a set of three speech samples obtained by sampling the author's (JM) voice at 8 kHz. Figure 8.4 shows the set of observed signals (these were formed by mixing with a random 5×3 matrix and adding Gaussian noise). Since we know what the hidden sources are, from figure 8.3, it is possible to identify each of the hidden sources in the observed mixtures. By observation of the mixtures alone, it is not obvious what the hidden sources are. As before, the number of sources could be inferred by testing a number of models with varying numbers of sources or by assuming that $M = N$ and seeing how many sources are switched off.

Figure 8.5 shows the recovered sources. Three of these sources match the original sources although the signs of two have been flipped, this is due to the invariance of the ICA model with respect to scaling. Two of the recovered sources have been switched off, showing that a model with $M = 3$ would be a better model. The algorithm has recovered the sources without using extra sources to model the noisy observed data.

Figure 8.6 shows the distributions of the recovered sources. We can compare these with the mixture of Gaussians source model that is learnt for each source. We can see that the learnt model is a close match to

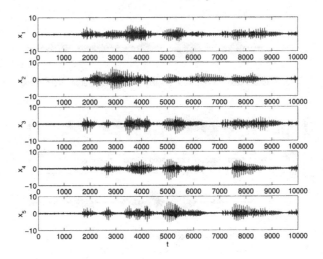

Figure 8.4. **Observed samples:** *The mixtures of sound samples obtained by mixing the source samples in figure 8.3 by a random 5 × 3 matrix and adding Gaussian noise.*

recovered sources and so the MOG model is an adequate model for source separation of some real world signals.

8.3 Separation of images

The previous sections have used a mixture of Gaussians prior to model the prior distribution for the sources. While this mixture prior works for many problems (for instance sound samples) it is not necessarily going to be the best prior for all situations. One obvious point is that the mixture prior allows for the sources to have negative values. In many experiments the results that are obtained are not going to be formed from mixtures of sources which are both positive and negative. For example, the following datasets will all consist of positive data values:

- imaging data from telescopes, cameras, etc. where each pixel value is an intensity [Gull & Daniell, 1978];
- Nuclear Magnetic Resonance (NMR) power spectra [Ochs *et al.*, 1999];
- Face/Digit recognition, where each pixel ranges from white to black (or 0 to 1) [Lee & Seung, 1999].

In order to model these datasets more accurately, we should include

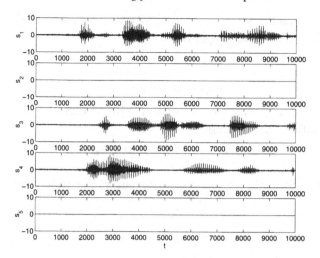

Figure 8.5. **Recovered source samples:** *The sound samples obtained by applying the EL–ICA algorithm to the observations in figure 8.4. Three of the recovered sources match the hidden sources in figure 8.3. The remaining recovered sources have zero amplitude showing that the data could be modelled by three hidden sources.*

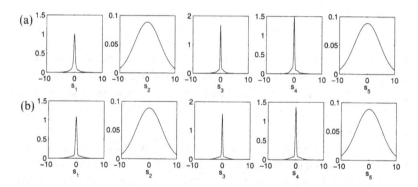

Figure 8.6. **Source probability densities:** *(a) shows the approximate posterior densities for each of the recovered sources. Two of the sources, s_2 and s_5, have been switched off and so are Gaussian. The remaining recovered sources are non-Gaussian; (b) shows the mixture of Gaussians model for each of the sources. The plots use the mean values for the π and β parameters, the variances of these parameters are insignificant. We can see that the MOG distributions match the recovered distributions.*

a positivity constraint which will be a better model of the sources. Intuitively we can see that by having a prior that does not allow for negative values, we are increasing the evidence in favour of positive values by about 1 bit per pixel. Therefore it seems likely that the evidence values for a model which forces positivity for each of these datasets will be greater than for the simple ICA model.

8.3.1 Forcing positivity

One way to force positivity is to use a rectified Gaussian prior for the sources rather than a Gaussian:

$$\mathcal{G}^{(R)}\left(s_{mt}\,|a,b\right) \propto e^{-\frac{b}{2}(s_{mt}-a)^2}. \tag{8.50}$$

In order to favour more sparse source sources, a mixture could be used:

$$P\left(s_{mt}\,|\mathcal{H}\right) = \sum_{c=1}^{L} \pi_{mc}\mathcal{G}^{(R)}\left(s_{mt}\,|0,\beta_{mc}\right). \tag{8.51}$$

Alternatively the prior could be a mixture of exponentials:

$$P\left(s_{mt}\,|\mathcal{H}\right) = \sum_{c=1}^{L} \pi_{mc}\mathrm{Expon}\left(s_{mt}\,|\beta_{mc}\right), \tag{8.52}$$

where

$$\mathrm{Expon}\left(s_{mt}\,|b\right) = be^{-bs_{mt}}. \tag{8.53}$$

If the prior is a mixture model, the prior allows for sparser sources, but the single exponential can still be modelled since it is a sub-set of the mixture distribution. Either prior can be used to enforce positivity in an EL–ICA algorithm. Here we will show the derivation using the rectified Gaussian prior.

Our model for image separation will be the ICA model, equation (8.5), but t now labels the pixel in the images. The positivity constraint is applied by the choice of the mixture of rectified Gaussians source prior. By using the EL approach we can obtain a bound on the evidence for each of the models, so we can compare the prior with a positivity constraint,

$$P\left(s_{mt}\,|\mathcal{H}\right) = \sum_{c=1}^{L} \pi_{mc}\mathcal{G}^{(R)}\left(s_{mt}\,|0,\beta_{mc}\right), \tag{8.54}$$

with the prior without a positivity constraint,

$$P\left(s_{mt}\,|\mathcal{H}\right) = \sum_{c=1}^{L} \pi_{mc}\mathcal{G}\left(s_{mt}\,|0,\beta_{mc}\right). \tag{8.55}$$

In order to enforce positivity of the mixing matrix, we use a rectified Gaussian prior for the mixing matrix,

$$P\left(A_{nm} | \mathcal{H}\right) = \mathcal{G}^{(R)}\left(A_{nm} | 0, \alpha_m\right). \tag{8.56}$$

The hyperpriors for the parameters of the prior distributions are the same as for the EL–ICA model. Additionally we will assume there is Gaussian noise added to the model. In order to preserve the positivity constraint we assume that the noise has zero mean and additionally we assume that the noise has equal variance for all observations:

$$P\left(\mathbf{x}_t | \Lambda, \mathcal{H}\right) = \mathcal{G}\left(\mathbf{x}_t | A\mathbf{s}_t, \Lambda I\right). \tag{8.57}$$

We derive an EL image separation algorithm in the same way as for the more general ICA algorithm. We minimise the cost function, C_{KL}, with respect to the approximate posterior distribution, Q, over the latent variables. In order to reduce memory requirements and to make the code more efficient, we choose the distribution to be of the separable form

$$Q\left(\mathbf{s}, \pi, \beta, A, \alpha, \Lambda\right) = \prod_{m=1}^{M} \prod_{t=1}^{T} Q\left(\mathbf{s}_{mt}\right) \times \prod_{n=1}^{N} \prod_{m=1}^{M} Q\left(A_{nm}\right)$$
$$\times Q\left(\pi\right) Q\left(\beta\right) Q\left(\alpha\right) Q\left(\Lambda\right). \tag{8.58}$$

When the positivity constraint is enforced, the optimal posterior distributions are found to be rectified Gaussians rather than Gaussians,

$$Q\left(\mathbf{s}_{mt}\right) = \mathcal{G}^{(R)}\left(\mathbf{s}_{mt} \left| m_{mt}^{(s)}, \Sigma_{mt}^{(s)}\right.\right), \tag{8.59}$$

$$Q\left(A_{nm}\right) = \mathcal{G}^{(R)}\left(A_{nm} \left| m_{nm}^{(A)}, \Sigma_{nm}^{(A)}\right.\right). \tag{8.60}$$

The choice of a separable distribution for the posterior allows the expectations under the rectified Gaussian to be evaluated using error functions,

$$\langle x \rangle_Q = a + \sqrt{\frac{2}{\pi b}} \frac{1}{\text{erfcx}\left(-a\sqrt{\frac{b}{2}}\right)}, \tag{8.61}$$

$$\langle x^2 \rangle_Q = a^2 + b^{-1} + a\sqrt{\frac{2}{\pi b}} \frac{1}{\text{erfcx}\left(-a\sqrt{\frac{b}{2}}\right)}. \tag{8.62}$$

If the full covariance matrix is obtained for the rectified Gaussian distribution, using expressions similar to equations (8.25-8.37), the expectations must be found by sampling from the distribution.

Otherwise the distributions are the same as for the algorithm without a positivity constraint. Therefore the update rules are the same as in (8.25-8.37). Although it appears that the algorithms are now the same with or without the positivity constraint, it should be remembered that the update rules depend on the expectations under the approximate distributions for s and A and so the parameter values will be different when positivity is required.

If instead of rectified Gaussians, the priors are chosen to be exponentials, the approximate posterior distributions are still rectified Gaussians, but the parameters satisfy

$$\Sigma_{mt}^{(s)} = \sum_{n=1}^{N} \left\langle A_{nm}^2 \Lambda \right\rangle_Q , \tag{8.63}$$

$$\Sigma_{mt}^{(s)} m_{mt}^{(s)} = -\sum_{c=1}^{L} \lambda_{mtc} \left\langle \beta_{mc} \right\rangle_Q , \tag{8.64}$$

$$+ \sum_{n=1}^{N} \left\langle A_{nm} \Lambda \left(\mathbf{x}_{nt} - \sum_{m' \neq m} A_{nm'} \mathbf{s}_{m't} \right) \right\rangle_Q , \tag{8.65}$$

$$\Sigma_{nm}^{(A)} = \sum_{t=1}^{T} \left\langle \Lambda \mathbf{s}_{mt}^2 \right\rangle_Q , \tag{8.66}$$

$$\Sigma_{nm}^{(A)} m_{nm}^{(A)} = -\left\langle \alpha_m \right\rangle_Q + \sum_{t=1}^{T} \left\langle \Lambda \left(\mathbf{x}_{nt} - \sum_{m' \neq m} A_{nm'} \mathbf{s}_{m't} \right) \mathbf{s}_{mt} \right\rangle_Q , \tag{8.67}$$

where α and β are the scale hyperparameters for the priors.

8.3.2 Application to handwritten digits

We can consider separation of some real world images. Figure 8.7 contains the first 64 '3's from the MNIST handwritten digit dataset. White corresponds to a pixel value of zero and black corresponds to a pixel value of one. We can separate these digits into a smaller basis of prototype digits. Figure 8.8 shows the results of performing EL–ICA without a positivity constraint on the images. While some of the images are based on '3's or their deformations, it is hard to understand where some of the images are derived from.

We can instead enforce a positivity constraint on the elements of s and A. Since $N \gg M$ and $T \gg M$, we can consider both s and A to be conceptually very similar, both can be expressed as rectangular matrices. Therefore it makes sense to model the two matrices in a similar way and

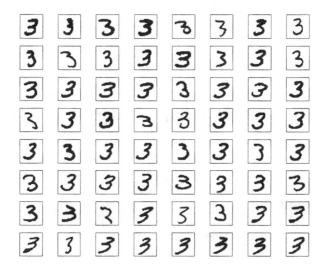

Figure 8.7. **MNIST digits:** *Sample digits from the MNIST handwritten dataset. There is a considerable range of styles for each of the digits. This range extends as far as digits that do not look like their assigned class, '3's that could be '2's, '7's that could be '9's,etc.*

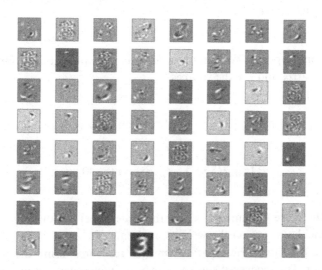

Figure 8.8. **Independent digits:** *Recovered sources obtained by separating the first 256 '3's into 64 images. Some of the images look like '3's or distortions to '3's (several images have negative regions next to positive regions which, when added to a prototype '3', will have the effect of moving the digit strokes). Many of the digits are not obviously recognisable as digit parts.*

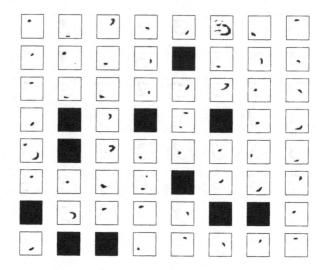

Figure 8.9. *Positive independent digits:* The recovered source images obtained when the positivity constraint is applied. The all-black images are the sources that have been switched off, that is there is no evidence to support their existence and so the posterior distributions for those images match the prior. The remaining images are all recognisably strokes that could be used to construct a digit. Each of the images is a localised feature of a digit.

to use similar priors. We can use a mixture of exponentials prior for the mixing matrix and for the sources,

$$P\left(A_{nm}\,|\mathcal{H}\right) = \sum_{c=1}^{L} \pi_{mc}^{(A)}\mathrm{Expon}\left(A_{nm}\,|\alpha_{mc}\right), \tag{8.68}$$

$$P\left(\mathbf{s}_{mt}\,|\mathcal{H}\right) = \sum_{c=1}^{L} \pi_{mc}^{(s)}\mathrm{Expon}\left(\mathbf{s}_{mt}\,|0\right)\beta_{mc}, \tag{8.69}$$

where there are Gamma priors on the scale hyper-parameters, α and β, and Dirichlet priors on the weights, $\pi^{(A)}$ and $\pi^{(s)}$.

Figure 8.9 shows the separated images recovered using the positivity constraint. The recovered source images are now separated into different strokes in the digits. Enforcing the positivity constraint has caused the hidden images to represent regions of the digits and so the separated images have become localised features rather than the images in figure 8.8 which were global features.

Figure 8.10 shows the reconstructions of the digits in figure 8.7 using

Figure 8.10. **Digit reconstructions:** *Reconstructions of the digits in figure 8.7 using the recovered images in figure 8.9. The digits are recognisable as the original digits, although in some cases the digits have been distorted to be more like a standard '3'.*

the recovered source images. The results show that a reduced basis of positive images can represent the dataset of digits.

We can extend this model further by considering separation of multiple digit classes. This could be useful for digit classification. One method would be to optimise a model for each class of digit and see which model best represents a trial digit. This could be viewed as wasteful since we believe that the hidden images are localised features of the digits and many of these will be the same for several classes of digits, for instance '2's and '3's are similar and so many of the features for the tops of the digits will be the same.

We can separate all the digits at once by splitting the mixing matrix into a matrix for each class of digit,

$$A = \begin{bmatrix} A^{(0)} \\ A^{(1)} \\ \vdots \\ A^{(9)} \end{bmatrix}, \qquad (8.70)$$

where $A^{(d)}$ is the mixing matrix that maps the hidden images to the images of the digits of class d. We can now choose a separate prior for the element of the mixing matrix for each different class, since we believe

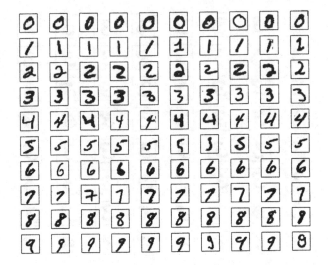

Figure 8.11. **Multiple digits classes:** *Examples of the digits that were used. The training set consisted of 256 examples of each class of digit.*

that the difference between a '2' and a '3' is that the digits are made with different amounts of each of the hidden images,

$$P\left(A_{nm}^{(d)}|\mathcal{H}\right) = \sum_{c=1}^{L} \pi_{mc}^{(A,d)} \text{Expon}\left(A_{nm}|\alpha_{mc}^{(d)}\right). \qquad (8.71)$$

Figure 8.11 shows some of the sample digits used when optimising the models. Figure 8.12 shows the hidden images when 256 of each class ('0' to '9') are separated into 64 hidden images. As before, the hidden images are localised features of the digits. Figure 8.13 shows the reconstructions of the original images using the learnt basis of hidden images. The reconstructions match the original digits showing that the set of 64 hidden images can represent the much larger set of 2560 digit images.

8.4 Deconvolution of images

A variation on image separation is the problem of image deconvolution. One example of the need to perform image deconvolution is astronomical imaging [Gull & Daniell, 1978]. When the sky is observed through a radio telescope, the recovered image is blurred by the beam pattern of the telescope. In order to obtain a better image, the image must be deconvolved. If the images are noisy, the deconvolution process is

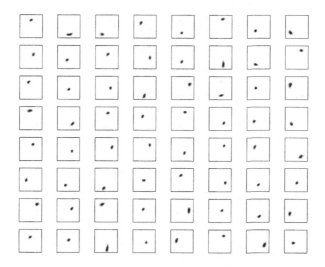

Figure 8.12. **Independent digits:** *Hidden images found when 256 examples from each class of digit ('0' to '9') are represented by a set of 64 hidden images. Unlike in figure 8.9, all of the hidden images are used since there are 10 times as much data and more evidence for each hidden image. The images represent localised features within the set of all digits but are qualitatively similar to those in figure 8.9.*

ill-conditioned and can result in a negative region in the image. This is unphysical since it corresponds to absorption of energy from the telescope by the sky. We can obtain a better reconstruction by reconstructing with a positivity constrain on the source pixels.

Our model for the convolution process is

$$\mathbf{x}_{ij} = \sum_{k=-K}^{K} \sum_{l=-L}^{L} A_{kl} \mathbf{s}_{i-k,j-l} + \mathbf{n}_{ij}, \qquad (8.72)$$

where the convolution filter, A, extends to size $(2K + 1) \times (2L + 1)$ and the observed data are $I \times J$ pixels. Figure 8.14 shows an example of this blurring process. The blind deconvolution problem is similar to the blind separation problem in that we have to infer A and $\mathbf{s}$ given $\mathbf{x}$.

Since we observe $I \times J$ pixels, any pixel in the range $-K < i \leqslant I + K$ and $-L < j \leqslant J + L$ in the source image will have an effect on the observed pixels. We can infer values for pixels outside the observed image. Therefore the inferred image will be an image of $(I + 2K) \times (J + 2L)$ pixels.

We use rectified Gaussian priors on the elements of A and $\mathbf{s}$. We optimise the model by minimising C_{KL}. If we choose the same separable

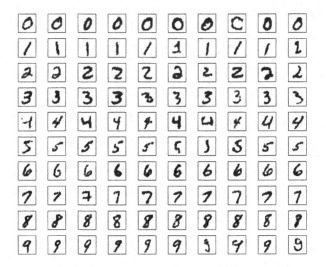

Figure 8.13. **Digit reconstructions:** *Reconstructions of the digits in figure 8.11 using the hidden images in figure 8.12.*

distribution as for the image separation process we obtain a set of rectified Gaussians but now the parameters are determined by

$$\Sigma_{ij}^{(s)} = \sum_{c=1}^{L} \lambda_{ijc} \langle \beta_c \rangle_Q + \sum_{kl} \langle A_{kl}^2 \Lambda \rangle_Q, \tag{8.73}$$

$$\Sigma_{ij}^{(s)} m_{ij}^{(s)} = \sum_{kl} \left\langle A_{kl} \Lambda \left(x_{i+k,j+l} - \sum_{k'l' \neq kl} A_{k'l'} s_{i+k-k',j+l-l'} \right) \right\rangle_Q, \tag{8.74}$$

$$\Sigma_{kl}^{(A)} = \langle \alpha \rangle_Q + \sum_{ij} \langle \Lambda s_{i-k,j-l}^2 \rangle_Q, \tag{8.75}$$

$$\Sigma_{kl}^{(A)} m_{kl}^{(A)} = \sum_{ij} \left\langle \Lambda \left(x_{ij} - \sum_{k'l' \neq i-k,j-l} A_{k'l'} s_{i-k,j-l'} \right) s_{i-k,j-l} \right\rangle_Q, \tag{8.76}$$

where the ranges of the summations are over those values for which s, A and x are defined.

8.4.1 Toy problem

Figure 8.15 shows the recovered source images obtained when the algorithm is optimised for varying sizes of convolution filters. When K is too small, the recovered source image is incorrect. But for $K \geqslant 2$

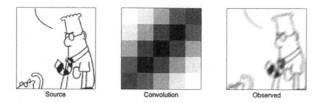

Figure 8.14. *Image blurring: Example of blurring by a localised convolution filter. The image is $I = 100$ by $J = 100$ pixels and the convolution filter is 5 by 5 pixels. Choosing a model where all of the pixels in the convolution are independent (i.e., not governed by a fixed functional form) allows for considerable variation in the shape of the filter, even for small sizes. [Dilbert image Copyright ©1997 United Feature Syndicate, Inc., used with permission.]*

Figure 8.15. *Deconvolved images: Recovered source images found from deconvolving the observation in figure 8.14 when the size of the convolution filter is varied. Here it is assumed that the filter is square, $L = K$. For $K < 2$ the filter is too small and so the reconstructed source is incorrect. For $K \geq 2$ the filter is large enough and the recovered source images match the hidden source. [Dilbert image Copyright ©1997 United Feature Syndicate, Inc., used with permission.]*

the recovered source matches the hidden source. We can view this is a model selection problem: how big must the filter be to perform a correct deconvolution of a noisy image? Figure 8.16 shows how C_{KL} varies as K varies. We can see that the model that minimises C_{KL} has $K = 2$ and so the correct filter size optimises C_{KL}.

Additionally there is a correct reconstruction of the image up to 2 pixels outside the observed image. This means that edge effects can be handled since an inference will be made of the pixels outside the observed region and the convolved image will match the data. The variance of the

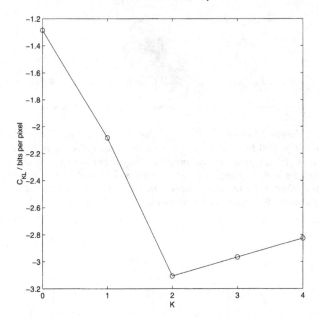

Figure 8.16. **Model selection:** *Variation of C_{KL} as K is varied for the deconvolution process. For $K < 2$ the filter is too small and so the deconvolution is incorrect. For $K > 2$ the filter is too large and so there are too many parameters. $K = 2$ optimises C_{KL} for this family of models.*

parameters outside the observed data is larger since the number of data points with which to make an inference is smaller. For $K > 2$ there is a border around the recovered image, these pixels are the pixels which have no influence on the observed data due to the learnt filter only being non-zero in a 5×5 patch. Therefore the posterior distribution for the pixels in the border tends to the prior.

Ensemble Learning allows us to search through the space of all possible parameters, varying K, L, L, etc., to find the model that optimises the deconvolution process. Alternatively we can see that if K is too large the deconvolution is still possible but it may be more computationally intensive.

8.5 Conclusion

We have shown how Ensemble Learning can be applied to the ICA problem to derive a simple algorithm that is able to perform separation of a mixture of sources into their independent components. We have shown that by choosing a set of priors that includes the idea of relevance, the model is able to switch off sources that are not required and so the model will not overfit to the data by including too many sources. We have shown that the cost function can be used as a bound on the evidence and so the EL–ICA model can be compared with other models (or compared with other EL–ICA models with different parameters).

The EL–ICA model has been extended to include the idea of positivity of the elements of A and s so that the algorithm can be applied to datasets in which it is unrealistic to assume that the sources can be negative valued. Finally we have shown that a blind deconvolution algorithm can be derived using the same principles.

9

Image processing methods using ICA mixture models

T.-W. Lee

M.S. Lewicki

An unsupervised classification algorithm is derived by modelling observed data as a mixture of several mutually exclusive classes that are each described by linear combinations of independent, non-Gaussian densities. The algorithm estimates the density of each class and is able to model class distributions with non-Gaussian structure. It can improve classification accuracy compared with standard Gaussian mixture models. When applied to images, the algorithm can learn efficient codes (basis functions) for images that capture the statistical structure of the images. We applied this method to the problem of unsupervised classification, segmentation and de-noising of images. This method was effective in classifying complex image textures such as trees and rocks in natural scenes. It was also useful for de-noising and filling in missing pixels in images with complex structures. The advantage of this model is that image codes can be learned with increasing numbers of classes thus providing greater flexibility in modelling structure and in finding more image features than in either Gaussian mixture models or standard ICA algorithms.

9.1 Introduction

Recently, Blind Source Separation by Independent Component Analysis has been applied to signal processing problems including speech enhancement, telecommunications and medical signal processing. ICA finds a linear non-orthogonal coordinate system in multivariate data determined by second- and higher-order statistics. The goal of ICA is to linearly transform the data in such a way that the transformed variables are as statistically independent from each other as possible [Jutten & Herault, 1991, Comon, 1994, Bell & Sejnowski, 1995, Cardoso & Laheld, 1996, Lee et al., 2000b]. ICA generalizes the technique of Principal

234

Component Analysis (PCA) and, like PCA, has proven a useful tool for finding structure in data.

In a mixture model (see, for example, [Duda & Hart, 1973]), the observed data can be categorized into several mutually exclusive classes. When the data in each class are modeled as multivariate Gaussian, it is called a Gaussian mixture model. We generalize this by assuming that the data in each class are generated by a linear combination of independent, non-Gaussian sources, as in the case of ICA. We call this model an ICA mixture model. This allows modelling of classes with non-Gaussian structure, e.g., platykurtic or leptokurtic probability density functions. The algorithm for learning the parameters of the model uses gradient ascent to maximize the log likelihood function.

In this chapter we are interested in finding structures in images. The application of ICA to sensory information processing is currently a vivid area of research and the efficient encoding of visual sensory information is an important task for image processing systems as well as for the understanding of coding principles in the visual cortex. Barlow [1961a] proposed that the goal of sensory processing is to transform the input signals in such a way as to reduce the redundancy between the inputs. Recently, several methods have been proposed to learn image codes that utilize a set of linear basis functions. Olshausen & Field [1996] used a sparseness criterion and found codes that were similar to localized and oriented receptive fields. Similar results were obtained by Bell & Sejnowski [1997] and Lewicki & Olshausen [1999] using the infomax ICA algorithm and a Bayesian approach respectively. The results in this chapter are along the lines of research on finding efficient codes. The main difference is the modelling of the underlying structure in mutually exclusive classes with an ICA mixture model.

This chapter is organized as follows. We present the ICA mixture model and show how to infer the parameters for this model. Detailed derivations are presented in Appendix 1. Section 9.3 shows how this method can be used to learn codes for images of different types. Section 9.4 uses the learned codes to classify and segment individual images with complex structure. Section 9.5 extends this model to de-noising images and filling in missing pixels in images. Finally, section 9.6 relates these methods to other algorithms and gives future directions of this line of research.

9.2 The ICA mixture model

Assume that the data $X = \{\mathbf{x}_1, \ldots, \mathbf{x}_T\}$ are drawn independently and generated by a mixture density model [Duda & Hart, 1973]. The likelihood of the data is given by the joint density

$$p(X|\Theta) = \prod_{t=1}^{T} p(\mathbf{x}_t|\Theta). \qquad (9.1)$$

The mixture density is

$$p(\mathbf{x}_t|\Theta) = \sum_{k=1}^{K} p(\mathbf{x}_t|C_k, \theta_k) p(C_k), \qquad (9.2)$$

where $\Theta = (\theta_1, \ldots, \theta_K)$ are the unknown parameters for each $p(\mathbf{x}|C_k, \theta_k)$, called the component densities. C_k denotes the class k and it is assumed that the number of classes, K, is known in advance. The number of classes can be also estimated using a split and merge algorithm described in [Bae et al., 2000]. Assume that the component densities are non-Gaussian and the data within each class are described by

$$\mathbf{x}_t = A_k \mathbf{s}_k + \mathbf{b}_k, \qquad (9.3)$$

where A_k is an $N \times M$ scalar matrix† and $\mathbf{b}_k$ is the bias vector for class k. The vector $\mathbf{s}_k$ is called the source vector‡ (these are also the coefficients for each basis function).

It is assumed that the individual sources $s_{k,i}$ within each class are mutually independent across a data ensemble. For simplicity, we consider the case where the number of sources (M) is equal to the number of linear combinations (N). Figure 9.1 shows a simple example of a dataset describable by an ICA mixture model. Each class was generated from (9.3) using a different A_k and $\mathbf{b}_k$. Class 'o' was generated by two uniformly distributed sources, whereas class '+' was generated by two Laplacian distributed sources ($p(s) \propto \exp(-|s|)$). The task is to classify the unlabelled data points and to determine the parameters for each class, $\{A_k, \mathbf{b}_k\}$, and the probability of each class $p(C_k|\mathbf{x}_t, \Theta)$ for each data point.

The iterative learning algorithm (derived in the Appendix 1) which performs gradient ascent on the total likelihood of the data in (9.2) has the following steps.

---

† This matrix is called the mixing matrix in ICA papers and specifies the linear combination of independent sources. Here, we refer to A as the basis matrix to distinguish this from the word mixture in the mixture model.

‡ Note that we have omitted the data index t for $s_{k,t}$.

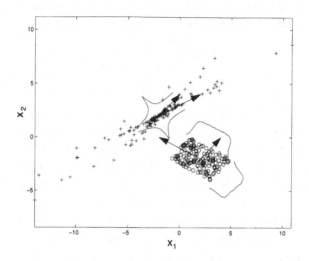

Figure 9.1. *A simple example for classifying with an ICA mixture model: There are two classes, '+' and 'o'; each class was generated by two independent variables, two bias terms and two basis vectors. Class 'o' was generated by two uniformly distributed sources as indicated next to the data class. Class '+' was generated by two Laplacian distributed sources with a sharp peak at the bias and heavy tails. The inset graphs show the distributions of the source variables, $s_{i,k}$, for each basis vector.*

- Compute the log likelihood of the data for each class:

$$\log p(\mathbf{x}_t | C_k, \theta_k) = \log p(\mathbf{s}_k) - \log(\det |A_k|), \tag{9.4}$$

where $\theta_k = \{A_k, \mathbf{b}_k\}$. Note that $\mathbf{s}_k$ is implicitly modeled for the adaptation of A_k.

- Compute the probability for each class given the data vector $\mathbf{x}_t$:

$$p(C_k | \mathbf{x}_t, \Theta) = \frac{p(\mathbf{x}_t | \theta_k, C_k) p(C_k)}{\sum_k p(\mathbf{x}_t | \theta_k, C_k) p(C_k)}. \tag{9.5}$$

- Adapt the basis functions A_k and the bias terms $\mathbf{b}_k$ for each class. The basis functions are adapted using gradient ascent:

$$\Delta A_k \propto \frac{\partial}{\partial A_k} \log p(\mathbf{x}_t | \Theta)$$

$$= p(C_k | \mathbf{x}_t, \Theta) \frac{\partial}{\partial A_k} \log p(\mathbf{x}_t | C_k, \theta_k). \tag{9.6}$$

This gradient can be approximated using an ICA algorithm, as shown below. The gradient can also be summed over multiple data points. An

approximate update rule was used for the bias terms (see Appendix 1
for an on-line update version for $\mathbf{b}_k$ and the derivations):

$$\mathbf{b}_k = \frac{\sum_t \mathbf{x}_t \, p(C_k|\mathbf{x}_t, \Theta)}{\sum_t p(C_k|\mathbf{x}_t, \Theta)}, \tag{9.7}$$

where t is the data index $(t = 1, \ldots, T)$.

The gradient of the log of the component density in (9.6) can be approximated using an ICA model. There are several methods for adapting the basis functions in the ICA model [Comon, 1994, Cardoso & Laheld, 1996, Bell & Sejnowski, 1995, Hyvärinen & Oja, 1997, Lee *et al.* 1999b]. One of the differences between the ICA algorithms is the use of higher-order statistics such as cumulants versus models that use a pre-defined density model. In our model, we are interested in iteratively adapting the class parameters and modelling a wider range of distributions. The extended infomax ICA learning rule is able to blindly separate unknown sources with sub- and super-Gaussian distributions.† This is achieved by using a simple type of learning rule first derived by Girolami [1998]. The learning rule in [Lee *et al.*, 1999b] uses the stability analysis of [Cardoso & Laheld, 1996] to switch between sub- and super-Gaussian regimes:

$$\Delta A_k \propto -p(C_k|\mathbf{x}_t, \Theta)A_k \left[I - K \tanh(\mathbf{s}_k)\mathbf{s}_k^\mathsf{T} - \mathbf{s}_k \mathbf{s}_k^\mathsf{T} \right], \tag{9.8}$$

where k_i are elements of the N-dimensional diagonal matrix K and $\mathbf{s}_k = W\mathbf{x}_t$. $W = A^{-1}$ is called the filter matrix. The source density parameters are adapted via the $k_{k,i}$s [Lee *et al.*, 1999b]:

$$k_{k,i} = \operatorname{sign} \left(E\{\operatorname{sech}^2(s_{k,i})\}E\{s_{k,i}^2\} - E\{[\tanh(s_{k,i})]s_{k,i}\} \right). \tag{9.9}$$

The source distribution is super-Gaussian when $k_{k,i} = 1$ and sub-Gaussian when $k_{k,i} = -1$. For the log likelihood estimation in (9.4) the term $\log p(\mathbf{s}_k)$ can be approximated as follows:

$$\log p(\mathbf{s}_{k,t}) \propto -\sum_{i=1}^{M} \left(k_{k,i} \log(\cosh s_{k,i,t}) - \frac{s_{k,i,t}^2}{2} \right). \tag{9.10}$$

Super-Gaussian densities are approximated by a density model with heavier tails than the Gaussian density; sub-Gaussian densities are approximated by a bimodal density [Girolami, 1998]. This source density

† A distribution that is more sharply peaked than a Gaussian around the mean and
has heavier tails is called super-Gaussian (a leptokurtic distribution) and a distribution
with flatter peak such as a uniform distribution is called sub-Gaussian (a platykurtic
distribution).

approximation is adequate for most problems [Lee *et al.*, 1999b].† The extended infomax algorithm is used for finding the parameters in Figure 9.1. A continuous parameter is inferred that fits a wide range of distributions.

When only sparse representations are needed, a Laplacian prior ($p(s)$ $\propto \exp(-|s|)$) can be used for the weight update, which simplifies the infomax learning rule:

$$\Delta A_k \propto -p(C_k | \mathbf{x}_t, \Theta) A_k \left[I - \text{sign}(\mathbf{s}_k) \mathbf{s}_k^T \right], \tag{9.11}$$

$$\log p(\mathbf{s}_k) \propto - \sum_i |s_{k,i}| \quad \text{(Laplacian prior)}. \tag{9.12}$$

A complete derivation of the learning algorithm is given in the Appendix 1. Note that the above adaptation rule is the learning rule that we applied to learning the image features. The use of other ICA algorithms is briefly discussed in the Appendix 2. Although the Laplacian prior was imposed on the coefficients, a more flexible prior such as the generalized Gaussian density model [Box & Tiao, 1973, Lewicki, 2000, Lee & Lewicki, 2000] was applied to the same dataset. The results were very similar to the results with the Laplacian prior ICA, suggesting that enforcing independence among the outputs results in sparse source densities.

9.3 Learning efficient codes for images

Recently, several methods have been proposed to learn image codes that utilize a set of linear basis functions. Olshausen & Field [1996] used a sparseness criterion and found codes that were similar to localized and oriented receptive fields. Similar results were presented in [Bell & Sejnowski, 1997] using the infomax ICA algorithm and in [Lewicki & Olshausen, 1998] using a Bayesian approach. By applying the ICA mixture model we present results that show a higher degree of flexibility in encoding the images. We used images of natural scenes obtained from [Olshausen & Field, 1996] and text images of scanned newspaper articles. The dataset consisted of 12 by 12 pixel patches selected randomly from both image types. Figure 9.2 illustrates examples of those image patches. Two complete basis vectors A_1 and A_2 were randomly initialized. Then, for each gradient in (9.6), a stepsize was computed as a function of the amplitude of the basis vectors and the

---

† Recently, we have replaced this with a more general density using an exponential power distribution [Lee & Lewicki, 2000] (see also section 1.5).

ıy Picture-Perfect Slice of the

ing on Route 4 over a dark and winding mountain pass, the visitor suddenly emerges into a "Lost Horizon" world of hot springs, trout streams and meadows of wildflowers, where cattle and the state's largest elk herd graze side by side.

But the same sense of wide-open Western independence evoked by the vistas has prevented the sale of the land for years. And the deal that is being negotiated for the ranch, which has been owned by one family for almost 40 years, is as much about Western attitudes toward public land as it is about money.

The Administration has long supported the purchase of the ranch, which has been called "the hole in the doughnut" because it is an island surrounded by the Santa Fe National Forest. Last February on a visit to

New Mexico, President had Air Force One mal fly over the ranch for a l its dominant feature — wide crater of the dorm

Republicans, noting one-third of New Mexi owned by the Federal have long opposed l chases. But in August sentiment began shift cally.

Under legislation dra tor Pete V. Domenici, l New Mexico, the Baca separate unit of the Na system, owned by the l Forest Service, but m trust, comprised of n pointed by the Presider

Continued on Pa

Figure 9.2. *Example of natural scene and text image: The 12 by 12 pixel image patches were randomly sampled from the images and used as inputs to the ICA mixture model.*

number of iterations. The algorithm converged after 100 000 iterations and learned two classes of basis functions. Figure 9.3 (top) shows the learned basis functions corresponding to natural images. The basis functions show Gabor†-like structure as previously reported [Olshausen & Field, 1996, Bell & Sejnowski, 1997, Lewicki & Olshausen, 1998]. However, the basis functions corresponding to text images (Figure 9.3 (bottom)) resemble bars with different lengths and widths that capture the high-frequency structure present in the text images. Note that unlike the case in K-means clustering or clustering with spherical Gaussians, the classes can be spatially overlapping. In the example of the natural images and newspaper text, both classes had zero mean and the pattern vectors were only distinguished by their relative probabilities under the different classes.

9.3.1 Comparing coding efficiency

We have compared the coding efficiency between the ICA mixture model and similar models using Shannon's theorem to obtain a lower bound on

---

† A Gaussian modulated sinusoid.

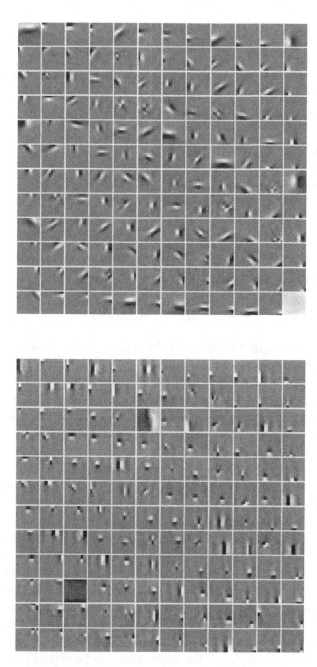

Figure 9.3. *ICA basis functions: (Top) Basis function class corresponding to natural images. (Bottom) Basis function class corresponding to text images.*

Table 9.1. *Comparing coding efficiency*

Data set and model	Test data (bits/pixel)		
	Nature	Text	Nature and text
ICA mixtures	4.7	5.2	5.0
Nature-adapted ICA	4.7	9.6	7.2
Text-adapted ICA	5.0	5.2	5.1
Nature- and text-adapted ICA	4.8	5.3	5.1
PCA	6.2	6.0	6.1

Note: Coding efficiency (bits per pixel) of five methods is compared for three test sets. Coding precision was set to 7 bits (nature, $\sigma_x = 0.016$ and text, $\sigma_x = 0.029$).

the number of bits required to encode the pattern [Lewicki & Sejnowski, 2000, Lewicki & Olshausen, 1999]:

$$\#\text{bits} \geqslant -\log_2 P(\mathbf{x}_t|A_k) - N \log_2(\sigma_x), \tag{9.13}$$

where N is the dimensionality of the input pattern $\mathbf{x}_t$ and σ_x is the coding precision (standard deviation of the noise introduced by errors in encoding). Table 9.1 compares the coding efficiency of five different methods. It shows the number of bits required to encode three different test datasets (5000 image patches from natural scenes, 5000 image patches from text images and 5000 image patches from both image types) using five different encoding methods (ICA mixture model, nature-adapted ICA, text-adapted ICA, nature- and text-adapted ICA, and PCA adapted on all three test sets). The ICA basis functions adapted on natural scene images exhibited the best encoding only for natural scenes (column: nature). The same occurred when text images were used for adapting and testing (column: text). Note that text adaptation yielded a reasonable basis for both datasets but nature adaptation gave a good basis only for nature data. The ICA mixture model gave the same encoding power for the individual test datasets, and it had the best encoding when both image types are present. The difference in coding efficiency between the ICA mixture model and PCA was significant (more than 20%). ICA mixtures yielded a small improvement over ICA adapted on both image types. We expect the size of the improvement to be greater in situations where there are greater differences among the classes. An advantage of the mixture model is that each image patch is automatically classified.

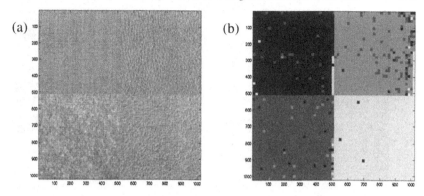

Figure 9.4. **Texture segmentation:** *(a) Texture of four different materials: (top-left) herringbone weave, (top-right) woollen cloth, (bottom-left) calf leather and (bottom-right) raffia. (b) The labels found by the algorithm are shown in different grey levels. Mis-classified patches of size 16 by 16 pixels are isolated patches in a different grey level than the square region of the texture.*

9.4 Unsupervised image classification and segmentation

In the previous section we applied the ICA mixture model to learn two classes of basis functions for newspaper text images and images of natural scenes. The same approach can be used to identify multiple classes in a single image. The learned classes are mutually exclusive and by dividing the whole image into small image patches and classifying them we can identify a cluster of patches which encode a certain region or texture of the image. Two examples illustrate how the algorithm can identify texture in images by unsupervised classification. In the first example, four texture images were taken from the Brodatz texture dataset and put into one image. Figure 9.4a shows the texture of four different materials: (top-left) herringbone weave, (top-right) woollen cloth, (bottom-left) calf leather and (bottom-right) raffia. Four classes of basis functions were adapted using the ICA mixture model by randomly sampling 8 by 8 pixel patches from the whole image, i.e., no label information was taken into account. One million patches were processed which took five hours on a Pentium II 400 MHz processor. The learned classes corresponded to the true classes 95% of the time. The automatic classification of the image as shown in figure 9.4b was done by dividing the image into adjacent non-overlapping 16 by 16 pixels patches. The mis-classified patches are shown in different grey levels than the square region of the texture. On larger problems (up to 10 classes and textures), the classification error rate was not significantly

(a)　(b)

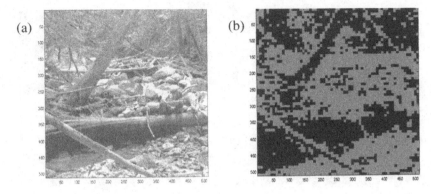

Figure 9.5. **Segmentation of natural scenes:** *(a) Example of natural scene with trees and rocks. (b) The classification of patches (8 by 8 pixels) using the learned two sets of basis functions. The cluster of class labels can be used to roughly segment the image into trees and rocks.*

different. In all experiments we used the merge and split procedure in [Ghahramani & Roweis, 1999] which helped to speed up convergence and avoid local minima. Another example of unsupervised image classification using the ICA mixture model is the segmentation of natural scenes. Figure 9.5a shows an example of a natural scene with trees and rocks. The 8 by 8 pixel patches were randomly sampled from the image and used as inputs to the ICA mixture model. Two classes of basis functions were adapted. The classification of the patches is shown in figure 9.5b. The cluster of class labels can be used to roughly segment the image into trees and rocks. Note that the segmentation may have been caused by brightness. However, very similar results were obtained on the whitened image.

9.5 Image enhancement

The ICA mixture model provides a good framework for encoding different image types. The learned basis functions can be used for de-noising images and filling in missing pixels. Each image patch is assumed to be a linear combination of basis functions plus additive noise: $\mathbf{x}_t = A_k \mathbf{s}_k + \mathbf{n}$. Our goal is to infer the class probability of the image patch as well as the coefficients $\mathbf{s}_k$ for each class that generate the image. Thus, $\mathbf{s}_k$ is inferred from $\mathbf{x}_t$ by maximizing the conditional probability density $p(\mathbf{s}_k | A_k, \mathbf{x}_t)$ as shown for a single class in [Lewicki & Olshausen, 1999]:

$$\hat{s}_k = \max_{s_k} \left[\log p(\mathbf{x}_t | A_k, \mathbf{s}_k) + \log p(\mathbf{s}_k) \right] \qquad (9.14)$$

$$= \min_{s_k} \left[\frac{\lambda_k}{2} |\mathbf{x}_t - A_k \mathbf{s}_k|^2 + \alpha_k^{\mathsf{T}} |\mathbf{s}_k| \right], \qquad (9.15)$$

where α_k is the width of the Laplacian p.d.f. and $\lambda_k = 1/\sigma_{k,n}^2$ is the precision of the noise for each class. The inference model in (9.15) computes the coefficients $\hat{s}_k$ for each class A_k, reconstructs the image using $\hat{\mathbf{x}}_t = A_k \hat{s}_k$, and computes the class probability $p(C_k | A_k, \hat{\mathbf{x}}_t)$. For signal to noise ratios above 20 dB the mis-classification of image patches was less than 2%. However, the error rate was higher when the noise variance was half the variance of the signal.

9.5.1 De-noising

To demonstrate how well the basis functions capture the structure of the data we applied the algorithm to the problem of removing noise in two different image types. In figure 9.6 (top-left) a small image was taken from a natural scene and a newspaper text. The whole image was corrupted with additive Gaussian noise that had half of the variance of the original image. The Gaussian noise changes the statistics of the observed image in such a way that the underlying coefficients **s** are less sparse than the original data. By adapting the noise level it is possible to infer the original source density by using (9.15). The adaptation using the ICA mixture model is better than the standard ICA model because the ICA mixture model is allowed to switch between different image models and therefore is more flexible in reconstructing the image. In this example, we used the two basis functions learned from natural scenes and newspaper text. For de-noising, the image was divided into small 12 by 12 pixel image patches. Each patch was first de-noised within each class and then classified by comparing the likelihood of the two classes. Figure 9.6 shows the original image, the noisy image with the signal to noise ratio (SNR) of 13 dB, the reconstructed image by using Wiener filtering, which is a standard de-noising method with SNR=15 dB, and the results of the ICA mixture model (SNR=21 dB). The classification error was 10%.

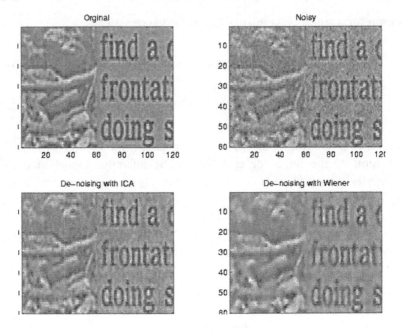

Figure 9.6. *Image de-noising:* Top-left: the original image. Top-right: the noisy image (SNR=13 dB). Bottom-left: the results of the Wiener filtering de-noising method (SNR=15 dB). Bottom-right: the reconstructed image using the ICA mixture model (SNR=21 dB).

9.5.2 Filling in missing data

In some image processing applications pixel values may be missing. This problem is similar to the de-noising problem and the ICA mixture model can be used as a technique to solve this problem. In filling in missing pixels, the missing information can be viewed as another form of noise. Figure 9.7 (top-right) shows the same image with now 50% of the pixels missing. The SNR improved from 7 dB to 14 dB using the ICA mixture model (figure 9.7 (bottom-left)). The reconstruction by interpolating with splines gave SNR = 11 dB (Figure 9.7 (bottom-right)). The classification error was 20%.

9.6 Discussion

The algorithm for unsupervised classification presented here is based on a mixture model using ICA to model the structure of the classes. The parameters are estimated using maximum likelihood. This method

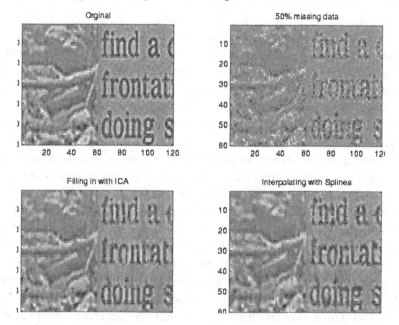

Figure 9.7. *Image de-noising: Top-left: the original image. Top-right: the image with 50% missing pixels replaced with grey pixels (SNR=7 dB). Bottom-left: the reconstructed image using the ICA mixture model (SNR=14 dB). Bottom-right: the reconstructed image using splines (SNR=11 dB).*

is similar to other approaches including the mixture density networks by Bishop [1994] in which a neural network was used to find arbitrary density functions. This algorithm reduces to the Gaussian mixture model when the source priors are Gaussian. Purely Gaussian structure, however, is rare in real datasets. Here we have used super-Gaussian and sub-Gaussian densities as priors. These priors could be extended as proposed by Attias [1999a]. The ICA mixture model was used for learning a complete set of basis functions without additive noise. However, the method can be extended to take into account additive Gaussian noise and an overcomplete set of basis vectors [Lewicki & Sejnowski, 1998, Lewicki & Sejnowski, 2000]. The structure of the ICA mixture model is also similar to the mixtures of factor analyzers proposed by Ghahramani & Hinton [1997]. The difference here is that the coefficient distribution $p(s)$ and hence the distribution $p(X|\Theta)$ are assumed to be non-Gaussian. Another extension of this into modelling temporal information by Penny *et al.* [2000] could be considered.

We have demonstrated that the algorithm can learn efficient codes to represent different image types such as natural scenes and text images and was a significant improvement over PCA encoding. Single class ICA models showed image compression rates comparable to or better than traditional image compression algorithms such as JPEG [Lewicki & Olshausen, 1999]. Using ICA mixtures to learn image codes should yield additional improvement in coding efficiency. We have investigated the application of the ICA mixture model to the problem of unsupervised classification and segmentation of images as well as de-noising, and filling in missing pixels. Our results suggest that the method is capable of handling these problems successfully. Furthermore, the ICA mixture model is able to increase the performance over Gaussian mixture models or standard ICA models when a variety of image types are present in the data. However, the unsupervised segmentation of images by discovering image textures remains a difficult problem. Since the segmentation technique presented here is based on the classification of small image patches, the global information of the image is not taken into consideration. The multi-resolution problem may be overcome by including a multi-scale hierarchical structure into the algorithm or by re-applying the algorithm with different scales of the basis functions and combining the results. This additional process would smooth the image segmentation and the ICA mixture model could serves as a baseline segmentation algorithm. These results need to be compared with other methods, such as those proposed by De Bonet & Viola [1998] which measured statistical properties of textures coded with a large-scale, fixed wavelet basis. In contrast, the approach here models image structure by adapting the basis functions themselves. The application of ICA for noise removal in images as well as filling in missing pixels will result in significant improvement when several different classes of images are present in the image. Fax machines, for example, transmit text as well as images. Since the basis functions of the two image models are significantly different [Lee *et al.*, 1999c] the ICA mixture model will improve in coding and enhancing the images. The technique used here for de-noising and filling in missing pixels was proposed in [Lewicki & Sejnowski, 2000, Lewicki & Olshausen, 1999]. The same technique can be applied to multiple classes as demonstrated in this chapter. The main concern of this technique is the accuracy of the coefficient prior. A different technique for de-noising using the fixed point ICA algorithm was proposed in [Hyvärinen *et al.*, 1999b].

The ICA mixture model has the advantage that the basis functions of several image types can be learned simultaneously. Compared with algorithms that use one fixed set of basis functions, the results presented here are promising and may provide further insights in designing improved image processing systems.

9.7 Appendix 1: derivation of the ICA mixture model algorithm

We assume that $p(X|\Theta)$ as given by (9.1) is a differentiable function of Θ. The log likelihood $\mathcal{L}$ is then

$$\mathcal{L} = \sum_{t=1}^{T} \log p(\mathbf{x}_t|\Theta) \tag{9.16}$$

and, using (9.2), the gradient for the parameters of each class k is

$$
\begin{aligned}
\nabla_{\theta_k}\mathcal{L} &= \sum_{t=1}^{T} \frac{1}{p(\mathbf{x}_t|\Theta)}\nabla_{\theta_k}p(\mathbf{x}_t|\Theta) \\
&= \sum_{t=1}^{T} \frac{\nabla_{\theta_k}\left[\sum_{k=1}^{K} p(\mathbf{x}_t|C_k,\theta_k)p(C_k)\right]}{p(\mathbf{x}_t|\Theta)} \\
&= \sum_{t=1}^{T} \frac{\nabla_{\theta_k}p(\mathbf{x}_t|C_k,\theta_k)p(C_k)}{p(\mathbf{x}_t|\Theta)}.
\end{aligned}
\tag{9.17}
$$

Using the Bayes relation, the class probability for a given data vector $\mathbf{x}_t$ is

$$p(C_k|\mathbf{x}_t,\Theta) = \frac{p(\mathbf{x}_t|\theta_k,C_k)p(C_k)}{\sum_k p(\mathbf{x}_t|\theta_k,C_k)p(C_k)}. \tag{9.18}$$

Substituting (9.18) in (9.17) leads to

$$
\begin{aligned}
\nabla_{\theta_k}\mathcal{L} &= \sum_{t=1}^{T} p(C_k|\mathbf{x}_t,\Theta)\frac{\nabla_{\theta_k}p(\mathbf{x}_t|\theta_k,C_k)p(C_k)}{p(\mathbf{x}_t|\theta_k,C_k)p(C_k)} \\
&= \sum_{t=1}^{T} p(C_k|\mathbf{x}_t,\Theta)\nabla_{\theta_k}\log p(\mathbf{x}_t|C_k,\theta_k).
\end{aligned}
\tag{9.19}
$$

The log likelihood function in (9.19) is the log likelihood for each class. For the present model, the class log likelihood is given by the log likelihood for the standard ICA model:

$$
\begin{aligned}
\log p(\mathbf{x}_t|\theta_k,C_k) &= \log \frac{p(\mathbf{s}_t)}{|\det A_k|} \\
&= \log p(A_k^{-1}(\mathbf{x}_t - \mathbf{b}_k)) - \log|\det A_k|.
\end{aligned}
\tag{9.20}
$$

Gradient ascent is used to estimate the parameters that maximize the log likelihood. The gradient parameters for each class are the gradient of the basis functions and the gradient of the bias vector $\nabla_{\theta_k}\mathcal{L} = \{\nabla_{A_k}\mathcal{L}, \nabla_{\mathbf{b}_k}\mathcal{L}\}$. We consider each in turn.

9.7.1 Estimating the basis matrix

Adapt the basis functions for each class A_k with (9.19):

$$\nabla_{A_k}\mathcal{L} = \sum_{t=1}^{T} p(C_k|\mathbf{x}_t, \Theta)\nabla_{A_k} \log p(\mathbf{x}_t|C_k, \theta_k). \qquad (9.21)$$

The adaptation is performed by using gradient ascent with the gradient of the component density with respect to the basis functions giving

$$\Delta A_k \propto p(C_k|\mathbf{x}_t, \Theta)\frac{\partial}{\partial A_k} \log p(\mathbf{x}_t|C_k, \theta_k). \qquad (9.22)$$

In the basis function adaptation, the gradient of the component density with respect to the basis functions A_k is weighted by $p(C_k|\mathbf{x}_t, \Theta)$.

9.7.2 Estimating the bias vectors

We can use (9.19) to adapt the bias vectors for each class A_k.

$$\nabla_{\mathbf{b}_k}\mathcal{L} = \sum_{t=1}^{T} p(C_k|\mathbf{x}_t, \Theta)\nabla_{\mathbf{b}_k} \log p(\mathbf{x}_t|C_k, \theta_k). \qquad (9.23)$$

The adaptation is performed by using gradient ascent with the gradient of the component density with respect to the bias vector $\mathbf{b}_k$ giving

$$\Delta \mathbf{b}_k \propto p(C_k|\mathbf{x}_t, \Theta)\frac{\partial}{\partial \mathbf{b}_k} \log p(\mathbf{x}_t|C_k, \theta_k). \qquad (9.24)$$

Using (9.20) in (9.24) we can adapt $\mathbf{b}_k$ as follows:

$$\Delta \mathbf{b}_k \propto p(C_k|\mathbf{x}_t, \Theta)\frac{\partial}{\partial \mathbf{b}_k} \left[\log p(A_k^{-1}(\mathbf{x}_t - \mathbf{b}_k)) - \log|\det A_k|\right]. \qquad (9.25)$$

Instead of using the gradient we may also use an approximate method for the adaptation of the bias vectors. The maximum likelihood estimate $\hat{\Theta}$ must satisfy the condition

$$\sum_{t=1}^{T} p(C_k|\mathbf{x}_t, \hat{\Theta})\nabla_{\theta_k} \log p(\mathbf{x}_t|C_k, \hat{\theta}_k) = 0, \qquad k = 1,\dots,K. \qquad (9.26)$$

We can use (9.26) to adapt the bias vector or mean vector $\mathbf{b}_k$.

$$\nabla_{\mathbf{b}_k} \mathcal{L} = 0, \tag{9.27}$$

$$\sum_{t=1}^{T} p(C_k|\mathbf{x}_t, \Theta) \nabla_{\mathbf{b}_k} \log p(\mathbf{x}_t|\theta_k, C_k) = 0. \tag{9.28}$$

Substituting (9.20) into (9.28) shows that the gradient of the first term in (9.20) must be zero. From this it follows that

$$\nabla_{\mathbf{b}_k} \log p(A_k^{-1}(\mathbf{x}_t - \mathbf{b}_k)) = 0. \tag{9.29}$$

Assuming that we observe a large amount of data $\mathbf{x}_t$ and the probability density function of the prior $p(\mathbf{s}_t)$ is symmetric and differentiable, then $\log p(\mathbf{s}_t)$ will be symmetric as well and the bias vector can be approximated by the weighted average of the data samples

$$\mathbf{b}_k = \frac{\sum_t \mathbf{x}_t \, p(C_k|\mathbf{x}_t, \Theta)}{\sum_t p(C_k|\mathbf{x}_t, \Theta)}. \tag{9.30}$$

9.8 Appendix 2: ICA learning algorithm

The gradient of the log component density for each class $\log p(\mathbf{x}_t|C_k, \theta_k)$ can be computed using ICA.

The goal of ICA is to find a linear transformation W of the dependent sensor signals $\mathbf{x}$ that makes the outputs $\mathbf{a}$ as independent as possible so that $\mathbf{a}$ is an estimate of the sources. The sources are exactly recovered when W is the inverse of A up to a permutation and scale change. A learning algorithm for adapting the basis functions can be derived using the information maximization principle [Bell & Sejnowski, 1995] or the maximum likelihood estimation (MLE) method [Gaeta & Lacoume, 1990, MacKay, 1996, Pearlmutter & Parra, 1996, Pham & Garrat, 1997, Cardoso, 1997b]. The learning rule is obtained by maximizing the log likelihood with respect to A and using the natural gradient extension [Cardoso & Laheld, 1996, Amari, 1998]:

$$\Delta A \propto AA^{\mathsf{T}} \frac{\partial}{\partial A} \log p(\mathbf{x}|A) = -A \left[I - \phi(\mathbf{s})\mathbf{x}^{\mathsf{T}} \right] \tag{9.31}$$

where $\phi(\mathbf{s}) = -\frac{\partial p(\mathbf{s})/\partial \mathbf{s}}{p(\mathbf{s})}$. The learning rule (9.31) is the general ICA learning rule and involves the prior knowledge on $p(\mathbf{s})$ which is necessary to implement the application specific ICA learning rule. It has been shown that the general learning algorithm in (9.31) can be derived from several theoretical viewpoints such as MLE [Pearlmutter & Parra, 1996], info-max [Bell & Sejnowski, 1995] and negentropy maximization [Girolami &

Fyfe, 1997b]. Lee *et al.* [2000b] review these techniques and show their relation to each other; see also Chapter 1. The parametric density estimate $p_i(s_i)$ plays an essential role in the success of the learning rule in (9.31). Local convergence is assured if $p_i(s_i)$ is an estimate of the true source density [Pham & Garrat, 1997]. For example, the sigmoid function used in the Bell & Sejnowski [1995] learning algorithm is suited to separating super-Gaussian sources

A way of generalizing the learning rule to sources with either sub-Gaussian or super-Gaussian distributions is to derive a separate learning rule for sub-Gaussian and super-Gaussian components was described by Girolami [1998] as

$$\Delta A \propto -A \left[I - K \tanh(\mathbf{s})\mathbf{s}^\mathsf{T} - \mathbf{s}\mathbf{s}^\mathsf{T} \right], \quad \begin{cases} k_i = 1, & \text{super-Gaussian,} \\ k_i = -1, & \text{sub-Gaussian,} \end{cases}$$

(9.32)

where k_i are elements of the N-dimensional diagonal matrix K. The k_is can be derived from the generic stability analysis [Cardoso, 1998a] of separating solutions. This yields the choice of k_is used by Lee *et al.* [1999b],

$$k_i = \text{sign} \left(E\{\text{sech}^2(s_{i,t})\} E\{s_{i,t}^2\} - E\{[\tanh(s_{i,t})]s_{i,t}\} \right), \quad (9.33)$$

which ensures stability of the learning rule [Lee *et al.*, 1999b]. Instead of the binary switching of k_i one can derive a learning rule using a generalized Gaussian density model [Box & Tiao, 1973]. The source densities are modeled by generalized Gaussians [Box & Tiao, 1973] that provide a general method for modelling non-Gaussian statistical structure of univariate distributions that have the form $p(x) \propto \exp(-|x|^q)$. By inferring q, a wide class of statistical distributions can be characterized including uniform, Gaussian, Laplacian, and other sub- and super-Gaussian densities. Details of the learning rule derivation are given in [Lewicki, 2000]. The extension of the generalized Gaussian model into the ICA mixture model is described in [Lee & Lewicki, 2000]. Note that the type of generalized Gaussian for ICA was described by Everson & Roberts [1999a] who used a maximum likelihood model for inferring the parameters.

9.8.1 ICA mixture model learning rules

We can write (9.32) and (9.33) in terms of the basis functions for each class A_k in (9.22):

$$\Delta A_k \propto -p(C_k|\mathbf{x}_t, \Theta)A_k \left[I - K \tanh(\mathbf{s}_k)\mathbf{s}_k^\mathsf{T} - \mathbf{s}_k\mathbf{s}_k^\mathsf{T} \right], \qquad (9.34)$$

where

$$\mathbf{s}_k = A_k^{-1}(\mathbf{x}_t - \mathbf{b}_k), \qquad (9.35)$$

and

$$k_{k,i} = \text{sign} \left(E\{\text{sech}^2(s_{k,i})\}E\{s_{k,i}^2\} - E\{[\tanh(s_{k,i})]s_{k,i}\} \right). \qquad (9.36)$$

The source distribution is super-Gaussian when $k_{k,i} = 1$ and sub-Gaussian when $k_{k,i} = -1$. The adaptation of the log prior $\log p(\mathbf{s}_k)$ can be approximated as follows:

$$\log p(\mathbf{s}_{k,t}) \propto -\sum_{i=1}^{N} \left(k_{k,i} \log(\cosh s_{k,i,t}) - \frac{s_{k,i,t}^2}{2} \right). \qquad (9.37)$$

These are the formulae used for unsupervised classification and automatic context switching in the examples given in the text.

For the learning of image codes a Laplacian model was used to learn sparse representations. The simplified learning rule uses (9.22) and (9.38):

$$\Delta A_k \propto -p(C_k|\mathbf{x}_t, \Theta)A_k \left[I - \text{sign}(\mathbf{s}_k)\mathbf{s}_k^\mathsf{T} \right]. \qquad (9.38)$$

The log prior simplifies to

$$\log p(\mathbf{s}_k) \propto -\sum_i |s_{k,i}| \qquad \text{(Laplacian prior)}. \qquad (9.39)$$

We have also applied the extended infomax rule as well as the generalized Gaussian model to learning image codes. It turned out that the basis functions and coefficients had very similar statistics to the results with the simple Laplacian ICA mixture model. Again, this suggests that enforcing statistical independence among the outputs of the linear transformation yields sources that have sparse densities.

10

Latent class and trait models for data classification and visualisation

M.A. Girolami

10.1 Introduction

Independent Component Analysis (ICA), as a signal processing tool, has shown great promise in many application domains, two of the most successful being telecommunications and biomedical engineering. With the growing awareness of ICA many other less obvious applications of the transform are starting to appear, for example financial time series prediction [Back & Weigend, 1998] and information retrieval [Isbell & Viola, 1999, Girolami, 2000a, Vinokourov & Girolami, 2000]. In such applications ICA is being used as an unsupervised means of exploring and, hopefully, uncovering meaningful latent traits or structure within the data. In the case of financial time series prediction the factors which drive the evolution of the time series are hopefully uncovered, whereas within information retrieval the latent concepts or topics which generate key-words that occur in the documents are sought after. The strong assumption of independence of the hidden factors in ICA is difficult to argue for when there is limited *a priori* knowledge of the data, indeed it is desired that the analysis uncover *informative components* which may, or may not, be independent. Nevertheless the independence assumption allows analytically tractable statistical models to be developed.

This chapter will consider how the standard ICA model can be extended and used in the unsupervised classification and visualisation of multivariate data. Prior to the formal presentation, to set the context of the remainder of the chapter, a short review of the ICA signal model and the corresponding statistical representation is given. The remaining sections propose ICA inspired techniques for the unsupervised classification and visualisation of multivariate data.

10.2 Latent variable models

The standard signal model for ICA is given as

$$\mathbf{x} = A\mathbf{s} + \mathbf{n} \tag{10.1}$$

where, usually, $\mathbf{x} \in \mathbb{R}^N$, $\mathbf{s} \in \mathbb{R}^M$ and $\mathbf{n} \in \mathbb{R}^N$. We will however consider a range of possible source and observation representations. This has the following associated statistical model:

$$p(\mathbf{x}|A) = \int p(\mathbf{x}|\mathbf{s}, A)p(\mathbf{s})d\mathbf{s} \tag{10.2}$$

The form of the source or latent factor density $p(\mathbf{s})$ is crucial and indeed makes the distinction between what are termed latent trait and latent class models [Agresti, 1990]. If the latent space is known to consist of continuous statistically independent components such that $p(\mathbf{s}) = \prod_{i=1}^{M} p(s_i)$ then (10.2) yields the standard ICA statistical model with additive noise, where the noise model $p(\mathbf{x}|\mathbf{s}, A)$ can be any member of the exponential family of distributions in which case a Laplace approximation to the likelihood (10.2) can be made. In most applications the noise is taken to have a multivariate Gaussian distribution.

On the other hand, if the latent space consists of discrete factors or sources which have K distinct states each with a prior probability of occurrence given by $P(\mathbf{s}_k)$ then the model can be described as

$$p(\mathbf{x}|A) = \sum_{k=1}^{K} p(\mathbf{x}|\mathbf{s}_k, A)P(\mathbf{s}_k). \tag{10.3}$$

In telecommunications engineering transmitted symbols are discrete. These are, possibly, emitted from the alphabet with known prior probabilities and after transmission, the received signals will be a noise contaminated mixture. Equation (10.1) has been used as a signal model for this process [Belouchrani & Cardoso, 1994]. The corresponding statistical model is (10.3) and this has been used to develop an ICA method for recovering discrete sources from their noise (Gaussian) contaminated unknown mixture [Belouchrani & Cardoso, 1994].

It is interesting to note that if the latent space is modelled as a finite number K of discrete uniformly spaced points on an M-dimensional grid then (10.3) reduces to

$$p(\mathbf{x}|A) = \frac{1}{K} \sum_{k=1}^{K} p(\mathbf{x}|\mathbf{s}_k, A). \tag{10.4}$$

If for the purposes of visualisation $M = 2$ and the noise distribution is modelled as an isotropic Gaussian then (10.4) exactly describes the Generative Topographic Mapping (GTM) form of latent trait model [Bishop, 1998]. Indeed, both the GTM and the ICA method proposed by Belouchrani & Cardoso [1994] yield (perhaps unsurprisingly, but worthy of note) identical parameter estimation methods.

An alternative interpretation of the GTM, from the perspective of the ICA signal model, is that the M sources are each continuous uniformly distributed signals and so drawing K Monte Carlo samples from this distribution gives the approximation to the observation density as

$$p(\mathbf{x}|A) \approx \frac{1}{K} \sum_{k=1}^{K} p(\mathbf{x}|\mathbf{s}_k, A). \tag{10.5}$$

The uniform distribution has been termed sub-Gaussian. Now multimodal distributions exhibit sub-Gaussian characteristics, such as negative kurtosis. The uniform sampling then provides an approximation of drawing samples from the multimodal distributions, and this is one reason why the GTM has proven to be most successful in visualising clustered structure in multivariate continuous data.

In contrast to latent trait models a latent class model assumes a discrete latent space which is formed by a K-dimensional hyper-cube where each latent point is formed by the individual vertices of the hyper-cube. In this case the generative model is also given by equation (10.3); now, however, each $\mathbf{s}_k$ is a K-dimensional vector which has only one non-zero element signifying a vertex of the hyper-cube. It should be noted that these latent vectors are therefore categorical and nominal and as such have no topographic meaning [Agresti, 1990], they are in effect the labels of each vertex. So $P(\mathbf{s}_k)$ is the proportion of points associated with the kth vertex. In the case where the conditional density is taken as Gaussian then this is a standard Gaussian-Mixture model from which standard clustering methods such as soft-assignment K-means follow [Jain & Dubes, 1988]. In fact the soft-assignment K-means clustering method is the latent class equivalent of the continuous GTM as both assume a Gaussian class conditioned likelihood.

Latent trait and class models have been briefly reviewed here and the probabilistic model which describes ICA also describes methods such as the GTM and indeed the two techniques are identical in the case of mixtures of discrete symbols emitted from a finite alphabet and contaminated with Gaussian noise.

The notion of utilising ICA as a means of clustering (unsupervised classification) has previously been proposed in [Roberts *et al.*, 1999], [Lee *et al.*, 1999a] and [Girolami, 1998]. The following section introduces a hierarchic method for clustering multiclass (polychotomous) data and demonstrates how this is closely linked to ICA

10.3 ICA clustering using binary decision trees

Decision trees are a common methodology for inductive inference. Their benefits include fast computational properties and a representation that may be easy to interpret in terms of decisions. Typically they are used when data is discrete-valued but extensions to continuous-valued data exist.

Decision trees can be used for solving classification and regression problems. Binary trees provide a computationally effective solution, since only $\log_2 n$ decisions have to be made for a tree with n leaves. Furthermore, if the decisions are linear, then each decision is essentially an inner product between a data vector and a normal vector of a separating hyperplane.

A binary decision tree works by recursively partitioning the dataset into two. This series of decisions implicitly defines a binary tree, where the decisions are made at the nodes. Depending on the result of each decision, the observed sample continues down the tree to a child node or leaf. Finally, each observation ends up in a leaf and hence the tree has classified the data.

The typical problem where decision trees are applied is when the observed data is a set of multivariate attribute values, e.g., $\mathbf{x}(k) = [age(k), sex(k), height(k)]$. In basic methods, the decisions are made by choosing one of the attributes and computing a threshold, which then implements a binary decision on all observations. For example, we might choose the attribute $sex(k)$ as the deciding attribute and then separate the observations into classes *male* and *female*.

The choice of attribute in the ID3 algorithm [Quinlan, 1986] is based on the concept of *information gain*. The attribute which reduces entropy the most is selected for implementing the decision. This measure, however, depends on using training data in which we know the correct classes for each observation. The information gain then chooses the decision that gives the best partitioning with respect to classification performance. The algorithm can therefore be interpreted as a greedy optimisation method for minimising classification error using a binary tree.

10.3.1 Linear decisions at tree nodes using ICA

The basic approaches, e.g., ID3, have been extended in various directions. Continuous-valued attributes have been considered and decisions made by thresholding linear combinations of continuous-valued attributes. However, the decisions are made by depending on known class labels for the observations. In contrast to this we consider implementing the decisions by thresholding linear combinations without depending on class labels, i.e., we depend alone on the data distribution $p(\mathbf{x})$.

If a multivariate dataset is considered in the classification problem, each decision divides the dataset in two. Intuitively, it is desirable to divide the dataset so that different types of samples go to different parts of the tree. With known class labels this can be achieved using one of various information gain measures, or simply by computing the optimal separating hyperplane. However, it is our purpose to construct a decision tree without knowing the class labels.

Essentially a single ICA vector can be used to compute the decision rule in each node. The ICA vector $\mathbf{w}$ defines the direction in which the dataset has most 'structure' as explained below. The decision rule is then implemented as a separating hyperplane with normal $\mathbf{w}$ [Pajunen & Girolami, 2000].

In Independent Component Analysis it is normally assumed that the observed multivariate data is generated by the signal model defined in equation (10.1) and described by the statistical model (10.2). ICA is often solved, in the noiseless case, by extracting one component $\hat{s}_i = \mathbf{w}^T\mathbf{x}$ at a time by imposing certain restrictions on the separating matrix. Consequently, one is looking for directions that *minimise entropy*. A single row vector of the separating matrix gives one component $a = \mathbf{w}^T\mathbf{x}$.

Entropy can be interpreted as a measure of structure in the data if we accept the notion that certain non-Gaussian distributions imply more structure than Gaussian distributions. This can be demonstrated for example considering multimodal distributions which have clearly non-Gaussian distributions when we consider directions which would retain the multimodal distribution in projections. Other directions where the different modes would overlap in projections are closer to Gaussian and simultaneously do not have the visible multimodal structure. For exploratory data analysis looking for such directions has been proposed in [Friedman & Tukey, 1974].

From the viewpoint of unsupervised classification, we would like to implement a decision that effectively separates different types of data samples to different outcomes of the decision. Looking to implement a linear binary decision means that we need to define a hyperplane which separates the samples into two classes (creates a dichotomy). If we choose this hyperplane as the one defined by $\mathbf{w}$ as the normal vector, then the hyperplane will be orthogonal to the minimum entropy direction.

This can be interpreted in another way: the linear transformation $a = \mathbf{w}^T\mathbf{x}$ is a change of variables into a new variable which has most bimodal structure. The decision rule may then simply be a thresholding operation on the new variable. However, in the following section we consider the estimation of the hyperplane and show that standard ICA methods yield the maximum posterior estimate of the Fisher linear discriminant for dichotomies.

10.4 Maximum negentropy classification

The transformed data negentropy has been proposed as a suitable ICA contrast and adopted by a number of researchers in their work, for example useful approximations are developed by Hyvärinen [1999a]. Consider then the case where we are seeking to dichotomise the data into two clusters of self-similar points. As with Gaussian mixture modelling we can assume that the projection will consist of a mixture of two univariate Gaussians and so the projection vector will be a Gaussian linear discriminant. Using a two element mixture model and maximising the negentropy of the projected data will find a projection which will be maximally bimodal [Girolami, 1998]. In addition however this will be a minimum entropy projection and so will minimise the overlap between the two clusters.

The estimate of negentropy based on T samples of the zero-mean data $\mathbf{x}$, i.e., $\frac{1}{T}\sum_t \mathbf{x}_t = 0$, is given as

$$\mathcal{D} = \sum_{t=1}^{T} \log\{p(a_t|\mathbf{w})\} + \frac{1}{2}\log\{2\pi e \mathbf{w}^T R_\mathbf{x} \mathbf{w}\}. \qquad (10.6)$$

Here $R_\mathbf{x} = \frac{1}{T}\sum_{t=1}^{T} \mathbf{x}_t\mathbf{x}_t^T$ and $p(a_t)$ is the distribution of the tth sample, being defined as the mixture of two Gaussians such that the marginal probability of the transformed observations satisfies

$$p(a_t|\mathbf{w}) = \sum_{k\in\{\mathcal{C}_1,\mathcal{C}_2\}} p(a_t|\mathcal{C}_k,\mathbf{w})P(\mathcal{C}_k)$$
$$= \mathcal{N}(\alpha_1,\beta_1)P(C_1) + \mathcal{N}(\alpha_1,\beta_1)P(C_2).$$

The derivative of the negentropy follows as:

$$\frac{\partial \mathcal{D}}{\partial \mathbf{w}} = \frac{1}{T} \sum_{t=1}^{T} \frac{p'(a_t|\mathbf{w})}{p(a_t|\mathbf{w})} \mathbf{x}_t + (\mathbf{w}^T R_\mathbf{x} \mathbf{w})^{-1} R_\mathbf{x} \mathbf{w}, \qquad (10.7)$$

with

$$\frac{p'(a_t|\mathbf{w})}{p(a_t|\mathbf{w})} = -\beta_1 P(\mathcal{C}_1|a_t)a_t - \beta_2 P(\mathcal{C}_2|a_t)a_t$$
$$+\alpha_1 \beta_1 P(\mathcal{C}_1|a_t) + \alpha_2 \beta_2 P(\mathcal{C}_2|a_t).$$

The optimisation can be constrained in such a way that $\|\mathbf{w}^T R_\mathbf{x} \mathbf{w}\| = 1$. Setting the gradient to zero and defining the posterior estimates of the sufficient statistics $\langle \mathbf{x}|\mathcal{C}_k \rangle = \frac{1}{T} \sum_{t=1}^{T} P(\mathcal{C}_k|a_t)\mathbf{x}_t$ and $\langle \mathbf{x}\mathbf{x}^T|\mathcal{C}_k \rangle = \frac{1}{T} \sum_{t=1}^{T} P(\mathcal{C}_k|a_t)\mathbf{x}_t\mathbf{x}_t^T$ gives the following:

$$\mathbf{w} = R_t^{-1} \left[\alpha_1 \beta_1 \langle \mathbf{x}|\mathcal{C}_1 \rangle - \alpha_2 \beta_2 \langle \mathbf{x}|\mathcal{C}_2 \rangle \right], \qquad (10.8)$$

where $R_t = \beta_1 \langle \mathbf{x}\mathbf{x}^T|\mathcal{C}_1 \rangle + \beta_2 \langle \mathbf{x}\mathbf{x}^T|\mathcal{C}_2 \rangle - R_\mathbf{x}$.

Now for simplicity we can assume that the two class covariance matrices are equal and so $\beta_1 = \beta_2 = \beta$. This is clearly unrealistic in many cases; however, it has been shown that linear discriminants are quite robust to departures from the equal class covariance matrix assumption [Bishop, 1995]. The final simplifying assumption is that the two means are the same about the pooled data sample mean in which case

$$\mathbf{w} = \frac{\alpha\beta}{\beta - 1} R_\mathbf{x}^{-1} \left[\langle \mathbf{x}|\mathcal{C}_1 \rangle - \langle \mathbf{x}|\mathcal{C}_2 \rangle \right]. \qquad (10.9)$$

This is a rather interesting result in that equation (10.9) can be interpreted as an unsupervised estimate of the solution to Fisher's linear criterion where the class means estimated by the labelled training data are now replaced by the posterior class mean estimates. The within class scatter matrix is proportional to the sample covariance matrix and so (10.9) can be regarded as the best unsupervised estimate of Fisher's linear discriminant. The class priors can be updated using their maximum likelihood estimates $P^{new}(\mathcal{C}_k) = \frac{1}{T} \sum_{t=1}^{T} P(\mathcal{C}_k|a_t)$. Now an iterative estimate of the separating hyperplane has to be made.

A second-order estimation method may be used and so the following matrix is required:

$$\frac{\partial^2 \mathcal{D}}{\partial \mathbf{w}^2} = 4\alpha\beta \langle \mathbf{x}\mathbf{x}^T|\mathcal{C}_1\mathcal{C}_2 \rangle + (1 - \beta)R_\mathbf{x}. \qquad (10.10)$$

Note that as the partition probabilities become more certain, each $P(\mathcal{C}_1|\mathbf{x}_t)P(\mathcal{C}_2|\mathbf{x}_t) \to 0$ and so $\langle \mathbf{x}\mathbf{x}^T|\mathcal{C}_1\mathcal{C}_2 \rangle \to \mathbf{0}$. Then $\langle \mathbf{x}\mathbf{x}^T|\mathcal{C}_1\mathcal{C}_2 \rangle \to$

$R_x \langle P(\mathcal{C}_1|\mathbf{x})P(\mathcal{C}_2|\mathbf{x}) \rangle$ provides a valid and convenient approximation; hence the inverse of the information matrix can be approximated by

$$\left\{ \frac{\partial^2 \mathcal{D}}{\partial \mathbf{w}^2} \right\}^{-1} = \frac{1}{\delta} R_x^{-1}, \tag{10.11}$$

where $\delta = 4\alpha\beta \langle P(\mathcal{C}_1|\mathbf{x})P(\mathcal{C}_2|\mathbf{x}) \rangle + 1 - \beta$. A second-order update for the vector $\mathbf{w}^{new}$ is therefore:

$$\mathbf{w}^{new} = \mathbf{w}^{old} - \left\{ \frac{\partial^2 \mathcal{D}}{\partial \mathbf{w}^2} \right\}^{-1} \frac{\partial \mathcal{D}}{\partial \mathbf{w}}$$

$$= \mathbf{w}^{old} - \frac{\alpha\beta}{\delta} R_x^{-1} \left[\langle \mathbf{x}|\mathcal{C}_1 \rangle - \langle \mathbf{x}|\mathcal{C}_2 \rangle \right] + \frac{(1-\beta)}{\delta} \mathbf{w}^{old}.$$

Note that with some simple manipulation the estimation of the vector can be written in a similar form to the Fixed-Point ICA algorithm developed in [Hyvärinen, 1999a] and so we have

$$\mathbf{w} = \mathbf{w}^{old}\gamma + R_x^{-1} \left[\langle \mathbf{x}|\mathcal{C}_1 \rangle - \langle \mathbf{x}|\mathcal{C}_2 \rangle \right], \tag{10.12}$$

where $\gamma = \{(1-\beta)(1-\frac{1}{\alpha\beta}) - 4\alpha\beta \langle P(\mathcal{C}_1|\mathbf{x})P(\mathcal{C}_2|\mathbf{x}) \rangle\}$ and the normalisation of the vector is achieved using $\mathbf{w}^{new} = \mathbf{w}/\sqrt{\|\mathbf{w}^T R_x \mathbf{w}\|}$.

It is rather interesting to note that by assuming equal class priors and setting the mean and variance of each Gaussian to be equal, for pre-whitened data such that $R_x = I$ equation (10.12) reduces exactly to the Fixed-Point ICA algorithm where the contrast function $\log(\cosh(a))$ is used [Hyvärinen, 1999a]. We can then see that the standard one unit ICA methods can be interpreted as providing the minimum entropy partition of the observed data which will be the posterior estimate of Fisher's linear discriminant.

Whereas for the purposes of ICA it is oftentimes desirable to pre-whiten the observations, in the case of classification, this is not an entirely beneficial form of processing. The scaling of each feature may have a particular discriminating effect and thus pre-whitening can give a reduction in the discriminating power of the particular features. Because of this no pre-whitening is carried out in the experiments reported.

10.5 Constructing the binary decision tree

The available unlabelled data sample $\mathbf{x}_1, \ldots, \mathbf{x}_T$ can be used to implement a binary decision tree as follows.

(i) Estimate the mean of the observations $\mathbf{x}_t$ and transform by subtracting the sample mean: $\mathbf{x}_t' = \mathbf{x}_t - E\{\mathbf{x}\}$.

(ii) Use the zero-mean observations to find an ICA dichotomising vector $\mathbf{w}$ yielding the structured variable $a_t = \mathbf{w}^T \mathbf{x}_t'$.

(iii) Partition the observations into two classes:

$$\mathbf{w}^T \mathbf{x}_t' \in \begin{cases} \text{Class 1} & \mathbf{w}^T \mathbf{x}_t' \geqslant 0, \\ \text{Class 2} & \mathbf{w}^T \mathbf{x}_t' < 0. \end{cases}$$

(iv) Repeat the above steps for appropriate subclasses.

The construction of the binary tree is limited by the number of observed samples since reliable estimation of ICA requires a sufficient amount of data. However, this limitation is somewhat less severe compared to regular ICA since only one component is computed at each node.

10.6 Selecting the size of the decision tree

The above method for constructing the decision tree did not include any methods for model selection, i.e., deciding the size of the tree. Growing the tree as large as possible suffers from *overfitting* which means that properties of the available data are being modelled that do not generalise to unobserved data.

There are two general ways to limit the size of the decision tree:

- stopping rules, which prevent further splitting of the nodes;
- pruning rules, which discard decisions after the tree has been constructed.

Most of the methods require knowledge of the class labels. For example validation sets can be used to test the usefulness of further splitting. If the performance increases on the validation set, then the new decision is included.

The approach taken in this case however is driven by selecting the most probable number of splits and the nodes to split at each level which will provide a minimum entropy tree. As the tree is binary, the number of leaf nodes in the tree will correspond to the number of classes or clusters inherent in the data. The decision regarding which nodes to split is based on the minimum partition entropy principle [Roberts *et al.*, 1999]. For example, in a two class problem, partitioning a sample of data which consists of sufficient examples of both classes will yield a smaller partition entropy than that achieved by a binary partition of a sample which has examples of only one class, assuming, of course, that each class is compact. The appropriate number of leaf nodes is estimated using the entropy change at each split assuming a flat prior for each number of leaf nodes [Roberts *et al.*, 1999]. In the experiments which have been carried out using typical test datasets, this procedure has provided a promising criterion. Further investigation is required to assess how robust this measure is over a large number of datasets.

10.7 Experiments

A range of datasets have been investigated to test the proposed ICA classification method. Results on two standard benchmark datasets are given here by way of example. The first is the well worn IRIS† dataset. The data consists of fifty four-dimensional samples of each of the three classes which form the data. One of the classes is linearly separable and well separated from the other two classes. The remaining two classes are overlapping and have a large intra-cluster scatter.

The root node was presented with the data and the proposed method was used to create an ICA separating hyperplane. It is important to emphasise that this is also the minimum entropy or minimum overlap partition. Figure (10.1) shows the development of the tree. The root node partitions the data in such a way that the left-hand leaf is correctly assigned all the samples from Class 1 with all the remaining samples of both Class 2 and Class 3 being assigned to the right-hand leaf. The partition entropy and evidence are computed for this partition. At the second level the left-hand node is partitioned and the model evidence and entropy for the tree are given. The right-hand node, which contains all samples from Classes 2 and 3, is then partitioned. Comparing the two splits it is clear that the partition entropy is minimised when the right-hand node is split further into the second and third classes. The model evidence for the two partitions for this layer is similar. Moving on to the third layer and further partitioning gives a much smaller value of the model evidence and so the leaf nodes are taken at the first and second levels denoted by the tree with the minimum entropy: figure (10.1). The overall result of the partitioning given in terms of mis-classification is 98%. The class posterior probabilities are given in figure (10.2), as expected there are no errors in the discrimination of Class 1 from the others and three errors – due to the class overlap – in discriminating

† Available from http://www.ics.uci.edu/~mlearn/MLSummary.html

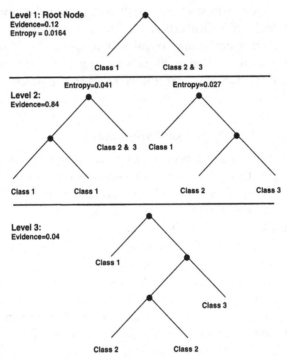

Figure 10.1. **Partition tree:** *The partition trees and associated entropy values for the IRIS dataset.*

between examples of Class 2 and Class 3. It is worth highlighting that this result equals the best reported by any unsupervised classification method that has been applied to this particular dataset and significantly outperforms techniques such as K–means clustering.

One further example is given using the oil pipeline data originally used in [Bishop, 1998]. The data consists of twelve-dimensional samples each of which is classified into one of three possible classes. The dataset contained 1000 samples, first, all samples were assigned to the root of the tree and after removing the mean value a single ICA vector was computed and the process described above was carried out. The classification accuracy measured on the dataset was 88%. This illustrates how well the proposed algorithm is able to represent the classes in the data. Remember that the representation was computed *without* using the class labels.

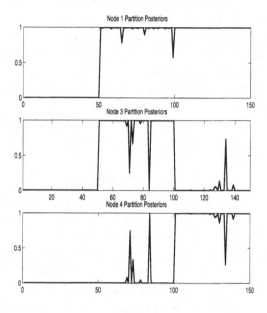

Figure 10.2. *The posterior class probabilities at each level of the tree for the IRIS dataset: The top plot shows the posterior probability of each of the second level nodes, Class 1 (the first fifty points) has been completely separated from Classes 2 & 3. The middle and bottom plots show the second level partition probabilities. There are only three misclassifications.*

10.8 Discussion

The previous sections have shown how ICA can be used to partition data in a hierarchic manner using binary decision trees. The maximisation of an ICA criterion such as negentropy yields a maximum certainty partition and indeed for the two class case gives the unsupervised (maximum posterior) estimate of Fisher's linear discriminant. The results presented herein have indicated that this simple method of partitioning polychotomous data via a hierarchy of dichotomies is as effective as more sophisticated methods. Of course this is a linear discriminant and so for the large class of problems which are not linearly separable this will be found wanting. However, the nonlinear transformation of the feature vectors into some high-dimensional feature space can then render the problem linearly separable. Indeed this is precisely the method adopted in [Girolami, 2000b] where the notion of Kernel-ICA is proposed for the partitioning of non-linearly separable data.

The visualisation of multivariate data is a method extensively employed in data-mining. Indeed ICA has been considered as a method of finding alternative informative projections to that of principal component analysis [Hyvärinen, 1999a, Girolami, 1999a]. The following section looks at the problem of data visualisation from the perspective of the statistical generative models discussed in the opening section of this chapter and extends the generative topographic mapping to deal with binary data.

10.9 Data visualisation

The Generative Topographic Mapping (GTM) originally proposed by Bishop [1998] is a latent trait model for continuous data which assumes an isotropic Gaussian noise model and performs uniform sampling from a two-dimensional latent space. It has already been remarked that the GTM model† and the associated parameter estimation method are exactly the same as those for ICA of mixtures of discrete sources which have been distorted with Gaussian noise. In both models the assumption of knowledge of the prior *symbol* or *latent variable* distributions is made. Indeed the GTM has been investigated as a potentially useful method for performing nonlinear ICA (see [Pajunen & Karhunen, 1997] and Chapter 4).

The application of ICA to data mining applications for data visualisation is gaining some degree of interest and novel applications of ICA such as text mining and information retrieval are being investigated [Isbell & Viola, 1999]. In applications such as text mining there is a problem with the standard ICA model in that a Gaussian likelihood is assumed. In the case of vector space representations of text-based documents the Bernoulli or multinomial event models predominate in which case the observations (in ICA parlance) are also discrete and not continuous. Another example is binary coded images such as handwritten letters or digits, the observations are discrete and binary. Because of this the standard ICA model is inappropriate for such data and a more appropriate model is required and it is this which the following section seeks to address.

Despite the success of methods such as ICA and GTM when applied to continuous data for exploratory data analysis the development of a similar latent trait model for discrete (binary or frequency counts) data has been hindered due, in part, to the nonlinear link function inherent

---

† Where the transformation from latent space to data space is strictly linear.

in the exponential distributions which describe the data under consideration, for example the Bernoulli for binary data or the Poisson for discrete frequency counts. This link function yields a log likelihood that is nonlinear in the model parameters and so closed form expressions of the maximum-likelihood parameter estimates are not available. However, an effective method for the parameter estimation of a binary latent trait model – a binary version of the GTM – is proposed by adopting a variational approximation to the Bernoulli likelihood. This approximation thus provides a log likelihood which is quadratic in the model parameters and so obviates the necessity of an iterative M-step in the Expectation Maximisation (EM) algorithm. The power of this method is demonstrated on two significant application domains, handwritten digit recognition and text-based document organisation and retrieval. This method can easily be extended to other members of the exponential family.

10.10 Binary variables

Multivariate binary data accounts for a significant amount of the increasing information that is stored in large data repositories. Handwritten customer signatures are stored by financial institutions for biometric verification purposes, text documents stored in digital libraries such as the US Patent Office and, of course, the World Wide Web are all potential sources of multivariate binary data. The latter example of multivariate binary data, text-based documents, forms an important and challenging domain of application for many models of unsupervised learning [McCallum & Nigam, 1998, Isbell & Viola, 1999, Landatter & Harshman, 1990, Kohonen, 1995].

Generative latent variable models have recently been proposed as probabilistic tools for the visualisation and analysis of high-dimensional data [Tipping, 1999, Bishop, 1998]. The Generative Topographic Mapping was proposed as a means of visualising high-dimensional continuous data by the topographic ordering of the data on a two-dimensional grid. In this respect it shares many common features with the Self-Organising Map (SOM) [Kohonen, 1995], both compute the Euclidean distance between data and reference points; however, the GTM fully describes a generative statistical model of the observed data. The GTM is essentially based on a nonlinear mapping from a two-dimensional uniform grid of points in latent space $s \in \mathbb{R}^2$ to a D-dimensional observation space $x \in \mathbb{R}^D$. The probability of the observations conditioned on the latent variables and the model parameters A is given as $p(\mathbf{x}|\mathbf{s}, A)$ and is chosen as an isotropic Gaussian, indicating that $p(\mathbf{x}|\mathbf{s}, A) = \prod_{i=1}^{D} p(x_i|\mathbf{s}, A)$. The choice of the uniform sampling of each point in latent space gives the observation data probability as an equally weighted mixture of isotropic Gaussians. The observation data density which describes this particular model is given by the following expression:

$$p(\mathbf{x}|A) = \frac{1}{K} \sum_{k=1}^{K} \left\{ \prod_{i=1}^{D} p(x_i|\mathbf{s}_k, A) \right\}. \qquad (10.13)$$

Recently a latent trait model, which deals specifically with binary data, has been developed for visualisation purposes in [Tipping, 1999]. In this case however as the observations are binary the conditional distribution in (10.13) is given as a univariate single trial Bernoulli distribution $P(x_i|\mathbf{s}) = \mu_i^{x_i}(1 - \mu_i)^{1-x_i}$ where μ_i is the expected value of the Bernoulli variable. The key assumption made in [Tipping, 1999] is that the latent space is distributed as a zero-mean, unit-variance Gaussian. By introducing a quadratic variational approximation for the logistic function [Jaakkola & Jordan, 1997] in the conditional element of (10.13) it is noted that the exponential introduced will be quadratic in $\mathbf{s}$ and as the Gaussian prior is also quadratic in $\mathbf{s}$ the integral of the variational approximation can be solved analytically and so the required parameter estimates can be given in closed form. However, by imposing a Gaussian prior on the continuous latent space the model defined in [Tipping, 1999] will effectively provide an approximate singular value decomposition of the binary observations onto the plane associated with the two most significant singular values. Taken as a single model the latent space visualisation possible in using the method proposed in [Tipping, 1999] will in essence be an approximation of a projection of the data onto the principal axes. However, the probabilistic basis of the model may allow for more general extensions. Nevertheless a means of topographically organising and visualising multivariate binary data is therefore still a requirement.

Whereas the method to be developed is generic for any multivariate binary data the primary motivation for this work is to be able to define an alternative *semantically dense* [Landatter & Harshman, 1990] representation of a vector space text-based document model based on the multivariate Bernoulli event model [McCallum & Nigam, 1998]. It is interesting to note that the conditional independence of the observation probability density embodied in the product of marginal probabilities is a direct match to the multivariate conditional independence of the *Bag-of-words* document representation [McCallum & Nigam, 1998]. The restructuring of a vector space document model using ICA [Girolami *et al.*, 1998] has been proposed in [Isbell & Viola, 1999]. However, as already mentioned, the current linear ICA data models appear to be inappropriate for visualising the mapping from *concept* space into word space. It is with this in mind that we turn to probabilistic generative models for defining the potential text generation mechanism. As already mentioned the proposed method is general for any form of multivariate binary data and the experiments reported demonstrate this.

10.11 Algorithm

Let us consider a latent class representation of ordinal categorical points $s_k \in \{s_1, \dots, s_K\}$. Each K-dimensional vector s_k (which has only a single non-zero element, whose value is one) may, in some sense, represent a class or topic label. The matrix S whose rows are each s_k is a $K \times K$ identity matrix. It is worth noting that in this case A defines the model parameters which will be the logit transformed individual class means.

The EM estimation of the class means has a common M-step for any distribution from the exponential family and is given below where the matrix F is a $K \times D$ matrix and each row is an individual class mean $\mu_k \in \mathbb{R}^D$.

$$F \stackrel{\text{def}}{=} G^{-1}RX \qquad (10.14)$$

The $K \times K$ diagonal matrix whose k^{th} diagonal element is $\sum_t P^{old}(s_k|x_t)$ is defined as G and the $T \times D$ matrix X represents the binary data matrix. The matrix of the *old* posterior estimates is defined as R which is a $K \times T$ matrix with individual elements $P^{old}(s_k|x_t)$.

The E-step of course will be specific to each particular distribution model, and for the case of multivariate Bernoulli distributed data the elements of the posterior probability or responsibility [Bishop, 1998] matrix are given below.

$$P^{old}(s_k|x_t) = \frac{\prod_{i=1}^{D}(\mu_{ik}^{new})^{x_{it}}\{1 - \mu_{ik}^{new}\}^{(1-x_{it})}}{\sum_{k'}\prod_{i=1}^{D}(\mu_{ik'}^{new})^{x_{it}}\{1 - \mu_{ik'}^{new}\}^{(1-x_{it})}}. \qquad (10.15)$$

This is a standard means of *soft* clustering data and we propose to utilise this approach in assigning class labels to each observation. Of course the labelling of the data provides no means of topographically organising

the data in latent space to enable meaningful visualisation of the data.
Therefore a corresponding latent trait model is now considered.

For this model the latent variables s_k will form points on a uniformly spaced grid. An optional nonlinear mapping from the latent
space is denoted here in keeping with the form of generalised linear
model transformation proposed in [Bishop, 1998]. The generalised linear model [McCullagh & Nelder, 1983] for Bernoulli response variables
proposes the use of the logit- (sigmoid-) based link function from the
latent space to data space. The logit transformation is then given as the
following:

$$E\{x_i|s_k\} = \mu_{ik} = \frac{\exp(A_i^\mathsf{T}\phi(s_k))}{1 + \exp(A_i^\mathsf{T}\phi(s_k))}, \tag{10.16}$$

where A_i is the ith column vector which defines the linear transformation
to data space or the mixing matrix in ICA terms. The estimation of
the *new* model parameters can be found in a straightforward manner
[Bishop, 1995]. However, due to the nonlinear link function the estimation
of the new conditional probabilities requires an inner iterative loop to
estimate the model parameters A_i. The following derivative of the log
likelihood, $\mathcal{L} = \sum_t \log\{p(\mathbf{x}_t|A)\}$, with respect to each A_{mi}, is required:

$$\frac{\partial \mathcal{L}}{\partial A_{mi}} = \sum_{t,k} P^{old}(s_k|\mathbf{x}_t)\{x_{it} - \mu_{ik}\}\phi_m(s_k). \tag{10.17}$$

If we are to use Newton or pseudo-Newton type optimisation approaches
which require the inverse of the Hessian then the second-order derivatives
with respect to A_{mi} have to be computed. Note that as the expression for
the posterior probabilities $P^{old}(s_k|\mathbf{x}_t)$ is fixed within this step it does not
form part of the expression for the derivative.

$$\frac{\partial^2 \mathcal{L}}{\partial A_{mi}\partial A_{m'i}} = -\sum_{t,k} P^{old}(s_k|\mathbf{x}_t)\mu_{ik}\{1 - \mu_{ik}\}\phi_m(s_k)\phi_{m'}(s_k) \tag{10.18}$$

Both of these expressions can be given in convenient matrix format by
defining the following additional set of matrices. The $K \times M$ matrix Φ
has individual elements $\phi_m(s_k)$ and A is an $M \times D$ matrix with elements
A_{mi}. Z_i is the $K \times K$ diagonal matrix with elements $\mu_{ik}(1 - \mu_{ik})$. As
stated above, the estimation of the parameters A, which define each
$P^{new}(x_{it}|s_k) = \mu_{ik}^{x_{it}}(1 - \mu_{ik})^{(1-x_{it})}$, in this M-step is iterative and a number
of efficient optimisation techniques are available to us. In the case of a
simple gradient ascent then the matrix of parameters A can be updated

using the following iterative procedure:

$$A^{n+1} = A^n + \delta_n \left[\Phi^T RX - \Phi^T GF^n \right], \tag{10.19}$$

where δ_n is the step size at each nth update iteration. Note that only the matrix of binomial distribution means μ_{ik} requires to be updated at each step. The new value of this matrix is denoted in the usual way by F^n. The iterative re-weighted least-squares approach [McCullagh & Nelder, 1983] can also be used noting that we can write the Hessian matrix for each conditionally independent element x_i as $H_i = -\Phi^T GZ_i\Phi$. This completes the M-step estimation of the *new* parameters. The main problem here is that the likelihood is not guaranteed to monotonically increase during the iterative estimation of the parameters A. The additional computational complexity of each iterative M-step, for the gradient update of (10.19), is $O\{MTD + MK(T + D + K)\}$ which can be costly if the dimensionality of the data is high.† Also it should be noted that the complexity scales quadratically in the number of latent points and there is no guarantee of a monotonic increase in the likelihood. Because of these drawbacks we consider an alternative approach.

10.12 A variational approach to the binary GTM

Now it is desirable to remove the requirement for the iterative M-step as defined in the previous section. In [Tipping, 1999] the variational approximation for the logistic function, originally proposed in [Jaakkola & Jordan, 1997], is used in maximising the likelihood of the observations given that the latent variables have a Gaussian prior distribution $\mathcal{N}(0, I)$ in latent space. The approach taken in this chapter is to use the uniform grid of points as our prior distribution in latent space as originally proposed in [Bishop, 1998]. The key to this approach is the adoption of a variational approximation to the conditional distribution [Jaakkola & Jordan, 1997]. We define

$$\tilde{p}(x_{in}|\mathbf{s}_k, A, \xi) = \sigma(\xi_{in}) \exp\{(B_{ink} - \xi_{in})/2 + \lambda(\xi_{in})(B_{ink}^2 - \xi_{in}^2)\}, \tag{10.20}$$

where $B_{ink} = (2x_{in} - 1)(A_i^T\phi(\mathbf{s}_k))$, the negative function is $\lambda(\xi_{in}) = \frac{-1}{4\xi_{in}}\tanh(\xi_{in}/2)$ and $\sigma(\xi_{in})$ is the logistic function. As detailed in [Jaakkola & Jordan, 1997] this provides a lower bound on the likelihood $p(x_{in}|\mathbf{s}_k, A)$ and this bound is maximised by the optimisation of the additional variational parameters ξ_{in}. Nevertheless we now have a means of removing

---

† Vector space models of text-based documents can have several thousand distinct terms.

the iterative M-step to estimate the model parameters as the log likelihood will now be quadratic in the parameters. The derivative of the log likelihood with respect to the variational parameters gives

$$\frac{\partial \mathcal{L}}{\partial \xi_{it}} = \sum_{k,l,m}^{K,M,M} \tilde{r}_{kt} A_{il} A_{im} \phi_l(\mathbf{s}_k) \phi_m(\mathbf{s}_k) - \sum_{k}^{K} \tilde{r}_{kt} \xi_{it}^2, \qquad (10.21)$$

where $\tilde{r}_{kt}$ denotes $\tilde{P}^{old}(\mathbf{s}_k|\mathbf{x}_t)$. Now setting the gradient to zero and noting that $\sum_k r_{kt} = 1$ we have the expression

$$\xi_{it}^2 = \sum_{k,l,m} \tilde{r}_{kt} A_{il} A_{im} \phi_l(\mathbf{s}_k) \phi_m(\mathbf{s}_k), \qquad (10.22)$$

which in matrix notation is

$$\Lambda \bullet \Lambda = R^{\mathsf{T}} \left\{ (\Phi A) \bullet (\Phi A) \right\}. \qquad (10.23)$$

The $T \times D$ matrix of variational parameters ξ_{it} is Λ and the symbol $\bullet$ denotes element-wise multiplication. The derivative of the log likelihood with respect to the model parameters is given by the following expression.

$$\frac{\partial \mathcal{L}}{\partial A_{ij}} = \sum_{t,k,l}^{T,K,M} r_{kt} \left\{ \frac{1}{2}(2x_{it} - 1) + 2\lambda(\xi_{it}) A_{il} \phi_l(\mathbf{s}_k) \right\} \phi_j(\mathbf{s}_k) \qquad (10.24)$$

Setting the gradient to zero gives the following after some manipulation:

$$2\sum_{t,k,l} r_{kt}\lambda(\xi_{it}) A_{il} \phi_l(\mathbf{s}_k)\phi_j(\mathbf{s}_k) = \sum_{t,k} r_{kt} \left(\frac{1}{2} - x_{it} \right) \phi_j(\mathbf{s}_k), \qquad (10.25)$$

and in vector notation

$$\Phi^{\mathsf{T}}\Theta_i \Phi A_i = \Phi^{\mathsf{T}} R X_i, \qquad (10.26)$$

where Θ_i is the $K \times K$ diagonal matrix with elements $\theta_{kk}^i = R\Gamma_{ik}$, that is, a diagonal matrix with elements equal to the elements of the ith row of the matrix $R\Gamma$, and $\Gamma = 2\lambda(\Lambda)$ (the function operates element-wise on the matrix) and the $T \times D$ matrix X now has elements $0.5 - x_{it}$. The solutions of the above systems of equations (10.23) and (10.26) form the M-step estimates of A^{new} and Λ^{new}. Consider further the posterior probability $\tilde{P}(\mathbf{s}_k|\mathbf{x}_t)$ which defines the E-step. The posterior takes the form of

$$\tilde{P}(\mathbf{s}_k|\mathbf{x}_t) = \frac{\prod_{i=1}^{D} \sigma(\xi_{it}) \exp\{\zeta_{tk}\}}{\sum_{k'=1}^{K} \prod_{i=1}^{D} \sigma(\xi_{it}) \exp\{\zeta_{tk'}\}} = \frac{\exp\{\zeta_{tk}\}}{\sum_{k'=1}^{K} \exp\{\zeta_{tk'}\}}, \qquad (10.27)$$

where $\zeta_{tk} = \sum_{i=1}^{D}[(B_{itk} - \xi_{it})/2 + \lambda(\xi_{it})(B_{itk}^2 - \xi_{it}^2)]$ which simplifies to the standard *softmax* form as the product terms in the numerator and the denominator cancel. The exponential term simplifies to $\zeta_{tk} = \sum_{i=1}^{D}(B_{itk}/2 + \lambda(\xi_i)B_{itk}^2)$ which in matrix form is given as $\frac{1}{2}((\Phi A) \bullet (\Phi A))\Gamma^{\mathsf{T}} - \Phi A X^{\mathsf{T}}$. The posterior matrix then follows as the expression below:

$$R = softmax\left\{\frac{1}{2}((\Phi A) \bullet (\Phi A))\Gamma^{\mathsf{T}} - \Phi A X^{\mathsf{T}}\right\} \tag{10.28}$$

As the form of this posterior is normalised, we can re-arrange the numerator in such a way that

$$\zeta_{tk} = -\frac{1}{2}\sum_{i=1}^{D}\{A_i^{\mathsf{T}}\Phi(\mathbf{s}_k) - 2x_{it}A_i^{\mathsf{T}}\Phi(\mathbf{s}_k)$$
$$+ 2\lambda(\xi_{it})\Phi(\mathbf{s}_k)^{\mathsf{T}}A_iA_i^{\mathsf{T}}\Phi(\mathbf{s}_k)\}. \tag{10.29}$$

This takes the form of a multivariate Gaussian where the standard exponential term is $-\frac{1}{2}(\Phi(\mathbf{s}_k) - \mu_t)^{\mathsf{T}}C_t^{-1}(\Phi(\mathbf{s}_k) - \mu_t)$. It is straightforward to compare the terms and so the posterior induced by the variational approximation will be Gaussian such that $\tilde{p}(\Phi(\mathbf{s}_k)|\mathbf{x}_t, A, \xi) \sim \mathcal{N}(\mu_t, C_t)$ where

$$C_t = \left[2\sum_{i=1}^{D}|\lambda(\xi_{it})|A_iA_i^{\mathsf{T}}\right]^{-1} , \quad \mu_t = C_t\left\{\sum_{i=1}^{D}(x_{it} - 1/2)A_i\right\}.$$

So we also have a closed form method of computing the mean position in latent space of the tth data point and in addition the covariance of the posterior around the mean.

Unlike the method proposed in [Tipping, 1999] the sufficient statistics do not arise naturally from the expression of the induced posterior distribution but have to be explicitly computed. However, imposing the Gaussian prior, although providing estimates of the sufficient statistics in closed form, causes the approach taken in [Tipping, 1999] to reduce to an approximate singular value decomposition. The nonlinear transformation of the non-Gaussian uniform grid provides a potentially more powerful method of visualising binary data, as argued originally in [Bishop, 1998] for the case of continuous data. Therefore by defining the following matrix $\Omega = \Phi A$ the EM parameter estimation procedure follows.

- **Initialisation**

  ```
  Initialise the matrices A and Λ.
  Set Ωinit = ΦAinit
  iterate until log likelihood maximised
  ```

  – **E-step**

  $$R = softmax\left\{\frac{1}{2}(\Omega_{new} \bullet \Omega_{new})\Gamma_{new}^{\mathsf{T}} - \Omega_{new}X^{\mathsf{T}}\right\}$$

  – **M-step for variational parameters**

  $$\Lambda_{new} = \sqrt{R^{\mathsf{T}}\{(\Omega_{new} \bullet \Omega_{new})\}}$$

  – **M-step for model parameters**

  $$A_i^{new} = (\Phi^{\mathsf{T}}\Theta_i\Phi)^{-1}\Phi^{\mathsf{T}}RX_i \quad \forall\, i\,:\, 1, \ldots, D$$

  $$\Omega_{new} = \Phi A_{new}$$

The square root taken in the variational M-step is taken element-wise. This completes the presentation of the model. Due to the possibly high dimensionality of the data to which this method may be applied many of the posterior probabilities may be very small, typically less than 10^{-200}, and we need to be careful with the finite-precision numerical representations of the data. A standard method of numerical scaling is used in this case where each posterior is computed by $p_i = \exp(l_i - \gamma)/\sum_{i'}\exp(l_{i'} - \gamma)$ where each $\gamma = \max_i(l_i)$, this method is used in the implementation of the algorithm.

10.13 Simulations

The first reported experiment concerns a dataset† consisting of the handwritten numerals ('0'–'9') extracted from a collection of Dutch utility maps. There are two hundred samples of each digit amounting to two thousand samples each of which is a 15×16 binary pixel image. For the purposes of this simulation two hundred examples of each of the digits '0', '1', '2', '3', '4' were used. The dataset therefore consisted of a 1000×240 binary data matrix. For comparative purposes the method proposed in [Tipping, 1999] was also used in this simulation.

A 50×50 grid was created and nine Gaussian basis functions were used for this model. The variational approximation only required two

† http://www.ics.uci.edu/~mlearn/MLSummary.html

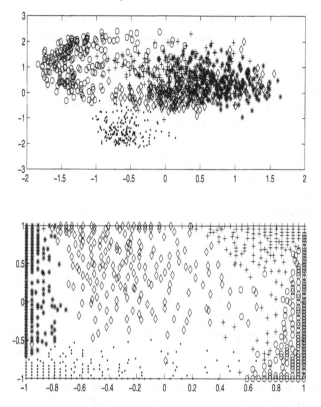

Figure 10.3. **Data visualisation:** *The posterior mean of 1000 binary representations of the handwritten digits '0'–'4' plotted on the two-dimensional latent grid. The top plot shows the results when a Gaussian prior is imposed on the latent space. The bottom plot gives the results from the 'Binary-GTM' presented herein. The class labels are used to differentiate the individual digits and the clear and distinct topographic organisation is evident. The following symbols are used to denote the following digits . = 0; o = 1; * = 2; ◇ = 3; + = 4.*

M-steps for the estimation of the variational parameters as noted in [Jaakkola & Jordan, 1997]. The log likelihood was maximised in ten EM steps of the proposed algorithm. Figure (10.3) shows the results from both of the methods developed in [Tipping, 1999] and the method presented here. As has been discussed, the imposition of a Gaussian prior produces results similar to a PCA projection, whereas the non-Gaussian uniform grid of points clearly shows the topographic relations between the individual digits.

The main motivation for this work is to develop probabilistic models which will be able to represent the word generation process within text documents and provide a means to represent documents in an efficient manner. Latent Semantic Analysis (LSA) [Landatter & Harshman, 1990] performs a singular value decomposition on the term document matrix representations of document corpora and the dimensions associated with the most significant singular values are retained. The absence of a probabilistic model and the difficulty in interpreting the transformed representation motivate the search for other representations. Both the SOM and standard Independent Component Analysis (ICA) [Kohonen, 1995, Isbell & Viola, 1999] have been applied to this domain, it can be argued that the claimed shortcomings of LSA are also found with these methods.

For this experiment an arbitrary collection of three thousand documents was created. One thousand documents were taken from each of the following newsgroups in the **CMU-Newsgroups** collection: alt.atheism, talk.politics.guns, sport.hockey.† A vocabulary size of one hundred terms was used throughout in the document representations which were represented by a binary variable signifying the occurrence of a term in the document. The number of classes (*concepts or topics* in information retrieval parlance) was taken as six and a latent class model was used to fit the data. Three distinct *concepts* were identified which, because of the distinct nature of the three newsgroups, coincided with the manual labels given to the documents. Two hundred samples from each group were then used in the 'training' of the variational approach proposed in [Tipping, 1999] to visualise the documents with the results shown in figure (10.4). The 'Binary-GTM' was set using a 40×40 grid, nine basis functions and run for twenty iterations, the results of which are shown in figure (10.4).

Figure (10.4) shows the posterior mean for each of the six hundred documents and it is clear that the 'Binary-GTM' has been able to define a topographic ordering in latent space which reflects the topical grouping of the documents within the corpora. In addition, however, due to the probabilistic nature of the model it is then possible to garner further information about the data from this model. Note that for each point in latent space the expectation probability $E\{p(x_i|\mathbf{s}_k)\}$ which comes directly from the model will give the likelihood of a word being related to specific latent points. This then allows a representation where the most probable words occurring in a document are assigned to the corresponding point in latent space. This is somewhat similar to the *Semantic Maps* produced

---

† http://www.cs.cmu.edu/~textlearning

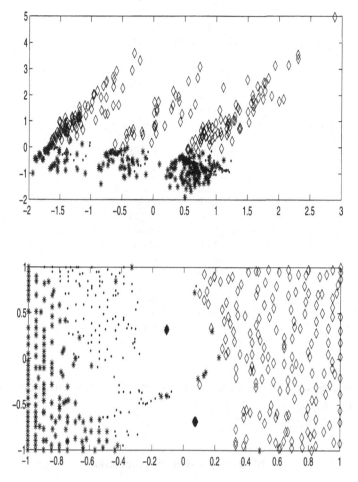

Figure 10.4. **Document visualisation:** *The top plot shows the posterior mean for each of the documents. The topographic organisation induced by the Binary-GTM is given in the bottom plot. The following symbols denote documents from the various groups. . = alt.atheism, * = talk.politics.guns, ◇ = sport.hockey.*

by the SOM [Oja & Kaski, 1999]. By way of an example four points were chosen in the four quadrants of the grid shown in figure 10.4 and the ten most probable words (ranked by the taking the sigmoid of the elements of the $K \times D$ matrix (ΦA)) are shown in Table 10.1.

It is clear that the words in the first upper-left quadrant correspond to the *alt.atheism* group of documents, the point from the lower-left-hand quadrant clearly has probable words which are relevant to discussion on *politics.guns* whilst the two right-hand points refer to *sport.hockey*. This

Table 10.1.

god	cup
article	stanley
belief	pittsburgh
religion	islanders
religious	year
bible	article
atheist	play
objective	people
atheism	fans
clinton	players
article	year
police	hockey
year	bruins
gun	season
people	team
rights	fan
boston	nhl
firearms	wings
guns	goals
argument	game

can of course be extended to cover the relevant range of points in the latent space.

10.14 Discussion and conclusion

Based on the theoretical basis of latent trait and ICA modelling a version of the GTM for binary data (the experiments used sparse high-dimensional binary data) has been proposed. In this contribution the method has been applied to the organisation and analysis of handwritten digits and the analysis of binary represented documents which may have a number of dimensions in excess of 1000 and yet only a small number of elements will be non-zero. The results have been most encouraging and further work into Latent Trait/Class document representations is under way. This proposed method is, however, suitable for binary data in general. The unsupervised classification of data using a form of one unit ICA has been proposed and it is notable that, with certain assumptions and restrictions, this method yields the best estimate of the Fisher linear discriminant in the absence of labelled data.

Acknowledgements

This work is supported by a grant from the British Library and Information Commission, Grant Number LIC/GC/991 'Improved Online Information Access'. The author is grateful to Dr. P. Pajunen for minimum entropy discussions on certain aspects of this work. Routines from the GTM toolkit available on http://www.ncrg.aston.ac.uk/GTM were utilised in writing the code to implement the proposed Binary-GTM.

11

Particle filters for non-stationary ICA

R.M. Everson

S.J. Roberts

11.1 Introduction

One may think of blind source separation as the problem of identifying speakers (sources) in a room given only recordings from a number of microphones, each of which records a linear mixture of the sources, whose statistical characteristics are unknown.

Here we consider the blind source separation problem when the mixing of the sources is non-stationary. Pursuing the speakers in a room analogy, we address the problem of identifying the speakers when they (or equivalently, the microphones) are moving. The problem is cast in terms of a hidden state (the mixing proportions of the sources) which we track using particle filter methods, which permit the tracking of arbitrary state densities. Murata *et al.* [1997] have addressed this problem by adapting the learning rate and we mention work by Penny *et al.* [2000] on hidden Markov models for ICA which allows for abrupt changes in the mixing matrix with stationary periods in between.

We first briefly re-review classical Independent Component Analysis. ICA with non-stationary mixing is described in terms of a hidden state model and methods for estimating the sources and the mixing are described. Particle filter techniques are then introduced for the modelling of state densities. Finally, we address the non-stationary mixing problem when the sources are independent, but possess temporal correlations.

11.2 Stationary ICA

Classical ICA belongs to the class of latent variable models which model observed data as being generated by the linear mixing of latent sources. We assume that there are M sources whose probability density functions (p.d.f.) are $p_m(s^m)$. Observations, $\mathbf{x}_t \in \mathbb{R}^N$, are produced by the instantaneous linear mixing of the sources by A:

$$\mathbf{x}_t = A\mathbf{s}_t. \tag{11.1}$$

In order for the problem to be well posed, the mixing matrix, A, must have at least as many rows as columns ($N \geqslant M$), so that the dimension of each observation is at least as great as the number of sources. The aim of ICA methods is to recover the latent sources $\mathbf{a}_t$. This may, for example, be by finding W, the (pseudo-) inverse of A:

$$\mathbf{a}_t = W\mathbf{x}_t. \tag{11.2}$$

As was discussed in Chapter 1 the probability density of the observations is related [Papoulis, 1991] to the joint density over the recovered source estimates by

$$p(\mathbf{x}_t | A) = \frac{p(\mathbf{a})}{|\det A|}. \tag{11.3}$$

Hence the normalised log likelihood of a set of observations $t = 1, \ldots, T$ is therefore

$$\mathcal{L} = -\log|\det A| + \frac{1}{T} \sum_{t=1}^{T} \log p(\mathbf{a}_t). \tag{11.4}$$

To proceed further some assumptions or prior knowledge about the nature of $p(\mathbf{s}_t)$, and hence $p(\mathbf{a}_t)$, must be incorporated into the model. Physical considerations may provide strong constraints on the form of $p(\mathbf{s}_t)$ (see, for example, Miskin and MacKay, Chapter 8). The assumption that the sources are linearly decorrelated leads to an $M(M-1)$-dimensional manifold of separating matrices [Everson & Roberts, 1999a]. The further constraint that the sources are normally distributed with zero mean and unit variance leads to variations of principal component analysis, PCA [Jolliffe, 1986] (see also section 1.3).

Independent component analysis assumes that the sources are independent so that the joint p.d.f. of the recovered sources factorises into the product of marginal densities:

$$p(\mathbf{a}_t) = \prod_{m=1}^{M} p(a_t^m). \tag{11.5}$$

Using this factorisation, the likelihood for a single observation is

$$\log \ell_t = -\log |\det A| + \sum_{m=1}^{M} \log p_m(a_t^m) \qquad (11.6)$$

and the normalised log likelihood of a set of T observations is therefore [Cardoso, 1997, MacKay, 1996, Pearlmutter & Parra, 1996]

$$\mathcal{L} = -\log |\det A| + \frac{1}{T} \sum_{t=1}^{T} \sum_{m=1}^{M} \log p_m(a_t^m). \qquad (11.7)$$

Traditionally the optimum A may then be found by maximisation of $\mathcal{L}$ with respect to A, assuming some specific form for the marginal densities $p(a_t^m)$.

Successive gradient ascents on $\log \ell_t$ (equation (11.6)) leads to the Bell & Sejnowski stochastic learning rule for ICA [Bell & Sejnowski, 1995], while batch learning is achieved by maximising $\log \mathcal{L}$. Learning rates may be considerably enhanced by modifying the learning rule to make it covariant [Amari *et al.*, 1996, MacKay, 1996]; see also page 44. A common choice is $p(s_t^m) \propto 1/\cosh(s_t^m)$, which leads to a tanh nonlinearity in the learning rule. Although the source model is apparently fixed, scaling of the mixing matrix tunes the model to particular sources (see [Everson & Roberts, 1999a] and section 1.5, and with a tanh nonlinearity platykurtic (heavy-tailed) sources can be separated, although not leptokurtic ones. Cardoso [1998b] has elucidated the conditions under which the true mixing matrix is a stable fixed point of the learning rule.

Adoption of more flexible models for the source densities permits the separation of a wider range of source densities. Attias [1999a] has used mixtures of Gaussians to model the sources, which permits multimodal sources, and Lee *et al.* [1999b] switch between sub- and super-Gaussian source models. In the work presented here a generalised exponential model is used.

We emphasise that since the likelihood is unchanged if A is premultiplied by a diagonal matrix D or a permutation matrix P, the original scale of the sources cannot be recovered. The separating matrix W is therefore only the inverse of A up to a diagonal scaling and permutation, that is,

$$WA = PD. \qquad (11.8)$$

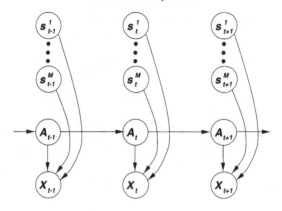

Figure 11.1. *Graphical model describing non-stationary ICA.*

11.3 Non-stationary ICA

Figure 11.1 depicts the graphical model describing the conditional independence relations of the non-stationary ICA model. In common with static Independent Component Analysis, we adopt a generative model in which M independent sources are linearly mixed at each instant. Unlike static ICA, however, the mixing matrix A_t is allowed to vary with time. We also assume that the observation $\mathbf{x}_t$ is contaminated by normally distributed noise with zero mean and covariance R:

$$\mathbf{x}_t = A_t \mathbf{s}_t + \mathbf{n}_t. \tag{11.9}$$

We denote the density of the observational noise by

$$p(\mathbf{n}_t) = \mathcal{G}(\mathbf{n}_t, R). \tag{11.10}$$

The p.d.f. of observations $p(\mathbf{x}_t | A_t)$ is given by

$$p(\mathbf{x}_t | A_t) = \int p(\mathbf{x}_t | A_t, \theta, \mathbf{s}_t) p(\mathbf{s}_t | \theta) \, d\mathbf{s}_t, \tag{11.11}$$

where θ are parameters pertaining to the particular source model (in our case the parameters of the generalised exponential source model). Since the *sources* are assumed stationary the likelihood of $\mathbf{x}_t$ given a particular mixing matrix is

$$p(\mathbf{x}_t | A_t) = \int p(\mathbf{x}_t | A_t, \mathbf{s}) p(\mathbf{s} | \theta) \, d\mathbf{s}. \tag{11.12}$$

As with static ICA, the assumption of the independence of the sources permits the source density to be written in factorised form (equation (11.5)) so that the likelihood becomes

$$p(\mathbf{x}_t | A_t) = \int \mathcal{G}(\mathbf{x}_t - A_t \mathbf{s}, R) \prod_{m=1}^{M} p_m(s^m) \, d\mathbf{s}. \tag{11.13}$$

We emphasise that it is in equation (11.13) that the independence of the sources is modelled by writing the joint source density in factored form.

The dynamics of A_t are modelled by a first-order Markov process, in which the elements of A_t diffuse from one observation time to the next. If we let $\vec{A}_t = \text{vec}(A_t)$ be the $(N \times M)$-dimensional vector obtained by stacking the columns of A_t, then $\vec{A}_t$ evolves according to the state equation:

$$\vec{A}_{t+1} = F\vec{A}_t + \mathbf{v}_t, \tag{11.14}$$

where $\mathbf{v}_t$ is zero-mean Gaussian noise with covariance Q, and F is the state transition matrix; in the absence of *a priori* information we take F to be the identity matrix. The state equation (11.14) and the statistics of $\mathbf{v}_t$ together define the density $p(\vec{A}_{t+1} | \vec{A}_t)$.

A full specification of the hidden state must include the parameter set $\theta = \{\theta_m\}, m = 1, \ldots, M$, which describes the independent source densities. We model the source densities with generalised exponentials, as described in subsection 11.3.1. Since the sources themselves are considered to be stationary, the parameters θ are taken to be static, but they must be learned as data are observed.

The problem is now to track A_t and to learn θ as new observations $\mathbf{x}_t$ become available. If X_t denotes the collection of observations $\{\mathbf{x}_1, \ldots, \mathbf{x}_t\}$, then the goal of filtering methods is to deduce the probability density function of the state $p(\vec{A}_t | X_t)$. This p.d.f. may be found recursively in two stages: prediction and correction. If $p(\vec{A}_{t-1} | X_{t-1})$ is known, the state equation (11.14) and the Markov property that $\vec{A}_t$ depends only on $\vec{A}_{t-1}$ permits prediction of the state at time t:

$$p(\vec{A}_t | X_{t-1}) = \int p(\vec{A}_t | \vec{A}_{t-1}) p(\vec{A}_{t-1} | X_{t-1}) \, d\vec{A}_{t-1}. \tag{11.15}$$

The predictive density $p(\vec{A}_t | X_{t-1})$ may be regarded as an estimate of $\vec{A}_t$ prior to the observation of $\mathbf{x}_t$. As the datum $\mathbf{x}_t$ is observed, the prediction may be corrected via Bayes' rule:

$$p(\vec{A}_t | X_t) = Z^{-1} p(\mathbf{x}_t | \vec{A}_t) p(\vec{A}_t | X_{t-1}), \tag{11.16}$$

where the likelihood of the observation given the mixing matrix, $p(\mathbf{x}_t | \vec{A}_t)$, is defined by the observation equation (11.9). The normalisation constant Z is known as the innovations probability:

$$Z = p(\mathbf{x}_t | X_{t-1}) = \int p(\mathbf{x}_t | \vec{A}_t) p(\vec{A}_t | X_{t-1}) \, d\vec{A}_t. \tag{11.17}$$

The prediction (11.15) and correction/update (11.16) pair of equations may be used to step through the data online, alternately predicting the subsequent state and then correcting the estimate when a new datum is observed. The corrected state at time t is then the basis for the prediction of the state at $t + 1$.

11.3.1 Source model

In order to be able to separate light-tailed sources a more flexible source model than the traditional $1/\cosh$ density is needed. It is difficult to use a switching model [Lee *et al.*, 1999b] (see also page 37) in this context. Attias [1999a] has used mixtures of Gaussians to model the sources, which permits multimodal sources (see page 35 and Chapter 3); we use generalised exponentials, which provide a good deal of flexibility and do not suffer from the combinatorial complexities associated with mixture models.

Each source density is modelled by

$$p(a^m | \theta_m) = z \exp - \left| \frac{a^m - \mu_m}{\sigma_m} \right|^{r_m} \tag{11.18}$$

where the normalising constant is

$$z = \frac{r_m}{2\sigma_m \Gamma(1/r_m)}. \tag{11.19}$$

The density depends upon parameters $\theta_m = \{\mu_m, \sigma_m, r_m\}$. The location of the distribution is set by μ_m, its width by σ_m and the weight of its tails is determined by r_m. Clearly p is Gaussian when $r_m = 2$, Laplacian when $r_m = 1$, and the uniform distribution is approximated in the limit $r_m \to \infty$. More details on the generalised exponential model are given in section 1.5 and [Everson & Roberts, 1999a].

11.4 Particle filters

Practical implementation of the filtering equations (11.15 and 11.16) requires a representation of the predicted and corrected state densities: $p(\vec{A}_t | X_{t-1})$ and $p(\vec{A}_t | X_t)$. In the Kalman filter [Kalman & Bucy, 1961,

Jazwinski, 1973], whose observation equation is linear, the state densities are Gaussian and thus easily represented. Nonlinear and non-Gaussian tracking problems must either approximate the state density by a tractable form (usually Gaussian) or use a sampling method. Particle filters, which date back to the Sampling Importance Resampling (SIR) filter introduced by Gordon *et al.* [1993], represent the state density $p(\vec{A}_t|X_{t-1})$ by a collection or swarm of 'particles' each with a probability mass. Each particle's probability mass is modified using the state and observation equations after which a new independent sample is obtained from the posterior $p(\vec{A}_t|X_t)$ before proceeding to the next prediction/observation step. Alternatively, particle filters may be viewed as a Monte Carlo integration method for the integrals involved in the state and observation equations. Isard and Blake [1996] give a nice introduction to tracking using particle filters.

The SIR algorithm finds a swarm of N_p equally weighted particles which approximate the posterior $p(\vec{A}_{t-1}|X_{t-1})$ at time $t-1$. The swarm of particles is regarded as an approximate sample from the true posterior density. At time t we assume that $\{\vec{A}_{t-1}^n\}_{n=1}^{N_p}$ is the swarm of N_p particles distributed as an independent sample from $p(\vec{A}_{t-1}|X_{t-1})$. Filtering proceeds as follows.

Initialisation

The filter is initialised by drawing N_p samples from the prior $p(\vec{A}_1)$. In the absence of additional information we choose $p(\vec{A}_1)$ to be Gaussian-distributed with a mean found by performing static ICA on the first, say, 100 observations.

Prediction

Draw N_p samples $\{v_t^1, v_t^2, \ldots, v_t^{N_p}\}$ from the state noise density $\mathcal{N}(0, Q)$. Each particle is then propagated through the state equation (11.14) to form a new swarm of particles, $\{\vec{A}_{t|t-1}^1, \ldots, \vec{A}_{t|t-1}^{N_p}\}$, where

$$\vec{A}_{t|t-1}^n = F\vec{A}_t^n + v_t^n. \tag{11.20}$$

If the particles $\{\vec{A}_{t-1}^n\}$ are an independent sample from $p(\vec{A}_{t-1}|\mathbf{x}_{t-1})$ the particles $\vec{A}_{t|t-1}^n$ are an independent sample from $p(\vec{A}_t|X_{t-1})$, so the prediction stage implements equation (11.15).

The prediction stage is rapidly achieved since sampling from the Gaussian distribution is efficient.

Filtering

On the observation of a new datum $\mathbf{x}_t$ the prediction represented by the swarm $\{\vec{A}^n_{t|t-1}\}$ can be corrected. Each particle is weighted by the likelihood of the observation $\mathbf{x}_t$ being generated by the mixing matrix represented by $\vec{A}^n_{t|t-1}$. Thus probability masses q^n_t are assigned by

$$q^n_t = \frac{p(\mathbf{x}_t \mid \vec{A}^n_{t|t-1})}{\sum_{k=1}^{N_p} p(\mathbf{x}_t \mid \vec{A}^k_{t|t-1})}. \tag{11.21}$$

This procedure can be regarded as a discrete approximation to equation (11.16), where the prior $p(\vec{A}_t \mid X_{t-1})$ is approximated by the sample $p(\vec{A}_t \mid X_{t-1})$.

Laplace's approximation can be used to approximate the convolution of equation (11.13) for any fixed A_t when the observational noise is small (see Appendix, page 297). Otherwise the integral can be evaluated by Monte Carlo integration; however, since the integral must be evaluated for every particle, Monte Carlo integration is usually prohibitively time consuming.

Re-sampling

The particles $\vec{A}^n_{t|t-1}$ and weights q^n_t define a discrete distribution approximating $p(\vec{A}_t \mid \mathbf{x}_t)$. These are then re-sampled with replacement N_p times to form an approximate sample from $p(\vec{A}_t \mid \mathbf{x}_t)$, each particle carrying an equal weight. This new sample can now be used as the basis for the next prediction.

Although many variants and improvements to the basic SIR filter exist (see [Fearnhead, 1999] for a review), we have found the basic SIR filter to be adequate for non-stationary ICA.

11.4.1 Source recovery

Rather than making strictly Bayesian estimates of the model parameters $\theta^m = \{r_m, \sigma_m, \mu_m\}$, the maximum *a posteriori* (MAP) or mean estimate of A_t is used to estimate $\mathbf{a}_t$, after which maximum likelihood estimates of the parameters are found from sequences $\{a^m_\tau\}^t_{\tau=1}$. Finding maximum likelihood parameters is readily and robustly accomplished [Everson & Roberts, 1999a]. Subsequently each $\mathbf{a}_t$ is found by maximising $\log p(\mathbf{a}_t \,|\, \mathbf{x}_t, A_t)$, which is equivalent to minimising

$$(\mathbf{x}_t - A_t^* \mathbf{a}_t)^\mathsf{T} R^{-1} (\mathbf{x}_t - A_t^* \mathbf{a}_t) + \sum_{m=1}^{M} \left| \frac{a_t^m - \mu_m}{\sigma_m} \right|^{r_m}, \qquad (11.22)$$

where A_t^* is the MAP estimate for A_t. The minimisation can be carried out with a pseudo-Newton method, for example. If the noise variance is small, $\mathbf{a}_t \approx A_t^\dagger \mathbf{x}_t$, where $A_t^\dagger = (A_t^\mathsf{T} A_t)^{-1} A_t^\mathsf{T}$ is the pseudo-inverse of A_t, and this estimate provides a good starting guess for a numerical minimisation.

11.5 Illustration

Here we illustrate the method with two examples.

In the first example a Laplacian source ($p(s) \propto e^{-|s|}$) and a source with uniform density are mixed with a mixing matrix whose components vary sinusoidally with time:

$$A_t = \begin{bmatrix} \cos \omega t & \sin \omega t \\ -\sin \omega t & \cos \omega t \end{bmatrix}. \qquad (11.23)$$

Note, however, that the oscillation frequency doubles during the second half of the simulation making it more difficult to track. Figure 11.2 shows the true mixing matrix and the tracking of it by non-stationary ICA. The smooth solid line marks the mean of the particle swarm. As can be seen from the figure the particle mean tracks the mixing matrix well, although the tracking is poorer in the second half of the simulation where the mixing matrix is changing more rapidly.

Like ICA for stationary mixing, this method cannot distinguish between a column of A_t and a scaling of the column. In figure 11.2 the algorithm has 'latched on' to the negative of the first column of A_t (shown dashed) which is then tracked for the rest of the simulation.

We resolve the scaling ambiguity between the variance of the sources and the scale of the columns of A_t by insisting that the variance of each source is unity; i.e., we ignore the estimated value of σ_m (equation (11.18)), instead setting $\sigma_m = 1$ for all m and allowing all the scale information to reside in the columns of A_t.

To provide an initial estimate of the mixing matrix and source parameters static ICA was run on the first 100 samples. At times $t > 100$ the generalised exponential parameters were re-estimated every 10 observations.

To illustrate the particle filter, the location of every 50th particle at every 10th timestep is shown in Figure 11.3. There were 1000 particles

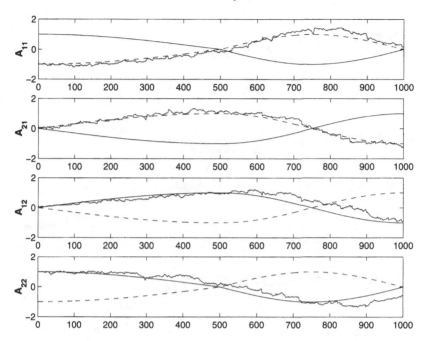

Figure 11.2. **Example 1:** *Tracking a mixture of Laplacian and Gaussian sources. The smooth solid and dashed lines are, respectively, the time variation of the elements of A and −A.*

in total. The thick solid line here shows the true mixing matrix, whose elements change discontinuously at $t = 600$ and $t = 1200$.

Estimates of the tracking error are provided by the covariance of the state density, which is found from the particle swarm. In this case the true A_t lies within one standard deviation of the estimated A_t almost all the time (see figure 11.3). We remark that it appears to be more difficult to track the columns associated with light-tailed sources than heavy-tailed sources. We note, furthermore, that the Gaussian case appears to be most difficult. In figure 11.2, A_{11} and A_{21} mix the Laplacian source, and the uniform source is mixed by A_{12} and A_{22} which are tracked less well, especially during the second half of the simulation. We suspect that the difficulty in tracking columns associated with nearly Gaussian sources is due to the ambiguity between a Gaussian source and the observational noise which is assumed to be Gaussian.

It is easy to envisage situations in which the mixing matrix might briefly become singular. For example, if the microphones are positioned

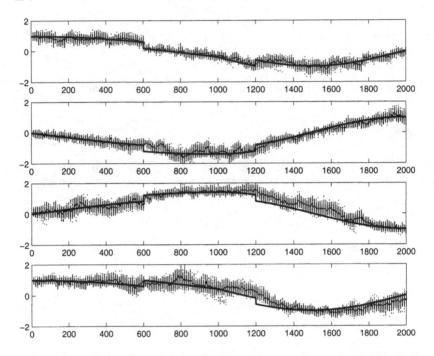

Figure 11.3. **Example 2:** *The swarm of particles tracking the mixing matrix for a mixture of a Laplacian and a Gaussian source. Thick solid lines mark the true mixing matrix; thin solid lines mark the mean of the particle swarm. Every 50th particle is plotted every 10th time-step.*

so that each receives the same proportions of each speaker the columns of A_t are linearly dependent and A_t is singular. In this situation A_t cannot be inverted and source estimates (equation (11.22)) are very poor. To cope with this we monitor the condition number of A_t; when it is large, implying that A_t is close to singular, the source estimates are discarded for the purposes of inferring the source model parameters, $\{r_m, \sigma_m, \mu_m\}$.

In figure 11.4 we show non-stationary ICA applied to Laplacian and uniform sources mixed with the matrices

$$A_t = \begin{bmatrix} \cos 2\omega t & \sin \omega t \\ -\sin 2\omega t & \cos \omega t \end{bmatrix} \qquad (11.24)$$

where ω is chosen so that A_{1000} is singular. Clearly the mixing matrix is tracked through the singularity, although not so closely as when A_t is well-conditioned. Figure 11.5 shows the condition number of the MAP A_t. The

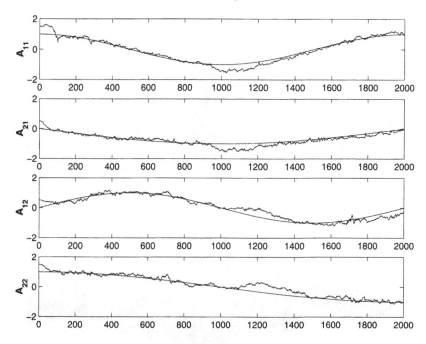

Figure 11.4. **Tracking through a singularity:** *The mixing matrix is singular at* $t = 1000$.

normalising constant $Z = p(\mathbf{x}_t | X_{t-1})$ in the correction equation (11.16) is known as the innovations probability (equation (11.17)) and measures the degree to which a new datum fits the dynamic model learned by the tracker. Discrete changes of state are signalled by low innovations probability. The innovations probability is approximated by

$$p(\mathbf{x}_t | X_{t-1}) \approx \sum_{n=1}^{N_p} p(\mathbf{x}_t | \vec{A}_{t|t-1}^n) \qquad (11.25)$$

when the state density is represented by particles. Figure 11.5 shows the innovations probability for the mixing shown in Figure 11.4: the presence of the singularity is clearly reflected.

Note also that the simulation shown in figure 11.4 was deliberately initialised fairly close to, but not exactly at, the true A_1. The 'latching on' of the tracker to the correct mixing matrix in the first 100 observations is evident in the figure.

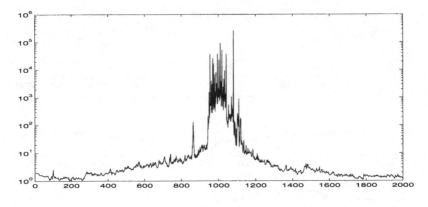

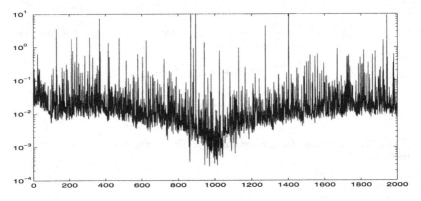

Figure 11.5. *Condition number and innovations probability: Top: Condition number of the MAP estimate of A_t. At $t = 1000$ the true mixing matrix is singular. Matrices with condition numbers greater than 10 were not used for estimating the source parameters. Bottom: Innovations probability $p(\mathbf{x}_t | X_{t-1})$.*

11.6 Smoothing

The filtering methods presented estimate the mixing matrix as $p(A_t | X_t)$. They are therefore strictly causal and can be used for online tracking. If the data are analysed retrospectively future observations ($\mathbf{x}_\tau$, $\tau > t$) may be used to refine the estimate of A_t. The Markov structure of the generative model permits the p.d.f. $p(\vec{A}_t | X_T)$ to be found from a forward pass through the data, followed by a backward sweep in which the influence of future observations on $\vec{A}_t$ is evaluated. See, for example, [Ghahramani & Roweis, 1999] for a detailed exposition of forward-backward recursions.

In the forward pass the joint probability

$$p(\vec{A}_t, \mathbf{x}_1, \ldots, \mathbf{x}_t) \equiv \alpha_t = \int \alpha_{t-1} p(\vec{A}_t | \vec{A}_{t-1}) \, p(\mathbf{x}_t | \vec{A}_t) \, d\vec{A}_{t-1} \qquad (11.26)$$

is recursively evaluated. In the backward sweep the conditional probability

$$p(\mathbf{x}_{t+1}, \ldots, \mathbf{x}_T | \vec{A}_t) \equiv \beta_t = \int \beta_{t+1} \, p(\vec{A}_{t+1} | \vec{A}_t) p(\mathbf{x}_{t+1} | \vec{A}_{t+1}) \, d\vec{A}_{t+1} \qquad (11.27)$$

is found. Finally the two are combined to produce a smoothed non-causal estimate of the mixing matrix:

$$p(\vec{A}_t | \mathbf{x}_1, \ldots, \mathbf{x}_T) \propto \alpha_t \beta_t. \qquad (11.28)$$

The forward density α_t and the backward density can each be approximated by a swarm of particles. However, combining them to produce the smoothed estimate (equation (11.28)) necessitates storing the entire history of the particles during the forward sweep [Kitagawa, 1996]. The storage problems inherent in this method can be somewhat alleviated by ignoring the influence of observations outside some window around the current observation. An alternative, which we have adopted, is to calculate the mean and covariance of the particle swarm approximating α_t at each t on the forward sweep. These are then combined with a Gaussian approximation to β_t from the backward sweep. The Gaussian approximation makes the calculation of equation (11.28) particularly simple and only two quantities, the mean and covariance of α_t, need be stored.

Figure 11.6 illustrates tracking by both smoothing and causal filtering. As before, the elements of the mixing matrix vary sinusoidally with time except for discontinuous jumps at $t = 600$ and 1200. Both the filtering and forward-backward recursions track the mixing matrix; however, the smoothed estimate is less noisy and more accurate, particularly at the discontinuities. Note also that following the discontinuity at $t = 1200$ the negative of the first column of A_t is tracked.

11.7 Temporal correlations

The graphical model in figure 11.1 assumes that successive samples from each source are independent, so that the sources are stochastic. When temporal correlations in the sources are present the model must be modified to include the conditional dependence of s_t^m on s_{t-1}^m. In this case the hidden state is now comprised of $\vec{A}_t$ and the states of the sources $\mathbf{s}_t$, and predictions and corrections for the full state should be made. Since

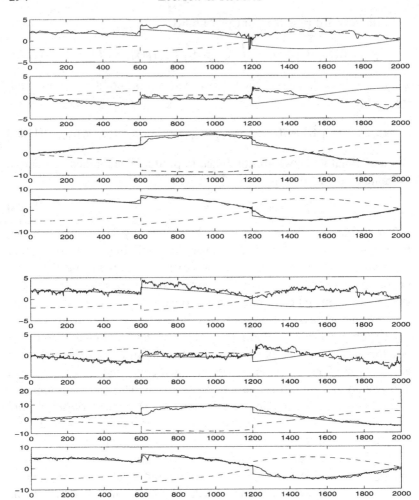

Figure 11.6. **Smoothing and filtering:** *Top four: Retrospective tracking with forward-backward recursions. Bottom four: Online filtering of the same data. Dashed lines show the negative of the mixing matrix elements.*

the sources are independent, predictions for each source and $\vec{A}_t$ may be made independently and the system is a factorial hidden Markov model [Ghahramani & Roweis, 1999].

A number of source predictors have been implemented, including the Kalman filter, autoregressive (AR) models and Gaussian mixture models. However, we find that in all these cases the combined tracker is unstable. The instability arises because the change in observation from $\mathbf{x}_t$ to $\mathbf{x}_{t+1}$

cannot be unambiguously assigned to either a change in the mixing matrix or a change in the sources. Small errors in the prediction of the sources induce errors in the mixing matrix estimates, which in turn lead to errors in subsequent source predictions; these errors are then incorporated into the predictive model for the sources and further (worse) errors in the prediction are made. This problem is not present in the stochastic case because the source model is much more tightly constrained.

Under the assumption that the sources evolve on a rapid time scale compared with the mixing matrix, the effect of temporal correlations in the sources may be removed by averaging over a sliding window. That is, the likelihood $p(\mathbf{x}_t | A_t)$ used in the correction step (equation (11.16)) is replaced by

$$\left\{ \prod_{\tau=-L}^{L} p(\mathbf{x}_{t+\tau} | A_{t+\tau}) \right\}^{\frac{1}{2L+1}}. \tag{11.29}$$

The length of the window $2L + 1$ is chosen to be of a typical time scale of the sources. Tracking using the averaged likelihood is computationally expensive because at each t the $p(\mathbf{x}_{t+\tau} | A_{t+\tau})$ must be evaluated for each τ in the sliding window. An alternative method of destroying the source temporal correlations is to replace the likelihood $p(\mathbf{x}_t | A_t)$ with $p(\mathbf{x}_{t+\tau} | A_{t+\tau})$ with τ chosen at random from within the sliding window $(-L \leqslant \tau \leqslant L)$. This is no more expensive than using $p(\mathbf{x}_t | A_t)$ and effectively destroys the source correlations.

Figures 11.7 and 11.8 illustrate the tracking of a mixing matrix with temporally correlated sources. The window length was $L = 50$. Tracking is not as accurate as in the stochastic case; however, the mixing matrix is followed and the sources are recovered well.

If more precise knowledge about the sources is available it might be incorporated into the source evolution equations in the form of a Bayesian prior. With sufficient information to constrain the sources this might permit the tracking and separation of temporally correlated sources without recourse to temporal averaging.

11.8 Conclusion

We have presented a method for independent component analysis when the mixing proportions are non-stationary. The Sampling Importance Re-sampling particle filter permits easy tracking of the state density even though the density is non-Gaussian and the observation equation

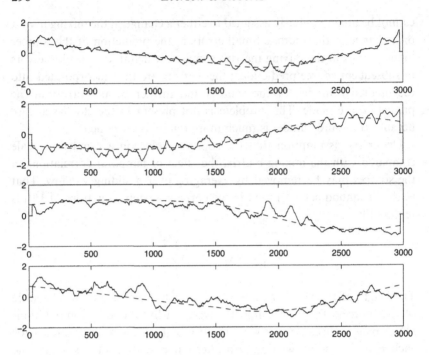

Figure 11.7. **Tracking temporally correlated sources:** *Elements of the mixing matrix during tracking of temporally correlated sources. Dashed lines show the true mixing matrix elements.*

is nonlinear. The method is strictly causal and can be used for online tracking (or 'filtering'). If data are analysed retrospectively forward-backward recursions may be used for smoothing rather than filtering. The mixing of temporally correlated sources may be tracked by averaging or sampling from within a sliding window.

In common with most tracking methods, the state noise covariance Q and the observational noise covariance R are parameters which must be set. Although we have not addressed the issue here, it is straight-forward, though laborious, to obtain maximum likelihood estimates for them using the EM method [Ghahramani & Roweis, 1999]. It would also be possible to estimate the state mixing matrix F in the same manner.

Although we have modelled the source densities here with generalised exponentials, which permits the separation of a wide range of sources, it is possible to both generalise and restrict the source model. More complicated (possibly multimodal) densities may be represented by a mixture of Gaussians. On the other hand, if all the sources are restricted

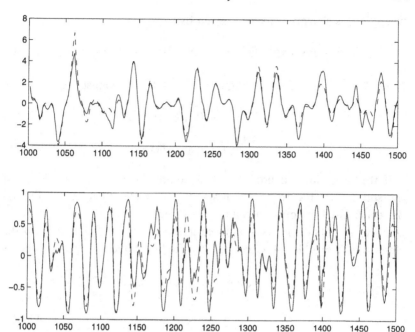

Figure 11.8. *Source estimation: Recovered sources and the true sources (dashed) for times 1000–1500 for the tracking shown in figure 11.7.*

to be Gaussian the method becomes a tracking factor analyser. In the zero noise limit the method performs non-stationary principal components analysis.

11.9 Appendix: Laplace's approximation for the likelihood

Here we use Laplace's approximation to evaluate the convolution integral (11.13) which gives the likelihood of an observation $\mathbf{x}$ given the mixing matrix A:

$$p(\mathbf{x}|A) = \int \mathcal{G}(\mathbf{x} - A\mathbf{s}, R) \prod_{m=1}^{M} p_m(s^m) \, d\mathbf{s}. \qquad (11.30)$$

The source densities are taken to be generalised exponentials (11.18).

Laplace's approximation [O'Ruanaidth & Fitzgerald, 1996] for the N-dimensional integral

$$I = \int f(\mathbf{y}) \exp\{-h(\mathbf{y})\} \, d\mathbf{y}, \qquad (11.31)$$

where $h(\mathbf{y})$ is sharply peaked, is given by

$$I \approx \int f(\hat{\mathbf{y}}) \exp\{-h(\hat{\mathbf{y}}) - (\mathbf{y} - \hat{\mathbf{y}})^\mathsf{T} H(\mathbf{y} - \hat{\mathbf{y}})/2\} \, d\mathbf{y}. \qquad (11.32)$$

Here $H = \frac{\partial^2 h}{\partial y_i y_j}$ is the Hessian and $\hat{\mathbf{y}}$ is the $\mathbf{y}$ that minimises h. Thus

$$I \approx f(\hat{\mathbf{y}}) \exp\{-h(\hat{\mathbf{y}})\} \sqrt{\det 2\pi H^{-1}} \qquad (11.33)$$

$$= \frac{(2\pi)^{\frac{N}{2}}}{\sqrt{\det H}} f(\hat{\mathbf{y}}) \exp\{-h(\hat{\mathbf{y}})\}. \qquad (11.34)$$

If the observational noise is small compared with the amplitude of the sources we regard the Gaussian term in (11.30) as $\exp\{-h\}$ and the generalised exponential and normalising factors as f. Then $h(\mathbf{s}) = (A\mathbf{s} - \mathbf{x})^\mathsf{T} R^{-1}(A\mathbf{s} - \mathbf{x})/2$ is minimised at $\hat{\mathbf{s}} = (A^\mathsf{T} C^{-1} A)^{-1} A^\mathsf{T} R^{-1} \mathbf{x}$ and the Hessian is $H = A^\mathsf{T} R^{-1} A$. Consequently the likelihood is approximated as

$$p(\mathbf{x}|A) \approx \rho \exp\{-(A\hat{\mathbf{s}} - \mathbf{x})^\mathsf{T} R^{-1}(A\hat{\mathbf{s}} - \mathbf{x})/2\} \, \exp - \sum_{m=1}^{M} \left| \frac{\hat{s}_m - \mu_m}{\sigma_m} \right|^{r_m} \qquad (11.35)$$

where the normalising factor ρ is

$$\rho = \frac{Z}{\sqrt{\det(A^\mathsf{T} R^{-1} A) \det(R)}} \qquad (11.36)$$

Comparison with Monte Carlo integration shows that this approximation is good over a wide range of noise covariances. Evaluation of the likelihood using (11.35) is much more efficient than Monte Carlo integration or other numerical quadratures.

Acknowledgement

We gratefully acknowledge funding from British Aerospace plc.

12

ICA: model order selection and dynamic source models

W.D. Penny

S.J. Roberts

R.M. Everson

12.1 Introduction

In this chapter we investigate ICA models in which the number of sources, M, may be less than the number of sensors, N: so-called non-square mixing.

The 'extra' sensor observations are explained as observation noise. This general approach may be called Probabilistic Independent Component Analysis (PICA) by analogy with the Probabilistic Principal Component Analysis (PPCA) model of Tipping & Bishop [1997]; ICA and PCA don't have observation noise, PICA and PPCA do.

Non-square ICA models give rise to a likelihood model for the data involving an integral which is intractable. In this chapter we build on previous work in which the integral is estimated using a Laplace approximation. By making the further assumption that the unmixing matrix lies on the decorrelating manifold we are able to make a number of simplifications. Firstly, the observation noise can be estimated using PCA methods, and, secondly, optimisation takes place in a space having a much reduced dimensionality, having order M^2 parameters rather than $M \times N$. Again, building on previous work, we derive a model order selection criterion for selecting the appropriate number of sources. This is based on the Laplace approximation as applied to the decorrelating manifold. This is then compared with PCA model order selection methods on music and EEG datasets.

Standard ICA, if there is such a thing, is not a proper time-series model, as each source is considered to be Independent and Identically Distributed (i.i.d.). But with dynamic source models, temporal information can be used and, as we show, this can lead to much improved source estimation. The second part of this chapter looks at the use of such dy-

299

namic source models, where the sources are modelled using a generalised autoregressive (GAR) process. This is the usual autoregressive process but where the noise has a Generalised Exponential (GE) distribution instead of the usual Gaussian.

This chapter has six further sections. The first describes the probability model for non-square ICA and derives the Laplace approximation required to calculate the data likelihood. Section 12.3 describes the decorrelating manifold and section 12.4 describes ICA and PCA model order selection methods. Section 12.5 describes different source models including the GAR process. This includes a description of its own model order criterion for determining the optimal number of taps in the GAR filter. Section 12.6 describes results from applying the above methods to the unmixing of music and EEG sources and the chapter is concluded in section 12.7.

12.2 A probabilistic model

The observed variables $\mathbf{x}$, of dimension N, are modelled as

$$\mathbf{x} = A\mathbf{s} + \mathbf{n} \tag{12.1}$$

where $\mathbf{n}$ is zero-mean Gaussian observation noise having an isotropic covariance matrix with precision β, A is the mixing matrix, and the underlying sources $\mathbf{s}$ are statistically independent:

$$p(\mathbf{s}) = \prod_{i=1}^{M} p(s_i), \tag{12.2}$$

where the sum runs over the M sources. The distribution of the observations conditioned on the mixing matrix and sources is

$$p(\mathbf{x}|A, \mathbf{s}) = \mathcal{N}(\mathbf{x}; A\mathbf{s}, (1/\beta)I) \tag{12.3}$$

where $\mathcal{N}(\mathbf{x}; \mu, \Sigma)$ is a normal distribution with mean μ and covariance Σ. The likelihood of a data point is given by

$$p(\mathbf{x}|A) = \int p(\mathbf{x}|A, \mathbf{s})p(\mathbf{s})\, d\mathbf{s}. \tag{12.4}$$

With a non-square ICA model, optimisation takes place in two iterated steps: source estimation and mixing matrix estimation.

12.2.1 Source estimation

The sources can be estimated by noting that their posterior distribution

$$p(\mathbf{s}|A, \mathbf{x}) \propto p(\mathbf{x}|A, \mathbf{s})p(\mathbf{s}) \tag{12.5}$$

is proportional to the 'prior' distribution, $p(\mathbf{s})$, and the source-dependent likelihood $p(\mathbf{x}|A, \mathbf{s})$. An iterative gradient-based scheme exists for estimating the Maximum *A Posteriori* (MAP) sources, $\mathbf{s}_{\text{MAP}}$. This consists of two terms: (i) the gradient of the source-dependent log likelihood and (ii) the gradient of the log source densities, both of which are given in later parts of this chapter. Because estimation of $\mathbf{s}_{\text{MAP}}$ requires a separate optimisation for each data point it is computationally expensive.

Alternatively, the prior can be ignored and the sources set to their Maximum Likelihood (ML) source values, $\mathbf{s}_{\text{ML}}$. These are recovered via an unmixing matrix

$$\mathbf{s}_{\text{ML}} = W\mathbf{x}, \tag{12.6}$$

which is given by the pseudo-inverse of the mixing matrix

$$W = (A^{\mathsf{T}}A)^{-1}A^{\mathsf{T}}. \tag{12.7}$$

This unmixing minimises the squared reconstruction error, and therefore maximises the data likelihood. Computation of the MAP sources will not improve on the ML reconstruction error or the squared error of source estimation, but it will reduce 'cross-talk' between the sources, i.e., make them more independent. An empirical demonstration of this is given in [Attias, 1999a].

12.2.2 Mixing matrix estimation

To compute the likelihood of an observation we must be able to calculate the integral in equation (12.4). If we assume that the distribution over sources is dominated by a single peak, $\hat{\mathbf{s}}$, then the integral can be performed using Laplace's method [Kass *et al.*, 1991]:

$$\int p(\mathbf{x}|A, \mathbf{s})p(\mathbf{s})d\mathbf{s} \approx p(\mathbf{x}|A, \hat{\mathbf{s}})p(\hat{\mathbf{s}})(2\pi)^{M/2} \det(F)^{-1/2}, \tag{12.8}$$

where

$$F = -\left[\frac{d^2 \log p(\mathbf{x}|A, \mathbf{s})p(\mathbf{s})}{d\mathbf{s}_i d\mathbf{s}_j}\right]_{\mathbf{s}=\hat{\mathbf{s}}}. \tag{12.9}$$

In this chapter we use a simplified variant of Laplace's method where the above matrix is replaced by the Hessian [Kass *et al.*, 1991]:

$$H = - \left[\frac{d^2 \log p(\mathbf{x}|A, \mathbf{s})}{ds_i ds_j} \right]_{\mathbf{s}=\hat{\mathbf{s}}}. \tag{12.10}$$

As discussed by Kass, this variant is less accurate but is easier to compute. We have

$$\log p(\mathbf{x}|A, \mathbf{s}) = \frac{N}{2} \log \left(\frac{\beta}{2\pi} \right) - \frac{\beta}{2} (\mathbf{x} - A\mathbf{s})^\mathsf{T} (\mathbf{x} - A\mathbf{s}) \tag{12.11}$$

giving

$$H = \beta A^\mathsf{T} A. \tag{12.12}$$

The log likelihood of an observation, $\mathcal{L} \equiv \log p(\mathbf{x}|A)$, is therefore given by

$$\mathcal{L} = \frac{N - M}{2} \log \left(\frac{\beta}{2\pi} \right) - \frac{\beta}{2} (\mathbf{x} - A\hat{\mathbf{s}})^\mathsf{T} (\mathbf{x} - A\hat{\mathbf{s}})$$
$$+ \log p(\hat{\mathbf{s}}) - \frac{1}{2} \log \det(A^\mathsf{T} A). \tag{12.13}$$

The mixing matrix, A, can be optimised by following the gradient $d\mathcal{L}/dA$ using a Broyden-Fletcher-Goldfarb-Shanno (BFGS) optimiser as shown in [Roberts, 1998]. The noise precision can then be estimated using a fixed point of the above likelihood:

$$\frac{1}{\beta} = \frac{1}{N - M} \langle (\mathbf{x} - A\hat{\mathbf{s}})^\mathsf{T} (\mathbf{x} - A\hat{\mathbf{s}}) \rangle, \tag{12.14}$$

where the expectation is taken over all observations.

Fitting a non-square ICA model therefore consists of iterating estimates of the mixing matrix with estimates of the noise precision and the sources. The sources can be estimated either by their MAP or ML values, i.e., $\hat{\mathbf{s}} = \mathbf{s}_{\text{MAP}}$ or $\hat{\mathbf{s}} = \mathbf{s}_{\text{ML}}$, as shown in the previous subsection. Because estimation of the MAP sources is computationally expensive, ML source estimation is the preferred method during this optimisation. In previous work Roberts [1998] used ML sources.

12.3 The decorrelating manifold

In previous work [Everson & Roberts, 1999a] we have constrained the unmixing matrix to be a decorrelating matrix. The motivation for this is that, for sources to be statistically independent, they must be at least linearly decorrelating. Therefore, by ensuring that they are decorrelating, we are at least some way to finding the ICA solution. The corresponding mixing matrix is defined as follows.

If X is an $N \times T$ matrix of zero-mean data vectors, and each entry is normalised by $1/T$, and the Singular Value Decomposition (SVD) of X is given by

$$X = U\Lambda V, \tag{12.15}$$

then U contains the principal components of the observation covariance matrix and $\Lambda = [\lambda_1, \lambda_2, \ldots, \lambda_N]$ contains the standard deviations of the corresponding principal components. The mixing matrix is then given by

$$A = U_M \Lambda_M Q^\mathsf{T} D^{-1}, \tag{12.16}$$

where U_M and Λ_M are the first M columns of U and Λ. The transform is also parameterised by a diagonal scaling matrix D and an orthonormal matrix Q which are both of dimension $M \times M$. The matrices Q and D constitute the ICA transform proper.

12.3.1 Source and noise estimation

The ML source estimates are, as before, given by the pseudo-inverse of the mixing matrix

$$W = (A^\mathsf{T} A)^{-1} A^\mathsf{T} \tag{12.17}$$

$$= DQ\Lambda_M^{-1} U_M^\mathsf{T} \tag{12.18}$$

operating on the observations

$$\mathbf{s}_{\mathrm{ML}} = W\mathbf{x}. \tag{12.19}$$

The reconstructed observations are given by

$$A\mathbf{s}_{\mathrm{ML}} = U_M U_M^\mathsf{T} \mathbf{x}, \tag{12.20}$$

which gives an average reconstruction error of

$$E = \langle (\mathbf{x} - A\mathbf{s}_{\mathrm{ML}})^\mathsf{T} (\mathbf{x} - A\mathbf{s}_{\mathrm{ML}}) \rangle \tag{12.21}$$

$$= \mathrm{Tr}[(X - U_M U_M^\mathsf{T} X)^\mathsf{T} (X - U_M U_M^\mathsf{T} X)]$$

$$= \mathrm{Tr}[X^\mathsf{T} X - X^\mathsf{T} U_M U_M^\mathsf{T} X]. \tag{12.22}$$

By noting that the projection onto the first M principal components is $Y = X^\mathsf{T} U_M$, and their covariance is $YY^\mathsf{T} = X^\mathsf{T} U_M U_M^\mathsf{T} X$, E is seen to be the variance of the data not explained by the first M components. Hence

$$E = \sum_{i=M+1}^{N} \lambda_i^2 \qquad (12.23)$$

and

$$\frac{1}{\beta} = \frac{1}{N-M} \sum_{i=M+1}^{N} \lambda_i^2. \qquad (12.24)$$

This is the same as the noise estimate in the probabilistic PCA model. Therefore, if ICA is constrained to the decorrelating manifold and ML source estimates are used, the observation noise level is not dependent on D or Q, i.e., the ICA transform proper. It can therefore be calculated ahead of optimising D and Q and fixed to its calculated value.

12.3.2 Mixing matrix estimation

In previous work [Everson & Roberts, 1999a], we showed that for flexible source models (see later), the mixing matrix can be constrained to have rows of length one. For these cases we have $D = I$. The matrix Q is constrained to be orthonormal by writing it as

$$Q = \exp(Z) \qquad (12.25)$$

where Z is a skew-symmetric matrix ($Z^\mathsf{T} = -Z$) whose non-zero entries z_{ij} are known as Cayley coordinates [Minka, 2000].

By substituting in the average reconstruction error and our chosen form for the mixing matrix, the log likelihood becomes

$$\mathcal{L} = \frac{N-M}{2} \log\left(\frac{\beta}{2\pi e}\right) + \log p(\mathbf{s}_{\mathrm{ML}})$$
$$+ \log \det(D) - \log \det(Q) - \log \det(\Lambda_M). \qquad (12.26)$$

As Q is an orthonormal matrix, we always have $\det(Q) = 1$. Therefore the only term in the likelihood that depends on Q is the log source density where the dependence is introduced via equations (12.17) and (12.19).

In previous work [Everson & Roberts, 1999a] we show how to compute the derivative of this term and combine it with an expression for dQ/dZ. This then gives the gradient of the likelihood with respect to the Cayley coordinates. Fitting the ICA model therefore corresponds to simply following this gradient using, for example, a BFGS optimiser. We refer to the decorrelating manifold approach as the ICADEC algorithm.

12.4 Model order selection

The optimal number of sources, $\hat{M}$, can be computed by plotting the log likelihood, $\log p(\mathbf{x}|A)$, as a function of M and choosing the maximum. For most signal processing models, e.g., autoregressive models, wavelets or neural networks, model order selection using a maximum likelihood criterion is doomed to failure. This is because as more basis functions are *added* the likelihood increases monotonically; the optimal model order is therefore infinite. ICA, however, is more like a product model than an additive model, because the sources are independent. As too many sources are postulated, the independence criterion is violated thus reducing the overall likelihood. ICA model order selection using ML is therefore plausible.

For the case of Gaussian sources the ICA model reduces to PCA. We are then able to use PCA model order selection methods such as the Laplace approximation used by [Minka, 2000]. By using conjugate priors for the eigenvectors, eigenvalues and noise level and parameterising the eigenvectors using Cayley coordinates, [Minka, 2000] shows that the evidence for a PCA model with M sources is

$$p(X|M) \approx p(U) \left(\prod_{j=1}^{M} \lambda_j \right)^{-T/2} \beta^{T(N-M)/2} (2\pi)^{(m+M)/2} |A_Z|^{-1/2} T^{-M/2}.$$

(12.27)

Here $m = NM - M(M+1)/2$, β is given in equation (12.24) and

$$p(U) = 2^{-M} \prod_{i=1}^{M} \Gamma((N-i+1)/2) \pi^{-(N-i+1)/2}, \tag{12.28}$$

where

$$|A_Z| = \prod_{i=1}^{M} \prod_{j=i+1}^{N} (\hat{\lambda}_j^{-1} - \hat{\lambda}_i^{-1})(\lambda_i - \lambda_j) T \tag{12.29}$$

and λ_i^2 are the eigenvalues from PCA, and $\hat{\lambda}_i^2$ are identical except for $i > M$ where $\hat{\lambda}_i^2 = 1/\beta$. Minka's experiments and our own show this to be a remarkably consistent model order criterion, even with very few data points. Moreover, Minka produces empirical evidence to show that for selected non-Gaussian sources (sound samples with skewed and kurtotic densities), accurate model order selection is still feasible.

12.5 Source models

12.5.1 Reciprocal cosh sources

In [Bell & Sejnowski, 1995] the source densities are assumed to be reciprocal cosh densities

$$p(s_i) = \frac{1}{\pi \cosh(s_i)}. \tag{12.30}$$

This form arises from the hyperbolic tangent squashing function used in the neural network implementation, as discussed in [MacKay, 1996]; see also Chapter 1. A drawback of the RC density, however, is its inability to model sub-Gaussian densities, such as the uniform density. This can be overcome by using the 'flexible' source models described in the next two subsections.

12.5.2 Generalised exponential sources

A more general parametric form which can model super-Gaussian, Gaussian *and* sub-Gaussian forms is the 'exponential power distribution' or 'generalised exponential (GE)' density

$$p(s_i) \equiv G(s_i; r_i, \sigma_i) = \frac{r_i}{2\sigma_i \Gamma(1/r_i)} \exp\left(-\left|\frac{s_i}{\sigma_i}\right|^{r_i}\right). \tag{12.31}$$

This density has zero mean, a kurtosis determined by the parameter r_i and a variance which is then determined by $1/\sigma_i$. Everson & Roberts [1999a] show how to calculate the derivative of the log source density and describe an embedded line search method for estimating r_i and σ_i.

12.5.3 Generalised autoregressive sources

Pearlmutter & Parra [1997] have proposed a 'contextual-ICA' algorithm where the sources are conditioned on previous source values. Their work focuses on using generalised autoregressive (GAR) models for modelling each source. The term 'generalised' is used because the AR models incorporate additive noise which is non-Gaussian. Specifically, Pearlmutter and Parra used a logistic density noise distribution.

Pearlmutter and Parra have shown that contextual-ICA can separate sources which cannot be separated by standard (non-contextual) ICA algorithms. This is because the standard methods only use information from the cumulative histograms; temporal information is discarded.

In this chapter we use GAR models with p filter taps and additive noise drawn from a generalised exponential distribution; for $p = 0$ these models therefore reduce to the GE sources described in the previous subsection. The density model is

$$p(s_i) = G(e_i[t]; r_i, \sigma_i), \tag{12.32}$$

where $e_i[t] = s_i[t] - \hat{s}_i[t]$ is the GAR prediction error and $\hat{s}_i[t]$ is the GAR prediction

$$\hat{s}_i[t] = -\sum_{k=1}^{p} c_i(k) s_i[t-k], \tag{12.33}$$

where $c_i(k)$ are the GAR coefficients for the ith source which can collectively be written as a vector c_i. The GAR coefficients can be estimated by minimising the error

$$E = \sum_{t=1}^{T} |e_i[t]|^{r_i}. \tag{12.34}$$

Penny *et al.* [2000] derive the corresponding gradients and, again, use BFGS for optimisation. This procedure is embedded within the algorithm for estimating the unmixing matrix, W, where the GAR models are re-estimated once for every ten updates of W.

The optimal number of filter taps, $\hat{p}$, can be chosen using a Minimum Description Length (MDL) model order selection criterion. For a dataset $\mathcal{D}$ and estimated parameters $\hat{\theta}$ of dimension p, the MDL criterion is given by

$$MDL(p) = -\log p(\mathcal{D}|\hat{\theta}) + \frac{p}{2} \log T, \tag{12.35}$$

where T is the number of data points. For a GAR model this gives

$$MDL_{\text{GAR}}(p) = -T \log \left(\frac{r\sigma^{(1/r)}}{2\Gamma(1/r)} \right) + \sum_{t=1}^{T} \beta |e_t|^R + \frac{p}{2} \log T. \tag{12.36}$$

For $r = 2$, if we ignore terms not involving p or σ, this reduces to the well-known MDL criterion for an AR model:

$$MDL_{\text{AR}}(p) = -\frac{T}{2} \log \beta + \frac{p}{2} \log T. \tag{12.37}$$

This criterion can be applied to each GAR source in an ICA model, allowing each to have a different number of taps, thus reflecting the dynamic complexity or otherwise of each source.

12.6 Results

12.6.1 Selecting the number of sources

We now give some results of applying the various model order selection methods for estimating the optimal number of sources. The first method, which we call ICADEC-L, uses the Laplace approximation and constrains the unmixing matrix to be on the decorrelating manifold. This results in the likelihood expression in equation (12.26).

The above measure is compared with PCA model order selection methods. The first of these methods, which we call PCA-L, uses Minka's Laplace approximation described earlier. The second, which we call PCA-MDL, uses an MDL criterion described in [Wax & Kailath, 1985]. The last method, which we call PCA-EV, is the evidence method described in [Rajan & Rayner, 1997].

The methods are applied to four datasets. The first consists of two music sources (the top two in figure 12.1) which are mixed into six observations to which is then added observation noise of variance $1/\beta$. The second dataset consists of all four music sources which are again mixed into six observations to which we add observation noise. All music sources were normalised to zero mean and unit variance. Fifty datasets of each type were created, where each time, the mixing matrix was set randomly according to a Gaussian distribution. The observation noise sequence was generated afresh each time.

Tables 12.1 and 12.2 show the number of times each criterion selected the correct order, for 100 data points and various noise levels. The PCA-L and PCA-MDL criteria appear to offer the best performance, with PCA-L being slightly better. The ICADEC-L criterion always degrades more rapidly in the presence of noise. The PCA-EV criterion is inconsistent; outperforming all methods on the four-source task (and actually getting better with increasing noise level!), but doing poorly on the two-source task.

The next two datasets involve EEG sources which were derived as follows. We applied ICADEC to a 22-channel EEG recording, over a time period for which the signal statistics were considered to be stationary (this was found by embedding the ICA model in a hidden Markov process; see [Penny *et al.*, 2000] for details). The true number of sources underlying these data is unknown, but applying PCA-L gave an answer of 15. We then extracted two datasets; one consisting of three sources, shown in figure 12.2, and one consisting of ten sources (not shown). All sources were normalised to zero-mean and unit variance. These

Table 12.1. *Model order selection with two music sources and observational noise variance of $1/\beta$. The numbers indicate the percentage of times the correct model order was selected.*

$1/\beta$	PCA-L	PCA-MDL	PCA-EV	ICADEC-L
0.1	100	100	100	100
0.3	94	96	64	86
0.5	96	94	0	62
1.0	78	71	0	8

Table 12.2. *Model order selection with four music sources and observational noise variance of $1/\beta$. The numbers indicate the percentage of times the correct model order was selected.*

$1/\beta$	PCA-L	PCA-MDL	PCA-EV	ICADEC-L
0.01	100	96	56	100
0.1	94	94	58	88
0.3	86	82	82	76
0.5	72	70	96	66

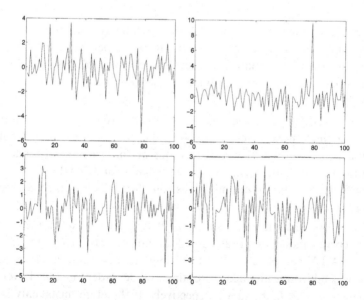

Figure 12.1. *Music sources used in model order selection experiments.* The left two are samples of Beethoven and the right two are samples of Bessie Smith.

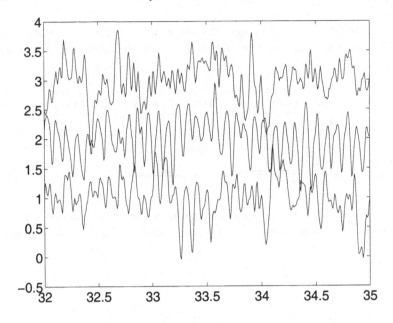

Figure 12.2. *Three EEG sources.*

sources were then mixed up to form 20-dimensional observations to which noise was added. Fifty datasets of each type were created, where each time, the mixing matrix was set randomly according to a Gaussian distribution and the observation noise sequence was generated afresh each time.

The ICADEC-L criterion was applied to only 10 datasets of each type, and at a single noise level $(1/\beta = 0.1)$, due to the excessive amount of computation required; the PCA methods perform a single eigendecomposition of the 20-dimensional space, whereas for ICADEC-L we have to perform 20 separate optimisations (one for each hypothesised model order; actually 19 as $\hat{M} = 1$ is not considered.

For the three-source EEG dataset, PCA-L and PCA-MDL achieved 100% correct model order selection at all noise levels $(1/\beta = 0.1, 0.3, 0.5, 1.0)$. PCA-EV completely failed at all but the first noise level; as more noise was added it estimated the optimal model order (averaged over the 50 datasets) as 3, 6, 9 and 13 respectively. It therefore mistakenly interprets the extra observation noise as extra sources. ICADEC-L also failed completely on the (limited) data it was applied to, again overestimating

Table 12.3. *Model order selection with 10 EEG sources of unit variance.*
The numbers indicate the percentage of times the correct model order was
selected.

$1/\beta$	PCA-L	PCA-MDL	PCA-EV
0.1	100	100	100
0.3	80	72	50
0.5	58	36	8
1.0	12	4	0

the model order. It chose $\hat{M} = 4$ for 9 out of 10 of the datasets and
$\hat{M} = 5$ on the remaining one.

The results for the ten-source EEG dataset are shown in table 12.3.
Again, PCA-L performs the best, followed by PCA-MDL. PCA-EV again
fails at high noise levels, interpreting the extra noise as extra sources.
ICADEC-L performed poorly on the limited data it was tried on; getting
only 7 out of 10 correct at the first noise level (for which all PCA methods
were 100% correct).

12.6.2 Comparing source models

Our second set of results compares the different source models, namely,
reciprocal cosh (RC), Generalised Exponential (GE) and Generalised
Autoregressive (GAR). For the GAR model, application of the MDL
criterion to the music sources suggested using a model order of 10.
Figures 12.3 and 12.4 show the correlations between true and estimated
music sources using ICADEC with the RC and GAR source models
respectively. This was for a dataset containing six observations mixed up
from two music sources, as described earlier. The variance of the observation noise was $1/\beta = 0.001$. The corresponding Normalised Mean
Squared Errors (NMSE, the squared source estimation error normalised
by the variance of the true sources) were 0.0272 for RC, 0.1946 for
GE and only 0.0014 for GAR. Table 12.4 shows how unmixing accuracy is dependent on the level of observation noise (we omit the
results for the GE model as it is not a good source model for this
dataset). At low noise levels there is an order of magnitude benefit in
using a GAR model, whereas at high noise levels the benefit is modest.

Penny, Roberts & Everson

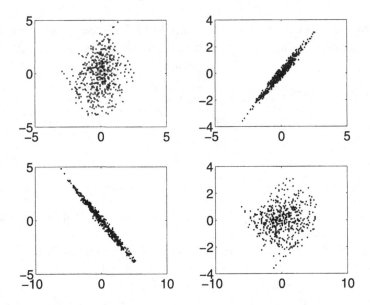

Figure 12.3. *Source estimation using a reciprocal cosh source model.* Plots of true versus estimated sources.

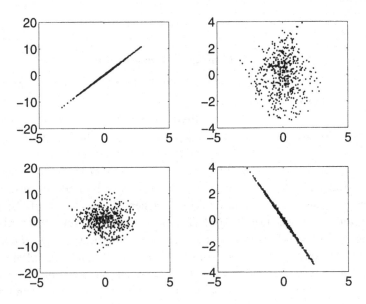

Figure 12.4. *Source estimation using a GAR source model.* Plots of true versus estimated sources.

Table 12.4. *Normalised mean squared error of unmixing using reciprocal cosh (RC) and Generalised Autoregressive (GAR) source models, for various levels of added observation noise, $1/\beta$. The final column shows the relative error. At low noise levels (top half of table) there is an order of magnitude benefit in using a GAR model, whereas at high noise levels the benefit is modest.*

$1/\beta$	RC	GAR	RC/GAR
0.001	0.0309	0.0013	24
0.005	0.0315	0.0027	12
0.01	0.0328	0.0045	7.3
0.05	0.0412	0.0195	2.1
0.1	0.0577	0.0360	1.6
0.3	0.1111	0.0902	1.2
0.5	0.1587	0.1200	1.3
1.0	0.1807	0.1640	1.1

12.7 Discussion

Of the model order criteria investigated the method of choice is PCA-L, a Bayesian PCA criterion derived by Minka [2000]. Not only is it accurate, it is also fast. This is important as ICA is increasingly being applied to datasets of a higher dimensionality where, for example in EEG or fMRI analysis, we have tens or hundreds of observations.

Mathematically, the use of a PCA model order criterion in an ICA context is only suitable when the sources are Gaussian. The experiments in this paper, on music and EEG sources, suggest that the PCA-L criterion is robust to departures from Gaussianity. It even appears to be robust to departures from unimodality; experiments with mixtures of Gaussian sources show that, at low observation noise levels, the criterion performs well even with several modes per source.

The relatively poorer performance of the ICADEC-L criterion is not really surprising as it is, in fact, a maximum likelihood criterion; in its derivation we have not integrated out the mixing matrix or the observation noise. In future, we intend to do this by extending the use of the conjugate priors used in PCA-L to the ICADEC situation; this is a natural extension as, in ICADEC, the mixing matrix component Q is also parameterised using Cayley coordinates.

The use of dynamic source models can, at low noise levels, improve source estimation accuracy by an order of magnitude. In the future, we envisage applying the GAR model order criterion at the same time as mixing matrix estimation. This could be used to allow the overall algorithm to extract only those sources with a high temporal information content. The consequent reduction in the number of sources produced may help to speed up interpretation of the various ICA components.

References

[Agresti, 1990] Agresti, A. (1990). *Categorical Data Analysis*. Wiley.

[Aine *et al.*, 1998] Aine, C.J., Huang, M., Christner, R., Stephen, J., Meyer, J., Silveri, J., & Weisend, M. (1998). New developments in source localization algorithms: clinical examples. *International Journal of Psychophysiology*, **30**, 198.

[Akaike, 1973] Akaike, H. (1973). Information theory and the extension of the maximum likelihood principle. *Pages 267–281 of:* Petrov, B.N., & Csaki, F. (eds), *Second International Symposium on Information Theory*. Akademiai Kiado.

[Amari, 1985] Amari, S.-I. (1985). *Differential Geometrical Methods in Statistics*. Lecture Notes in Statistics, vol. 28. Springer.

[Amari, 1997] Amari, S.-I. (1997). Neural learning in structured parameter spaces - natural Riemannian gradient. *Pages 127–133 of: Advances in Neural Information Processing Systems*, vol. 9. MIT Press.

[Amari, 1998] Amari, S.-I. (1998). Natural gradient works efficiently in learning. *Neural Computation*, **10**(2), 251–276.

[Amari *et al.*, 1996] Amari, S.-I., Cichocki, A., & Yang, H. (1996). A new learning algorithm for blind signal separation. *Pages 757–763 of:* Touretzky, D., Mozer, M., & Hasselmo, M. (eds), *Advances in Neural Information Processing Systems*, vol. 8.

[Amari *et al.*, 1997] Amari, S.-I., Chen, T.-P., & Cichocki, A. (1997). Stability analysis of adaptive blind source separation. *Neural Networks*, **10**(8), 1345–1351.

[Amari *et al.*, 1998] Amari, S.-I., Douglas, S.C., & Cichocki, A. (1998). Multichannel blind deconvolution and source separation using the natural gradient. *IEEE Transactions on Signal Processing*, 101–104.

[Atick & Redlich, 1990] Atick, J.J., & Redlich, A.N. (1990). Towards a theory of early visual processing. *Neural Computation*, **2**, 308–320.

[Atick *et al.*, 1995] Atick, J.J., Griffin, P.A., & Redlich, A.N. (1995). Statistical approach to shape from shading: reconstruction of 3-dimensional face surfaces from single 2-dimensional images. *Neural Computation*, **8**(6), 1321–1340.

[Attias, 1999a] Attias, H. (1999a). Independent factor analysis. *Neural Computation*, **11**(5), 803–852.

[Attias, 1999b] Attias, H. (1999b). Inferring parameters and structure of latent variable models by variational Bayes. *Pages 21–30 of: Proceedings of the*

Fifteenth Conference on Uncertainty in Artificial Intelligence.

[Attias, 2000] Attias, H. (2000). A variational bayesian framework for graphical models. T. Leen *et al.* (eds), *Advances in Neural Information Processing Systems*, vol. 12. MIT Press. Available from http://www.gatsby.ucl.ac.uk/~hagai/papers.html.

[Attias & Schreiner, 1998] Attias, H., & Schreiner, C.E. (1998). Blind source separation and deconvolution - the dynamic component analysis algorithm. *Neural Computation*, **10**(6), 1373–1424.

[Back & Weigend, 1998] Back, A.D., & Weigend, A.S. (1998). A first application of independent component analysis to extracting structure from stock returns. *International Journal on Neural Systems*, **8**(4), 473–484.

[Bae *et al.*, 2000] Bae, U.-M., Lee, T.-W., & Lee, S.-Y. (2000). Blind signal separation in teleconferencing using the ICA mixture model. *IEE Electronics Letters*, **36**(7), 680–682.

[Barber & Bishop, 1998] Barber, D., & Bishop, C.M. (1998). Ensemble learning in Bayesian neural networks. *Pages 215–237 of:* Jordan, M.I., Kearns, M.J., & Solla, S.A. (eds), *Advances in Neural Information Processing Systems*, vol. 10. MIT Press.

[Barlow, 1961a] Barlow, H.B. (1961a). The coding of sensory messages. *Pages 330–360 of:* Thorpe, & Zangwill (eds), *Current Problems in Animal Behavior*. Cambridge University Press.

[Barlow, 1961b] Barlow, H.B. (1961b). Possible principles underlying the transformation of sensory messages. *Pages 217–234 of:* Rosenblith, W.A. (ed), *Sensory Communication*. MIT Press.

[Barlow, 1989] Barlow, H.B. (1989). Unsupervised learning. *Neural Computation*, **1**, 295–311.

[Bar-Ness *et al.*, 1982] Bar-Ness, Y., Carlin, J., & Steinberger, M. (1982). Bootstrapping adaptive cross-pol canceller for satellite communications. *Pages 4F.5.1–4F.5.5 of: Proc IEEE Int Conf Comunications.*

[Barros & Ohnishi, 1999] Barros, A.K., & Ohnishi, N. (1999). Removal of quasi-periodic sources from physiological measurements. *Pages 185–190 of: Proceedings of First International Conference on Independent Component Analysis and Blind Source Separation: ICA'99.*

[Bartlett *et al.*, 1997] Bartlett, M.S., Stewart, M., & Sejnowski, T.J. (1997). Viewpoint invariant face recognition using independent component attractor networks. *Pages 817–823 of:* M. Mozer, M. Jordan, T. Petsche (ed), *Advances in Neural Information Processing Systems*, vol. 9. Available from http://www.cnl.salk.edu/~marni.

[Bartlett *et al.*, 1998] Bartlett, M.S., Lades, H.M., & Sejnowski, T.J. (1998). Independent components representations for face recognition. *Pages 528–539 of:* Rogowitz, & Pappas (eds), *Proceedings of the SPIE Symposium on Electronic Imaging: Science and Technology: Conference on Human Vision and Electronic Imaging III*, vol. 3299. SPIE Press. Available from http://www.cnl.salk.edu/~marni.

[Beale & Mallows, 1959] Beale, E.M.L., & Mallows, C.L. (1959). Scale mixing of symmetric distributions with zero means. *Annals of Mathematical Statistics*, **30**, 1145–1151.

[Bell & Sejnowski, 1995] Bell, A.J., & Sejnowski, T.J. (1995). An information maximization approach to blind separation and blind deconvolution. *Neural Computation*, **7**(6), 1129–1159.

[Bell & Sejnowski, 1997] Bell, A.J., & Sejnowski, T.J. (1997). The "independent components" of natural scenes are edge filters. *Vision Research*, **37**(23), 3327–3338.

[Belouchrani & Cardoso, 1994] Belouchrani, A., & Cardoso, J.-F. (1994). Maximum likelihood source separation for discrete sources. *Pages 768–771 of: Proc EUSIPCO*.

[Belouchrani & Cardoso, 1995] Belouchrani, A., & Cardoso, J.-F. (1995). Maximum likelihood source separation by the expectation-maximization technique: deterministic and stochastic implementation. *Pages 49–53 of: Proceedings of 1995 International Symposium on Non-Linear Theory and Applications*.

[Belouchrani et al., 1993] Belouchrani, A., Abed Meraim, K., Cardoso, J.-F., & Moulines, E. (1993). Second order blind separation of correlated sources. *Pages 346–351 of: Proceedings of International Conference on Digital Signal Processing*.

[Belouchrani et al., 1997] Belouchrani, A., Abed Meraim, K., Cardoso, J.-F., & Moulines, E. (1997). A blind source separation technique based on second order statistics. *IEEE Transactions on Signal Processing*, **45**(2), 434–44.

[Ben-Tal & Zibulevsky, 1997] Ben-Tal, A., & Zibulevsky, M. (1997). Penalty/barrier multiplier methods for convex programming problems. *SIAM Journal on Optimization*, **7**(2), 347–366.

[Bezdek, 1981] Bezdek, J.C. (1981). *Pattern Recognition with Fuzzy Objective Function Algorithms*. Plenum Press.

[Bingham & Hyvärinen, 2000] Bingham, E., & Hyvärinen, A. (2000). A fast fixed-point algorithm for independent component analysis of complex-valued signals. *International Journal of Neural Systems*, **10**(1), 1–8.

[Bishop, 1994] Bishop, C.M. (1994). *Mixture density networks*. Tech. rept. Neural Computing Research Group, Aston University.

[Bishop, 1995] Bishop, C.M. (1995). *Neural Networks for Pattern Recognition*. Oxford University Press.

[Bishop, 1998] Bishop, C.M. (1998). GTM: the generative topographic mapping. *Neural Computation*, **10**, 215–234.

[Bishop, 1999] Bishop, C.M. (1999). Variational principal components. *Pages 509–514 of: International Conference on Artificial Neural Networks*.

[Bofill & Zibulevsky, 2000a] Bofill, P., & Zibulevsky, M. (2000a). Blind separation of more sources than mixtures using the sparsity of the short-time Fourier transform. Pajunen, P. (ed), *International Workshop on Independent Component Analysis and Blind Signal Separation*.

[Bofill & Zibulevsky, 2000b] Bofill, P., & Zibulevsky, M. (2000b). *Sparse underdetermined ICA: estimating the mixing matrix and the sources separately*. Tech. rept. UPC-DAC-2000-7. Universitat Politecnica de Catalunya. Available from http://www.ac.upc.es/homes/pau/sounds.html.

[Box & Tiao, 1973] Box, G., & Tiao, G. (1973). *Bayesian Inference in Statistical Analysis*. Wiley.

[Bradwood, 1978] Bradwood, D. (1978). Cross-coupled cancellation systems for improving cross-polarisation discrimination. *Pages 41–45 of: Proceedings of IEEE International Conference on Antennas and Propagation*, vol. I.

[Brandwood, 1983] Brandwood, D. (1983). A complex gradient operator and its application in adaptive array theory. *IEE Proceedings*, **130**(1), 11–16.

[Bregman, 1990] Bregman, A.S. (1990). *Auditory Scene Analysis*. MIT Press.

[Brehm & Stammler, 1987] Brehm, H., & Stammler, W. (1987). Description and generation of spherically invariant speech-model signals. *Signal Processing*, **12**, 119–141.

[Buckheit *et al.*, 1995] Buckheit, J., Chen, S.S., Donoho, D.L., Johnstone, I., & Scargle, J. (1995). *About WaveLab*. Tech. rept. Department of Statistics, Stanford University. Available from `http://www-stat.stanford.edu/~donoho/Reports/`.

[Burel, 1992] Burel, G. (1992). Blind separation of sources: A nonlinear neural algorithm. *Neural Networks*, **5**, 937–947.

[Cardoso, 1994] Cardoso, J.-F. (1994). On the performance of orthogonal source separation algorithms. *Pages 776–779 of: Proceedings of EUSIPCO*.

[Cardoso, 1997] Cardoso, J.-F. (1997). Infomax and maximum likelihood for blind separation. *IEEE Signal Processing Letters*, **4**(4), 112–114.

[Cardoso, 1998a] Cardoso, J.-F. (1998a). Blind signal separation: statistical principles. *Proceedings of the IEEE. Special issue on blind identification and estimation*, **9**(10), 2009–2025.

[Cardoso, 1998b] Cardoso, J.-F. (1998b). On the stability of source separation algorithms. *Pages 13–22 of:* Costantinides, A., Kung, S.-Y., Niranjan, M., & Wilson, E. (eds), *Neural Networks for Signal Processing VIII*. IEEE.

[Cardoso, 1999a] Cardoso, J.-F. (1999a). High-order contrasts for independent component analysis. *Neural Computation*, **11**, 157–192.

[Cardoso, 1999b] Cardoso, J.-F. (1999b). *JADE for real-valued data*. Available from `http://sig.enst.fr:80~cardoso/guidesepsou.html`.

[Cardoso, 2000] Cardoso, J.-F. (2000). On the stability of source separation algorithms. *Journal of VLSI Signal Processing Systems*, **26**(1), 7–14. Available from `http://tsi.enst.fr/~cardoso/`.

[Cardoso & Comon, 1996] Cardoso, J.-F., & Comon, P. (1996). Independent component analysis, a survey of some algebraic methods. *Pages 93–96 of: Proceedings of ISCAS'96*, vol. 2. Available from `ftp://sig.enst.fr/pub/jfc/Papers/iscas96_algebra.ps.gz`.

[Cardoso & Laheld, 1996] Cardoso, J.-F., & Laheld, B. (1996). Equivariant adaptive source separation. *IEEE Transactions on Signal Processing*, **45**(2), 434–444.

[Cardoso & Souloumiac, 1993] Cardoso, J.-F., & Souloumiac, A. (1993). Blind beamforming for non-Gaussian signals. *IEE Proceedings F*, **140**(6), 362–370.

[Cardoso & Souloumiac, 1996] Cardoso, J.-F., & Souloumiac, A. (1996). Jacobi angles for simultaneous diagonalization. *SIAM Journal of Matrix Analysis and Applications*, **17**(1), 161–164.

[Chen *et al.*, 1995] Chen, S.S., Donoho, D.L., Saunders, M.A., Johnstone, I., & Scargle, J. (1995). *About Atomizer*. Tech. rept. Department of Statistics, Stanford University. Available from `http://www-stat.stanford.edu/~donoho/Reports/`.

[Chen *et al.*, 1996] Chen, S.S., Donoho, D.L., & Saunders, M.A. (1996). *Atomic decomposition by basis pursuit*. Tech. rept. Department of Statistics, Stanford University. Available from `http://www-stat.stanford.edu/~donoho/Reports/`.

[Chevalier *et al.*, 1999] Chevalier, P., Capdevielle, V., & Comon, P. (1999). Performance of HO blind source separation methods: experimental results on ionospheric HF links. *Pages 443–448 of: Proceedings of First International Conference on Independent Component Analysis and Blind Source Separation: ICA'99*.

[Chin *et al.*, 1999] Chin, E., Weigend, A.S., & Zimmermann, H. (1999).

Computing portfolio risk using Gaussian mixtures and independent component analysis. *Proceedings of the 1999 IEEE/IAFE/INFORMS Conference on Computational Intelligence for Financial Engineering (CIFEr'99).* IAFE.

[Choi et al., 1998] Choi, S., Cichocki, A., & Amari, S.-I. (1998). Flexible independent component analysis. *Pages 83–92 of:* Costantinides, A., Kung, S.-Y., Niranjan, M., & Wilson, E. (eds), *Neural Networks for Signal Processing VIII.* IEEE.

[Choudrey et al., 2001] Choudrey, R., Penny, W., & Roberts, S. (2001). An ensemble learning approach to independent component analysis. *Neural Networks for Signal Processing X.* IEEE. Available from http://www.robots.ox.ac.uk/~sjrob/pubs.html.

[Cichocki & Unbehauen, 1996] Cichocki, A., & Unbehauen, R. (1996). Robust neural networks with on-line learning for blind identification and blind separation of sources. *IEEE Transactions on Circuits and Systems,* 43(11), 894–906.

[Cichocki et al., 1999] Cichocki, A., Zhang, L., Choi, S., & Amari, S.-I. (1999). Nonlinear dynamic independent component analysis using state-space and neural network models. *Pages 99–104 of: Proceedings of First International Conference on Independent Component Analysis and Blind Source Separation: ICA'99.*

[Coifman & Wickerhauser, 1992] Coifman, R.R., & Wickerhauser, M.V. (1992). Entropy-based algorithms for best-basis selection. *IEEE Transactions on Information Theory,* 38, 713–718.

[Coifman et al., 1992] Coifman, R.R., Meyer, Y., & Wickerhauser, M.V. (1992). Wavelet analysis and signal processing. *Pages 153–178 of:* Ruskai, M.B. (ed), *Wavelets and their applications.* Jones and Barlett.

[Comon, 1994] Comon, P. (1994). Independent component analysis, a new concept? *Signal Processing,* 36, 287–314.

[Comon et al., 1991] Comon, P., Jutten, C., & Herault, J. (1991). Blind separation of sources. Part II: problems statement. *Signal Processing,* 24(1), 11–20.

[Cook et al., 1993] Cook, D., Buja, A., & Cabrera, J. (1993). Projection pursuit indexes based on orthonormal function expansions. *Journal of Computational and Graphical Statistics,* 2(3), 225–250.

[Cover & Thomas, 1991] Cover, T., & Thomas, J. (1991). *Elements of Information Theory.* Vol. 1. Wiley.

[De Bonet & Viola, 1998] De Bonet, J.S., & Viola, P. (1998). A non-parametric multi-scale statistical model for natural images. Jordan, M.I., Kearns, M.J., & Solla, S.A. (eds), *Advances in Neural Information Processing Systems,* vol. 10. MIT Press.

[deCharms & Merzenich, 1998] deCharms, C.R., & Merzenich, M.M. (1998). Characteristic neurons in the primary auditory cortex of the awake primate using reverse correlation. *Pages 124–130 of:* Jordan, M.I., Kearns, M.J., & Solla, S.A. (eds), *Advances in Neural Information Processing Systems,* vol. 10.

[Deco & Brauer, 1995] Deco, G., & Brauer, W. (1995). Higher order statistical decorrelation by volume conserving neural architectures. *Neural Networks,* 8, 525–535.

[Deco & Obradovic, 1996] Deco, G., & Obradovic, D. (1996). *An Information Theoretic Approach to Neural Computing.* Perspectives in Neural Computing. Springer.

[Delfosse & Loubaton, 1995] Delfosse, N., & Loubaton, P. (1995). Adaptive blind separation of independent sources: a deflation approach. *Signal Processing*, **45**, 59–83.

[Dempster *et al.*, 1976] Dempster, A.P., Laird, N.M., & Rubin, D.B. (1976). Maximum likelihood from incomplete data via the EM algorithm. *Journal of the Royal Statistical Society, Series B*, **39**, 1–38.

[Deville *et al.*, 1999] Deville, Y., Damour, J., & Charkani, N. (1999). Improved multi-tag radio-frequency identification systems based on new source separation neural networks. *Pages 449–454 of: Proceedings of First International Conference on Independent Component Analysis and Blind Source Separation: ICA'99.*

[Donoho, 1981] Donoho, D. (1981). On minimum entropy deconvolution. *Pages 565–608 of:* Findley, D.F. (ed), *Applied Time Series Analysis II*. Academic Press.

[Douglas & Kung, 2000] Douglas, S.C., & Kung, S.Y. (2000). Gradient adaptive algorithms for contrast-based blind deconvolution. *VLSI Signal Processing Journal*, **26**(1), 47–61.

[Duda & Hart, 1973] Duda, R.O., & Hart, P.E. (1973). *Pattern Classification and Scene Analysis*. Wiley.

[Everitt, 1984] Everitt, B.S. (1984). *An Introduction to Latent Variable Models*. Chapman and Hall.

[Everson & Roberts, 1999a] Everson, R.M., & Roberts, S.J. (1999a). ICA: a flexible non-linearity and decorrelating manifold approach. *Neural Computation*, **11**(8), 1957–1983.

[Everson & Roberts, 1999b] Everson, R.M., & Roberts, S.J. (1999b). Non-stationary independent components analysis. *Proceedings of International Conference on Artificial Neural Networks (ICANN'99)*. IEE.

[Everson & Roberts, 2000a] Everson, R.M., & Roberts, S.J. (2000a). Independent component analysis. *Pages 153–168 of:* Lisboa, P.J.G., Ifeachor, E.C., & Szczepaniak, P.S. (eds), *Artificial Neural Networks in Biomedicine*. Perspectives in Neural Computing. Springer.

[Everson & Roberts, 2000b] Everson, R.M., & Roberts, S.J. (2000b). Inferring the eigenvalues of covariance matrices from limited, noisy data. *IEEE Transactions on Signal Processing*, **48**(7), 2083–2091.

[Everson & Roberts, 2000c] Everson, R.M., & Roberts, S.J. (2000c). *Measuring mutual information*. Tech. rept. Exeter University. Available from http://www.dcs.ex.ac.uk/academics/reverson.

[Fearnhead, 1999] Fearnhead, P. (1999). *Sequential Monte Carlo methods in filter theory*. Ph.D. thesis, University of Oxford.

[Fety & Van Ulffelen, 1988] Fety, L., & Van Ulffelen, J.P. (1988). New methods for signal separation. *Pages 226–230 of: Proceedings of 4th International Conference of HF radio systems and techniques*. IEE.

[Flury & Gautschi, 1986] Flury, B.N., & Gautschi, W. (1986). An algorithm for the simultaneous orthogonal transformation of several positive definite symmetric matrices to nearly orthogonal form. *SIAM Journal of Scientific and Statistical Computing*, **7**(1), 169–184.

[Fraser & Swinney, 1986] Fraser, A.M., & Swinney, H.L. (1986). Independent coordinates for strange attractors from mutual information. *Physical Review*, **33A**(2).

[Friedman, 1987] Friedman, J. (1987). Exploratory projection pursuit. *Journal of the American Statistical Association*, **82**(397), 249–266.

[Friedman & Tukey, 1974] Friedman, J., & Tukey, J. (1974). A projection pursuit algorithm for exploratory data analysis. *IEEE Transactions on Neural Networks*, **23**, 881–889.

[Gaeta & Lacoume, 1990] Gaeta, M., & Lacoume, J.-L. (1990). Source separation without prior knowledge: the maximum likelihood solution. *Pages 621–624 of: Proceedings of EUSIPO.*

[Ghahramani & Beal, 2000] Ghahramani, Z., & Beal, M.J. (2000). Variational inference for Bayesian mixtures of factor analysers. *Advances in Neural Information Processing Systems*, vol. 12. MIT Press.

[Ghahramani & Hinton, 1997] Ghahramani, Z., & Hinton, G.E. (1997). *The EM algorithm for mixtures of factor analyzers*. Tech. rept. Department of Computer Science, University of Toronto.

[Ghahramani & Jordan, 1997] Ghahramani, Z., & Jordan, M.I. (1997). Factorial hidden Markov models. *Machine Learning*, **29**, 245–273.

[Ghahramani & Roweis, 1999] Ghahramani, Z., & Roweis, S. (1999). Learning nonlinear dynamical systems using an EM algorithm. *Pages 599–605 of:* Kearns, M.S., Solla, S.A., & Cohn, D.A. (eds), *Advances in Neural Information Processing Systems*, vol. 11. MIT Press.

[Gill et al., 1995] Gill, P.E., Murray, W., & Wright, M.H. (1995). *Practical Optimization*. 10th edn. Academic Press.

[Girolami, 1997] Girolami, M. (1997). *Self-organising artificial neural networks for signal separation*. Ph.D. thesis, Department of Computing and Information Systems, Paisley University.

[Girolami, 1998] Girolami, M. (1998). An alternative perspective on adaptive independent component analysis algorithms. *Neural Computation*, **10**(8), 2103–2114.

[Girolami, 1999a] Girolami, M. (1999a). Hierarchic dichotomizing of polychotomous data – an ICA based data mining tool. *Pages 197–202 of: Proceedings of First International Conference on Independent Component Analysis and Blind Source Separation: ICA'99.*

[Girolami, 1999b] Girolami, M. (1999b). *Self-Organising Neural Networks – Independent Component Analysis and Blind Source Separation*. Springer.

[Girolami, 2000a] Girolami, M. (2000a). Document representations based on generative multivariate Bernoulli latent topic models. *Pages 194–201 of: Proceedings of the 22nd Annual Colloquium on Information Retrieval Research.*

[Girolami, 2000b] Girolami, M. (2000b). *Kernel based clustering and visualisation in feature space*. Tech. rept. ISSN 1461-6122. Computing and Information Systems, University of Paisley.

[Girolami & Fyfe, 1997a] Girolami, M., & Fyfe, C. (1997a). Extraction of independent signal sources using deflationary exploratory projection pursuit network with lateral inhibition. *IEE Proceedings on Vision, Image and Signal Processing*, **14**(5), 299–306.

[Girolami & Fyfe, 1997b] Girolami, M., & Fyfe, C. (1997b). Generalised independent component analysis through unsupervised learning with emergent Bussgang properties. *Pages 1788–1891 of: Proceedings of International Conference on Neural Networks.*

[Girolami et al., 1998] Girolami, M., Cichocki, A., & Amari, S.-I. (1998). A common neural network model for exploratory data analysis and independent component analysis. *IEEE Transactions on Neural Networks*, **9**(6), 1495–1501.

[Goldman, 1976] Goldman, J. (1976). Detection in the presence of spherically symmetric random vectors. *IEEE Transactions on Information Theory*, **22**(1), 52–59.

[Gordon *et al.*, 1993] Gordon, N., Salmond, D., & Smith, A.F.M. (1993). Novel approach to nonlinear/non-Gaussian Bayesian state estimation. *IEE Proceedings-F*, **140**, 107–113.

[Gull & Daniell, 1978] Gull, S.F., & Daniell, G.J. (1978). Image reconstruction from incomplete and noisy data. *Nature*, **272**(5655), 686–690.

[Hansen, 2000] Hansen, L.K. (2000). Blind separation of noisy image mixtures. *Pages 161–182 of:* Girolami, M. (ed), *Advances in Independent Component Analysis*. Perspectives in Neural Computing. Springer.

[Haykin, 1994] Haykin, S. (1994). *Blind Deconvolution*. Information and System Sciences. Prentice-Hall.

[Haykin, 1998] Haykin, S. (1998). *Neural Networks – a Comprehensive Foundation*. 2nd edn. Prentice-Hall.

[Hecht-Nielsen, 1995] Hecht-Nielsen, R. (1995). Replicator neural networks for universal optimal source coding. *Science*, **269**, 1860–1863.

[Hecht-Nielsen, 1996] Hecht-Nielsen, R. (1996). Data manifolds, natural coordinates, replicator neural networks, and optimal source coding. *Pages 41–45 of: Proceedings of 1996 International Conference on Neural Information Processing (ICONIP'96)*.

[Herault & Jutten, 1986] Herault, J., & Jutten, C. (1986). Space or time processing by neural network models. Denker, J.S. (ed), *Proceedings AIP Conference: Neural Networks for Computing*, vol. 151. American Institute for Physics.

[Hinton & Sejnowski, 1998] Hinton, G., & Sejnowski, T.J. (eds). (1998). *Unsupervised Learning: Foundations of Neural Computation*. MIT Press.

[Hinton & van Camp, 1993] Hinton, G.E., & van Camp, D. (1993). Keeping neural networks simple by minimizing the description length of the weights. *Pages 5–13 of: Proceedings of the Sixth Annual Conference on Computational Learning Theory*.

[Hochreiter & Schmidhuber, 1999] Hochreiter, S., & Schmidhuber, J. (1999). Feature extraction through LOCOCODE. *Neural Computation*, **11**, 679–714.

[Holmstrom & Bjorkman, 1999] Holmstrom, K., & Bjorkman, M. (1999). The TOMLAB NLPLIB. *Advanced Modeling and Optimization*, **1**, 70–86. Available from http://www.ima.mdh.se/tom/.

[Horn & Johnson, 1985] Horn, R.A., & Johnson, C.R. (1985). *Matrix Analysis*. Cambridge University Press.

[Huang *et al.*, 1998] Huang, M., Leahy, R.M., Mosher, J.C., & Spencer, M.E. (1998). Comparing the source localization accuracy of EEG and MEG for different head modeling techniques using a human skull phantom. *International Journal of Psychophysiology*, **30**, 200.

[Huber, 1985] Huber, P. (1985). Projection pursuit. *Annals of Statistics*, **13**(2), 435–475.

[Hyvärinen, 1997] Hyvärinen, A. (1997). One-unit contrast functions for independent component analysis: a statistical analysis. *Pages 388–397 of: Proceedings of IEEE Workshop on Neural Networks for Signal Processing VII*.

[Hyvärinen, 1998a] Hyvärinen, A. (1998a). New approximations of differential entropy for independent component analysis and projection pursuit. *Pages 273–279 of: Advances in Neural Information Processing Systems*, vol. 10. MIT Press.

[Hyvärinen, 1998b] Hyvärinen, A. (1998b). *The FastICA MATLAB toolbox.* Helsinki Univ. of Technology. Available at http://www.cis.hut.fi/projects/ica/fastica/.

[Hyvärinen, 1999a] Hyvärinen, A. (1999a). Fast and robust fixed-point algorithms for independent component analysis. *IEEE Transactions on Neural Networks,* **10**(3), 626–634.

[Hyvärinen, 1999b] Hyvärinen, A. (1999b). The fixed-point algorithm and maximum likelihood estimation for independent component analysis. *Neural Processing Letters,* **10**(1), 1–5.

[Hyvärinen, 1999c] Hyvärinen, A. (1999c). Gaussian moments for noisy independent component analysis. *IEEE Signal Processing Letters,* **6**(6), 145–147.

[Hyvärinen, 1999d] Hyvärinen, A. (1999d). Survey on independent component analysis. *Neural Computing Surveys,* **2**, 94–128. Available from http://www.icsi.berkeley.edu/~jagota/NCS.

[Hyvärinen & Oja, 1997] Hyvärinen, A., & Oja, E. (1997). A fast fixed-point algorithm for independent component analysis. *Neural Computation,* **9**(7), 1483–1492.

[Hyvärinen & Oja, 1998] Hyvärinen, A., & Oja, E. (1998). Independent component analysis by general nonlinear Hebbian-like learning rules. *Signal Processing,* **64**(3), 301–313.

[Hyvärinen & Pajunen, 1999] Hyvärinen, A., & Pajunen, P. (1999). Nonlinear independent component analysis: existence and uniqueness results. *Neural Networks,* **12**, 209–219.

[Hyvärinen et al., 1999a] Hyvärinen, A., Cristescu, R., & Oja, E. (1999a). A fast algorithm for estimating overcomplete ICA bases for image windows. *Pages 894–899 of: Proceedings of International Joint Conference on Neural Networks.*

[Hyvärinen et al., 1999b] Hyvärinen, A., Hoyer, P., & Oja, E. (1999b). Sparse code shrinkage: denoising by nonlinear maximum likelihood estimation. *Pages 473–479 of:* Kearns, M.S., Solla, S. A., & Cohn, D.A. (eds), *Advances in Neural Information Processing Systems,* vol. 11. MIT Press.

[Hyvärinen et al., 1999c] Hyvärinen, A., Särelä, J., & Vigário, R. (1999). Spikes and bumps: artefacts generated by independent component analysis with insufficient sample size. *Pages 425–430 of: Proceedings of First International Conference on Independent Component Analysis and Blind Source Separation: ICA'99.*

[Hyvärinen et al., 2000] Hyvärinen, A., Hoyer, P.O., & Inki, M. (2000). Topographic independent component analysis: Visualizing the independence structure. *Proceedings of International Workshop on Independent Component Analysis and Blind Signal Separation (ICA2000).*

[Ikram & Morgan, 2000] Ikram, M., & Morgan, D. (2000). Exploring permutation inconsistency in blind separation of speech signals in a reverberant environment. *ICASSP 2000.*

[Isard & Blake, 1996] Isard, M., & Blake, A. (1996). Contour tracking by stochastic density propagation of conditional density. *Pages 343–356 of: Proceedings of European Conference Computer Vision.*

[Isbell & Viola, 1999] Isbell, B.L., & Viola, P. (1999). Restructuring sparse high dimensional data for effective retrieval. *Pages 480–486 of:* Kearns, M.S., Solla, S. A., & Cohn, D.A. (eds), *Advances in Neural Information Processing Systems,* vol. 11. MIT Press.

[Jaakkola & Jordan, 1997] Jaakkola, T.S., & Jordan, M.I. (1997). Bayesian logistic regression: a variational approach. *Pages 283–294 of: Proceedings of the 1997 Conference on Artificial Intelligence and Statistics.*

[Jain & Dubes, 1988] Jain, A.K., & Dubes, R. (1988). *Algorithms for Clustering Data.* Prentice-Hall.

[Jänich, 1977] Jänich, K. (1977). *Einführung in die Funktionentheorie.* Springer.

[Jazwinski, 1973] Jazwinski, A.H. (1973). *Stochastic Processes and Filtering Theory.* Academic Press.

[Jolliffe, 1986] Jolliffe, I.T. (1986). *Principal Component Analysis.* Springer.

[Jones & Sibson, 1987] Jones, M., & Sibson, R. (1987). What is projection pursuit? *Journal of the Royal Statistical Society, series A,* **150,** 1–36.

[Jordan, 1999] Jordan, M.I. (ed). (1999). *Learning in Graphical Models.* MIT Press.

[Jung et al., 1998] Jung, T.-P., Humphries, C., Lee, T.-W., Makeig, S., McKeown, M.J., Iragui, V., & Sejnowski, T.J. (1998). Extended ICA removes artifacts from electroencephalographic recordings. Jordan, M.I., Kearns, M.J., & Solla, S.A. (eds), *Advances in Neural Information Processing Systems,* vol. 10. MIT Press.

[Jung et al., 1999a] Jung, T.-P., Makeig, S., Westerfield, M., Townsend, J., Courchesne, E., & Sejnowski, T.J. (1999a). Analyzing and visualizing single-trial event-related potentials. *Pages 118–124 of:* Kearns, M.S., Solla, S.A., & Cohn, D.A. (eds), *Advances in Neural Information Processing Systems,* vol. 11. MIT Press.

[Jung et al., 1999b] Jung, T.-P., Makeig, S., Westerfield, M., Townsend, J., Courchesne, E., & Sejnowski, T.J. (1999b). Independent component analysis of single-trial event-related potentials. *Pages 173–178 of: Proceedings of First International Conference on Independent Component Analysis and Blind Source Separation: ICA'99.*

[Jung et al., 2000] Jung, T.-P., Humphries, C., Lee, T.-W., McKeown, M.J., Iragui, V., Makeig, S., & Sejnowski, T.J. (2000). Removing electroencephalographic artifacts by blind source separation. *Psychophysiology,* **37,** 163–178.

[Jutten & Herault, 1991] Jutten, C., & Herault, J. (1991). Blind separation of sources, part I: an adaptive algorithm based on neuromimetic architecture. *Signal Processing,* **24,** 1–10.

[Kalman & Bucy, 1961] Kalman, R., & Bucy, R. (1961). New results in linear filtering and prediction theory. *Journal of Basic Engineering, Transactions of ASME series D,* **83**(95-108).

[Karhunen & Joutsensalo, 1994] Karhunen, J., & Joutsensalo, J. (1994). Representation and separation of signals using nonlinear PCA type learning. *Neural Networks,* **7,** 113–127.

[Karhunen & Malaroiu, 1999a] Karhunen, J., & Malaroiu, S. (1999a). Local independent component analysis using clustering. *Pages 43–48 of: Proceedings of First International Conference on Independent Component Analysis and Blind Source Separation: ICA'99.*

[Karhunen & Malaroiu, 1999b] Karhunen, J., & Malaroiu, S. (1999b). Locally linear independent component analysis. *Pages 882–887 of: Proceedings of the International Joint Conference on Neural Networks (IJCNN'99).*

[Kass et al., 1991] Kass, R.E., Tierney, L., & Kadane, J.B. (1991). Laplace's method in Bayesian analysis. *Contemporary Mathematics,* **115,** 89–99.

[Kawamoto et al., 1998] Kawamoto, M., Matsuoka, K., & Ohnishi, N. (1998). A method of blind separation for convolved non-stationary signals.

Neurocomputing, **22**, 157–171.

[Kendal & Stuart, 1969] Kendal, M.G., & Stuart, A. (1969). *The Advanced Theory of Statistics*. Charles Griffin.

[Kirby & Sirovich, 1990] Kirby, M., & Sirovich, L. (1990). Application of the Karhunen-Loève procedure for the characterization of human faces. *IEEE Transactions on Pattern Analysis and Machine Intelligence*, **12**(1), 103–108.

[Kisilev *et al.*, 2000] Kisilev, P., Zibulevsky, M., Zeevi, Y.Y., & Pearlmutter, B.A. (2000). *Multiresolution framework for sparse blind source separation*. Tech. rept. Technion Israel Institute of Technology.

[Kitagawa, 1996] Kitagawa, G. (1996). Monte Carlo filter and smoother for non-Gaussian nonlinear state space models. *Journal of Computational and Graphical Statistics*, **5**, 1–25.

[Kiviluoto & Oja, 1998] Kiviluoto, K., & Oja, E. (1998). Independent Component Analysis for parallel economic time series. *Pages 895–898 of: Proceedings of ICONIP'98*, vol. 2.

[Knuth, 1998a] Knuth, K.H. (1998a). Bayesian source separation and localization. *Pages 147–158 of:* Mohammad-Djafari, A. (ed), *SPIE'98 Proceedings: Bayesian Inference for Inverse Problems*.

[Knuth, 1998b] Knuth, K.H. (1998b). Difficulties applying recent blind source separation techniques to EEG and MEG. *Pages 209–222 of:* Rychert, J.T., & Smith, C.R. (eds), *Maximum Entropy and Bayesian Methods*. Kluwer.

[Knuth, 1999] Knuth, K.H. (1999). A Bayesian approach to source separation. *Pages 283–288 of: Proceedings of First International Conference on Independent Component Analysis and Blind Source Separation: ICA'99*.

[Koehler & Orglmeister, 1999] Koehler, B.-U., & Orglmeister, R. (1999). Independent component analysis using autoregressive models. *Pages 359–364 of: Proceedings of First International Conference on Independent Component Analysis and Blind Source Separation: ICA'99*.

[Kohonen, 1995] Kohonen, T. (1995). *Self-Organizing Maps*. Springer.

[Kolenda *et al.*, 2000] Kolenda, T., Hansen, L.K., & Sigurdsson, S. (2000). Independent component analysis in text. *Pages 236–256 of:* Girolami, M. (ed), *Advances in Independent Component Analysis*. Perspectives in Neural Computing. Springer.

[Kowalski *et al.*, 1996] Kowalski, N., Depireux, D.A., & Shamma, S.A. (1996). Analysis of dynamic spectra in ferret primary auditory cortex: I. Characteristics of single unit responses to moving ripple spectra. *Journal of Neurophysiology*, **76**(5), 3503–3523.

[Landatter & Harshman, 1990] Landatter, T.K., & Harshman, R. (1990). Indexing by Latent Semantic Analysis. *Journal of American Society for Information Science*, **41**(391-407).

[Lappalainen, 1999] Lappalainen, H. (1999). Ensemble learning for independent component analysis. *Pages 7–12 of: Proceedings of First International Conference on Independent Component Analysis and Blind Source Separation: ICA'99*.

[Lappalainen & Honkela, 2000] Lappalainen, H., & Honkela, A. (2000). Bayesian nonlinear independent component analysis by multi-layer perceptrons. *Pages 93–121 of:* Girolami, M. (ed), *Advances in Independent Component Analysis*. Springer.

[Lappalainen & Miskin, 2000] Lappalainen, H., & Miskin, J. (2000). Ensemble learning. *Pages 75–92 of:* Girolami, M. (ed), *Advances in Independent Component Analysis*. Springer.

[Lappalainen *et al.*, 2000a] Lappalainen, H., Giannakopoulos, X., Honkela, A., & Karhunen, J. (2000a). Nonlinear independent component analysis using ensemble learning: experiments and discussion. *Proceedings of the 2nd International Workshop on Independent Component Analysis and Blind Signal Separation.*

[Lappalainen *et al.*, 2000b] Lappalainen, H., Giannakopoulos, X., Honkela, A., & Karhunen, J. (2000b). Nonlinear independent component analysis using ensemble learning: theory. *Proceedings of the 2nd International Workshop on Independent Component Analysis and Blind Signal Separation.*

[Lee, 1998] Lee, T.-W. (1998). *Independent Component Analysis - Theory and Applications.* Kluwer.

[Lee & Lewicki, 2000] Lee, T.-W., & Lewicki, M.S. (2000). The generalized Gaussian mixture model using ICA. *Proceedings of the 2nd international workshop on ICA.*

[Lee & Seung, 1999] Lee, D.D., & Seung, H.S. (1999). Learning the parts of objects by non-negative matrix factorisation. *Nature, 401*, 788–791.

[Lee *et al.*, 1997] Lee, T.-W., Bell, A.J., & Lambert, R. (1997). Blind separation of delayed and convolved sources. *Pages 758–764 of:* Mozer, M.C., Jordan, M.I., & Petsche, T. (eds), *Advances in Neural Information Processing Systems*, vol. 9. MIT Press.

[Lee *et al.*, 1998] Lee, T.-W., Lewicki, M.S., Girolami, M., & Sejnowski, T.J. (1998). Blind source separation of more sources than mixtures using overcomplete representations. *IEEE Signal Processing Letters.*

[Lee *et al.*, 1999a] Lee, T.-W., Lewicki, M.S., & Sejnowski, T.J. (1999a). ICA mixture models for unsupervised classification and automatic context switching. *Pages 209–214 of: Proceedings of First International Conference on Independent Component Analysis and Blind Source Separation: ICA'99.*

[Lee *et al.*, 1999b] Lee, T.-W., Girolami, M., & Sejnowski, T.J. (1999b). Independent component analysis using an extended infomax algorithm for mixed sub-Gaussian and super-Gaussian sources. *Neural Computation, 11*, 417–441.

[Lee *et al.*, 1999c] Lee, T.-W., Lewicki, M.S., & Sejnowski, T.J. (1999c). Unsupervised classification with non-Gaussian mixture models using ICA. *Pages 508–514 of:* Kearns, M.S., Solla, S. A., & Cohn, D.A. (eds), *Advances in Neural Information Processing Systems*, vol. 11. MIT Press.

[Lee *et al.*, 2000a] Lee, D.D., Rokni, U., & Sompolinsky, H. (2000a). Algorithms for independent component analysis and higher order statistics. *Advances in Neural Information Processing Systems*, vol. 12. MIT Press.

[Lee *et al.*, 2000b] Lee, T.-W., Girolami, M., Bell, A.J., & Sejnowski, T.J. (2000b). A unifying framework for independent component analysis. *International Journal on Mathematical and Computer Models, 39*(11), 1–21. Available from http://www.cnl.salk.edu/~tewon/Public/mcm.ps.gz.

[Lewicki, 2000] Lewicki, M.S. (2000). A flexible prior for independent component analysis. *Neural Computation.* (Submitted).

[Lewicki & Olshausen, 1998] Lewicki, M.S., & Olshausen, B. (1998). Inferring sparse, overcomplete image codes using an efficient coding framework. *Pages 556–562 of:* Jordan, M.I., Kearns, M.J., & Solla, S.A. (eds), *Advances in Neural Information Processing Systems*, vol. 10.

[Lewicki & Olshausen, 1999] Lewicki, M.S., & Olshausen, B.A. (1999). A probabilistic framework for the adaptation and comparison of image codes. *Journal of the Optical Society of America A, 16*(7), 1587–1601.

[Lewicki & Sejnowski, 1998] Lewicki, M.S., & Sejnowski, T.J. (1998). Learning nonlinear overcomplete representations for efficient coding. *Pages 815–821 of:* Jordan, M.I., Kearns, M.J., & Solla, S.A. (eds), *Advances in Neural Information Processing Systems 10*, vol. 10.

[Lewicki & Sejnowski, 2000] Lewicki, M.S., & Sejnowski, T.J. (2000). Learning overcomplete representations. *Neural Computation*, **12**(2), 337–365.

[Liavas & Regalia, 1998] Liavas, A.P., & Regalia, P.A. (1998). Acoustic echo cancellation: do IIR models offer better modeling capabilities than their FIR counterparts? *IEEE Transactions on Signal Processing*, **46**, 2499–2504.

[Lin, 1999] Lin, J.K. (1999). Factorizing probability density functions: generalizing ICA. *Pages 313–318 of: Proceedings of First International Conference on Independent Component Analysis and Blind Source Separation: ICA'99.*

[Lin et al., 1997] Lin, J.K., Grier, D., & Cowan, J. (1997). Faithful representation of separable distributions. *Neural Computation*, **9**, 1305–1320.

[Linsker, 1989] Linsker, R. (1989). An application of the principle of maximum information transfer to linear systems. Touretzky, D.S. (ed), *Advances in Neural Information Processing Systems*, vol. 1. Morgan Kaufmann.

[Linsker, 1992] Linsker, R. (1992). Local synaptic learning rules suffice to maximise mutual information in a linear network. *Neural Computation*, **4**, 691–702.

[MacKay, 1994] MacKay, D.J.C. (1994). Bayesian non-linear modelling for the energy prediction competition. *ASHRAE Transactions*, **100**, 1053–1062.

[MacKay, 1995] MacKay, D.J.C. (1995). Developments in probabilistic modelling with neural networks – ensemble learning. *Pages 191–198 of: Neural Networks: Artificial Intelligence and Industrial Applications. Proceedings of the 3rd Annual Symposium on Neural Networks.*

[MacKay, 1996] MacKay, D.J.C. (1996). *Maximum likelihood and covariant algorithms for independent component analysis*. Tech. rept. University of Cambridge. Available from http://wol.ra.phy.cam.ac.uk/mackay/.

[MacKay, 1999] MacKay, D.J.C. (1999). Monte Carlo methods. *Pages 175–204 of:* Jordan, M.I. (ed), *Learning in Graphical Models*. Kluwer.

[Makeig, 1999] Makeig, S. (1999). *ICA/EEG toolbox*. Computational Neurobiology Laboratory, The Salk Institute. Available from http://www.cnl.salk.edu/~tewon/ica_cnl.html.

[Makeig et al., 1996] Makeig, S., Bell, A.J., Jung, T.-P., & Sejnowski, T.J. (1996). Independent component analysis of electroencephalographic data. *Pages 145–151 of:* Touretzky, D., Mozer, M., & Hasselmo, M. (eds), *Advances in Neural Information Processing Systems*, vol. 8. MIT Press.

[Makeig et al., 1997a] Makeig, S., Jung, T.-P., Bell, A.J., Ghahremani, D., & Sejnowski, T.J. (1997a). Blind separation of auditory event-related brain responses into independent components. *Proceedings of the National Academy of Sciences*, **94**, 10979–84.

[Makeig et al., 1997b] Makeig, S., Jung, T-P, Bell, A., Ghahremani, D., & Sejnowski, T.J. (1997b). Transiently time-locked fMRI activations revealed by independent components analysis. *Proceedings of the National Academy of Sciences*, **95**, 803–810.

[Makeig et al., 1999] Makeig, S., Westerfield, M., Townsend, J., Jung, T.-P., Courchesne, E., & Sejnowski, T.J. (1999). Functionally independent components of early event-related potentials in a visual spatial attention task. *Philosophical Transactions of the Royal Society: Biological Sciences*,

354, 1135–1144.

[Mallat, 1998] Mallat, S. (1998). *A Wavelet Tour of Signal Processing*. Academic Press.

[Manduchi & Portilla, 1999] Manduchi, R., & Portilla, J. (1999). Independent component analysis of textures. *IEEE International Conference on Computer Vision*.

[Matsuoka et al., 1995] Matsuoka, K., Ohya, M., & Kawamoto, M. (1995). A neural net for blind separation of nonstationary signals. *Neural Networks*, **8**(3), 411–419.

[McCallum & Nigam, 1998] McCallum, A., & Nigam, K. (1998). A comparison of event models for naive Bayes text classification. *AAAI-98 Workshop on Learning for Text Categorisation*. Available from http://www.cs.cmu.edu/~mccallum.

[McCullagh & Nelder, 1983] McCullagh, P., & Nelder, J.A. (1983). *Generalized Linear Models*. Chapman and Hall.

[McKeown et al., 1998a] McKeown, M.J., Makeig, S., Brown, G.G., Jung, T.-P., Kindermann, S.S., Bell, A.J., & Sejnowski, T.J. (1998a). Analysis of fMRI data by blind separation into independent spatial components. *Human Brain Mapping*, **6**, 160–188.

[McKeown et al., 1998b] McKeown, M.J., Jung, T.-P., Makeig, S., Brown, G.G., Kindermann, G., Lee, T.-W., & Sejnowski, T.J. (1998b). Spatially independent activity patterns in functional magnetic resonance imaging data during the Stroop color-naming task. *Proceedings of the National Academy of Sciences*, **95**, 803–810.

[Minka, 2000] Minka, T.P. (2000). *Automatic choice of dimensionality for PCA*. Tech. rept. 514. MIT. Available from ftp://whitechapel.media.mit.edu/pub/tech-reports/.

[Mohammad-Djafari, 1999] Mohammad-Djafari, A. (1999). A Bayesian approach to source separation. *19th International Workshop on Maximum Entropy and Bayesian Methods (MaxEnt99)*.

[Molgedey & Schuster, 1994] Molgedey, L., & Schuster, H.G. (1994). Separation of a mixture of independent signals using time delayed correlations. *Physical Review Letters*, **72**(23), 3634–3637.

[Moreau & Macchi, 1993] Moreau, E., & Macchi, O. (1993). New self-adaptive algorithms for source separation based on contrast functions. *Pages 215–219 of: Proceedings of IEEE Signal Processing Workshop on Higher Order Statistics*.

[Moulines et al., 1997] Moulines, E., Cardoso, J.-F., & Gassiat, E. (1997). Maximum likelihood for blind separation and deconvolution of noisy signals using mixture models. *Pages 3617–20 of: Proceedings of ICASSP'97*, vol. 5.

[Murata et al., 1997] Murata, N., Ikeda, S., & Ziehe, A. (1997). Adaptive on-line learning in changing environments. *Pages 599–605 of:* Mozer, M.C., Jordan, M.I., & Petsche, T. (eds), *Advances in Neural Information Processing Systems*, vol. 9. MIT Press.

[Nadal & Parga, 1994] Nadal, J.-P., & Parga, N. (1994). Non-linear neurons in the low noise limit: a factorial code maximises information transfer. *Network*, **5**, 565–581.

[Neal & Hinton, 1993] Neal, R.M., & Hinton, G.E. (1993). A view of the EM algorithm that justifies incremental, sparse, and other variants. *Pages 355–368 of:* Jordan, M.I. (ed), *Learning in Graphical Models*. Kluwer.

[Ochs et al., 1999] Ochs, M., Stoyanova, R., Arias-Mendoza, F., & Brown, T. (1999). A new method for spectral decomposition using a bilinear Bayesian approach. *Journal of Magnetic Resonance*, **137**, 161–176.

[Oja & Kaski, 1999] Oja, E., & Kaski, S. (eds). (1999). *Kohonen maps*. Elsevier.

[Oja et al., 1997] Oja, E., Karhunen, J., Hyvärinen, A., Vigário, R., & Hurri, J. (1997). Neural independent component analysis - approaches and applications. *Pages 167–188 of:* Amari, S.-I., & Kasabov, N. (eds), *Brain-Like Computing and Intelligent Information Systems*. Springer.

[Olshausen & Field, 1996] Olshausen, B., & Field, D. (1996). Emergence of simple-cell receptive field properties by learning a sparse code for natural images. *Nature*, **381**, 607–609.

[Olshausen & Field, 1997] Olshausen, B.A., & Field, D.J. (1997). Sparse coding with an overcomplete basis set: a strategy employed by V1? *Vision Research*, **37**, 3311–3325.

[O'Ruanaidth & Fitzgerald, 1996] O'Ruanaidth, J.J.K., & Fitzgerald, W.J. (1996). *Numerical Bayesian Methods Applied to Signal Processing*. Springer.

[O'Toole et al., 1991a] O'Toole, A.J., Abdi, H., Deffenbacher, K.A., & Bartlett, J.C. (1991a). Classifying faces by race and sex using an autoassiciative memory trained for recognition. *Pages 847–851 of:* Hammond, K.J., & Gentner, D. (eds), *Proceedings of the Thirteenth Annual Conference of the Cognitive Science Society*. Lawrence Erlbaum.

[O'Toole et al., 1991b] O'Toole, A.J., Deffenbacher, K.A., Abdi, H., & Bartlett, J.C. (1991b). Simulating the "other-race effect" as a problem in perceptual learning. *Connection Science*, **3**(2), 163–178.

[Pajunen & Girolami, 2000] Pajunen, P., & Girolami, M. (2000). Implementing decisions in binary decision trees using independent component analysis. *Second International Workshop on Independent Component Analysis (ICA2000)*.

[Pajunen & Karhunen, 1997] Pajunen, P., & Karhunen, J. (1997). A maximum likelihood approach to nonlinear blind separation. *Pages 541–546 of: Proceedings of 1997 International Conference on Artificial Neural Networks*.

[Pajunen et al., 1996] Pajunen, P., Hyvärinen, A., & Karhunen, J. (1996). Non-linear blind source separation by self-organizing maps. *Pages 1207–1210 of: International Conference on Neural Information Processing*. Springer.

[Papoulis, 1991] Papoulis, A. (1991). *Probability, Random Variables and Stochastic Processes*. McGraw-Hill.

[Parra, 1998a] Parra, L. (1998a). *An Introduction to Independent Component Analysis and Blind Source Separation*. Tech. rept. Princeton University. Available from http://www.humanism.org/~lucas/.

[Parra, 1998b] Parra, L. (1998b). *Blind source separation based on multiple decorrelations*. http://www.sarnoff.com/career_move/tech_papers/BSS.html.

[Parra & Spence, 2000a] Parra, L., & Spence, C. (2000a). Convolutive blind source separation of non-stationary sources. *IEEE Transactions on Signal Processing*, 320–327.

[Parra & Spence, 2000b] Parra, L., & Spence, C. (2000b). On-line convolutive blind source separation of non-stationary sources. *VLSI Signal Processing Journal*, **26**(1), 39–46.

[Parra et al., 1995] Parra, L. C., Deco, G., & Miesbach, S. (1995). Redundancy reduction with information-preserving maps. *Network: Computation in*

Neural Systems, **6**, 61–72.

[Parra *et al.*, 1996] Parra, L., Deco, G., & Miesbach, S. (1996). Statistical independence and novelty detection with information-preserving nonlinear maps. *Neural Computation,* **8**, 260–269.

[Parra *et al.*, 2000] Parra, L., Spence, C., Sajda, P., Ziehe, A., & Müller, K.-R. (2000). Unmixing hyperspectral data. *Advances in Neural Information Processing Systems,* vol. 12.

[Pearlmutter & Parra, 1996] Pearlmutter, B.A., & Parra, L.C. (1996). A context-sensitive generalization of ICA. *Pages 151–157 of: International Conference on Neural Information Processing (ICONIP'96).* Springer. Available from
http://www.cs.unm.edu/~bap/papers/iconip-96-cica.ps.gz.

[Pearlmutter & Parra, 1997] Pearlmutter, B.A., & Parra, L.C. (1997). Maximum likelihood blind source separation: a context-sensitive generalization of ICA. *Pages 613–619 of:* Mozer, M.C., Jordan, M.I., & Petsche, T. (eds), *Advances in Neural Information Processing Systems,* vol. 9. MIT Press.

[Pearson, 1894] Pearson, K. (1894). Contributions to the mathematical study of evolution. *Philosophical Transactions of the Royal Society, series A,* **185**(71).

[Pearson, 1901] Pearson, K. (1901). On lines and planes of closest fit to systems of points in space. *Philosophical Magazine,* **6**, 559.

[Penny *et al.*, 2000] Penny, W.D., Everson, R.M., & Roberts, S.J. (2000). Hidden Markov independent components analysis. *Pages 1–22 of:* Girolami, M. (ed), *Advances in Independent Component Analysis.* Springer.

[Pham, 1996] Pham, D.-T. (1996). Blind separation of instantaneous mixture of sources via an independent component analysis. *IEEE Transactions on Signal Processing,* **44**(11), 2668–2779.

[Pham, 1999] Pham, D.-T. (1999). *Joint approximate diagonalization of positive definite Hermitian matrices.* Tech. rept. Laboratoire de Modélisation et de Calcul. Submitted to Simax. Available from
http://www-lmc.imag.fr/lmc-sms/Dinh-Tuan.Pham/jadiag/.

[Pham & Cardoso, 2000a] Pham, D.-T., & Cardoso, J.-F. (2000a). *A Cramér-Rao bound for the separation of non-stationary non-Gaussian sources.* Available at http://tsi.enst.fr/~cardoso/CRBnSnG.ps and
http://www-lmc/lmc-sms/Dinh-Tuan.Pham/BBS/CRBnSnG.ps.

[Pham & Cardoso, 2000b] Pham, D.-T., & Cardoso, J.-F. (2000b). Blind separation of instantaneous mixtures of non-stationary sources. *Proceedings of 2nd International Conference on Independent Component Analysis and Blind Source Separation, ICA 2000.*

[Pham & Garrat, 1993] Pham, D.-T., & Garrat, P. (1993). Séparation aveugle de sources temporellement corrélées. *Pages 317–320 of: Proceedings of Gretsi.*

[Pham & Garrat, 1997] Pham, D.-T., & Garrat, P. (1997). Blind separation of mixture of independent sources through a quasi-maximum-likelihood approach. *IEEE Transactions on Signal Processing,* **45**(7), 1712–1725.

[Pham *et al.*, 1992] Pham, D.T., Garrat, P., & Jutten, C. (1992). Separation of a mixture of independent sources through a maximum likelihood approach. *Pages 771–774 of: European Signal Processing Conference.*

[Pinter, 1996] Pinter, I. (1996). Perceptual wavelet-representation of speech signals and its application to speech enhancement. *Computer Speech and Language,* **10**, 1–22.

[Porrill *et al.*, 2000] Porrill, J., Stone, J.V., Berwick, J., Mayhew, J., & Coffey, P. (2000). Analysis of optical imaging data using weak models and ICA.

Pages 217–233 of: Girolami, M. (ed), *Advances in Independent Component Analysis*. Perspectives in Neural Computing. Springer.

[Press et al., 1992] Press, W.H., Teukolsky, S.A., Vetterling, W.T., & Flannery, B.P. (1992). *Numerical recipes in C*. 2nd edn. Cambridge University Press.

[Quinlan, 1986] Quinlan, J. (1986). Induction of decision trees. *Machine Learning*, **1**, 81–106.

[Rabiner & Juang, 1993] Rabiner, L., & Juang, B.-H. (1993). *Fundamentals of Speech Recognition*. Prentice-Hall.

[Rajan & Rayner, 1997] Rajan, J.J., & Rayner, P.J.W. (1997). Model order selection for the singular value decomposition and the discrete Karhunen-Loeve transform using a Bayesian approach. *IEE Proceedings on Vision, Images and Signal Processing*, **144**(2), 116–123.

[Rangaswamy et al., 1993] Rangaswamy, M., Weiner, D., & Oeztuerk, A. (1993). Non-Gaussian random vector identification using spherically invariant random processes. *IEEE Transactions on Aerospace and Electronic Systems*, **29**(1), 111–123.

[Richardson & Green, 1997] Richardson, S., & Green, P.J. (1997). On Bayesian analysis of mixtures with an unknown number of components. *Journal of the Royal Statistical Society, series B)*, **59**(4), 731–758.

[Rissanen, 1978] Rissanen, J. (1978). Modeling by shortest data description. *Automatica*, **14**, 465–471.

[Ristaniemi & Joutsensalo, 1999] Ristaniemi, T., & Joutsensalo, J. (1999). On the performance of blind source separation in CDMA downlink. *Pages 437–442 of: Proceedings of First International Conference on Independent Component Analysis and Blind Source Separation: ICA'99*.

[Roberts, 1998] Roberts, S.J. (1998). Independent component analysis: source assessment and separation, a Bayesian approach. *IEE Proceedings, Vision, Image and Signal Processing*, **145**(3), 149–154.

[Roberts et al., 1999] Roberts, S.J., Everson, R.M., & Rezek, I. (1999). Minimum entropy data partitioning. *Pages 844–849 of: Proceedings of the International Conference on Artificial Neural Networks*, vol. 2.

[Roth & Baram, 1996] Roth, Z., & Baram, Y. (1996). Multidimensional density by shaping sigmoids. *IEEE Transactions on Neural Networks*, **7**(5), 1291–1298.

[Roweis, 1997] Roweis, S. (1997). EM algorithms for PCA and SPCA. *Pages 626–632 of: Jordan, M.I., Kearns, M.J., & Solla, S.A. (eds), Advances in Neural Information Processing Systems*, vol. 10.

[Roweis & Ghahramani, 1999] Roweis, S., & Ghahramani, Z. (1999). A unifying review of linear Gaussian models. *Neural Computation*, **11**(2), 305–346.

[Rubin & Thayer, 1982] Rubin, D., & Thayer, D. (1982). EM algorithms for ML factor analysis. *Psychometrica*, **47**, 69–76.

[Ruderman, 1998] Ruderman, D.L. (1998). Origins of scaling in natural images. *Vision Research*, **37**(23), 3385–3398.

[Rupp, 1993] Rupp, Markus. (1993). The behavior of LMS and NLMS algorithms in the presence of spherically invariant processes. *IEEE Transactions on Signal Processing*, **41**(3), 1149–1160.

[Saul & Jordan, 1996] Saul, L., & Jordan, M.I. (1996). Exploiting tractable structures in intractable networks. Touretzky, D., Mozer, M., & Hasselmo, M. (eds), *Advances in Neural Information Processing Systems*, vol. 8. MIT Press.

[Saul et al., 1996] Saul, L.K., Jaakkola, T., & Jordan, M.I. (1996). Mean field theory of sigmoid belief networks. *Journal of Artificial Intelligence Research*, **4**, 61–76.

[Schießl et al., 1999] Schießl, I., Stetter, M., Mayhew, J.E.W., Askew, S., McLoughlin, N., Levitt, J.B., Lund, J.S., & Obermayer, K. (1999). Blind separation of spatial signal patterns from optical imaging records. *Pages 179–184 of: Proceedings of First International Conference on Independent Component Analysis and Blind Source Separation: ICA'99.*

[Schießl et al., 2000] Schießl, I., Stetter, M., Mayhew, J.E.W., McLoughlin, N., Lund, J.S., & Obermayer, K. (2000). Blind signal separation from optical imaging recordings with extended spatial decorrelation. *IEEE Transactions on Biomedical Engineering*, **47**.

[Schoebben, 1998] Schoebben, D. (1998). *Real room recordings and separation results.* http://www.esp.ele.tue.nl/onderzoek/daniels/BSS.html.

[Schöner et al., 2000] Schöner, H., Stetter, M., Schießl, I., Mayhew, J.E.W., Lund, J.S., McLoughlin, N., & Obermayer, K. (2000). Application of blind separation of sources to optical recording of brain activity. *Advances in Neural Information Processing Systems*, vol. 12.

[Shalvi & Weinstein, 1993] Shalvi, O., & Weinstein, E. (1993). Super-exponential methods for blind deconvolution. *IEEE Transactions on Information Theory*, **39**(2), 504–519.

[Shalvi & Weinstein, 1994] Shalvi, O., & Weinstein, E. (1994). Universal methods for blind deconvolution. *Pages 8–59 of:* Haykin, S. (ed), *Blind Deconvolution*. Prentice-Hall.

[Sirovich, 1987] Sirovich, L. (1987). Turbulence and the dynamics of coherent structures. *Quarterly of Applied Mathematics*, **XLV**(3), 561–590.

[Sirovich & Everson, 1992] Sirovich, L., & Everson, R.M. (1992). Analysis and management of large scientific databases. *International Journal of Supercomputing Applications*, **6**(1), 50–68.

[Sirovich & Kirby, 1987] Sirovich, L., & Kirby, M. (1987). Low-dimensional procedure for the characterization of human faces. *Journal of the Optical Society of America*, **4A**(3), 519–524.

[Sivia, 1996] Sivia, D.S. (1996). *Data Analysis: a Bayesian Tutorial*. Clarendon.

[Souloumiac, 1995] Souloumiac, A. (1995). Blind source detection and separation using second order non-stationarity. *Pages 1912–1915 of: International Conference on Acoustics, Speech and Signal Processing.*

[Spence & Parra, 2000] Spence, C., & Parra, L. (2000). Hierarchical image probability (HIP) model. *Advances in Neural Information Processing Systems*, vol. 12. MIT Press.

[Stone et al., 1999] Stone, J.V., Porrill, J., Buchel, C., & Friston, K. (1999). Spatial, temporal and spatiotemporal independent component analysis of fMRI data. *Proceedings of the Conference on Spatio-temporal Modelling and its Applications, University of Leeds, UK.*

[Taleb & Jutten, 1999] Taleb, A., & Jutten, C. (1999). Source separation in post-nonlinear mixtures. *IEEE Transactions on Signal Processing*, **47**, 2807–2820.

[Tang et al., 1999] Tang, A.C., Pearlmutter, B.A., & Zibulevsky, M. (1999). Blind separation of neuromagnetic responses. *Computational Neuroscience*. In press as a special issue of *Neurocomputing*.

[Tang et al., 2000] Tang, A.C., Pearlmutter, B.A., Zibulevsky, M., Hely, T.A., & Weisend, M.P. (2000). An MEG study of response latency and variability in the human visual system during a visual-motor integration task. *Pages*

185–191 of: Advances in Neural Information Processing Systems, vol. 12. MIT Press.

[Theunissen & Doupe, 1998] Theunissen, F.E., & Doupe, A.J. (1998). Temporal and spectral sensitivity of auditory neurons in the nucleus HVc of male zebra finches. *Journal of Neuroscience*, **18**(10), 3786–3802.

[Thi & Jutten, 1995] Thi, H.-L.N., & Jutten, C. (1995). Blind source separation for convolutive mixtures. *Signal Processing*, **45**(2), 209–229.

[Tipping, 1999] Tipping, M.E. (1999). Probabilistic visualisation of high-dimensional binary data. *Pages 592–598 of:* Kearns, M.S., Solla, S. A., & Cohn, D.A. (eds), *Advances in Neural Information Processing Systems*, vol. 11. MIT Press.

[Tipping & Bishop, 1997] Tipping, M.E., & Bishop, C.M. (1997). *Probabilistic Principal Component Analysis*. Tech. rept. NCRG/97/010. Neural Computing Research Group, Aston University. Available from http://www.ncrg.aston.ac.uk.

[Tipping & Bishop, 1999] Tipping, M.E., & Bishop, C.M. (1999). Mixtures of probabilistic principal component analyzers. *Neural Computation*, **11**(2), 443–482.

[Tong & Liu, 1990] Tong, L., & Liu, R. (1990). Blind estimation of correlated source signals. *Proceeding of the Asilomar Conference*.

[Torkkola, 1996a] Torkkola, K. (1996a). Blind separation of convolved sources based on information maximization. *Pages 2097–2100 of: Proceedings of ICASSP*.

[Torkkola, 1996b] Torkkola, K. (1996b). Blind separation of convolved sources based on information maximization. *Neural Networks for Signal Processing*, vol. VI. IEEE.

[Torkkola, 1996c] Torkkola, K. (1996c). Blind separation of delayed sources based on information maximization. *Pages 423–432 of: IEEE Workshop on Neural Networks for Signal Processing*.

[Torkkola, 1999] Torkkola, K. (1999). Blind separation of audio signals: are we there yet? *Pages 239–244 of: Proceedings of First International Conference on Independent Component Analysis and Blind Source Separation: ICA'99*. Available from http://members.home.net/torkkola/bss.html.

[Tsatsanis & Kweon, 1998] Tsatsanis, M.K., & Kweon, C. (1998). Source separation using second order statistics: identifiability conditions and algorithms. *Pages 1574–1578 of: Proceedings of the 32nd Asilomar Conference on Signals, Systems, and Computers*. IEEE.

[T'so et al., 1990] T'so, D., Frostig, R.D., Lieke, E.E., & Grinvald, A. (1990). Functional organisation of primate visual cortex revealed by high resolution optical imaging. *Science*, **249**, 417–420.

[van Gerven & van Compernolle, 1995] van Gerven, S., & van Compernolle, D. (1995). Signal separation by symmetric adaptive decorrelation: Stability, convergence, and uniqueness. *IEEE Transactions on Signal Processing*, **43**(7), 1602–1612.

[van Hateren & Ruderman, 1998] van Hateren, J.H., & Ruderman, D.L. (1998). Independent component analysis of image sequences yields spatio-temporal filters similar to simple cells in primary visual cortex. *Proceedings of the Royal Society of London, series B*, **265**, 2315–2320.

[van Hateren & van der Schaaf, 1998] van Hateren, J.H., & van der Schaaf, A. (1998). Independent component filters of natural images compared with simple cells in primary visual cortex. *Proceedings of the Royal Society of*

334   References

London, series B, **265**, 359–366.

[Vetter *et al.*, 1999] Vetter, R., Vesin, J.-M., Celka, P., & Scherrer, U. (1999). Observer of the autonomic cardiac outflow in humans using non-causal blind source separation. *Pages 161–166 of: Proceedings of First International Conference on Independent Component Analysis and Blind Source Separation: ICA'99.*

[Vigário, 1997] Vigário, R. (1997). Extraction of ocular artifacts from EEG using independent component analysis. *Electroenceph. clin. Neurophysiol.*, **103**(3), 395–404.

[Vigário *et al.*, 1999] Vigário, R., Sarela, J., Jousmaki, V., & Oja, E. (1999). Independent component analysis in decomposition of auditory and somatosensory evoked fields. *Pages 167–172 of: Proceedings of First International Conference on Independent Component Analysis and Blind Source Separation: ICA'99.*

[Vigário *et al.*, 2000] Vigário, R., Särelä, J., Hämäläinen, M., & Oja, E. (2000). Independent component approach to the analysis of EEG and MEG recordings. *IEEE Transactions on Biomedical Engineering.*

[Vinokourov & Girolami, 2000] Vinokourov, A., & Girolami, M. (2000). A probabilistic hierarchical clustering method for organising collections of text documents. *Proceedings of 15th International Conference on Pattern Recognition.*

[Wainwright & Simoncelli, 2000] Wainwright, M.J., & Simoncelli, E.P. (2000). Scale mixtures of Gaussians and the statistics of natural images. *Advances in Neural Information Processing Systems*, vol. 12. MIT Press.

[Wallace & Boulton, 1968] Wallace, C.S., & Boulton, D.M. (1968). An information measure for classification. *Computer Journal*, **11**(2), 195–209.

[Waterhouse *et al.*, 1996] Waterhouse, S., Mackay, D.J.C., & Robinson, T. (1996). Bayesian methods for mixtures of experts. Touretzky, D., Mozer, M., & Hasselmo, M. (eds), *Advances in Neural Information Processing Systems*, vol. 8. MIT Press.

[Wax & Kailath, 1985] Wax, M., & Kailath, T. (1985). Detection of signals by information theoretic criteria. *IEEE Transactions on Acoustics, Speech, and Signal Processing*, **32**, 387–392.

[Weinstein *et al.*, 1993] Weinstein, E., Feder, M., & Oppenheim, A.V. (1993). Multi-channel signal separation by decorrelation. *IEEE Transactions on Acoustics, Speech, and Signal Processing*, **1**(4), 405–413.

[Weitzer *et al.*, 1997] Weitzer, D., Stanhill, D., & Zeevi, Y.Y. (1997). Nonseparable two-dimensional multiwavelet transform for image coding and compression. *Proceedings SPIE*, **3309**, 944–954.

[Wübbeler *et al.*, 2000] Wübbeler, G., Ziehe, A., Mackert, B.-M., Müller, K.-R., Trahms, L., & Curio, G. (2000). Independent component analysis of non-invasively recorded cortical magnetic DC-fields in humans. *IEEE Transactions on Biomedical Engineering*, **47**(5).

[Yang *et al.*, 1998] Yang, H., Amari, S.-I., & Cichocki, A. (1998). Information-theoretic approach to blind separation of sources in non-linear mixture. *Signal Processing*, **64**, 291–300.

[Yen & Zhao, 1999] Yen, K.-C, & Zhao, Y. (1999). Adaptive co-channel speech separation and recognition. *IEEE Transactions on Signal Processing*, **7**(2), 138–152.

[Ypma & Pajunen, 1999] Ypma, A., & Pajunen, P. (1999). Rotating machine vibration analysis with second-order independent component analysis.

Pages 37–42 of: Proceedings of First International Conference on Independent Component Analysis and Blind Source Separation: ICA'99.

[Ziehe *et al.*, 2000] Ziehe, A., Müller, K.-R., Nolte, G., Mackert, B.-M., & Curio, G. (2000). Artifact reduction in magnetoneurography based on time-delayed second-order correlations. *EEE Trans. on Biomedical Eng*, **47**(1), 75–87.

Index

Printed in the United States
By Bookmasters